OUT OF PRINT

5—

I Remember it Well

VINCENTE MINNELLI

I Remember it Well

With **HECTOR ARCE**

Foreword by **ALAN JAY LERNER**

SAMUEL FRENCH • HOLLYWOOD

NEW YORK • LONDON • TORONTO

First Samuel French edition 1990

Library of Congress Cataloging-in-Publication Data

Minnelli, Vincente
I remember it well/Vincente Minnelli, with Hector Arce.
p.   cm.
Reprint. Originally published: Garden City: Doubleday, 1974.
Includes index.
1. Minnelli, Vincente. 2. Motion picture producers and directors—United
States—Biography. I. Arce, Hector. II. Title.
PN1998.3.M56A3   1990   791.43'0233'092--dc20 [B]   90-3330

Grateful acknowledgment is made to the following for permission to reprint material:
From *The Magic Factory: How M-G-M Made "An American in Paris"* by Donald
Knox copyright © 1973 by Praeger Publishers, Inc., N.Y. Excerpted and reprinted
by permission.
From *Passport to Paris*, the Vernon Duke Autobiography, 1955, Little, Brown &
Company.
From *The Human Comedy*, by William Saroyan. Reprinted by permission of Harcourt
Brace Jovanovich, Inc.
From pp. 302–3 "Easter Parade" in *Steps in Time* by Fred Astaire, copyright © 1959
by Fred Astaire. Reprinted by permission of Harper & Row, Publishers, Inc.
Quotation from *Lyrics on Several Occasions* copyright 1959 by Ira Gershwin. Re-
printed by permission of Ira Gershwin.
Quote from *Fred Astaire: A Pictorial Treasury of His Films*. Edited by Howard
Thompson, 1970, Falcon Enterprises.

Cover design by Tony Gleeson

Printed and bound in the United States of America

Published and distributed by
Samuel French Trade
7623 Sunset Blvd.
Hollywood, CA 90046

To my daughters,
Liza and Tina . . .

Contents

Foreword

As everyone must surely know, Hollywood is now a subject for the Schliemanns, the Toynbees, and the Gibbons—a Pompeii buried in the ashes of accounts receivable, its Caesars long gone to their final resting or testing place, an occasional chipped column still standing amid the rubble as a lonely reminder, the sagas of its former glory told around the fires of middle-class barbecues, along the antiseptic corridors of TV studios and assembled in scholarly fashion by graduate students in theses on ancient history.

One of those remaining columns can be found on a small side street of a town of well-to-do squalor, gas stations, and oil derricks called Culver City. The figurative column is in fact an imposing, white stone edifice mounted at the top of two dozen building-wide steps still not old enough to be creviced by use. It bears the name of the Irving Thalberg Building and it stands next to a mortuary. Once upon a time it was the main office of Metro-Goldwyn-Mayer, the legendary "home of the stars." (Actually M-G-M is still there but I believe it now produces wide-lens hotels.) It was here that Garbo, Gable, Tracy and Hepburn, Garland, Kelly and Astaire, to name but a few, passed one another in the hall. At the far right end of the building is a door that once led to crowded sound stages, busy recording studios, lusciously filled dressing rooms, rows of offices, the Mississippi River, a town in the Old West, a street corner in Paris, the jungles of Africa, locomotives, chariots and steamboats, and all the other paraphernalia known as "the lot."

From the early 40's, to the mid 60's there used to come through that door a man of average height, slender, his dark hair brushed tightly against his head, his mouth twitching and his large, black, soft eyes in a chronic state of pop. (I can describe him thusly over so long a period because somehow he never changed.) He was usually on his way upstairs to see Arthur Freed, who was, for purposes of identification, the greatest producer of motion picture musicals the screen has ever known. The man on his way to see him was (and is, thank God) Vincente Minnelli, the greatest director of motion picture musicals the screen has ever known.

The fact that Vincente is a dear friend, a very dear friend, of long standing has nothing to do with this judgment. (It happens to be universal.) The fact that I had the marvelous good fortune to do four pictures with him most certainly has.

The direction of a motion picture musical requires very special skills that cover every color of the creative spectrum, very special instincts, very special training and from the beginning a clear, precise, unshakable view of the goal. Motion picture ledgers glow with the red ink of musical films directed by brilliant directors of straight pictures. Vincente not only has all those skills, all those instincts, all that training, but his view of the goal is so uniquely his that one can only say his talent goes too far beyond talent not to be called genius. A Minnelli musical has a look, an approach, a style and a patina that is as individual as his fingerprint. His best was the best there ever was. His worst was the kind of worst that only genuinely talented people can produce. I have always believed that only really accomplished people can do something really bad. As Jean Giraudoux once said, only the mediocre are always at their best.

Working with Vincente was an experience. His involvement was total, his enthusiasm limitless and irresistible. In fact, he was always so enthusiastic about what I had done that I hardly noticed he was saying he wanted it all done over. Many times I was never quite certain exactly what he meant, but I always rewrote the scene even if I liked what I had written because somehow I figured he knew better. And somehow he did.

They say that musicals, even in the theater, are a collaborative art form and it is undoubtedly true. But this I know: there has to be one person with his eye on the end of the road. One man has to be pointing so that all the others know where to look. And that's Vincente.

What a director! What a joy to work with! What a human being!
Thank you, dear Vincente. It was terrific.

Alan Jay Lerner
Centre Island
January 1974

Acknowledgments

In the telling of my story, I'm afraid I've tried the patience of friends and colleagues for the second time . . . first in the living of our mutual experiences and now in the reminiscing. But without their assistance, my faulty memory couldn't have described my life with even remote accuracy. My thanks, in alphabetical order of course, to an all-star cast of memory joggers: Carleton Alsop, Robert Anderson, Fred Astaire, Pandro Berman, Betty Comden, Fred de Cordova, Kirk Douglas, Lee and Ira Gershwin, Keogh Gleason, Adolph Green, John Houseman, Gene Kelly, Deborah Kerr, Alan Jay Lerner, Robert Mitchum, S. J. Perelman, Dorothy Ponedel, Kay Thompson. Special thanks to my daughter Liza for her contributions to the script, as well as for much of its supervision.

Introduction

I seem to be casting myself against type. Low key people who tiptoe through life don't presume to write autobiographies. We're more likely to apologize for our existence than to attempt to rationalize it.

This condition doesn't necessarily deny the existence of a healthy vanity. Those who probe beneath my bland surface will testify that, though it may be turned inward, my ego isn't all that submerged. It simply isn't obsessed with the need to tell all.

If I had no thought about writing my life story, the director in me had another reason. Why should I want to express myself on paper when there's a giant screen on which to create a far more entertaining tale?

I've noticed that some of my contemporaries insist on having it both ways. All the aesthetic and material rewards of long and successful careers weren't enough. Damned if they'll let the critics or the box office have the last word.

Their efforts should have been the final dissuader, for I admit such books often strike me as presumptuous and self-serving. Reminiscences need some fiber of truth, and the larger-than-life approach used in describing themselves seems aimed at creating a legend rather than revealing a man. Where are the insecurities that plague us all? If this is the film-maker's concept of honesty, then I hesitate to associate him with the lovely moments he created on the screen. I zealously guard the few illusions left to me.

Now, despite my reservations, I too have yielded to the irresistible temptation. So much for talk about *my* innate modesty.

In so doing, I know I risk destroying illusions for others. I have become part of that great assembly line which turns out one "definitive" film biography every fifteen minutes or so. But if my story is to have its quarter-hour in the spotlight, I want this show to beam at prime time . . . "tonight at eight-thirty."

The selection process can be interminable. Life tends to crowd out the ordinary reminiscences in favor of more vivid ones. I've had to dig deeply into my cluttered storehouse of memories and dust them all off. The jumbled segments of free association had to be pieced into a cohesive whole. At the same time I've had to guard against the all too human trap: showing myself in the most flattering light.

There is validity in describing the era I represent in the public's mind and in supplying insights about the fashioning of a career. But I've never believed in nostalgia for its own sake. It's a commodity too much with us these days.

The most bittersweet tragedy is the realization that one is on the brink of middle age, then just as suddenly he's beyond. In California, a season ends and another begins, with none of nature's fanfare. Years blend relentlessly into decades, and the Boy Wonder of yesterday becomes the Silver Screen's Tarnished Relic of today. Even if I could change that, I wouldn't. There's nothing drearier than to be current.

My work supplies no answers. How could it, when I often didn't know the questions? When critics praise my films, I respond, "Why, yes! Absolutely! That's exactly what I had in mind." But if they tear it to pieces, I let my insecurity sway me the other way. What could I have been thinking of? I become the penitent sackcloth-and-ashes figure, moaning, *"Mea culpa."*

Like Shakespeare's Lady I've protested—perhaps too much—that I had no obsession to write about my life. And yet—

Throughout my career, I seem to have been guided by invisible powers, unable to affect the direction in which they drove me.

Perhaps, I've done it again. I may not have gone deeply enough into my subconscious. All along I might have been planning to write my autobiography at some distant tomorrow, which has turned into today. For no one, after all, has asked me to do so until now.

I approach the task, hoping to conquer my lifelong reticence, to be as honest as taste and discretion allow. It's a difficult job.

xiv

I Remember It Well

What is the answer? (I was silent.) In that case, what is the question?

Gertrude Stein's last words
From *What Is Remembered*
by Alice B. Toklas
(New York: Holt, Rinehart and Winston, 1963)

1 | What Is the Question?

Answers, answers . . . we know all the answers.

We go through life, carrying ourselves with the smug knowledge that we've uncovered life's secrets . . . all of those, at any rate, that matter.

We've developed a special homing device to isolate think-alike spirits. In a flicker we categorize people as either with us or beneath us.

It's not too different from a slant I supplied Frank Sinatra and Dean Martin in *Some Came Running,* the picture we made together in 1958.

Both were playing ne'er-do-well gamblers, though Frank's part was that of a novelist of modest reputation and Dean's role was that of an irredeemable low life.

"I think you should approach each other," I suggested, "as if you were two matrons being introduced at a party in Beverly Hills. Both of you used to be hookers, but you're now married to producers and are totally respectable. But when you look at each other, you know . . . you both know."

This immediate recognition has always been with us. Can't you just imagine prehistoric cavemen looking on as one of their brothers drags his woman by the hair? They'd notice whether she was being carried off with proper style and panache. If he just grabs a hank of hair and pulls, he's not one of us. Doesn't he know that first you wind her hair around your wrist, then tug? How dreary, how common.

Which brings me to the first person. I too have that special radar. Unfortunately, it was designed by Rube Goldberg, and it operates in the most convoluted fits and sputters. It's out to lunch at the most inconvenient times. Its needle refuses to waver even as the planet is being destroyed by World War III and Armageddon and cigarette cough, for my mind has been too busy elsewhere. I've been preoccupied with nuance and detail of other times, an interest too consuming to be distracted by the immediacy of today and too specialized to share with others. There aren't many gaps in social conversations, after all, which one can fill with his knowledge of rococo furbelows.

Because of such distractions, it takes me longer to come up with the required answers. I always have to preface them, as friends will testify, with a "Beg pardon?" Then they know that to supply the answer, I've had to ask, "What is the question?"

Others may remember 1951 as the year Estes Kefauver headed the Senate hearings on Organized Crime, or the year that President Truman relieved General Douglas MacArthur of the Far East command. To me it was the year Liza was five.

We were driving home from Metro-Goldwyn-Mayer late one afternoon. My thoughts had been occupied with the French impressionist sets for the ballet in *An American in Paris* and with the very real problems of creating charm and style out of hot lights and sweat and knotted dancers' muscles. But that was before the chirping of my marvelous magpie began. After her first exuberant outburst, which lasted roughly half the distance between Culver City and Beverly Hills, Liza became pensive.

"Daddy—"

"Yes?"

"I want you to direct me."

"Of course!" I enthused. "As soon as we get home, I'll find a scene and we'll work on it."

"No," she answered firmly, "that's not what I mean."

"Do you want to do it at the studio?" Then, considering that she might be inhibited by the presence of others, I added, "We can practice when no one's around."

2

"No," Liza said, a note of exasperation creeping into her voice. "I want you to *direct* me."

I tried probing further, but to little success. Liza seemed unhappy with my obtuseness. Her look was accusatory. If she couldn't say exactly what she meant, my extrasensory antennae should have been working better.

She finally managed to blurt it out.

"I want you to get mad at me and shout! Just like you get mad at other people."

Once she decided on a career, it was inevitable that I would "shout" at Liza. We've been planning it for years. Sometimes our schedules didn't coincide. Other times the project was weighed down by insolvable problems and couldn't get off the ground.

And then it happened . . . with a book that had been knocking around for years.

When I first read the English translation of Maurice Druon's *Film of Memory,* I felt it would make a marvelous picture. It told the story of La Contessa, the toast of Europe in the early 1900s, who in her old age has been reduced to taking rooms in a once-fashionable hotel in Rome. There she meets a chambermaid, and in recalling her past triumphs to the impressionable country girl, the old lady regresses to a point in time where she is a young girl about to step out into the big world. It was a touching story with much inherent comedy.

Vivien Leigh had starred in the English provinces in a play based on the book, but it was not successful. She was too young for the part and, what's more, the work lacked focus. A French production also failed.

The book had been optioned by several film producers over the past ten years. Whenever I got my offer in, it was either too little or too late. I had given up hope that I'd ever be involved with that lovely story. It was frustrating, because my approach, I felt, could lick the problem. I thought the emphasis should be changed to concentrate on the effect the old woman's reminiscences have on the young girl, by having her fantasize herself as having lived La Contessa's life, thus being transformed at the end into an extraordinary creature herself.

Early in 1973, the property became available again. Though I hadn't seen Liza in the role at first, she had now grown to the point where the part would show still another facet to her extraordinary range. Liza was crazy about the idea.

We formed a partnership with Ed Grainger and Jack Skirball. Ed produced *Home from the Hill,* which I directed at Metro in 1959. Jack joined forces with him later. Together we obtained the film rights.

It was a dizzy pace. I found myself, in a way, auditioning the project before the money men. Though all the studios approached were receptive to the project, and we found ourselves in an enviable bargaining position, this New Hollywood was a fact of life I had to adjust to. It bore little resemblance to the way we did it when Leo the Lion's roar wasn't as muffled as it is today. I don't enjoy wrapping up packages.

The fall and winter of 1973 were spent in preparation for the spring shooting in Italy. The title of the picture was now *Carmela,* the character Liza plays, and it was time for the two of us to sit down with an interviewer to discuss where we were at and where we were heading. The meeting was conducted during Liza's record-breaking run at the Greek Theatre in Los Angeles, the two of us sitting on a sofa in my upstairs library . . . the same one I often discover Liza camped out on. Superstars, like other daughters, often fall asleep in front of the television instead of retiring to their own rooms.

Interviews are always artificial situations, but they never seem more manufactured than when two people are meeting with a third. You find yourself speaking to and about each other through a third person, and when the article is finally published, both of you usually sound exactly like the interviewer.

Yet, recording a conversation and printing it verbatim hardly makes interesting reading. The emphases and intonations which bring speech to life aren't there on the printed page. Now the reader knows what a director goes through when he pores over piles of scripts. He has to supply the conversational highs and lows in his own mind . . . as I am now asking the reader to do. Of course, he would never accept the constant interruptions and answering of each other's questions that Liza and I indulged in. But this was the reality of the situation, the one mind we share about so many things. I'm supplying an additional perception or two as a guide. The lady of the piece is adorable and adored . . . a marvelous reactor . . . supplying both quiet approval and uproarious laughter to her old man's pronouncements . . . speaking her own lines with that special full-throated way so much like her mother's, yet also so much her own. The man is a mixed metaphor, peacock-proud and purring as contentedly as a fat and spoiled house cat. Call her Liza, call me Vincente.

4

So, Mr. Interviewer, what is the question?

INTERVIEWER

Liza, your father told me once of an incident . . . you were driving home from the studio and you said, "I want you to direct me."

LIZA

Well, I used to be at the studio so much. I especially loved the musical numbers. I didn't quite understand the drama, because Daddy would go over and whisper quietly. Then the cameras would go. So that didn't interest me much as a kid . . . but the music numbers I thought were wonderful. I used to see how people would change after he talked to them. I wanted to know if I could do that . . . and to show off for him of course, because I always wanted to be perfect for him. He would sometimes say, "Okay, you're going to walk over here, pick this up and set that down, then say—" . . . and that wasn't what I had in mind at all—

VINCENTE

"No, no, you don't understand," she said. I couldn't find out what she meant.

LIZA

I was so frustrated—

VINCENTE

And then she said, "I want you to get mad at me and shout! Just like you get mad at other people." Oh, I thought, my God. What a monster I am. I was never conscious that I yelled at other people.

LIZA

No . . . it's incredible . . . well there are certain people who move with lightning speed, and move ahead of themselves even. And when you're on an idea, and you say let's try it like this. The mere fact someone isn't as fast and isn't right with you can be terribly frustrating. You have to stop to say, "Well I want this and da-dum-da-dum-da-dum." And you get clinical, and lose the inspiration of the moment that you had. The only time I would see you lose your temper was when people weren't keeping up with you or weren't listening.

VINCENTE

You have to find a phrase that would explain it to them. Sometimes it would be intelligible only to you and to them.

LIZA

My mother had a very funny line . . . and she said it in total jest . . . it was after a day at the studio . . . and it was horrendous. It was a scene in *The Clock,* where the minister has to marry them. Remember that

5

scene? And this poor man was a nervous wreck in that scene. Even when he came on.

VINCENTE

He was a bit player, but awfully good . . . though he would get confused . . . the door would shut behind him and he'd jump. Judy came to me and said, "Vincente, this man's a nervous wreck."

LIZA

So she said, "I'm going to open a home for bit players who have worked with you and gone mad. And call it the Minnelli Home for Bit Players and Extras."

VINCENTE

They had been used to coming to the studio and the assistant director would tell them what to do . . . "You cross the street here and stand there under the lamp post and you pick your nose." And they'd collect their money and go home at night. But I made them do all these things and say these crazy things, because I loved the bit players.

LIZA

There was an actor I met recently in Italy, who said he had been an extra in a party sequence . . . I guess it was in *Two Weeks in Another Town*. He said what was incredible . . . he'd done this a lot, played extras and bit players . . . he was impressed by the fact that you went to each person or each group of people and told them exactly what they were to talk about. Everything was specific as far as the atmosphere. Nothing was general.

VINCENTE

Well, they have to accomplish something. They can't just stand there saying, "Walla walla walla." They have to be reacting the way real people would do it. Because parties can be very revealing . . . a lot of dramatic things can happen there. It would drive me crazy if people weren't doing things you see them do at parties—

LIZA

—and talking about something.

VINCENTE

Yes.

LIZA

But the actor thought this was extraordinary. He'd never seen anything like that before.

INTERVIEWER

Liza, when did you decide you wanted to go into show business?

6

VINCENTE

I had just come back from Europe I remember, it was in New York, when she told me she wanted to stay there to study acting . . . the first time I'd known it, really, because you have to love it in order to do it at all . . . and to survive in it. So I was exuberant about it because she said she really wanted to do it.

LIZA

He told me I was going about it right too . . . my going to New York and studying.

VINCENTE

Yes, she had wonderful ideas, so her mother and I got together and we decided, yes, absolutely.

LIZA

I always liked to dance, I know . . . movement and all. I thought I was going to be an ice skater for a while.

VINCENTE

Yes, I thought Liza would be a dancer, because she was always working to records and improvising.

LIZA

And his sitting down for hours, after long hard days at the studio . . . and with my girl friends doing little plays for him . . . and he would sit there, and never get up and leave, he might have said, "Come on already, I'm a little tired."

INTERVIEWER

Who were the girls you performed with?

LIZA

Gayle Martin was the main one . . . and Amanda Levant too . . . the Levants were very close to us. I'm sure that Daddy told you that every time Oscar and June had a spat, Oscar would end up over here.

INTERVIEWER

Do you remember what these theatricals were about?

LIZA

Usually music or comedy things . . . always involving dancing.

INTERVIEWER

Would you write them yourself?

LIZA

Yeah, we'd make them up—

INTERVIEWER

Was there ever any dialogue you made up?

7

LIZA

Our first number we did for Daddy was a number from his show. I guess it was *The Band Wagon.* (crooning) I guess I'll have to change my plans. Gayle and I worked it out at recess at school. We did it first for Daddy . . . then we did it for Mama for her birthday.

VINCENTE

Do you remember when you and Gayle would make me sit downstairs?

LIZA.

Yes!

VINCENTE

And they would come upstairs and rehearse and rehearse—

LIZA (*laughing*)

And you would sit and sit there while we came upstairs to rehearse.

VINCENTE

I couldn't move, you know . . . then they would come downstairs and do it.

INTERVIEWER

You did it with no musical accompaniment?

LIZA

Yes, we would just do it ourselves. I said something once that got screwed up somewhere. The way they quoted me was, "My father gave me my dreams, but my mother my drive." And that's not what I said. I said, "My mother gave me my drive" . . . which is the basic way you know that I am . . . *"but* my father gave me my dreams." And it changed . . . it was switched around slightly . . . but that's very true . . . my father taught me that nothing was impossible, nothing was out of the question. There's always a way to accomplish something.

INTERVIEWER

You're getting along in years, Liza. You're now twelve or thirteen. You're not dancing any more.

LIZA

Oh, yeah! I danced every minute. There wasn't a *minute* that I didn't dance. I danced through all my years. We started to talk to each other more. Because when I was young, we lived on a schedule . . . our family . . . there was a schedule in that household. People got up and went to work, and Miss MacFarland or whatever her name was, burped me and fed me and whatever . . . and Mama and Daddy would come home . . . and they would have a martini or something like that . . . and then it was time for me to go to bed.

8

Do you remember that?

LIZA

Sure!

INTERVIEWER

You couldn't have been more than three or four at the time. How much do you remember?

LIZA

Daddy's not going to tell you this, but Mama loved beautiful things, and she never really had them . . . and she didn't know how to get them or find them . . . suddenly all the things that were deep down inside her . . . the real lady in her . . . were brought to the surface by many different things . . . not only incredible wit between these two people . . . conversation and laughter . . . for instance the house on Evanview . . . the colors in that room . . . the grey . . . I'll always remember that . . . the couches, and the shape of the martini things . . . and the time when everyone came home . . . the one time we were together . . . they were tired . . . but the fact there was this thing . . . you couldn't laugh at me . . . there was a time in my life when you *couldn't* laugh at me . . . so there was this incredible rapport between them . . . he would try to break my mother up . . . knowing that if he did it was disaster time and I would cry.

VINCENTE

I would say these things in a straight face that would make Judy want to laugh. She'd go through agony . . . Judy wouldn't dare laugh at Liza . . . this was when you were very little.

LIZA

And Mama's bathroom . . . she suddenly had things . . . her bathroom was absolutely beautiful . . . it had two blackamoors . . . weren't there, Daddy?

VINCENTE

Yes.

LIZA

. . . and I keep describing something that I want so much. It was an engagement ring . . . but it was more than that . . . it was set a certain way . . . it was a pink pearl set in a black shadow box made of ebony.

VINCENTE

It was an antique pearl we found and I designed a black enamel shadow box with gold . . . it was quite stunning. You know the coral

9

stuff in *The Pirate* Judy wore in her hair . . . and the earrings? That was an antique that I got for her too.

LIZA

But that remained with her for the rest of her life . . . and it was the first . . . it was like . . . it was something very special that never quite happened again . . . I know for *her* . . . and I've been lucky enough to have it happen to me all my life. There's a time and a place when Daddy . . . I guess it's his business . . . it's his job . . . which includes being a psychiatrist . . . a visual artist . . . you know, to know about what people do . . . to be able to do something like that which is absolutely perfect at the time. But the way things looked and smelled . . . and the first snowfall . . . when he woke me up to look at the snow . . . in the middle of the night.

VINCENTE

Yes, it was very unusual for it to snow out here.

INTERVIEWER

How old were you?

LIZA

I don't know . . . two or three? . . . and once by accident I kicked my mother in the head and she'd obviously had a terrible day . . . and I didn't know that though . . . and there was a scene . . . and Daddy came down and explained to me that she'd had a terrible day at the studio . . . so everything was okay. I always had someone to explain things to me . . . on terms I could understand at each age . . . he never threw anything at me that was too much for me to understand at any age.

INTERVIEWER

It's a very rare quality for any adult to be able to talk to a child at his level, and not talk down to him at the same time.

VINCENTE

Liza liked being talked to as an adult, didn't you?

LIZA

Well, yeah. It was a complicated existence in those days . . . for somebody to take the time to explain what was happening, was very important indeed.

VINCENTE

Up to that time everyone talked baby talk to her . . . and she was so serious . . . everyone went crazy about her.

LIZA

Do you remember the time I slugged you?

VINCENTE

It was at an enormous birthday party for Liza at the Gershwins. I was talking to Betty Bacall and some other mothers. And some little girl came over and she sat on my lap and I kissed her. And I didn't notice that Liza was watching. And she came over and punched me right in the nose. It was so completely unlike her. And I saw stars. She never did it again.

INTERVIEWER

You never kissed another little girl again, I wouldn't imagine.

VINCENTE

Yes, the attitude was . . . "That was for nothing. Now watch it!"

LIZA

We had wonderful times together . . . sitting in a pancake house on Sunset past La Brea—very bright place—right before Daddy started working in *On a Clear Day*—Daddy was having his coffee with cream— and we just had pancakes. He said, "I know what it's gotta be . . . I just know what it's gotta be." I said, "What what what *what?*" He said, "You've got to be so interested in those flashbacks that you can't wait to get back to them." Now we hadn't been talking about the film . . . but right away, I said, "Yeah!" because there's a bit of a shorthand . . . we do it once in a while . . . we can sit for hours and not say anything . . . then suddenly you'll say, "I think at the time that the—" and I'll know right where you are. See, I watched a great deal of the way he handled people . . . it was important . . . it was done with such care and logic! And if it wasn't logical to them he'd make it logical on their terms. And if they were illogical, then he'd make it logically illogical . . . and that's some trick, you know? I've heard him listen to actresses rattle for days . . . about small points . . . he'll say, "Yes, I think you're absolutely right." Then not say anything for a long time, then ask, "What do you think about—" and say something that is totally the opposite, but it sounds like something that they've said. "Oh, that's great! That's what it should be."

INTERVIEWER

You have been quoted as saying you inherited your singing voice from your father.

LIZA

Actually, my father taught me *how* to sing. He taught me all the songs that I know on the way to and from the studio . . . and he introduced me to good music. He'd say, "Listen to this," I'd say, "Who's this?" And he'd say, "Ella Fitzgerald." And it became, you know, salvation, really. But still when you hear a great song, you say, "Listen to this great song."

INTERVIEWER

You have always talked about the preparation . . . this is what really fascinates you . . . getting it right. Did you learn this from your father?

LIZA

Yes . . . absolutely.

VINCENTE

She digs down so deep . . . and brings out bits of characterization . . . it's wonderful. And unexpected things . . . that you don't expect this person to be . . . and somehow they're right.

LIZA

I learned that from Daddy, but I can't say how I learned it. By osmosis or something.

INTERVIEWER

Just by his example, maybe?

LIZA

Yes . . . just by hanging around.

INTERVIEWER

You've always talked about doing a film together. *Zelda* was the first time you actively made plans to do this?

VINCENTE

Yes, because it had to be something that was right—you know?—that was important.

LIZA

Oh, I know something—did I ever tell you this? About the time that I asked him for help . . . the first time I asked him for help? I was doing *The Diary of Anne Frank*. We were going to do it in Israel.

VINCENTE

She did it at school . . . and it was so successful that they took it to Israel and several other places in Europe.

LIZA

I was in school in New York, but I came back here to visit Daddy. There are all these long speeches in the play, speeches from the diary, and I asked, "Will you help me?" "Well," he said, "you know the director. Listen to the director." And I said okay. He kind of weaseled out of it, I thought. And then I later went into my bedroom. Two hours later, I heard this knock. Daddy came in, and said, "You know I was thinking" . . . and he taught me the most wonderful lesson that I've used in songs and acting . . . and it never fails . . . that is when you have a long

12

speech, and know the basic points you have to make, it's . . . Daddy, maybe you can explain it better than I . . . what you told me about the word: What you said about Spencer Tracy—

VINCENTE

Well, he knew how to pick out the basic words to get the message over. There are a thousand ways of bringing the words out, and making them important, without seeming to—

LIZA

And taking the unobvious one. Taking the words that seem terribly wrong, at first, so that you won't get stale. For instance, and this is the line he gave me: "You're as *thin* as a toothpick." The point is that you're as *thin* as a toothpick. But if you feel uncomfortable, or it seems stupid to you or something, you take the word that isn't the point in the sentence. Then raise your eyes on it: "You're as thin as a tooth*pick*." And it gets the attention, because it strikes the ear differently. And it's always worked.

VINCENTE

I gave her exercises to read, and told her to take the unimportant words and somehow . . . the unimportant word *of* or *from* . . . you can see the mental images changing in your mind.

INTERVIEWER

Can you give me an example of how you've applied this, Liza?

LIZA

Unhh . . . yes, in *The Sterile Cuckoo* . . . in the telephone scene . . . there's a line where I have to say, "I didn't have a sandwich with my father." And I used that lesson Daddy taught me, and made the most important word "sandwich" . . . "I didn't have a *sandwich* with my father." It was very, very, very important.

INTERVIEWER

Well, it was very poignant too . . . the sandwich was the extent of the communication you had with him.

LIZA

Yes, but it wasn't the obvious thing the line was saying.

INTERVIEWER

What other exercises?

VINCENTE

Well, you have to have a great many speeches, and you have to recall a great many . . . try out different words in different speeches . . . sometimes the unimportant word is the one you think most of and stumble on. It's like a lie-detector test.

13

LIZA

What about, Daddy, what you told me? It's never what you're saying. It's what you're *not* saying.

VINCENTE

Yes, because you monitor all your thoughts, you know? You don't want to say the wrong thing. But do you remember that Fourth of July weekend in New York?

LIZA

Yes, very clearly.

VINCENTE

I had to be in New York the entire weekend and there was no one in town, and Liza was rehearsing *The Fantasticks*. And I went to one of the rehearsals. The director was saying things to Liza, and I knew what he meant.

LIZA

I didn't know what he meant!

VINCENTE

I knew Liza didn't quite understand it. It was something about the words. How to get emotion into words without bringing sentimentality into it.

LIZA

Again in the dialogue. The choice of words people use is what they're thinking.

VINCENTE

They monitor words and are very careful—

INTERVIEWER

Well, a very trivial line can seem profound if it's read properly.

VINCENTE

Yes, there are famous lines created that you remember and it isn't the sense of them, it's the way the actors have done them.

INTERVIEWER

About your discussions on *Carmela*—

VINCENTE

We've talked a great deal. It's a very complicated part. Why this girl is so obsessed by the old woman . . . she's had no experience whatever . . . she works hard in this hotel. She comes inadvertently upon this Contessa.

LIZA

It hits right at the time when the girl is ready for something.

VINCENTE

Yes, you know she has enormous potential and imagination . . . and it just happens to hit her right.

14

I think you also know that if it hadn't happened, she'd merrily go on being a maid. The timing's right. It's like magic.

INTERVIEWER

How do you see your interpretation of the role?

LIZA

As honestly as possible . . . well, I learned something *very* early . . . and that's always listen to the director. My father taught me the key to it . . . the flashbacks worried me a little bit. I wasn't sure how to get ahold of the idea of how to do them. You know when you love somebody *so* much and care *so* much about them, that when they're telling you a story about themselves, you're there . . . you can see yourself there. Even if they're telling you how they're reacting, you know that you would be reacting the same way . . . as *yourself*. You're right there with them.

VINCENTE

But she's not prepared for them. The Contessa is completely unexpected, and never does anything conventionally . . . and it always turns out to be right, you know? The Contessa doesn't tell her stories . . . "Well this is what happened to me." She re-enacts them . . . and she first uses the girl as a gondolier in the boat . . . a rather hideous story . . . the Contessa's at that age where she has to buy love . . . and it upsets the girl terribly. The girl doesn't know . . . if the old woman is rambling or what. She keeps saying, "Shall I turn down your bed now?" Then she starts realizing that this woman is reliving parts of her past. Then she can't wait to get up to her room, to find out where she'll be in her memories. Then she gradually realizes the woman is living her life backwards.

LIZA

I think one of the most important things is . . . nothing much is happening with the Contessa that day. To her, the girl isn't Carmela. The Contessa calls her Jean, and the girl says yes. She lies.

VINCENTE

And when the Contessa has her take down this sari . . . and there's very little in the closet . . . so the girl pretends to take down a box. The Contessa says, "That's not the box. Get down the box." Then she takes out this sari, and dresses her in it, makes her up and fixes her hair . . . all the time telling her how to get jewels from a man. And nobody's ever taken the time to make the girl believe she's beautiful.

LIZA

It's strangely erotic and perverse too, because as she's dressing her and changing her and teaching her, it's her lover that she's sending the girl to

15

. . . as Jean or whatever. So she's sending the girl, but she's snapping too. There's a tinge of jealousy there. There's eight million different things going on at the same time. And the girl is watching herself being transformed . . .

VINCENTE

It's a very difficult role to make convincing. But Liza has gone through so much and shown so many different facets. And now she's ready for this. She's the one person I can think of who can make this role right. Liza has a wonderful new concept for make-up that she's working on . . . it's almost translucent, you know . . . the way the Contessa was, on which the novel was based . . . Liza and her make-up woman are trying it out.

LIZA

The concept of having a definite look started when I told Daddy I was going to do *Cabaret* . . . he asked, "What are you going to look like?" . . . and I got a blank expression on my face and said, "I don't know. What should I look like?" . . . and he answered, "I don't know." . . . end of conversation . . . then three days later I walked into his room, and on his bed were books and pictures and things to help me. You know, when you think of the Thirties, you think of Dietrich . . . you think of that very high cheekboned, incredibly sophisticated look . . .

VINCENTE

and those butterfly antenna eyebrows . . .

LIZA

Yes. For I didn't realize there was another look . . . and I was kind of worried about it too . . . and then we discussed Louise Brooks . . . and Daddy said, "You can do this sort of thing here. This will give you the effect that you want. Because you want to look special but you also have to look like you. It has to be a version of you, if you were in the Thirties." I've lived by that rule ever since, because it worked so well. I guess I work from the outside rather than the inside out . . . as soon as I find out how a person stands and looks, it all starts to fall into place for me . . . that was something that Daddy actually kind of taught me.

VINCENTE

She actually looked more like Louise Brooks in this . . . I thought in places you looked very much like her—

LIZA

Yeah—

VINCENTE

—and yet you looked completely natural.

16

So, on this note, you're experimenting now. What is your make-up on the new project evolving toward?

LIZA

Well, I'm just starting. I just listen to what Daddy says, and then I try to translate it. I take it to what I consider is the most marvelous make-up woman today, and we talk it over. She's kind of like Dotty Ponedel, Mama's make-up woman. The character was pale, but it was that see-through pale. There was something wonderful about her. It can't be dead-looking, like she was wearing white powder . . . and I throw out all these things I heard Daddy say . . . and Christina went to a chemist, literally, and we've tried out all these wonderful things . . . so we have all these little pots.

VINCENTE

Liza has two looks. One is a healthy, strapping farm girl of sixteen who is used to working, and works like crazy. And the other is when she gets into the rhythm of this Contessa, and later on starts to think of herself as the Contessa, and plays the young Contessa in her memoirs, you know?

INTERVIEWER

The range of your roles is considerably broader than your mother's. You said it couldn't have happened at a studio.

VINCENTE

Yes, even *The Sterile Cuckoo* couldn't have been done at an old studio. Because the implications are broader than they would allow in the old studio. It was much more mature, really.

INTERVIEWER

What about this range you've been allowed to show, that your mother didn't?

LIZA

Well I don't like . . . I think America has a terrible tendency to type cast. And if you can at all avoid that, it's marvelous. Because then you're never bogged down. Even though there are slight similarities in things, they're still very different.

VINCENTE

Well, Liza has been very lucky in having this variety of roles.

LIZA

Yeah, but each time I had to convince them that I could do it . . . because they were different from what I did last . . . I used Daddy's advice that you can talk anyone into doing anything if you go about it the right way. But this—he almost had to talk me into it a little bit. I said, "Do you think I can do that, Daddy? Do you really think I can?" And he said, "Yes." Just yes. He didn't say, "Of course you can." Then I thought . . . right! . . . then I can.

VINCENTE

There's no doubt in my mind. And actually there's no doubt in yours.

LIZA

No . . . there was a point there . . . five minutes maybe . . . because I was insecure about it, and I wanted it to be really good.

INTERVIEWER

And there's one song in the film, is that right?

VINCENTE

We don't know. If the film can stand it . . . but it's not a musical. It's a dramatic story. But if there's any song that will fit in well with what she's doing, fine. But the story won't be distorted in any way.

LIZA

The thing is . . . this girl . . . if the girl sings the song, it won't be done the way I would sing it. It would be part of the story.

INTERVIEWER

The fact that musical films are not being made in as great a number as in the past . . . you being a musical star . . . is this another reason why you might be allowed to show more range than your mother did?

LIZA

I've only done one musical . . . *Cabaret*.

VINCENTE

Everything else was dramatic.

LIZA

I think . . . maybe I'm wrong . . . but I think there had to come a time when I had to do a musical, so that the public could make that *final* comparison. And say, "There she is in a musical movie. And that's what her mom did. *And* she's holding her own."

INTERVIEWER

You did much more than that.

LIZA

Do you know what I mean?

INTERVIEWER

Did you have any hesitance?

LIZA

Not about *Cabaret*.

18

INTERVIEWER

You'd been offered a lot of other musicals?

LIZA

Oh! For days! A lot of Walt Disney musicals.

INTERVIEWER

Mary Poppins type things?

LIZA

Yes. When Walt Disney was still alive and doing, I thought, very good things.

VINCENTE

Her musical was done so beautifully—because all the numbers were done in the cabaret . . . and the cabaret became the symbol of Nazis and—

LIZA

—decadence.

INTERVIEWER

What kind of musicals would you like to do in the future?

LIZA

One that makes sense. It's a strange answer, I know.

INTERVIEWER

Do you think, then, that we're past the stage where the trivial, banal ones are still with us?

VINCENTE

There'll always be a musical to come around that will be quite unusual.

INTERVIEWER

What happened to all those musicals?

LIZA

Expense I think. Also people don't buy unreality as much as they used to. The escapism that people are trying to escape into is a worse reality than the one they're living in . . . rather than glamour. Also, it would be interesting to do . . . I liked *The Umbrellas of Cherbourg* . . . and I thought if you set up that you sang instead of talked and if you could do it really not as whacky as *Umbrellas of Cherbourg* as far as—

VINCENTE

Yes, that was the most successful of those, but it took a little getting used to . . . when you had the gas attendant singing, "Shall I Check the Carburetor?" it seemed forced. But once you got into it, the picture was enchanting.

LIZA

But there are kids now, for instance, whose whole lives are based on music . . . on rock . . . and when they're unhappy they don't necessarily sing to themselves unhappy songs. It's an interesting idea. If you have a kid whose whole life is just doing what they do, and living through music, their songs have nothing to do with what they're thinking, and yet show the energy level they're on at the time, that might be interesting.

VINCENTE

Yes . . . that bursting out of energy. But there are so few rock musicals that make any sense as pictures.

INTERVIEWER

How are you going to place yourself in the character?

LIZA

I'm terrible at that . . . I don't know yet.

VINCENTE

That needs time. The preparation. The trying out of costumes. And don't forget we don't have a script yet. But it is so rich that I have no doubt whatever—

INTERVIEWER

Your father's detail in film. How do you see it?

LIZA

It's always seemed normal to me. The detail always seemed part of the drama that was going on—

VINCENTE

—and the character.

LIZA

Rather than detail for detail's sake. It never came off like that.

VINCENTE

The things people are surrounded with . . . and the things they use.

LIZA

It's part of their lives.

VINCENTE

It explains them so well. Nobody's isolated and stands in front of a sheet, you know.

INTERVIEWER

Being exposed to tremendous talents all through your life, Liza, not only your parents but such people as Fred Astaire, Gene Kelly, and Cyd Charisse. What did you absorb from them?

LIZA

It's very strange, because you don't have any form of comparison. So it seems perfectly normal to you. Until you hit about thirteen, and it's your first time out of L.A. . . . that I was conscious that I was different, and lucky to have seen all this. And yet I did absorb this. My eyes were peeled. There were certain things I'll always remember.

VINCENTE

And subconsciously, all those things stick. They're there when you need them. And you don't know where they come from.

INTERVIEWER

Your attitude toward acting . . . instincts versus technique . . . do you depend more on one than the other? . . . or *can* you depend more on one than the other?

LIZA

I would like to have people think that it's instinct. Because then it becomes a more human ability. But a lot of it is technique. I think it's a combination of both. You start with the instinct, then you get the technique from the people you work with . . . the people who surround you. Like even our talks in there . . . in Daddy's yellow room. He said, "It's all a matter of choice. Here's all you have to know. Acting is hearing something for the first time. And then you have to make it look like you're saying it for the first time."

VINCENTE

And the kind of person you are, basically. How you react to situations that arise. Everybody reacts differently.

INTERVIEWER

Vincente, you and so many others say Spencer Tracy was the consummate screen actor. Are there any things he indirectly taught Liza?

LIZA

Oh, yeah. That thing about the toothpick. And the way he always seemed like he was saying it, as if it never came out of his mouth before.

VINCENTE

Yes, it was all spontaneous with him. He wasn't a method actor, and yet he arrived at the same sort of thing that the great method actors arrived at. He knew nothing about that at all. His great saying was, "Learn your lines and be on time." That's how simple it was for him. He found ways of saying things that made them sound spontaneous.

LIZA

It's a matter of believing things, really, isn't it?

VINCENTE

Yes.

LIZA

That's my technique. I *troo-ooly* believe. And until I truly believe, it doesn't seem right to me.

In getting a reaction from an audience. You don't cry to make them cry. You have to do something else.

LIZA

Oh, yeah! You have to try *not* to cry. It depends on whatever . . . people love bravery . . . bravery always makes people a little teary-eyed.

VINCENTE

The things that make me cry are not when everyone is beating Oliver Twist and being cruel to him, and you feel he's gone about as far as he can go with sadism. But let somebody be kind to him and pat him on the head and say, "Will you have a cup of coffee—"

LIZA

Yeah! Me too. That's it.

VINCENTE

It's when somebody is kind and understands.

LIZA

And there's communication . . . remember we talked about that word once. You said, "If I hear that word again, I'm going to kill myself."

VINCENTE

Yes, everything today is based on the lack of communication.

INTERVIEWER

Well, we don't communicate verbally a lot of times. But being a highly visual medium, that adapts itself well to film, doesn't it?

VINCENTE

Yes, you learn that every day. Language being what it is, it's impossible to indicate exactly . . . to make the other person understand exactly what you mean. You have to find ways to do it.

INTERVIEWER

Intellectualizing about any creative endeavor—what are your feelings on that?

VINCENTE

I feel that there are no rules. The minute you make a rule, you're dead. It's the matter of the moment, and how you put it. And when you find the right words that the actor understands, you can see it. There's always a key word that gives the actor the point of view that you want.

INTERVIEWER

But do you go into the psychological manifestations and implications . . . that sort of approach?

LIZA

I've seen Daddy do it.

INTERVIEWER

But does he do it on an intellectual level?

LIZA

Sure!

VINCENTE

With some people you have to.

LIZA

With George Peppard—remember that?

VINCENTE

Yes. The thing with George Peppard . . . he played the bastard son in *Home from the Hill* . . . he didn't want to make that big speech he had . . . he thought it was self-pitying. There was a way of doing it. He should be so completely honest when the time came he had to tell it . . . and he does it beautifully. "I didn't like it. When they tied me up like a dog out there. I didn't like it." That took the onus out of it. Once he understood how to do it, he did it brilliantly.

LIZA

Umm-hmm. Daddy taught me that too. He used to say to me, "There's nothing new. You can find a new way of doing something, or a different approach. But it all goes in circles."

INTERVIEWER

Does life in Hollywood go around in circles too?

LIZA

Well, there's an unreality to it all that . . . if you can get into it, you can enjoy it . . . and not worry about being kicked in the head when you're eight-and-a-half. It's a point of view, what you go through.

INTERVIEWER

Liza, you've suffered from the sob sister approach to writing. What do you think of it?

LIZA

Boring! I guess there's a market for it. I don't know.

VINCENTE

The poor little rich girl. They never change.

LIZA

People buy it and read it. For instance, in *The Parade's Gone By*, the book about silent pictures, it describes how *Photoplay* was then talking about the business. It was helping the film industry. Now it makes everyone seem like an idiot . . . an adulterer . . . it's forever ruining whatever images of Hollywood one were to hold with respect. I don't like that. Every time I've read an interview about myself . . . because my mind moves quickly and I jump . . . the writers make me sound so frantic. They don't say why you're thinking what you're thinking. They make it sound like you're in a frenzy of not knowing what you're saying.

VINCENTE

It's written with that idea in view.

INTERVIEWER

You've talked about the things you learned from your father in terms of show biz . . . cripes, show biz! . . . you say your mother taught you your drive. What else did she teach you?

LIZA

She was a good example of why not to take it too seriously. It was so way up in the air or down at the bottom. She always had a great sense of humor about the whole thing. But the pressure was enormous. But I was very lucky. People would be yelling to her for something or another. Again, the thing that annoys me is you read she'd done something like . . . an attempted suicide or something . . . they didn't tell you why. They didn't say what happened at ten-fifteen that morning or who'd done what to her or what happened or if it really was that at all. It's just headlines. But throughout all these pressures, I could always get in a cab and come here, and say to Daddy, "I don't understand," and have it explained to me.

INTERVIEWER

You don't take it as seriously. How does it feel when you're out there—

LIZA

—you know that your business is fantasy. That's what you've chosen to do. And first of all, that you can get paid for it, I think, is amazing. To do something you enjoy and get paid for it. You're dealing, you must always remember, in make-believe, and somewhere along the line you have to have your feet planted on what isn't make-believe. So that when six o'clock comes along . . . the time you finish work . . . come down. Get your laundry done, or whatever.

INTERVIEWER

When you're standing out there on the stage, and you get this mass outpouring . . . this frenzy you engender . . . how do you feel? You don't say, "I've got my feet planted firmly on the ground." You *have* to react to it. This adrenalin pouring out between you and the audience.

LIZA

Well, your first reaction is, "Isn't this *wonderful!*" Then you have your

24

kind of, "Oh, my God! One day they're going to rip away the mask and find out that I'm really nothing . . . and I really don't have all this talent . . . and I'm not that good." I go through that . . . the insecurity.

VINCENTE

Liza has the advantage of personal appearances. And you have all kinds of audiences. Sometimes they're cold, so the great challenge is to warm them up and get them excited. And sometimes they're with you and other times they're not, and you have to win them over to make them with you.

INTERVIEWER

The state of the movie business . . . do you feel the opportunities for you are as great as ten or fifteen years ago? Or do you feel lucky?

LIZA

I feel both. I feel terribly lucky . . . that I had the taste to choose what I did.

INTERVIEWER

Do you guide your own career?

LIZA

Yes.

VINCENTE

And she has this loyalty to people. Because the same people she started out with are the ones she's involved with now.

LIZA

The difference is that you suddenly find yourself in the position . . . you can't be the artist or director . . . you have to be a bit of a producer. You find yourself sitting in business meetings. It's not really what you do. But you have to be there because that's the way it works now. I find that confusing.

VINCENTE

Yes. And at the beginning it's a cold proposition. Those things have to be hot to come to life. It's very difficult to sit and talk business about something that's supposed to have some magic to it.

LIZA

We've sat through meetings together. I get a case of the giggles. I'm kind of drifting. I'm not staying with it. There are two things: I'm getting bored, and I don't really understand. I'm following it, but I'm wondering why I have to be there. At one point I was thinking, I wish we were working instead of sitting at this table. And I looked over, and Daddy had the same expression on his face. It broke me up, that here are these two people totally bewildered. The thing that cracks me up is that

25

Daddy sometimes looks like he doesn't understand, but he has heard *every* word. And he can repeat it to you verbatim. But I was really gone on some of those meetings. I didn't know what they were talking about.

INTERVIEWER

How broad is your range, Liza?

LIZA

I haven't a clue.

INTERVIEWER

But you haven't met your limitations yet.

VINCENTE

I don't think there are any.

INTERVIEWER

And you owe it *all* to your mother and father.

LIZA

Bob Hope got up on the stage with me the other night in Las Vegas, and said, "I worked with your mother when she was at the Paramount." They did a radio show together. Then he said, "And I adore your father. Two minutes before you asked me to come up on the stage you were sitting on a stool singing, and I thought, 'She looks exactly like Vincente.'" But it's true. Anybody who's known both Mama and Daddy, has always said I look more like Daddy. And yet, when I was with Mama, I looked like Mama. I think the only person I know who is also a combination of both her parents' looks is Geraldine Chaplin.

INTERVIEWER

Which brings to mind. Candy Bergen has written some very negative things about the Hollywood upbringing . . . the lavish parties and so on . . . the status things people did . . . what's your slant?

LIZA

Well, things go away. If you're ever lucky enough to have them . . . you were lucky enough to have them. I just feel it was great. I thought it was *terrific!*

VINCENTE

Candy brings it down, you know.

LIZA

But that's part of Candy's writing ability too.

INTERVIEWER

Yes, I think the best Rex Reed piece ever written was not written by him, but about him. She wrote it.

LIZA

Yes, Candy's wit is of the slashing kind. But at the time, our lives seemed

26

perfectly normal. Everybody else's birthday party was big and lavish. Now when I think back, I say, My God, I was so *lucky* to be able to have ponies at my birthday party . . . and that drunken clown who worked at every birthday party . . . so I just feel grateful. I wouldn't change one minute of my life for anything.

2 | Born in a Tent

I suppose Liza's career was almost preordained. Her mama was born in a trunk, and her papa was born in a tent.

The Minnelli Brothers Tent Theater owned by my father and Uncle Frank, with Mina Gennell—my mother—as leading lady, would do the summer circuit of small towns in Ohio, Illinois, and Indiana.

During the winter they'd be forced to go their separate ways. Father was a musical conductor and Mother was actress, singer, and dancer. Rarely did winter jobs become available in the same company. That was the case when I was born.

Mother had worked until the last moment, and as a very pregnant ingenue, she must have cut a very odd figure. Then, in Chicago, where her mother and sister lived, she left the company to await my birth. Father made his proper entrance at the lying-in before going on with his tour. Soon thereafter, with infant son in tow, Mother also went on with the show.

And it wouldn't be long before I too started paying my way, bringing c-u-l-t-u-r-e to the provinces.

The play was *East Lynne,* and it was an old chestnut even then. Mother, as star, had the dual part of Lady Isabel and Madam Vine. The wife elopes with a "scoundrel." Upon hearing that her son is critically ill, she returns, disguised, of course, in gray wig, cap, and spectacles. She passes herself off as a nursemaid and is hired by her former husband and his new wife to take care of the son.

I was to break into the act at the age of three-and-a-half, playing Little Willie, the adorable-but-dying son of the piece. Mother tried to rehearse me on stage. I, who would later sit in a packing crate in our back yard and will it into being as an airplane or an army tank, would have none of that. The two chairs on the bare stage, meant to simulate a bed, did absolutely nothing for me. It was decided to rehearse me at the boardinghouse instead.

"We are going to pretend," Mother told me. She coached me until I learned the lines for that heart-wrenching scene:

WILLIAM

Madam Vine, how long will it be before I die?

MADAM VINE

What makes you think you will die, William?

WILLIAM

I am certain of it, Madam Vine; but it is nothing to die when our Savior loves us; but why do you grieve so for me? I am not your child.

MADAM VINE

I know you are not my child, but I lost a little boy like you.

WILLIAM

It will be so pleasant to go up there, and never be tired or ill any more.

MADAM VINE

Pleasant? Ay, William, would that time were come.

WILLIAM

Madam Vine, do you think Mama will be there? I mean my own mama that was.

MADAM VINE

Ay, child, ere long, I trust.

WILLIAM

But how can I be sure that she will be there? You know she was not quite good to Papa or to us, and I sometimes think she did not grow good and ask Heaven to forgive her.

MADAM VINE

Oh William! Her whole life after she left you was one long scene of repentance—of seeking forgiveness; but her sorrow was greater than she could bear, and her heart broke in its yearning for you.

Those lines were the prelude to the finest death scene I was ever to have, and I'm sure I read them with great feeling.

29

Came the time for my debut. The scene was building nicely. I, dressed in a white nightgown and half-sitting up on the bed placed center stage, would have done the old man proud, had he not been in the box office outside counting the day's take. This whole acting dodge was going to be a breeze.

The tears of the audience were beginning to flow. Willie had just about had it. His father went to get the new wife. My mother, as Madam Vine, suddenly rose.

MADAM VINE

O Heaven! My punishment is more than I can bear. He has gone to bring that woman here that she may mingle her shallow sympathy with his deep grief. Oh, if ever retribution came to woman, it has come to me now. I can no longer bear it. I shall lose my senses. Oh William! In this last, dying hour try to think I am your mother.

WILLIAM

Papa has gone for her now.

MADAM VINE

No, not that woman there, not that woman. (*Throws off cap and spectacles*) Look at me, William, I am your mother! (*Catches him in her arms. He says* "Mother" *faintly, and falls back dead in her arms.*)

This was as far as we'd rehearsed the scene. I was totally unprepared for what came next.

MADAM VINE

Oh, he is dead!—he is dead! Oh William! Wake and call me mother once again! My child is dead—my child is dead!

Mother's sobs were more than I could bear. I sat up. "No, Mama, I'm not dead. I'm not dead. I was *acting!*"

Every performer remembers his first approving roar of audience laughter. This was mine. It went on so long that my father came running in to see what was wrong. I'd seen enough theater to know one should respond to such a reaction, so—as my parents later told me—I turned my head from side to side, smiling broadly and nodding. Mother somehow finished her speech. The fourth act curtain came down. So did the wrath of my father.

I appreciate the humor in this, my first in a series of less-than-adequate performances. But in the far reaches of my mind, there might have been

30

the memory of hearing my mother speak these lines before—in real life.

Before I was born, twin brothers had been carried off by mysterious childhood diseases endemic to the times. Another brother named Willie—curiously sharing the same name as the dying son in *East Lynne*—died when I was an infant.

Little wonder that Mother was overprotective of me, her last surviving son. Since I was born when she was in her midthirties, and Father was some fifteen to twenty years older, it wasn't likely they'd be having more children.

Though it wasn't my parents' style to tell me I was something special, I was made to understand that a lot was expected of me. My upbringing was so strict that I came to feel perhaps I was the original sin. But I can't blame my timidity and sense of guilt on their rigid Catholicism, combined as it was with the Puritan work ethic.

Astrologists say Pisceans are shy, imaginative, supersensitive . . . emotional, flexible, low key. If this accurately describes my makeup, I was quite young when I started fighting what the stars foretold about me. I knew how to bend, but I had to avoid swaying.

I had a short attention span. For me, life was free association, with my imagination leading me from one subject to another. I found it impossible to concentrate. It worried me. I remember staring at my reflection in the mirror on the medicine cabinet. "Here you are, nine years old," I told my image. "And what have you done? You're nothing . . . nothing but a failure."

I wish I could say this was the great breakthrough, but I took many more stumbling steps along the way.

One of the earliest lessons I learned was the existence of two codes of behavior. If I broke something at home, I was cautioned to be more careful in the future. If this happened on the road and involved a landlady's cherished possession, then watch out! There were many such punishments during my first bumbling years.

I suppose all this reflects badly on my parents. People now blame environment and press for more permissive upbringing, but it wasn't done in those times. They were good people, and devoted to each other. They gave me a sense of the commitment two people can have with each other. They married and stayed married. You couldn't prove the immoral image of show business by their example.

Father looked on his work as just another job and, as silent pictures began to cut into the take, not a well-paying one at that. Townspeople may have regarded him as an eminence—the well-known conductor and French horn player who also wrote Sousa-type marches. (One of them—"White Tops"—was played in every circus band.) But he knew the privations of show business. He encouraged most of my interests, but refused to allow me to study music. He knew what it had done to him.

On the other hand, Mother definitely lacked an emotional affinity for the theater. Never was there a more reluctant star. I can't imagine my gentle Grandmother Le Beau being the archetypal stage mother, but she was aware that her daughter had a talent. She began taking Mother to auditions in and around Chicago, where the family had settled after emigrating from France. Mother found it easy to get work, and adopted the stage name of Mina Gennell, the surname borrowed from a more obscure branch of the Le Beau family. But to those who loved her, particularly my father, she was simply known as May.

Her sister Amy had been one of two girls in a trapeze act with Ringling Brothers Circus, and her brother had been an equestrian. I don't remember much about this uncle, not even his name, except that he wasted away from some illness. He was reduced from his once proud role, first to clown and finally to candy butcher.

After their brother's death, Aunt Amy left the circus. She retired to Chicago, never marrying, looking after my grandmother until the older woman died. Mother, however, didn't find it as easy to quit. Though she was well on her way to becoming a star—a Dresden china doll, as famed Chicago critic Amy Leslie called her—acting was just a living to her, albeit one that supported the Le Beaus in comfort.

Mother's distaste for the stage would later rub off on me. I remember quite well her describing a tableau: "I once worked in a dime museum. We used to put on some fifteen shows a day, and we were so busy that everyone in the company had to live in the same building where we performed. There was an act on the bill that was patterned after one Buster Keaton did as a little boy. He would dress exactly like his father, wearing a half-bald Irish wig and donegals. In this case, the father played in black face, the mother was a black soubrette and the little boy went on in black face just like his father. They did a three-acter. I remember passing their dressing room very early one morning, on my way to my first performance. And there was the mother with the little boy in her lap, putting burnt cork on his face. He was still asleep. This came to represent everything I hate about show business."

I might have pointed to a more immediate example of a child unwillingly conscripted, had I thought of it. But having no other childhood with which to compare it, I never considered my upbringing horrendous. It even had a glamour of its own, as I could see whenever we arrived in a new town. The children there would seek me out to ask questions about life in the theater. Though I may have made it sound more fascinating than it actually was, it wasn't a cruel life.

Mother was on the bill of a road show company when she met my father, who was its musical conductor. They immediately fought over the music that was to accompany her act. As a result, he thought she was standoffish and she found him a snob. Their marriage, of course, was inevitable.

Father was a strapping, good-looking Italian. But to my mother, at the outset, he must have seemed as stern and disapproving as I found him when he occasionally flashed me warning looks while I was committing some public transgression.

He'd become a musician, like his father, *the* Professor Minnelli of Palermo, Italy, who moved to Delaware, Ohio, to head the music department at Ohio Wesleyan University. (After he settled in Delaware, the professor became known as the town eccentric. He was said to walk to work, singing to himself, whacking at flowers along the way with his rattan cane. He might look back half a block later, and come running back to administer the coup de grace to any flowers he missed along the way.

(He was possessed of a vagueness and distraction that only his absent-minded grandson could love, though he died long before I was born. His mind was too full of the masses and oratorios he composed to concern himself with the mundane. Professor Minnelli made it a practice to work in his garden before going to school each morning, wearing a black Prince Albert coat, heavily starched white shirt and white trousers. I'm sure he would be humming to himself, as I often catch myself doing, not fully concentrating on the garden or on keeping his clothes clean. Grandmother would often make him change his muddy clothes before he left for work. But that wasn't to be the case on one tragic morning. Professor Minnelli set out to prune the branches off a tree. He was sawing away. The branch fell. So did the professor. He'd been sitting on it. He died the following morning.)

After my parents married, Mother joined the Minnelli Brothers Tent Theater, which Father and Uncle Frank were in the process of forming. If she had to travel, this was the easiest way, with husband to lead the way.

My earliest memories are of Pullman trains churning along, taking us

33

from town to town . . . father, mother, uncle, son, eight actors, and a road manager. No sooner would we reach our destination than off I'd be spirited to early Mass with Mother, even before we checked into the boardinghouse where we'd be staying. Dad and Uncle Frank would supervise the setting up of the tent theater on a vacant lot rented by an advance man, who had also made arrangements for the troupe's housing and feeding.

The canvasmen of the troupe would ride in the baggage car along with the tent. They'd jump off the train, bustling to get over to the vacant lot. Then they'd go back to the train station to get the wagon where the wardrobe trunks had been placed. (As I grew older, my bicycle was tied to one of the trunks, enabling me to spend days exploring the towns we played.) The boss canvasman would then point out the spots where the yard-long metal poles would be pounded into the ground by his three men. The tent would gradually billow up.

The company opened that night, charging twenty-five cents for general admission. Those wanting reserved seats paid ten cents more, and those staying for the concert at the end of the play would be charged an additional five cents. The people of the small towns were so avid for entertainment that they accepted all the surcharges.

But then consider the luxurious appointments the Minnelli Brothers brought with them. The tent held five hundred people or more, much like conventional theaters, and we looked down our noses at a smaller tent show covering the same territory. We were also mildly contemptuous of another troupe whose only trick in its repertory bag was *Uncle Tom's Cabin*. During one particularly rough season they were reduced to multiplying the effect of the production. First they mounted a *Double Uncle Tom's Cabin*, with two Simon Legrees, two Little Evas, and two Topsys. When that didn't do well, they presented a *Triple Uncle Tom's Cabin*. I don't know how well that superspectacle did.

Our reserved seat section, with its folding chairs, was marked off by a rope and lots of red bunting. General admission bleachers, painted sky blue, formed a horseshoe around it. The elevated stage had a proscenium arch of red canvas decorated panels, complementing the red and white stripes of the tent's entrance. The piano box to the left of the stage was the same blue as the bleacher section. Sawdust had been spread on the ground to hold down the mud and to level the uneven terrain.

Behind the stage was a very long dressing room for the men, another for the women, and a third for Mother. Father made his headquarters in the box office outside, whenever he wasn't playing the piano.

34

I spent most of my time in the men's dressing room, watching the actors as they stood before the make-up table, which was constructed of two tall saw horses and a wooden plank. I might be eating bread with butter and brown sugar, a treat prepared by the canvasman who doubled as cook, and I'd look on the proceedings with a very jaundiced eye.

I was more greatly thrilled at one of those endless series of boardinghouses where we stayed, the landlady putting a piece of fruit or a toy in a stocking which I faithfully hung up every night.

Nor was I impressed by the motley assortment of has-beens and never-would-bes working in the company. The only good talent, as my young eyes saw it, was the comedian. He'd been in good shows, but he drank. Where no one else would have him, we were happy to be able to keep him. I suppose none of the troupe deserved the respectable salaries my father couldn't afford to pay.

The brightest spot backstage was Mike Kennedy, our stage manager. A steady, elderly man, he was enormously kind to me. He'd been a full-time actor early in his career—he still played occasional character parts for us—and he kept a white wig and a beard in the wardrobe trunk, a memento of a past portrayal of Rip Van Winkle. I'd pester him to show me those precious strands. Mike would gingerly undo the tissue paper in which they were wrapped. "These will be yours someday," he'd say. I knew I could lick the world when they were finally mine. But as I grew older, their appeal faded. They became a symbol of the third-rate magic we were creating.

We did pirated versions of Broadway shows, and we didn't pay royalties. The names of the characters were changed to protect us, the not-so-innocent. I was an active conspirator, playing all the child parts, many of them walk-ons. I'd squirm uneasily in Mother's lap as she put the make-up on my face. If I didn't have to perform, she would put me to bed before the evening's performance . . . I was allowed to be underfoot only during the day.

At no time was I more in the way than when I fell in love with one of the actresses in the troupe. To the rest of the world hers was a fading beauty, but to me she was almost as beautiful as Mother. She was a secret drinker, which I suppose grownups could discern just by looking at her, but Mother protected my fantasy. Realization came gradually . . . my heart broke for the first time.

But little matter. I was resilient. I still had my mother.

Though she was a simple person in real life, favoring white shirtwaists with dark skirts, she blossomed on stage. She had presence. She was *somebody* in those fancy dresses she wore for more glamorous roles. But those weren't the parts I remember best.

In *Tess of the Storm Country* she was incredibly young and daring, dressed in country clothes with shorter skirts. I was fascinated by her disguise as Madam Vine in *East Lynne*. But the part I loved most of all was the wrongly accused salesgirl of *Within the Law*. Sent off to prison for stealing, she becomes a gang leader upon her release, doing all her stealing "within the law." She marries the son of the man who'd accused her. Who can forget her curtain speech in the second act? "Five years ago, you took away my name and gave me a number," she says to her father-in-law. "Now I've given up the number and I have your name." *That* was writing.

During the winter I'd be sent off to stay with one of my grandmothers. I lived with my paternal grandmother in Delaware during my first year in school, arriving from the summer tour after the term had started. Never was I made to feel more unwelcome. I withered under the curious stares of my new classmates.

Grandfather Minnelli's untimely demise had become part of the local folklore. And there I stood, my muscular co-ordination having deserted me, speechless. Teacher and students alike surmised I was a mental deficient. Throughout that first school year I was treated like one, never called upon to recite, and whenever the class had art classes, another student would make an extra drawing or paste together a Valentine, suggesting I should pass it off as my own.

Later I went to St. Joseph's at Nottingham, outside of Cleveland, a boarding school run by nuns. I didn't have to live up to the responsibilities of the Minnelli name, and I loved it. It was so progressive that I was advanced several grades when I returned to Delaware.

Mother would come to see me every Sunday, and we'd try to crowd in a whole week of visiting before she'd have to rush back for her evening performance. Then came the Sunday she didn't show up.

We were putting on an entertainment. The boys in the upper grades staged a mock trial, prosecuting fashionable women for the crime of wearing endangered species of birds and animals. In those days ecology was known as conservation. We in the lower grades sang. I didn't see Mother before the performance, but I knew there'd be time afterward to get together. But she wasn't to be found. I went through agony the following week.

Sunday came again, and Mother reappeared. I went rushing to her, and she took me in her arms. "Why didn't you come last week?" I cried.

36

She comforted me. She'd come part way but the train she was to transfer to had been very late, and it wouldn't return on time for her evening performance. I never questioned the fact that this was the way it had to be.

One year I went to school in Wheeling, West Virgina, where Mother was appearing in stock. She'd get up each morning in time for early Mass, then return to wake me and fix breakfast, take me to school, then to her own rehearsals. She'd take me back to the boardinghouse for lunch, walk me back to school, then go back to the theater for the matinee.

After school, I'd go to the theater and watch her from the wings. If I got tired, I would plop onto the middle tray of her wardrobe trunk for a catnap. Her performance over, she would take me home, give me supper, put me to bed and return to the theater for the evening performance. I understood very well why she wanted to establish roots somewhere. I must have had similar vague yearnings.

Yet I wasn't unhappy. I would sing myself to sleep at night, which I was to do throughout my childhood, the made up tunes pouring out with exuberant gusto . . . and just incidentally holding at bay the goblins beneath the bed.

Then the time came when we finally left the theater. We made the final move to Delaware, setting up house across town from Grandmother and Aunt Anna. Mother considered it sheer luxury to be allowed to scrape along in near-poverty, to raise the family in a conventional way. And there certainly was no more conventional town than Delaware, the birthplace of Rutherford B. Hayes, a few miles north of Marion, where one Warren G. Harding ran a newspaper. It was a University town set in a semirural area of truck farms which serviced Columbus. Its houses were furnished in bilious green overstuffed sofas, tiny rosebuds in its ceiling and wall paper and pongee curtains which were so serviceable year-round.

Father wasn't as happy about the development. Motion pictures had finally done the tent theater in. From then on, with the exception of his tours as music conductor and Mother's rare stock company engagements, he made do with the occasional local engagements that came his way. Life for Father was to become more difficult as he gradually became incapacitated by rheumatism.

The house we moved to was at the end of the trolley line, one mile from the center of town. It wasn't as American Gothic as the one in *Meet Me in St. Louis*. In fact it was rather ordinary. But to Mother it was a marvel. Starting up housekeeping at a late age, she didn't have the Victorian hand-me-downs that other housewives did. She was more modern, with golden oak furniture and chintz fabrics. I learned to appreciate these fripperies by looking at them through her eyes.

The Minnellis' frugal, hand-me-down existence taught me to get as much use of my clothes as comfort and decency would allow. Waste was the cardinal sin. I had learned to recycle my experience in real life and applying them to my creative endeavors. I do it to this day.

The mental images, and the uses I put them to, come tumbling forth.

They stemmed back from my earliest days on the road. I couldn't have been more than seven when Mother took me to a matinee in the city—what city I can't remember. The curtains parted. There, sitting on a crescent moon, was a pink and blonde confection. She must have been all of ten. The stage was all black, and a spotlight was trained on this extraordinary vision singing "Shine on Harvest Moon." The moon started moving toward us. The effect was dazzling. Years later, I used the same device—a crane covered in black velvet being pushed around by men, also in black velvet—with Bea Lillie in *The Show Is On,* the third Broadway musical I directed for the Shuberts.

Then there was Aunt Anna. I used her time and again. (She was my father's half sister. After my grandfather was killed, my grandmother—a member of the South's famous Pickett family—married a farmer named Maine to give her sons a home. He was not a happy choice, though they had the one daughter. After the children were grown, they were divorced.) Anna never married. I borrowed the red tam-o'-shanter she constantly wore and put it on the maid in *Meet Me in St. Louis.* I turned her into Aunt Elsie in *The Long, Long Trailer.* "This is poor Elsie," Lucille Ball said by way of introduction. Desi Arnaz's eyebrows shot up. "Well, she's very shy," Lucy explained. "She doesn't meet people. She doesn't shake hands."

I also went back to my childhood to create the small-town carnival for *Some Came Running.* Booths would be set up in front of the stores on Sandusky—Delaware's main street—and spread over onto West Winter. A merry-go-round and Ferris wheel would be set up nearby. Banners and bunting would transform the dreary business streets during these fall Pumpkin shows. People would come from as far away as Marion and Worthington.

I even call on one of my father's old jokes whenever I'm asked to define the function of the director. "There was an old farmer," he used to say. "His cow had been lost for weeks in the hills and ravines around his farm.

He finally found her. He was asked how he did it. 'Well, I just asked myself, where would I go if I were a cow . . . and I did, and she had.' "

When one is as notoriously poor in remembering names, places, and dates as I am, it's such touches that flesh out the story. Many of them I can conjure up even now: a streetcar accident in front of our house and the unexpected reactions of people during the confusion; the infinite care my grandmother in Chicago took with Christmas, the crystal and china she saved for special occasions, the dancing Sambo she gave me which was one of the rare toys of my childhood; the sidelong disapproving glances of Grandmother Maine whenever Aunt Stella, Uncle Frank's second wife, was in the room. Stella was young and pretty. Consequently in Grandmother's Christian Scientist eyes, she was frivolous.

Stella was a far cry from Aunt Edna, Frank's first wife, who, after all, had money and made her husband a fine home—next door to Grandmother Maine's. Edna died of consumption. It was feared her daughter Francine would die of it too. Uncle Frank built her a special room in the house, and it was here I would come to visit. Francine was two or three years older and she liked me quite a bit, sharing with me her love of music and literature. After she too died of consumption I could sense the anxiety with which I was enveloped, even as the funeral cortege was leaving my uncle's house.

My flights of fantasy were boundless, it seems, placing me in the exotic locales of the books in Dad's library, from which he often read to me. I became such an expert on his books that all a person had to do was read me a few lines and I could tell from which work it came. It wasn't all that difficult to do, since my imagination had already absorbed them. I'd transport myself to Kipling's Barrack Rooms or place myself in the midst of an O. Henry denouement or I'd be far, far nobler than Sydney Carton in *A Tale of Two Cities*. I may not have cut it as an actor in the tent theater, but buried in those books, my acting range was limitless, specializing in the derring-do, which conflicted sharply with my parents' not so daring don'ts.

I could also quote from *Snappy Stories* and *Life*, the magazines Uncle Frank would lend me. He was flashier than Dad, and more current. Where my father treated me with grave courtesy, perhaps regretful that his son was so socially timid, Uncle Frank was a buddy. By exposing me to the publications of the day, he, more than anyone, taught me there was a far greater world of the theater out there.

But I didn't always need the catalyst of the printed page. Plopped on the floor, a sketch pad before me, I began creating my own images, placing myself somewhere in an upper stratosphere. Though they never thought of paying for art lessons, my parents encouraged me just the same. Father allowed me to use the chicken coop in the back yard as a studio. Many of my happiest—and loneliest—hours were spent there. But I had already learned to value such solitude.

This wasn't the age of organized sports. After school we were left on our own. I'd occasionally ride my bike with friends, or go skating, or swim in the abandoned quarry not far from the back of our house. I'd fight with the neighborhood kids for the privilege of swinging the trolley line around when the car reached the end of the tracks. But that was life in Delaware, and had as much significance to me as my charade as an altar boy. For I wasn't blessed with my mother's unyielding piety. I was already envisioning life on a grander secular scale. My father was inadvertently preparing me for it.

I'd run into the house to show him my latest work of art. He'd look at it very critically. "It's good," he'd slowly say, "but it isn't up to your usual standard." What that standard was, I'll never know. But in his own way he was teaching me not to be satisfied, to continually strive to improve. So I'd go back to the chicken coop, determined to do better by him and by me.

It wasn't the style of the times for parents to hang their children's drawings at home, nor were they shown in school. My audience was soon to be far larger than that.

While still in grade school, a sign painter offered me a job as his assistant. He'd paint show cards for display windows. My apprenticeship was rather short. He was the town drunk and, after one horrendous bender, I had to fill in for him to deliver an order on time. His pattern continued, and I found I'd inherited his customers.

Dad, in his professional travels, would often come home and regale us with a detailed account of his every waking hour away. Now it was my turn, for I was hired to go to Columbus—eighteen miles away—to do art work at conventions and to paint showcards.

I gave most of my wages to my parents. I had no personal extravagances, no taste in clothes or love of fine things. With money being so tight, I couldn't indulge myself anyway.

I was thirteen when my most ambitious assignment came: repainting the advertising curtain of the local cinema house. It was all painted pillars and draperies, with square boxes at each side to be filled in with ads for local businesses. A truck arrived at our house with this enormous curtain. Father helped me tack it up on the side of the barn, and I took out my watercolors and brushes to start work. Sometime during the week it took to finish the curtain, it began to rain. The colors started running. I was forced to finish the job, the center of an enormous sandwich: the curtain beneath and the canvas my dad hurriedly nailed over it to protect it from the elements.

He also protected me. One summer a friend got me a job helping a nearby farmer. I'd have to report to work at six every morning to help with the chores. I wasn't used to the grueling work. I came home dog tired after my first day. "How much is he paying you?" Dad asked. "A dollar a week." He didn't think it was very much.

The next day, the farmer came up to me, leading a steer by a rope, which he handed over to me. "Here," the farmer said, "hold this." I looked into the animal's soulful brown eyes. From out of nowhere, a sledge hammer came swinging over the farmer's head, hitting the steer right between the eyes. It let out this horrible painful sound, and blood trickled down its face. The front legs buckled, and the steer collapsed and died.

Maggots immediately began to form. The farmer made me hold a hose on the carcass as he proceeded to butcher it. I managed to control my nausea, but when I returned home at the end of the day, I was violently sick. Father didn't think it was a good idea for me to continue working for the farmer. I finished out the week and began looking for more fields to conquer.

Would I ever get any place? I had no definite goals. I turned to whatever was at hand, no doubt influenced by Mother's industriousness. She kept busy no matter what.

I continued my art work, striving to become more professional. An especially valuable mentor was Sister Patricia at St. Mary's, where I spent my first three years of high school. She was a tall and slim woman, regal in bearing, and she had enormous faith in me.

I supposed it was about then that I began to bloom. Still too shy to court the girls, I worshipped from afar. They were goddesses, to be placed on a pedestal. The only close relationship with a girl during this period was with a very bright and pretty classmate, who introduced me to F. Scott Fitzgerald's writing and, unfortunately, none of the other facts of life.

My timidity began to leave me during that last year at Willis High School, where I matriculated because St. Mary's had no twelfth grade. Suddenly, and with no particular overtures on my part, I was friends with the children of the area's upper middle class. Delaware, with its population of six thousand, was too small to have an upper class. We had to send out to Columbus for one. I shared many interests with these new friends. We loved Chaplin and Keaton. We were amused by those silent comedies in which Adolphe Menjou always seemed to be playing a headwaiter posing as a baron . . . or vice versa.

I was even intrepid enough to try acting again. I played Deadeye Dick in our school's production of *H.M.S. Pinafore*. I even played the lead in *The Fortune Hunter* at the Delaware Opera House, the theater in the courthouse complex which stood empty for long stretches of time since the town was dropped from the stock circuit. The one or two theater companies which stopped over each year weren't enough for us the culturally starved, so townspeople reopened the theater with productions which used local talent. That vague hunger for sophistication was assuaged, however inadequately.

My classmates started talking about the next school year, when most of them would be going to Ohio Wesleyan. Though I didn't know what career to pursue, being interested in everything, I felt going to college would help me decide.

Reality slapped me across the face. There was no money in the family to send me on to college, even though I would be getting my schooling in the same town and could live at home. I'd have to go to work.

So, at the age of sixteen and just graduated from high school, I left the lovely tree-shaded walks of Delaware for the wind-swept pavements of Chicago.

3 | "I will," said Chicago

It was a modest house on Polk Street, in the midst of the French colony and near the French Cathedral, where Grandmother Le Beau and Aunt Amy had lived for many years.

And it was from this house that I stuck my big toe into the current. Chicago was to be the great experiment, my halfway house between the small town of Delaware and the big time of New York.

O. Henry had taught me that I needed such a stopping place. Writing in *The Voice of the City*, he'd been able to guess the city's message: "Chicago says, unhesitatingly, 'I will.'" But the voice of New York, he conceded, was elusive. How could I, at such a tender age, grasp a message that dumfounded O. Henry?

I settled for Chicago's raucous vitality. The city enveloped me; through some form of osmosis, I absorbed its drive. I had as much right being there as the hog butcher, toolmaker, and stacker of wheat who'd come before me.

The area around my grandmother's house had deteriorated since my last visit. The change in the neighborhood, coming gradually, wasn't as obvious to those living there as it was to me. The houses weren't as well kept as I remembered them, and the streets seemed coated with grime.

43

The area would soon gain notoriety as the Fourteenth Ward, still another of the city's hell spots.

Grandmother sadly admitted the neighborhood had seen its best days. "But," she asked, "what can you expect with all those Italians moving in?"

My Italian blood should have boiled, but I knew I wasn't included in Grandmother's blanket condemnation . . . if you can call it that. Hers wasn't a prejudiced comment. It was instead the realization that the security of her insular life was being challenged. She didn't fault anyone for the change.

Grandmother had such extraordinary empathy that she unavoidably took on the accent of the black men or the Italians who began coming to her door to make deliveries. And she was so aware of their need for dignity that she hesitated to call them the milkman or the iceman. "The party that brought the milk," she'd say, or, "The party that brought the ice."

It was a loving climate, but cloying for a lively sixteen-year-old. My falling out as a practicing Catholic didn't help matters, though nothing was said about it. But the house was an adjunct to the church. Shortly after dawn, Grandmother and Aunt Amy would go off to early Mass, sometimes arriving before the priests opened the doors. The conversation every day over the breakfast table revolved around the doings of the nuns and priests. "Father Crepo didn't look well this morning," Grandmother might comment as she sat down. Aunt Amy would chime in, and it would continue through the housecleaning and cooking and ritual laundering of surplices and altar cloths.

Theirs was an unselfish, pastoral life, full of noble thoughts and good works. Grandmother's simple sweetness was a family legend. "I think you would have something nice to say abut the devil himself," Mother once observed. Grandmother paused for a while. "Well," she said, "I don't think he's as bad as he's painted."

When I moved in, Aunt Amy gave up her room to share Grandmother's brass bed in the room off the kitchen. Coming home late one night, and fixing myself a snack, I heard much creaking of bedsprings as the women were settling down for the night. "Move over, Amy." My aunt answered, "I'm over as far as I can get." There was a pause as the bedsprings creaked again. Apparently Grandmother was checking to see if Aunt Amy was telling the truth. "Go on, Amy," she instructed. "There's room for another party there."

I felt as much a displaced person as Aunt Amy, for I disturbed their

44

well-run household. And though I was given total freedom to come and go, I still felt inhibited. I planned to move into my own place as soon as I could afford it. But first I had to find a job.

Equipped with my portfolio of watercolors, I set out one morning. As I approached the intersection of Washington and State, I was seduced by an elaborate window display. The background was a Florence garden; in the foreground stood some merchandise, artfully arranged. I looked up at the store sign: *MARSHALL FIELD*.

I was directed to the top floor of the building and to a Mr. Frazier. I passed through a huge loft, where rolls of canvas were being transformed into painted backdrops, and found him in his cubbyhole, from which he functioned as chief designer and head of the display department. He looked at my portfolio and hired me on the spot. I was to be his fourth apprentice.

The job wasn't as creative as I'd hoped, but I was learning the trade in the best place possible. Despite their safe and traditional look, the windows at Marshall Field were considered the finest in the country, looked up to even by New York. Window displays were a logical progression of the department store concept which originated in Chicago. Later, New York took the lead. I suppose Savador Dali's windows for Bonwit Teller were the apotheosis.

I got to know my job and the city at the same time. I've never had a sense of money, but in retrospect I marvel at the lengths to which my minuscule salary went: I was able to pay Grandmother nominal room and board; I sent money home to supplement the income earned from the dancing school Mother started after I left home; I was able to set aside some savings for my first apartment. I had enough left over to indulge my renewed obsession in the theater and to take an occasional meal at Henrici's, the bakery-restaurant on Randolph Street where everyone of importance in Chicago seemed to hang out. It was an exciting and vital time for me. I didn't mind the Marshall Field experience too much. I was learning many valuable lessons.

I was never told that creativity was unmanly. Looking at Mr. Frazier's assistant, a William Bendix type, and talking to the other display men who were all married and raising families, I saw by their example that one could happily function as the male animal and still give vent to his so-called feminine traits. As a result, I wasn't cowed at this impressionable age into more conventionally male avenues of expression. I'm thankful for that. I'd make a miserable football coach.

The men also taught me the dedication and commitment of the true

45

professional. They had an easy confidence in their ability. I found such an attitude most attractive, and hoped that I could approach my craft in the same way.

Store windows were changed four times a year. Mr. Frazier, consulting with the merchandising people, concocted elaborate themes and brought in voluptuous statuary. The man who painted the backgrounds, a German, favored the gardens of Florence for his inspiration. If the windows were of a piece, they were its best rendition.

At the outset, I was assigned to the men's store across the street from the main building. But the infinite detail taken in deciding on the proper tie for that conservatively tailored suit was too much for even my exacting tastes. Working on the State Street windows, devoted to fashion, was the most coveted assignment in the department. I was realist enough to see there was a chain of succession, and promotions came slowly. So I asked to be transferred to the less desirable windows on Wabash Avenue, which displayed furniture, decorative accessories, and antiques. The request, happily, was granted.

Changing those windows every season was grueling work concentrated in brief snatches of time. We'd roll down the curtains over the windows to hide our activities from the street. Moving in furniture and setting it just so took all night. The curtains over the windows came up with the sun.

Having recently become transfixed by the work of Robert Edmond Jones on the stage, I came to see the many similarities between set design and window display, and started to develop ideas on how I would bring those already excellent windows into the twentieth century if I ever got the chance. Yet, as I learned soon enough, this wasn't what I wanted to do for the rest of my life.

I made a concrete start on my nebulous ambition to become a painter. But the classes at the Chicago Art Institute, where I enrolled, didn't inspire me, and I returned to working on my own.

I even made a half-hearted attempt at acting. A blind woman came in one day, accompanied by a young girl, asking to borrow some props from Mr. Frazier. She was with a group which put on plays in a theater behind the Radical Book Shop on North Clark Street. They were doing an O'Neill one-acter. "Would you like to join our group?" the woman asked.

I reported to the theater to read for one of the lesser parts, and went into rehearsal the same night. It was one of O'Neill's greatest exercises in foreboding doom . . . a retired sea captain going mad, along with his son . . . given to many pregnant pauses, it seemed to me, and to frequent trips to the roof in order to symbolically find the meaning of life, a vision he would receive through his trusty telescope. I was going mad along with the captain and his son.

Next door was a dance hall separated from the theater by a plywood partition. We were blitzed by the yelling and cussing that accompanied the frequent free-for-alls on the other side of that thin wall. Sometimes, when some battler was knocked against the partition, it looked as if we would be brought into the action . . . I fully expected it to happen whenever that wall finally toppled.

One evening, an Irishman came into the theater. He'd just been released from jail after serving a sentence for some sort of organized anarchy. "We won't stop," he screamed, "until we hang every capitalist from the highest lamp post!" The troupe reacted to his ranting as if it were a commonplace occurrence, which it probably was, meeting his outburst with desultory cheers. That did it for me. I packed my gear and walked out, turning my back on acting forevermore. If the performing arts lost a bright light you can blame it on the Bolsheviks.

My spare time would be devoted to the other side of the footlights, I decided. And there was a wealth of theatrical experiences to be enjoyed . . . and to be shared. I'd originally started going to the theater with Don Bernard, a friend from Delaware, who was studying voice in Chicago. But as those vital male juices started flowing, our relationship started to pall. No matter how much we liked each other, we liked girls better. My animal instincts overpowered my timidity, and I began courting the girls.

At first, it was all a hug and a tickle. "You're looking a little peaked," Mother observed on one of her occasional visits. I must have reddened. But there were some fevers—some frustrations—I'd rather not talk about.

But, as I became more assertive . . .

"You have nice color," Mother commented on a later visit. I smiled knowingly . . . to myself.

If I couldn't discuss with her the unraveling of life's greatest mystery, I could enthuse about our common interests. I'd describe the extraordinary theater touring in Chicago . . . the sophisticated comedies of Lonsdale and Behrman starring the dashing Ina Claire and Mary Nash . . . the costumes designed by James Reynolds for *Don Quixote,* patterned on Velásquez's paintings of Philip IV and the Spanish Infantas, using deep vibrant colors and innovative combinations of velvet,

47

satin, taffeta, and lace textures . . . the musical revues and vaudeville shows at McVicker's Theatre on Madison Street, particularly the *Ziegfeld Follies* with all those beads and feathers strategically placed on the form divine by designer John Harkrider.

I'd taken to sketching the actors and their costumes in the satirical style of Ralph Barton in *Vanity Fair*. They were much appreciated by my friends. Inspired by their reaction, I had them mounted and sold them backstage. I began doing so well with them that I was now able to move into my own place.

Grandmother and Aunt Amy reacted to my decision with perfect equanimity. They were polite, so they disguised their joy. The quarters had been cramped. They could spread out again. My moving would mean less work, and they knew I'd come often to visit.

One of the employees at Marshall Field, a dapper fellow in my department, told me there was space available in his rooming house on the far North Side. I snapped it up. I took the elevated train to work every day. At first I found commuting to be exciting. The unrelieved sameness of the trip, however, soon became a monotonous waste of time.

While backstage peddling my water colors one night, I was approached by a photographer by the name of Paul Stone, who was there hawking his own wares. "You know," he said, looking at my work, "you have a fine sense of composition. If you can do this sort of thing, you can become a fine photographer." The money he offered was right . . . more right, at any rate, than I was getting at Marshall Field.

It seemed fitting that I should now find digs more suitable for a cameraman about town. I explored the area on the near North Side around the Ambassador Hotel and came across one of the few brownstone buildings remaining there. The Gold Coast was being built up with more stately mansions. One of the most regal was Mrs. Potter Palmer's, its back turned to the comparatively modest building in which I found my L-shaped room. The apartment had comfort and charm. It would do very nicely.

I moved in with my few possessions. I wasn't acquisitive. My only concession to conspicuous consumption was my sparse record collection. I didn't collect art. Reproductions would do nicely. It would have been ruinous to indulge the gamut of styles and periods which captured my fancy.

All of Chicago, after all, belonged to me. And with my new job, it was mine to enjoy more than ever.

Paul Stone's business was equally divided among society and show business. His work was in the style of the best photography of the time. He wasn't Steichen or Karsh, but it wasn't for lack of trying.

His soft, cultivated voice went down well with the gentry; his high strung nervousness struck a responsive chord in frenetic show people.

I tried to emulate his rapport with clients. At first, I was very shy, keeping my head behind the camera. But I progressed to the point where, in order to get a better effect, I would shove a person off a bench if I had to.

The practical course I took in that studio, off State Street and in the heart of the theatrical district, would be of enormous value to me. I learned the different effects one creates with light. Stone's photography was soft, but in sharp focus, so that it could reproduce on the printed page. This taught me a way of creating mood. An easier way was the plain blue backdrop on rollers, over which we could throw different pieces of cloth to create many looks, particularly when we varied the dimmers on the lights. When all else failed, there was the considerable retouching which Stone favored. I shared this duty with the young fellow in the lab.

Another employee was a Spring Byington type, from a North Shore family which had seen better days. She was hired to drum up society business. Sitting in her cubicle, newspaper clippings before her, she would get on the telephone. She may have fluttered, but she sold.

One of her most minor selling points, though I took great pride in it nonetheless, was the instinctive way I had of placing the sitter's hands so that they wouldn't look awkward or arch.

Actresses like Ina Claire—and I still remember how I quaked with nervousness when I photographed her—were supposed to know their best angles and sides. They were often wrong. When I was assigned to photograph them in costume, I would have to jolly them out of their misconceptions. I suppose I learned to handle them quite well.

A few months after I started working for Stone, he had a nervous breakdown. It was now up to me to do all the shooting . . . the actresses, the society weddings, the businessmen's portraits. I took it in my stride. I developed such an efficient rhythm to my work that I continued to take most of the pictures for the studio after Stone returned to work. I'd also come to realize that in the hands of some people photography is an art. But not mine.

This vague feeling of dissatisfaction became magnified when I happened upon Pennell's biography of James McNeill Whistler in Stone's studio. My reading tastes had always been catholic . . . classic plays to detective stories in pulp magazines. But here was a man—and an artist—with whom I could identify.

A dandy and a rooster, Whistler originated epigrams that Oscar Wilde would later pass off as his own. I related to his penchant for titling his paintings with musical terms. I envied his childhood in the Russian court, his youth as a West Point cadet and starving artist in a Paris garret, his devotion to his distinguished wife.

His many facets enthralled me. He was a pioneer in interior design, introducing blue and white décor and Japanese china to London. He had an affinity for yellow, painting the walls of his house in its most sunny shading. His simplicity in the era of vulgarity and opulence was distinctive. He also invented the Sunday brunch . . . but nobody's perfect.

Whistler's, then, was the first biography of a painter I'd ever read. I was eager to read more. And since neither friends nor family had any such books in their collections, I explored the world of Brentano's. Even the process of selecting a book dazzled me. I saw customers come in and go directly to the book they wanted. How did one develop this homing instinct? What were all those worlds they were seeking?

A few years later, when we were both starting out at Metro, I told William Saroyan of this experience. He found my innocence so amusing that he adapted it in this way for *The Human Comedy:*

When the two boys entered this humble but impressive building, they entered an area of profound and almost frightening silence. It seemed as if even the walls had become speechless, and the floor and the tables, as if silence had engulfed everything in the building. There were old men reading newspapers. There were town philosophers. There were high school boys and girls doing research, but everyone was hushed, because they were seeking wisdom. They were near books. They were trying to find out. Lionel not only whispered, he moved on tiptoe. Lionel whispered because he was under the impression that it was out of respect for books, not consideration for readers. Ulysses followed him, also on tiptoe, and they explored the library, each finding many treasures, Lionel—books, and Ulysses—people. Lionel didn't read books and he hadn't come to the public library to get any for himself. He just liked to *see* them—the thousands of them. He pointed out a whole row of shelved books to his friend and then he whispered, "All of these—and these. And these. Here's a red one. All these. There's a green one. All these."

I wasn't quite as unread as the youngest Macauley and his little friend, but my reading would have to be the college education I never had, and I embarked on this curriculum with a vengeance.

50

Artists' biographies were supplanted by the English translations of de Maupassant and Chateaubriand, then by the romantic works of the Brontës, the fiction of Maugham, the plays of Shaw.

Inspired by the set designs of Gordon Craig and Robert Edmond Jones, and by the costumes of James Reynolds and Robert Locker, I looked toward New York now more than ever. It wasn't long before I started subscribing to the New York *World*, this in the days of Heywood Broun and Alexander Woollcott. Their viewpoint was what passed for sophistication in those days . . . in these days too. I was similarly trying to pass.

I might have more greatly appreciated Chicago of that era had my mind not been so full of New York. I was, however, aware of the art movements flourishing in Chicago during that time. Several of them didn't involve canvas and palette.

There was an art to living in Chicago . . . an impudent style with little class . . . an I'll-get-mine attitude that spawned the Al Capones and the Samuel Insulls . . . it was as directly flamboyant as the Chicago jazz movement sparked by Bix Beiderbecke, Eddie Condon, Jimmy McPartland, and Benny Goodman . . . it was writing with its sleeves rolled up as practiced by Carl Sandburg, Theodore Dreiser, and Sherwood Anderson.

I didn't know many painters in Chicago, though I was aware of a vital art movement in and around the Chicago Art Institute. It couldn't be ignored, what with its extraordinary collection of Impressionistic art.

The world of art was already one step beyond, and even we in the provinces were taken up with the surreal. Freud was starting to penetrate the consciousness of the world. There'd already been traces of surrealism in the work of Ronald Firbank and Aubrey Beardsley. Suddenly we were all interpreting dreams, and the talents of Duchamps, Ernst, and Dali burst wide open. They were followed by the experimental films of Cocteau and Buñuel. I was intrigued, but not very, being more taken with the accomplishments of earlier artists.

I yearned to be a participant like Whistler instead of a spectator, and I was itching to move on. I didn't concede to having an inconstant nature, for I was feeling my way, trying on everything for size and judging its wearability as I went along. Blame it on my youth.

At what other stage of life could one summon such brashness and presumption . . . to have the chutzpah to present myself as the savior of the Chicago Theatre?

With singleness of mind, I called on Frank Cambria, the head man there. He looked at my portfolio, which now included photographs as well as water colors.

"What do you have in mind, young man?"

"I think you should start your own costume department . . . and I should be in charge."

His eyes narrowed. I couldn't tell if he was affronted or amused.

The Chicago Theatre on State Street was part of the Balaban and Katz chain, and it presented quite elaborate one-hour stage presentations along with featured films. It was a format later copied by the Radio City Music Hall.

And here was I offering my unsolicited advice.

"What do you know about costume design?" Mr. Cambria asked.

"Well," I answered in a surprisingly cool tone, "I grew up in the theater. And I am very familiar with the work of James Roberts and Robert Locker and Lee Simonson."

"Do you sew?"

"No."

"Then how do you expect to accomplish this?"

"Well, I think I have a feel for it," I said. "Anything I don't know now I'll learn within a year."

Mr. Cambria turned pensive. Then he rose. "Come with me," he said.

He took me to meet A. J. Balaban. The interrogation procedure was repeated. They excused themselves and I was directed to an outer office while they discussed, I presumed, my inordinate gall.

The door opened and Mr. Cambria came out. "All right, young man, you're hired."

I didn't need any elevated to take me home that night. I must have walked, but my feet never touched the ground.

The Balaban and Katz organization had rented all its costumes in the past. My assignment was to give their shows a custom touch. I plowed right in. Nobody told me about budgets, so I was extravagant as I thought the traffic would bear. Months later, I was surprised to learn that the new department was operating considerably under the budget set up for it.

Women ran the sewing machines in the workroom which we installed in the cellar. Though we still rented some of the men's wardrobe, our department did the costumes for everyone else: the specialty acts, the chorus, the dancers.

I designed for very elaborate productions, and I was soon accomplished

52

in the baubles, bangles, braids, and spangles used in my craft. It was the hardest work I'd ever done.

The shows ran a week at each theater, opening at the Chicago, then moving on to the Tivoli and the Uptown. A. J. Balaban would tour the theaters with Mr. Cambria and me every Monday, when the shows changed.

We'd catch the first show at the Chicago downtown, then to the second show at the Tivoli. We'd have dinner before driving to the North Side and the last show at the Uptown.

The costumes I designed—as well as the scenery, as it came to pass— were then disassembled to be used another day. Those pieces of material and the flats of the sets were recycled time and again.

I truly don't know how good I was at this sort of thing. But I do know that I got much better, and notice was being taken of my work.

My active social life got even busier. I'd been rubbing—not bending— elbows with celebrated people. I was glad for the chance to finally meet them.

One of Chicago's most interesting salons was conducted by Lillian Rosedale Goodman, who'd been a concert singer. She'd also written, "Chérie, chérie, je t'aime." I was introduced to her, and was suddenly bombarded with invitations to her distinguished gatherings. A handsome older woman, she looked like a Russian opera star, with her black hair combed severely back and the long earrings which she favored.

I also began to pal around with Leo Stahr, a jolly German who designed sets. He and his wife would have me to dinner often, as would the Cambrias. An older man hired by the company as music arranger also befriended me. His name was Victor Young, and he later became a distinguished composer-conductor in films. Since he also worked at night, there were many occasions when we'd take a break, and he'd fascinate me with his stories of the theater in Poland and Russia, where he'd toured as a violin prodigy.

Then there were the girls. I'd seen the way one works in the theater, getting to know one's associates better than their wives did. I knew these intense relationships would end when we moved on to different projects. Emotional relationships, I realized, are also ephemeral in the theater. Showgirls and dancers came through the city. They were accessible, and seemed as wary of complications as I was.

As long as no one was hurt, the directness of it all made it so much easier to overcome my shyness.

Then, inevitably, it happened. I was having an affair with a beautiful girl, a specialty dancer several years older. When we first met, I vaguely remembered mention of her husband, an actor on tour. That vital piece of information soon slipped my mind.

Then I heard the husband was in town with his play. I felt uneasy.

One morning, there was a knock on my door. I opened it, and there stood a distinguished-looking man about forty. I swallowed hard. I knew.

"May I come in?" he asked in a friendly voice.

He entered stage left, straight into this Noël Coward confrontation.

"You're quite young," he observed.

I stuttered a reply.

"Don't be nervous," he said. "You have nothing to fear. I was just curious. I wanted to see who you were."

I breathed a little easier. We sat down to chat. I found him worldly and charming, and with a depth of understanding rare to my experience.

Even so, I had no stomach for this sort of intrigue. I can say that our meeting ended the affair . . . eventually.

I had already started cheating on the girl. For I'd started my flirtation with New York at last.

Balaban and Katz amalgamated with Paramount-Publix. The three-theater operation was now part of a national chain. I was taken to New York to occasionally work on shows which would tour later.

It was everything I expected it to be. Working on the shows at the Paramount Theater on Broadway, where the units originated, was my first taste of it all. Once the rigors of putting a new show together were completed, I could explore the rest of the city.

I was drawn time and again to Times Square and the color and fire of all that neon. Usually staying in a hotel on the East Side, I'd walk to the theater district, bathed in that awesome light. How well I understood G. K. Chesterton's observation when he'd seen the letters and trademarks advertising everything from pork to pianos: "What a glorious garden of wonders this would be, to any one who was lucky enough to be unable to read."

Life in Chicago seemed purposeless.

I was unaware that the New York theater was in less than blooming health. Vaudeville had laid an egg along with the stock market. Chicago hadn't felt the effect of their demise as yet. The city was too close to the soil and the stock yard to feel the immediate effect of paper phantoms. McVicker's, the Rialto, and the Balaban and Katz theaters still were running shows for big and unappreciative audiences.

54

Moving to New York became my foremost goal. Unknown to me, Balaban and Katz—for reasons of their own—had drawn the same conclusions.

Mr. Cambria delivered an ultimatum. If I wanted to stay with Balaban and Katz, I'd have to move with them to New York.

4 | The Greener Pastures

New York in 1931 was in the process of raising up one institution while tearing down another. The Empire State Building—the world's tallest—opened in May just as the Seabury Committee began the investigation which would eventually lead to Jimmy Walker's resignation as mayor.

The theater world was seeing similar ups and downs. Musical revues were supplanting the drawing-room comedies and Ruritanian operettas of the Twenties. Lavishly mounted and slickly directed, they were opulent distractions during the early days of the Depression. Successful musical revues that year, running 175 performances or more, included *The Band Wagon; Ziegfeld Follies of 1931; Earl Carroll's Vanities; George White's Scandals.*

Another musical, *Of Thee I Sing,* with a score by George and Ira Gershwin and book by George S. Kaufman and Morrie Ryskind, was continuing the book-show concept so effectively mounted four years previously by Florenz Ziegfeld with his production of the Jerome Kern-Oscar Hammerstein adaptation of Edna Ferber's *Show Boat.* That trailblazing approach would prove to be the musical theater's next new wave.

Though I related to the musical theater, I had no perception that this was the route it would soon be taking. I was too busy taking in all the musical world of the moment to look at it with any knowing overview.

I'd have to use the title of a non-musical production that year to describe my feelings. These, indeed, were *the green pastures.*

I arrived in New York to a tiny Greenwich Village nest, sublet from vagabond-dancer Jacques Cartier. It was hardly the proper setting for "*the* modern interpreter of rococo grace and master of Latin suavity and sense of color," as a theater critic was to describe me in a few years. But it was a well-kept secret at the time. Only one person knew I was the modern interpreter of rococo grace, et cetera, and I didn't have the knack of tooting my own horn. The apartment filled my needs very nicely and, what's more, it was across the street from Chumley's, the hangout for struggling artists and writers of the period. But the whole world was struggling at the time, the Depression more with us than ever.

Almost the first person I met was a charming young dynamo named Eleanor Lambert. She'd just married Seymour Berkson, one of Hearst's right-hand men, and was active herself in public relations. "I'm going to have to represent you very soon," she said after looking at my portfolio. "You're going to do great things." I accepted the remark as a friendly comment made by a very nice lady, but I certainly didn't consider Eleanor clairvoyant. Of course, she wasn't known as the high priestess of fashion as yet.

My work meshed smoothly with the other artists at Paramount. I was back to designing costumes exclusively, being precluded from doing sets because I didn't belong to the union. Brooks Costumes, just down the street from Paramount, ran up my designs. It was there that I met some of the people I'd only read about in Chicago—Robert Edmond Jones and James Reynolds. I was doing hard, creative work, putting costumes together for the production units doing the Paramount-Publix circuit. One such unit went out each week.

Somewhere in the back of my mind was the desire to go to Paris to paint, but it was as pressing an ambition as the diet the fat lady plans to start next week.

What was more vitally important was membership in the Society of Painters and Paper Hangers. Admission to the union local was difficult. Only a few budding set designers were accepted each year. Someone introduced me to Woodman Thompson, a prominent stage designer who also lived in the Village, and he began instructing me and a few others on techniques and scale. With his help, we were all accepted into the Society, and I remain a member to this day.

I continued, however, working only on costumes. At the outset, it was a full-time job designing the equivalent of a Broadway show every week.

57

Touring in these units was a young pianist named Oscar Levant. But we didn't meet until he retired a couple of years later at the age of twenty-seven to become the wise-cracking darling of the Gershwin set, with no visible means of support, but with a ready fund of jokes and sayings about his various neuroses and complexes.

The first member of the Gershwin salon that I met was E. Y. (Yip) Harburg. His social arena was broader than Oscar's, and we came upon each other at a party given by theater critic Gilbert W. Gabriel. I was drawn to his rare good nature, and he must have seen in me a kid who needed more polish and dash, which in his kindness he would help me acquire. I look back today and wonder where I got the time for such cake-frosting.

In addition to costuming a different show each week, I was also doing outside work. I first illustrated *Casanova's Memoirs* in the Aubrey Beardsley style for a publisher of semi-erotica in the Village. He would turn up at my one-room apartment and wait for me to finish whatever drawing was immediately needed. Sometimes we'd kibitz, but more often he'd fall asleep on the bed—the dominant piece of furniture in the room—while I worked into the night.

Next, I was hired by Earl Carroll to design a three-hundred-foot wide curtain for his 1931 *Vanities,* similar to the ones Erté did for the *Folies-Bergère*. I'd never done anything like that, but I eagerly went ahead with my Erté-inspired design . . . but for considerably less money than the original. I hadn't been to France, but I could see the way American craftsmen executed the Frenchman's ideas, since George White had been buying them for his *Scandals*.

My interpretation, using absinthe green chiffon seven times the width of the stage, incorporated silver embroidery in the gathered material. Strategically placed openings in the curtain had parts of showgirls' bodies peeping through, their coral costumes embroidered in gold and silver, with the girls wearing elaborate feather headdresses. The girls walked the seven widths of the curtain, gradually unveiling the tableau which was also being revealed as the lights slowly came up. I felt it came off effectively, even though Robert Benchley criticized the design for its "definitely Negroid sense of color." He, unfortunately, was ignorant of the traditional use of bold color in the European theater, particularly as inspired by Bakst and executed by Remisoff and Soudakin for the Ballet Russe. It was easier to go with the inaccurate stereotype, with its implication of riotous, mismatched colors, a slap at Negroes as well as at me.

But Carroll saw it differently, and he soon put me to designing both

58

sets and costumes for the 1932 *Vanities*. A young fellow named Harold Arlen was writing some of the music.

Spending my spare time at the Broadway Theatre, I became intrigued by the owner of one of those legs which peeped through my curtain the previous year. We became friendly . . . extremely. Then, someone told me she was Earl Carroll's girl friend. So much for that.

Carroll was a very thin man, soft-spoken, and with no nonsense about him. He was always in a smock, headphones over his ears during rehearsals, as he coolly put the girls through their paces. He put me through mine too. I finished the job, never having received an invitation to his sanctum, where it was rumored backers could look into the show-girls' dressing room.

Grace Moore then asked me to do the art direction for an operetta, *Du Barry*, scheduled to open in November 1932.

It had originally been produced abroad, and librettists Rowland Leigh and Desmond Carter were brought from England to revamp the work to Miss Moore's specifications and limitations.

I found the lady very much the artist, with definite ideas about what was seemly for her.

She was complimentary about a ballroom set done in chinoiserie style, but she was less than excited about a couple of other ideas I had. One scene had her inside a coach, being transported for her first meeting with Louis XV. The major-domo was giving her Pygmalion-like instructions on how to behave before royalty as they headed for the palace. The center of a black velvet curtain was cut out in a cloud shape, through which could be seen a portion of the coach and its revolving back wheel. I suggested the coach be rocked from side to side and up and down to go along with the wheel's movement. It didn't work out. The Madame got seasick. We had to settle on a less-satisfactory up and down movement.

Also, in an early scene in a brothel, I suggested Du Barry should wear a kimono-wrapper of sorts. Miss Moore didn't feel comfortable in the getup. We'd been rehearsing late into that particular night. She terminated our discussion by stalking angrily off the stage.

The friction was overcome, and the show moved to Boston for the out-of-town tryout. Our stay there was uneventful and, though the operetta was only modestly acclaimed, we prepared to bring it into New York.

My relations with the star were now cordial. It was only natural that I should send her an effusive good-luck telegram on opening night. It wasn't acknowledged.

A couple of days later, producer Morris Green came up to me. "She thinks you insulted her on purpose," he said.

"What?"

"The telegram you sent," Green answered. "I don't think it was very smart."

It was only then that the reason for Miss Moore's displeasure became known. I'd inadvertently addressed the message to Florence Moore, not Grace, and Florence was a singer-comedienne of mass appeal. Since Grace had high respect for her "art," I couldn't have been as bitchily insulting even if I'd tried.

There were many witnesses to my past vagueness and forgetfulness, and Miss Moore finally accepted my notorious lack of memory for names as an excuse. She could even laugh about it later. She was amused, at any rate, for the first eighty-seven performances. The show never saw its eighty-eighth.

With a track record of sorts behind me, Paramount executives broadened my duties to include set design. I was given the opportunity to arrange girls and glamour in costly tableaus, just as Ben Ali Haggin was doing for Ziegfeld. Shortly after, our operations moved to Astoria, Long Island, where Paramount Pictures' East Coast headquarters were located. I had to take a subway to work . . . but not for long. Paramount soon decided that traveling units weren't economically feasible, replacing them with a big band policy. In the cold winter of 1933, when the country was fearing much more than fear itself, I was out of a job.

Never having any sense of money, I'd spent every penny as I'd earned it, on books, art supplies, and girls . . . women, rather, for it was about this time that I discovered how much safer it was to get involved with ladies a few years older or with women who were discreetly not working at being married. I was down to my last dollar, so I bought a couple of pounds of beef, potatoes, and onions and cooked up a huge stew. It lasted for several days, but with only a nickel left in my pocket, my next recourse was the bread line.

I didn't quite make it. Like an improbable deus ex machina, the kind the audience groans at for its obviousness, I received a call from Radio City Music Hall. Would I be interested in a job as their chief costume designer?

I played hard to get . . . for a tenth of a second.

Radio City Music Hall, along with the Center Theatre, had opened in Rockefeller Center the previous December, its seating capacity of

60

6,200 making it the largest indoor theater in the world. The seventy-story Radio City office building would open the following November.

The Music Hall had been open only two months, presenting musical extravaganzas designed by Robert Edmond Jones. The Center Theatre was showing motion pictures. Neither of the concepts proved successful, and both theaters were temporarily closed. Jones left right after.

It was then that S. L. Rothafel was hired, and the Music Hall regeared to present motion pictures and vaudeville acts. Rothafel was better known as Roxy.

Vaudeville had passed its peak by this time, but being a great show-man Roxy was determined that this last stand would be the most success-ful. He brought in a precision dancing troupe of leggy girls from the Roxy Theatre which he egocentrically named the Roxyettes. A glee club and ballet were also formed as the permanent supporting cast for performers doing their specialty vaudeville turns. The new approach had been in operation only three weeks when I came on the staff.

It took a lot of costumes to fill that enormous stage. The first week was the toughest. Not only did I have to worry about mounting the show, I was very nervous about not having paid my rent. I hurried to the bank on payday, Monday, March 6. But it was closed. In one of his first directives as President, Roosevelt had declared a bank holiday. Many others were in the same financial pickle.

But that temporary problem was overcome. One that gave me much greater pause was trying to get along with the gruff-spoken, self-aggran-dizing Roxy. He was obstreperous and fault-finding, and he seemed to zero in on me. Perhaps, being the youngest, I seemed the most defenseless. He certainly proved it to me. I was no match for Roxy's caustic tongue.

Not that others were immune from his barbs. Art director Clark Robin-son, dance director Russell Markert, and I would work all through Wednesday night to prepare for the Thursday openings. No motion picture was held over in those days. It had its one-week run, as did the stage presentation.

Roxy would look at our work. "What will I do with it?" he'd ask himself in a loud, intensely dramatic soliloquy. "How will I save it? Well, I'll save it with lights." He'd sit at the big electric console experimenting with a lot of colored gelatins until our botched up handiwork was effectively camouflaged to his satisfaction. We'd suffer through his criticisms as we supervised the three shows on opening day, and got even more lip at the planning sessions held over Friday lunch. But who could eat?

Roxy obviously believed that keeping his underlings off balance and defensive was the best way to get work out of them. I don't know how effective this tactic is. To me, it's a contemptible practice.

I was at the Music Hall only a few weeks when Clark Robinson suddenly resigned. Roxy scrambled around trying to fill the gap. His eyes settled on me. I would be the new art director, in addition to retaining my duties as costume designer. Instead of doing the job of three men, I would now be doing the job of six . . . and getting a proportionally larger share of Roxy's sarcasms.

The first week of December 1933 marked the end of a historic era. Prohibition was repealed, but it was significant to me in another respect. The show that week was an unusually ambitious one, its highlight being the "Scheherazade Suite" of Rimsky-Korsakoff. I created very elaborate miniatures for the production, and the New York *Times* review marveled at "the Persian rugs, muezzins, elephants, janizaries, and veiled houris."

Roxy had the paper in front of him as we sat down in the enormous upstairs conference room for lunch. He looked over at me, then at the others. "You know, I've been picking on this fellow," Roxy said. "But all that picking brought fine results. He's an artist."

From that point on, my relations with Roxy were cordial . . . as cordial, at any rate, as you can have with a tin god. He started riding someone else, until that person too delivered. It was a painful way to whip someone into shape, but it did get results, and in a backhanded way I suppose I'm grateful. Roxy pushed me to creative heights that even I didn't know were in me.

The happy ending to the Roxy story would have had him transformed like some Ebenezer Scrooge from ruthless martinet to benevolent father figure, all of us soaring together to unparalleled heights. The Brothers Rockefeller had a different idea.

Roxy's abrasiveness proved too much for them, as did his extravagance and ego. He was unceremoniously sacked, the convenient "artistic differences" term given out, I suppose, so that Roxy would save face. There were no drawn-out tearful goodbyes to mark the transition.

W. G. Van Schmus, a New England banker type, was installed as vice-president and managing director. He proved to be soft-spoken, methodical, unflappable . . . and a surprisingly imaginative person.

The climate he created was such a welcome contrast from the Roxy regime that we didn't seem to mind any longer those sleepless nights and the endless rounds of work. Somehow I absorbed even more duties, replacing Roxy at the electric console to light the shows. I began to have some respect for his ability, as I jiggled through the very complicated technique, sometimes with as many as one hundred cues. I'd work through Wednesday night, the cast coming in at eight in the morning for final rehearsal, before the first of the three opening day shows went on at noon. I'd wake up from my weekly Thursday night collapse in time for the Friday lunch meeting, as did all my confreres.

Inspiration had to come as regularly as the 5:02, and many were the times that I just managed to creak into the station on time. Sometime during this madness I discovered an extraordinary record that miraculously supplied me with much-needed ideas. I wish I could say it was something by Scarlatti. But it was a less baroque work with more mass appeal, Claude Thornhill's "Tiajuana."

That we had time for a social life too amazes me today. Of course, we stole the time, not from our everyday activities, but from dispensable sleep. These were hours that were never replaced, but we were young and it made little difference. I'd occasionally double date with Russell Markert, who had started the dancing troupe under Roxy and supervised their change-over afterward as the Rockettes. He had a gorgeous redheaded girl friend, a showgirl named Lucille Ball. (I was then going with one of the well-known Giersdorf singing sisters.) Lucy and I didn't become friends until much later, for our early meetings were mostly at crowded parties. But I was struck at the time by her elegant humor and her enormous joie de vivre. *The Thin Man* had just made a big splash as a movie and, to me, she and Russell were Nora and Nick Charles come to life. If I had predicted her future then, I would have seen her as another Myrna Loy instead of the female Charlie Chaplin which she actually became.

If most of my socializing was with the kids I was working with, I was also preparing to move uptown . . . both to an apartment on East 52nd Street and into the Gershwin set. Yip Harburg took me to Leonore and Ira Gershwin's never-closing open houses. Talent seemed to be the only criterion for admission to that apartment on 72nd Street, and I was flattered to be there with such luminaries as Harpo Marx, Dashiell Hammett, Lillian Hellman, Heywood Broun, John O'Hara, Dorothy Parker, and Moss Hart.

Oscar Levant was the wit of the group, his lines coming fast, the ferocity aimed mostly at himself. He was friendly with everyone from newspaper publishers to gangsters and waiters. Everyone fought to have him, and since he wasn't very active professionally, he didn't fight back.

63

He was a sponger of the first order . . . and the second and the third. Yet he never wore out the welcome for himself and the constantly changing assortment of beautiful girls he took everywhere with him . . . most often one at a time.

Dotty Parker's humor was of a different sort. She was a quiet, darling girl. She'd look at you with those enormous innocent eyes and you would have trusted her with your bank book and your diary. But no sooner did you leave the room, than pow! No one was immune, and I probably was no exception.

The lovable mascot of the group was Moss Hart. His first huge success in 1930 with *Once in a Lifetime* found him socially unprepared, so he learned the proper graces in public . . . how to stir his teacup with a gold spoon, how to light a lady's cigarette with a gold lighter, where to place noted friends' pictures in their gold frames, and—probably—the proper way to tie his gold shoelaces. If Oscar was the original man who came to dinner, Moss was the original golden boy.

He told of the time soon after he made good that he was invited to be the guest of honor at a dinner party. He completely forgot about the engagement until the following day. What to do? It would have been bad enough if he'd been just an invited guest, but to be the honored one and not show up was another thing altogether. He was too ashamed to admit his error, yet some explanation was necessary. Moss decided to cool it until the following Friday. He rang his hosts' doorbell promptly at the appointed hour in black tie . . . but one week late. They received him in pajamas and wrappers, and after mutual apologies for the "misunderstanding," they all retired to the kitchen for potluck.

Then came his triumphant European tour, with the stately homes of England thrown open to him. At the first of a series of very elegant dinners, the ladies retired to the drawing room while the gentlemen stayed at the dining table for brandy and cigars. Moss rose with the ladies, and he fidgeted with embarrassment the rest of the evening over still another of his social gaffes . . . though he got much conversational mileage out of them later.

George Gershwin would occasionally come over from his apartment across the street. He was writing a folk opera to be called *Porgy and Bess* with his brother, and his muse accompanied him even on social occasions. I saw him often, but I didn't feel I knew George well. He was so lionized that there were always people three-deep around him.

He'd take over the piano and play all evening long. Other composers would throw darts at him, but George was oblivious to them. He knew

64

he was great, and there was no false modesty about it. Lee would laugh, "Isn't that just like George?" We'd agree, and how lucky we were to have him. Then, off he'd hurry, on his way to an engagement with a lady who was rarely identified . . . most probably because she was seldom the same one. He wasn't about to marry. He liked his freedom too much.

I suppose my exposure to these larger than life characters would have been somewhat limited if I'd only gone once or twice to the Gershwins. But Lee and Ira took me under their wing, and they became my most special friends.

Some people are even more attractive because they seem to be unaware of their charms. Ira was much like this. He didn't know how great a talent he had. He conceded that George was a genius, but he tended to dismiss himself as a not very gifted songsmith. With his brother he wrote such standards as "Embraceable You," "They Can't Take That Away From Me," "Who Cares?", "A Foggy Day in London Town," and "Lady Be Good," along with hundreds of others. But with other composers such as Kurt Weill, Vernon Duke, Jerome Kern, Harold Arlen, and Arthur Schwartz, his later output was no less impressive: "My Ship," "Long Ago and Far Away," "I Can't Get Started," and "The Man That Got Away." He was just as much a giant as his brother.

And his wife Lee was also an eminence . . . she still is. Charming and vivacious, all of Ira's friends were her friends. As long as the front light was on, their house was open to callers. Food and drink were always available, as was Lee's gentle kindness. She became as important a part of my life as Ira. Not only did she introduce me to many people, she was always there during the rough times, both in New York and in Hollywood. I love them both.

I was dating a girl named Nell O'Day by the time I became a regular at the Gershwins—she later married lyricist Ted Fetter—and through her I met a girl named Marian Herwood. The work at the Music Hall was getting so involved that it was decided I should have a secretary. I hired Marian.

Back at the Music Hall, I was being given every freedom. Mr. Van Schmus's only worry was that we shouldn't offend the conservative people sitting in the reserved mezzanine section. It was an enormous education, designing sets which used elevators and interlocking turntables and learning to look at effects from the slant of mechanical capability. I had to think up four or five scenes a week, and I could only work one week ahead of time. The ideas somehow came. I don't know what would have happened if any of us got sick.

65

I looked to every influence. Then suddenly one hit me between the eyes. Why not surrealism? I tried adding this touch to several productions. I occasionally stumbled. "Only Vincente Minnelli could make a tree like the one that figures in the superfluous number, 'Trees,' based on the Joyce Kilmer ballade," Bosley R. Crowther wrote in a New York *Times* review.

I continued experimenting. One week I might design Ferde Grofe's "Tabloid Suite" and use newspapers for the set and costumes. Then I might put together little vignettes using popular magazines of the day as backdrops. The possibilities were infinite, particularly when one experimented with color and all its shadings under a varied assortment of lighting effects.

As my responsibilities increased, so had my salary. With my move to East 52nd Street, I was able to hire a valet.

A young Japanese named Hara came for his interview, and looked around at the empty apartment. "The furniture hasn't arrived yet," I told him. "Can you start next Wednesday?"

The furniture still wasn't there when he showed up for his first day of work. He looked at me, surely wondering if there was any money to pay him. "You sure you want Japanese butler?" he asked. Assured, he moved in.

Hara was totally unexpressive, but highly opinionated. He could say the most outrageous things, which you wouldn't permit from your closest friends. He would come to the opening of each show, and the next day offer his severest unsolicited criticism. But what could I do? He was a character, and friends would invite themselves to dinner just to meet Hara.

One evening, Kay Swift—who was then going with George Gershwin and had written "Can't We Be Friends"—was in a group having dinner at my house. A piece of steak got caught in her throat. She was gasping for air, and the rest of us were frantically around her, trying to dislodge the piece of meat. Hara came over, pushed us all aside, and looked squarely into Kay's face. "I think she die."

Fortunately she didn't, but the episode added to the Hara folklore.

But with Hara taking care of the household needs, these were happy and challenging times. My blue and white apartment with its bright red bathroom was close enough to the Music Hall that I could walk to and from work. I could even take time to walk home for dinner on those late work nights. It was a comfortable existence, made even more so by the fact my parents could now move to St. Petersburg, where the sunshine

66

was a balm for my mother's angina and my father's rheumatism and liver trouble. They lived in the Florida house I bought for them until their death.

Late in 1934, Mr. Van Schmus decided several of us could try our hands at producing the weekly shows. The responsibility was alternated with conductor Leon Leonidoff, choreographer Florence Rogge, and Russell Markert.

My first show was scheduled for October 25. Yip Harburg immediately volunteered to write a song for it. He and Jerry Sears supplied an answer song to "Eadie Was a Lady" called "Jimmy Was a Gent." Duke Ellington's "The Mooch" was also to be introduced.

The show was called *Coast to Coast.* A chromium turntable opened the show, and as it turned around to reveal the Cote d'Azur in the style of Dufy, it threw enormous highlights all over the stage. Other sets were the Ascot royal enclosure for the Gold Coast, Negro sculpture for the Ivory Coast, a barroom set followed by a highly suggestive brass bed representing the Barbary Coast.

I was the guest of honor for the party which followed the opening in the upstairs penthouse, the site for many other receptions whenever a visiting star was in town. The kind words thrown my way were followed up by respectable press notices. The Music Hall's publicity office then got to work, sending out releases on Minnelli "and the satirical mood of his settings and costumes. He demonstrates a flair for the unusual and picturesque, sticking to his modern style. Modernistic dances and blue torch songs are the mediums in which he revels."

It was obvious to friends that I was becoming a known quantity in New York. Yip, Lee Gershwin, and I were walking out of the "21" restaurant one day when we bumped into a ticket broker named Harry Kaufman. Lee introduced us.

"Oh, yes," Kaufman said, "I know Minnelli. I know his work."

After he left us, Lee said, "He's now working with Lee Shubert. They're trying to create class productions. Do you think you might be interested in directing a Broadway show?"

I sure would, I told her.

5 | The Shuberts

I continued working at the Music Hall halfway into 1935, taking my monthly turn at producing a show in addition to my weekly art directing duties. The social candle was still being burned at both ends . . . and in the middle. Though youth was on my side, I was beginning to wonder if there was a limit to my energy.

Yes, I did want to direct a Broadway show . . . I wanted the time and reflection that goes into mounting one. Transferring to a more legitimate style of theater probably meant starting at the bottom. And the bottom in those days was the Shubert organization.

The Shuberts had started producing plays as far back as 1901, and they had great financial success in supplying the lowest common denominator to popular musical theater . . . first with Americanized operettas, then with inanely plotted musical comedies, and finally with revues just a step higher than the vaudeville of the Palace Theatre's heyday. They were a shlock operation, the theater's bargain basement. Jerry Stagg wrote in *The Brothers Shubert* that Lee Shubert subscribed to an old Willie Hammerstein adage: "The best seats in a theater for a producer are seats with asses in them." That seemed the only point Lee and his brother J.J. would vociferously agree on . . . had they been speaking. But Lee and Jake waged a love-hate relationship and had no personal

68

dealings with each other. Each headed his division of the company in separate-but-equal fashion.

They flourished by never underestimating the gullibility of the public. The Shuberts hired the finest musicians for a show's opening, then after the reviews were in, replaced them with lowly scale performers. If they had a success with a production one season, they'd open a ragtag version the following year, run it for two weeks and then ship it out to the provinces as "direct from Broadway." They were full of all sorts of cute tricks.

But now, Lee Shubert—with the prodding of Harry Kaufman—wanted respectability. He'd already produced two John Murray Anderson shows, the *Ziegfeld Follies* in 1933 and *Life Begins at 8:40* the following year. For the first time in his career, he had worked with such super talents as Fanny Brice, Bert Lahr, and Ray Bolger, and had employed such names of the music world as Ira Gershwin, Harold Arlen, and Yip Harburg.

Lee—with his deeply tanned face, dyed black hair, erect military carriage and impassive expression—had the look of a wooden cigar store Indian. In his soft flannel suits, though, he gave the impression of being a rather elegant one. Infrequently, I saw a flicker of reaction in his eyes. This proved to me that he didn't lack humor; he just didn't see the need to express it every other minute. He was of an indeterminate age and, though his career as well as his brother's was marked by the dirtiest of street-fighting tactics, he had developed a worldly and cultured patina.

He made all the right noises. "I want to move on to quality shows," he told me, "and I think you should be with us. How would you like to produce all the Shubert musicals?"

I was cautious. The Shubert reputation had preceded them. The matter was turned over to my attorney and a contract was ironed out. In it, I would have total control of the content of the shows for as long as they ran. I would also have the authority to hire everyone connected with the venture, from crew to musicians to cast members. It was an ideal situation, so I accepted the offer to produce three Shubert shows. Marian Herwood joined me in tendering my resignation at the Music Hall. She'd become so indispensable that I couldn't imagine working without her.

Boris Aronson had recently done the sets for *Three Men on a Horse*. I ran into him on the street around this time. "That was a great saloon set you did," I told him. "I liked those dingy shades of green and brown."

"Well," Boris answered, "the brown was for the cockroaches, and the green for the powder that exterminates them."

Seeing Boris jogged my memory, and I recommended the Music Hall hire him to replace me after my departure. He did take the job, but being a slow and methodical craftsman, he didn't like the accelerated pace.

Now that I was in the big time, I scouted around for a studio. I located it in a brownstone on East 53rd Street, next to the Museum of Modern Art. It was an enormous room with a carved ceiling and wall panels and two bay windows facing the street. Across the hall was a three-room apartment, which I was allowed to periodically use whenever there was an overflow in my studio. From these headquarters, I would design the show and hire composers and cast.

It quickly became the hangout for the likes of Yip Harburg, George Balanchine, the Gershwins, Paul Bowles, and Pavel Tchelitchev. Kay Swift, after her first visit there, gave my studio its name: The Minnellium.

We started rehearsing in July of 1935 and were scheduled to open amost three months later in New York. Nobody told me I couldn't continue performing all my Music Hall roles. With the longer lead time, I convinced myself that I could direct, design costumes, decorate sets, and supervise the lighting. Having the authority, I cast myself in all the parts.

Beatrice Lillie had already been signed as the star, and Howard Dietz and Arthur Schwartz were to do the score. The concept was to do a geographical revue, a musical holiday trip through Europe, Africa, Japan, and the West Indies. Our original title was *Not in the Guidebook,* but it was soon changed to *At Home Abroad.*

The cast fell into place. Eleanor Powell had already made her first big hit in pictures, but she was miraculously available to do the show, and she was signed as its tap dancing star. Ballet dancer Paul Haakon, who was working at the Music Hall and doing occasional concerts, came over to be her male counterpart. Reginald Gardiner was brought over from England to work with Bea. Ethel Waters and Herb Williams proved available.

The casting backstage went as easily. Howard Dietz, Marc Connelly, Dion Titheradge, and Raymond Knight supplied the sketches.

Working with the Shubert organization proved to be a huge surprise. I had total autonomy, and no expenses were spared in mounting the production. I had no contact with Jake Shubert. Though the show was being officially produced by both brothers, it was conceded that I was on Lee's side and all discussions went through him.

No huge hits came out of *At Home Abroad,* but the songs worked well within their context. Howard Dietz, however, was positive that two of them weren't up to standard. He ordered them dropped.

One was Paul Haakon's "Death in the Afternoon" ballet and the other was Eleanor Powell's "Lady With the Tap."

I didn't want to pull rank on Howard, for our relations were friendly up to then. The numbers were right for the show, I felt, so I politely insisted they remain.

The next thing I knew, Howard's lawyer was talking to my lawyer. They discovered that the Shuberts had given both Howard and me identical contracts. We were both led to believe that each of us had total autonomy. The Shuberts made themselves curiously scarce during our big fight. Lee might have wanted to be in the big time, but he still retained his bush-league ethics. Howard and I were at an impasse.

We prepared to travel to Boston for the first out-of-town tryout. Rehearsals had me so occupied that I didn't have a chance to look after my luggage. "Please pack my suitcases," I instructed Hara. His answer was a noncommittal grunt. "You do know how, don't you?" Hara nodded his head impatiently. The bags were deposited at the theater, to be sent on to the Boston hotel where we would be staying. I began to dress for dinner our first night there. I flipped open one suitcase. It was empty. So was the other. "Pack" must have been the Japanese word for "clean," since that appeared to be the only thing Hara had done to them. I had to buy a whole new wardrobe.

Prior to opening night in Boston, I was sitting in the front row of the theater, keying the orchestra on some last minute changes. I heard someone coming down the aisle. I looked up to see Howard Dietz coming over. "Look," he said, "it's you and me and to hell with the Shuberts. Let's talk this out." I was very pleased. I wanted to be friends.

The Powell and Haakon numbers remained. "Lady With the Tap" was a spoof on the Ernst Lubitsch spy drama. Eleanor was a spy who sent secret messages by tapping a code with her feet. It was outrageous fun.

"Death in the Afternoon" utilized some innovative lighting and sets in telling the story of a matador going from his dressing room to his fatal destiny. The sequence started with the torero and his two dressers, preparing for the bullfight. At center stage was a long red corridor leading to the bullring. A tango interlude in the middle of the number, introduced the bullfighter's sweetheart and her duena who forced their unauthorized way into the dressing room, because the girl had a premonition. The torero stuck with his decision to go on with the fight. The two

71

women leave, and minor toreros and picadors enter to watch the bullfighter finish dressing. He was now ready. He walked through the center corridor on his way to the bullring. It was constructed of louvers which were increasingly smaller, to suggest a deeper perspective than the stage would allow. As the matador made his way down the corridor, the lights suddenly changed, showing a hooded death's head as the orchestra glided into a tremolo passage. The red light returned, and the bullfighter continued on his way to the ring. It was highly dramatic and gripping with its foreboding effect.

One of Howard's favorite songs in the show—and mine too—was "Antonio." Bea Lillie didn't want to do it. The Italian accent wasn't particularly worrisome, she claimed. "It's just that the song has too many words, and I can't sing a song with too many words." Bea kept tripping over the fast tempo of the opening bars. The set was an arena for bicycle riders, with real ones wheeling stage front and being replaced by marionettes at stage rear.

Bea wanted to be in the "Get Yourself a Geisha" number toward the end of the show. I made a deal with her. She could do it at one of the tryout performances if she'd rehearse "Antonio" the following day. Agreed. When she did the geisha song with the chorus, I could see why Bea wanted to do it. All of the performers were in geisha costumes and wigs, Bea included, singing as a chorus. Toward the end of the song, Bea's solo voice piped up, "It's better with your shoes off," and the way she suggestively sang the line had the audience in hysterics . . . especially since they hadn't known Bea was one of the geisha chorus.

The next day, in the middle of the "Antonio" rehearsal, Bea burst into tears. "I can't do it . . . I can't do it." She went running to her dressing room. And so, the bicycle racer number was cut, though Bea continued to perform as the geisha with the double entendre to wonderfully comic effect.

Offstage, Bea was not very talkative, and she was seldom funny. But she was wonderful company, and had an enormous number of friends.

She was a huge star, and Bea, unconsciously I'm sure, assumed all her rightful prerogatives. Her career was at its height. Her every gesture on stage was hilarious. All she had to do was turn her profile or move a certain way or raise a finger.

She was superstitious about people laughing in rehearsals, however. All the time we were out of town, she was trying various effects. She'd do something brilliant one performance, then it would be missing from the next.

72

"What became of such and such?" I'd ask about some bit of business.

"What did I do?" she'd ask. "I don't remember." Her pose was that she was as completely intuitive as a child or an animal.

It was only at the opening in New York that she showed she was the greatest opening night performer I'd ever seen. All the effects were back with her. The laughs she'd deliberately lost out of town were remembered and dropped into place. She'd saved them all up for New York, and everyone went insane.

I also went mad. The stage at the Winter Garden wasn't as deep as the theaters in Boston and Philadelphia. We had a monstrous time getting the lights right. Several cues were missed on opening night. The show didn't seem to work. I was so close to the show, and so exhausted, that I was oblivious to audience reaction. I was suicidal.

All I could see was the many things that were going wrong. I knew Bea Lillie would emerge unscathed, but what about that refugee from the Music Hall? The performance limped along to its conclusion. I didn't care. I wanted to get out of there. People stopped me as I left the theater and said nice things. Kind words for a dying man.

I went straight to bed, and pulled the covers over my ears, knowing this insomniac night would be tossed and turned away. It must have been a couple of hours later—I felt it was a century—that the phone rang. I hesitantly answered.

"Where are you?" Howard's cheerful voice bellowed. I could hear the sound of laughter in the background. "We're waiting for you!"

"Be there soon," I answered. I got up and dressed. Might as well show a little class.

By the time I arrived at the opening night party in the Lombardy Hotel ballroom, the newspaper reviews had already been published. They were being read aloud. First came the *Times*'s Brooks Atkinson. "What gives *At Home Abroad* its freshest beauty is the scene and costume designing of Vincente Minnelli, who also staged the production. Without resorting to opulence, he has filled the stage with rich, glowing colors that give the whole work an extraordinary loveliness. Nothing quite so exhilarating as this has borne the Shubert seal before. Under his direction the revue has such unity of appearance that it is more difficult than usual to pluck out the best numbers. The whole thing stirs with the life of superior stage entertainment. Count Miss Lillie as one of the chief ornaments . . . All this young Mr. Minnelli has wrapped up in a handsome package . . . At last the season has begun."

Other reviewers were equally as generous, but I was too stunned and too tired to react. My colleagues, in their generous exuberance, did it for me. Some of them might have been rightly resentful over not being singled out in the reviews. But everyone was genuinely glad that the show was a hit, and sincerely congratulatory of my work. That's one selfless part of show business that I particularly like.

Taking in the reviews, I was finally getting an indication of what I was bringing to the theater. I'd approached my work with very personal instincts and perceptions. It took the critics to tell me what it was that I had accomplished. And make no mistake about it. Their words were gospel, as anyone who suffered through opening nights during that period can tell you.

A laudatory letter from a fan came a few days later. It was similar to several I'd received, being effusively complimentary of my innovative approach. In it, the writer also asked me to join him for a drink at the Hotel Lombardy. But how could it be? It was signed by a man who shared the name of my long-time idol, S. J. Perelman. Many were the times I would discuss his work with friends, all of whom seemed to have as great an affinity for his comic and picaresque writing as I did.

The appointed hour found me at the hotel bar. It was indeed *the* S. J. Perelman, and we became immediate friends.

Over the next few weeks, I found myself a lower case celebrity. I couldn't for the life of me say why, for my work didn't contrast that dramatically from my tenure at the Music Hall. I'd done many ballets before, and most of them had received scant mention in the press, though there was considerable word of mouth notice. The only difference now was the more money involved, and the greater artistic pretension.

Other publications started picking up the idea that I was the Great White Way's new white hope.

A few weeks later, *The New Yorker* ran a short profile. Its title: *Prodigy.* "It's time you know something about Vincente Minnelli, the youngster who directed *At Home Abroad,* and designed the settings and costumes. We're told that never before in the history of Broadway and musical shows has one man undertaken these three important jobs (at least nobody has tried it and got away with it). The impetuous Shuberts now have him under contract to do the same thing for five of their forthcoming shows.

"Up to a few years ago, he habitually dressed in a way to remind you of Easter Sunday in Harlem, but lately he has tapered off to gray suits and light-green ties. He reads Saki and Husmans more than he does any other writers, and has added Daumier and Roualt to his painting gods."

74

Eleanor Lambert had seen her prediction come true. Years later, Andy Warhol was quoted as saying that everyone is a celebrity for fifteen minutes during his lifetime . . . or similar words to that effect. Eleanor was partially responsible for my celebrity status. She took me on as a client, and suddenly the press descended. Not only had I established a reputation, they were trying to make me out a character, giving me a flamboyant personality I don't possess. "I'm not used to this," I told photographer George Platt Lynes during a sitting. "Well," he answered, "you'd better learn."

Mentions in the gossip columns inevitably followed. Walter Winchell reported that Marian and I were that way about each other, and wedding bells were imminent. My mother called from Florida. "You should have told me," she said, her personal hurt clearly coming through over the hundreds of miles of telephone wire.

"Mother," I protested, "there's no truth in that. Marian is my secretary and assistant. Yes, we go out a lot, because we're always working. We're good friends . . . we're not going to get married."

I thought I'd convinced her. Talk shifted to other matters. "Well, Mother," I said, winding up the conversation, "I'll talk to you soon."

"All right, son," she answered. There was a thoughtful pause. "You know," Mother said, "you *really* should have told me."

At Home Abroad was still in the midst of a highly successful run when Lee Shubert handed me the next plum. The *Ziegfeld Follies.*

The Shuberts had already mounted one previous *Follies,* in 1933, under Billie Burke Ziegfeld's aegis. John Murray Anderson was set to repeat his stage directing for another version the following year, but the Shuberts had difficulty getting title clearance. The show was mounted as *Life Begins at 8:40.* Now, in 1935, the Shubert's second *Follies,* again using Billie Burke's name as producer, was being prepared.

Lee Shubert had already contracted with John Murray Anderson to direct the show, and I gladly reduced my area of responsibility to costumes and set designs . . . provided this show was included as one of the three specified in my contract. I would return as director for the next show. With the Shuberts, one had to be as flexible as possible. You never knew when an untenable situation might develop, and it was sensible to fulfill all contractual obligations as quickly as possible.

John Murray Anderson and I were great friends, both before and after we worked together on the show. That's the nicest thing one can say about a professional association such as ours.

He was a founding father of the American revue, actually, a former dancer who began staging shows after his wife, who'd been his dancing partner, died. Many of the effects I was being praised for were actually started by John. Simplicity with taste was the standard he created in the *Greenwich Village Follies*, starting in 1919. Most bohemian types were already involved with the Washington Square Players, the progenitor of the Theatre Guild, or the Provincetown Players, who introduced Eugene O'Neill to the public. But there were enough free spirits left in the Village to present theater with a decided contrast. John's *Follies* were fey and casual . . . and just about the most happily infectious shows I'd ever seen. They were also the most stylish. The names that came out of his revues were to become the greatest names in the fields of costumes and high fashion: Howard Greer, Charles Le Maire, Adrian, and James Reynolds.

If such talents bloomed under his direction, it's a tribute to John's selfless character. There was no backbiting jealousy in his makeup. Everyone was allowed to shine, and everyone was treated with sincere affection and gentle humor.

He made up pet nicknames for everybody. As he did me. I'd told him of a time when I was still at the Music Hall. I had gone to Harlem on a tear with several colleagues. We got ahold of some marijuana—it was very accessible at the time. As the group sat in a bar puffing away, everything gradually got hysterically funny. We'd look down at our feet, and they seemed nine miles away. The evening ended at an eccentric old lady's apartment. She thought money was dirty—and she had a lot of it—so she would wash the bills and spread them out on newspapers to dry . . . at any rate, I *think* that's what happened. I woke the next day with no hangover, and with no special desire to monkey with cannabis again. After I told John the story, I was forever known as Mister Reefer.

John, more than any other, was the most influential in bringing the modern dance movement to middle America. He spotlighted such exponents as Martha Graham, Doris Humphrey, and Jack Cole in the *Greenwich Village Follies*.

Ironically, Fanny Brice—in the eyes of many—killed and buried the modern dance movement in the 1935 *Ziegfeld Follies* that John and I worked on. Ira Gershwin and Billy Rose wrote a number, "Modernistic Moe," for Fanny to sing. She was to come on wearing a long dank wig, large false feet and a jersey dress split up on both sides. After singing, she did a satirical dance. She was going at it one day at rehearsal when Ira called out, "Fanny! Revolt!" She yelled back, "Okay, kid."

Fanny stomped from one end of the stage to the other, striking dra-

76

matic poses as she stopped by each side curtain. "Rewolt! Rewolt! Oy, am I hungry!"

But there was another aspect to the movement that was featured for the first time on a Broadway stage: the surrealist ballet. George Balanchine, the Russian émigré now heading the New York City Ballet, was hired to choreograph. I directed the number, which starred Harriet Hoctor. Three dancing figures in green are seen at the opening, standing at the top of a ramp which angled down toward the audience. Three black-clad figures, lying at an angle from the dancers, suggest their shadows and repeat the dancers' movements from their prone positions. It was a striking effect which has been done hundreds of times since. The number ended with the men who had cast the shadows losing Harriet to the black silhouettes when they rise from the ground and spirit her away.

Ira teamed with Vernon Duke in putting the score together. David Freedman, the master of all sketch writers, was supplying some of his most comic work, including the now classic "Sweepstakes Ticket" sketch for Fanny.

In some of the sketches Fanny teamed with a rising young comedian, Bob Hope, who in turn was a continuing thread throughout the show in his avid pursuit of Eve Arden, all the while singing, "I Can't Get Started." The theme was hauntingly repeated in the pit by a young trumpet player named Bunny Berrigan and he became so associated with the number that most people forgot the song's origin and assumed it had been specifically written for him. Also in the cast were Gertrude Niesen, Judy Canova, and Josephine Baker.

Where I approached *At Home Abroad* with a flat design concept, much like a map filled in with bright, clear schoolbook colors, I attacked *Follies* in the spirit of fashion photography. Elegant, but with humor and style.

The opening was a teaser. The master of ceremonies sang an introduction which implied there'd be no emphasis on girls in this *Follies*. Then an enormous tableau was revealed, showing girls on mirrors and on swings. A Ziegfeld show without girls would obviously have to go by another name.

So many of the past *Follies* had used period costumes of the Louis XVI school that I decided an updating was needed. For "That Moment of Moments" I settled on the 1880s as inspiration, with their elaborate hair styles, their bustles and long trains on gowns.

The permanent setting was a highly adaptable three-foot ramp which was shoved around in several configurations, thus serving as a backdrop for the specialty numbers. From the suggestion of airplanes in "Night Flight," Harriet Hoctor's impressionistic dance number, it became an island surrounded by water and ships in Josephine Baker's "Island in the West Indies" number. Ira supplied her with one of his best lyrics. I supplied her with a very abbreviated costume ornamented by white tusks.

Josephine was returning to the United States after her long-running sensation at the *Folies-Bergère* and the Casino de Paris. I wanted her to look as glamorous as possible, and I designed costumes which suggested European influences. Her second number—"Maharanee"—a scene at the Longchamps night races—encased her svelte figure in a shimmering sari. This was followed by her autobiographical "Five A.M.," showing her return to a dusty pink room decorated with African sculpture. Her dress was made of gold mesh. I'd designed a dress in muslin and had it sent to a factory which manufactured metal mesh bags. They wove it exactly to specifications. The dress weighed almost one hundred pounds. With it Josephine wore a plum-colored ostrich cape. Critics may have complained that her thin, reedy voice didn't fill the theater, but none of them denied that her gorgeous figure did more than ample justice to the costumes.

As we got further into rehearsal, John Murray Anderson generously started turning over some of the directing duties to me. I was never to receive directorial credit for the show, but I had a whale of a time nevertheless.

When you're working at a job and loving every moment of it, you never know the way others see you. Vernon Duke, in his autobiography, described my work habits during the rehearsals for *Follies*: "I don't think there has ever been a greater disciplinarian or a more exacting perfectionist in the musical theater than Vincente Minnelli . . . Where other directors wasted a lot of valuable time wrangling with costume designers, arguing with overpaid stars or kidding around with chorus girls, with Vincente—once the rehearsals started—it was all work and no play. We all felt like cogs in Minnelli's magical wheel and kept ourselves well oiled." He went on to say many other extravagantly kind things. Yet, at the time, I had no idea that my voice was any more influential than anyone else's, Vernon's included. We were all working together to get a job done.

It was cause for uneasy concern when the Boston reviewers commented on the show's opening on December 30, 1935.

Elliott Norton's Boston *Post* review started, "Vincente Minnelli, who doesn't appear on the stage at all, is the star of the new 'Ziegfeld Follies,' which had its world premiere last night at the Boston Opera House."

I was thrilled by the review, naturally, but felt it unfairly slighted all the other top talents who'd worked so hard to put it together.

But again, I recall no animosity at being singled out. Neither does my friend, Fred de Cordova, who is now the producer of the Johnny Carson television show.

At the time, he was second assistant director; first assistant was Eddie Dowling. Freddie had known Jake Shubert's son John at Harvard, and he was now getting his start in show business.

"The show opened around New Year's Eve," Freddie recalls. "Eddie Dowling was my immediate boss. He set up a rule we couldn't fool around with the girls while in rehearsal. He said it was bad business. Eddie also felt being remote lent a fellow a great air of mystery.

"But the show was now open, and it was New Year's Eve. We subtly let it drop to several of the girls that we were finally going to be available to them. Eddie and I stocked up on booze and food in our hotel suite, and left the door ajar. No one showed up.

"Shortly after midnight, the doorbell rang. Minnelli walked in. He knew we'd be alone, and he didn't hide his amusement at our naiveté."

The girls, I'm sure, were snuggled in bed and resting up for the following day's matinee and evening performance.

We'd been playing in Boston a week when Elliott Norton did a follow up Sunday piece in the *Post*. "It will be hooted down in some quarters," he wrote. "And, here and there, it will probably serve to curl a well-rounded lip into an unbecoming sneer of derision.

"Nevertheless, it is the well-pondered opinion of this column that Vincente Minnelli, who designed the costumes and scenery for the current 'Ziegfeld Follies,' has a greater theatrical genius than the late Florenz Ziegfeld.

"This does not necessarily mean that Mr. Minnelli has, or will develop, a flair for self-publicization such as Ziegfeld had. Nor does it mean that he will make as picturesque a front-page figure as the late Great Glorifier.

"Furthermore, it does not necessarily signify that the Messrs. Shubert, to whom he is currently contracted, have any idea that he should become a personnae.

"What it does mean is that Florenz Ziegfeld, with all his vast capacity, never had any such amazing ability to create and project theatrical beauty as has this Italian-American.

"Veteran observers who have seen every Ziegfeld show, from the first 'Follies,' are agreed that this current version—whatever its other faults at present—is far and away the most beautiful of all.

"Mr. Minnelli, for one thing, manipulates colors in a way that would elicit bravos from a European audience.

"Perhaps his most striking flair is for using contrasting colors in combination—reds and greens, for instance—with results of rich beauty instead of what you would naturally expect.

"If you are one of those who like to follow names in the theater, you will do well to remember that of Vincente Minnelli.

"And if you are one of those who love the legitimate stage, you are urged to utter a fervent plea to the deities of the theater that the bogeymen of Technicolor don't get him for a while at least."

If movie moguls found the first act finale indicative of my regard for the film medium, I'm sure they considered my recruitment number 24,129 on their list of priorities.

It satirized the Golddiggers' Big Broadcast of the Broadway Melody type of musical, and it incorporated all the movie clichés of the time. The comedy scenes by David Freedman were played in the jerky rhythm that characterized such films.

The sketches which opened the sequence were a take-off of the Dick Powell-Ruby Keeler musicals. Fanny Brice played the chorus girl who fills in for the star on opening night and Bob Hope was her sweetheart.

The two kids meet in an agent's office. "Hey, you're different," the boy says. "You're different too," the girl answers. With that, they fall into a passionate embrace. All of these little scenes were mounted in black and white.

They were followed by the full-scale Technicolor production number, similar to the color finales to some of the black and white pictures of the time. A new dance "craze" was being introduced—"The Gazooka"—and it was similar to all the previous ones the public had come to expect: "First you take this step . . . and then you take another . . . and then you take . . . and then you take." And yet nothing ever happened.

To remain true to my inspiration, I decided the color sequence should be as blurred as most Technicolor films of the time. When the triangle discs came together to form the platform for the number, the color came on in the form of sets and dancers covered in colored cellophane, giving them similar blurred edges.

But what studio executives might have found offensive, the audience found irreverent fun.

I got out of Boston not a moment too soon, before I was either canonized or burned at the stake.

The reviews in Philadelphia didn't go overboard, but they were pleasing and more balanced in their comments.

On to New York, and the January 30, 1936, opening at the Winter Garden.

Brooks Atkinson in the New York *Times* review, wrote a more cogent observation, but offered a special bow. "Vincente Minnelli has burst into the Winter Garden with a whole portfolio of original splendors. Without being in the least sensational, he has managed this season to reanimate the art of scenic display and costumery. Although he is lavish enough to satisfy any producer's thirst for opulence, his taste is unerring and the 'Follies' that comes off his drawing-board is a civilized institution. Even the mediocre numbers, of which there are the usual number, look well when Mr. Minnelli dresses them."

The reviews were read at an opening night party hosted by Lorenz Hart. George Balanchine and I took a couple of girls home afterwards. They lived in Brooklyn . . . a fact we didn't discover until we were outside on the street. Well, on to the subway at Times Square. It was three in the morning. We went downstairs and passed a Child's Restaurant there. "These people," George said. "What they do here? I understand why we're . . . but why they're?"

Josephine Baker had put her West Indies song over to such effect that, as soon as the show was smoothly running, I agreed to go there with Lee and Ira Gershwin for a three-week holiday. I was so exhausted during the twenty-four-hour cruise on the S.S. *Britannica* that I slept the time away.

The first week in Barbados, Martinique, and Curacao was enchanting. We could hardly wait to get to Trinidad. On our way there, however, we crossed the interdenominational dateline.

Lent started the day we arrived. All merry-making was on forty-day leave. Trinidad was closed.

There were no planes to whisk us back. We'd have to wait two weeks for the boat. We created a schedule as best we could. In the morning, Ira and I would talk about a proposed book of his song lyrics, which he'd asked me to illustrate a couple of years previously. (When it was finally published, Ira had written so many additional great songs that there was no room for illustrations.) During this allotted time, Lee would go to the hairdresser, and wait . . . and wait. A deposed dictator from a South American banana republic was in residence at the hotel with his retinue, and his men took precedence at the hairdresser's. Then, after lunch, the three of us would prepare to sightsee or play tennis, but these plans were invariably rained out.

We'd sit and stare at each other. Lee in particular looked rather analytically at me. "Isn't it about time you started thinking of getting married?" she asked.

(Lee in the past had always made me get up at parties and tell of the untimely demise of my grandfather. For some reason everyone found it uproarious that the poor man had sawn a limb from under him and was killed. They'd look knowingly at me after that.)

"I've always wanted to get married," I told her. "But I'm afraid of passing on the Minnelli curse."

Lee and Ira giggled at the comment, decided to leave me alone and looked around for other distractions.

We discovered it in a handsome British establishment, an elegantly fitted tailor shop with mustachioed salesmen who spoke in distinguished low voices. The tailor offered the most beautiful tweeds and worsteds, and his suits were only twenty-five dollars each. Ira and I both decided to buy six. Late afternoons would be spent there, having numerous fittings. They were delivered on the day we left. I must have grown a hunchback and one arm must have extended three inches longer, because none of the suits fit when we returned to New York. Ira had the same problem. We gave the suits away, which meant that our late afternoons were also a total waste.

But not the evenings. There was one movie theater on the island, and the program changed twice a week. We'd be waiting in line every night for the doors to open. We saw a Warner Brothers musical, a Jerome Kern operetta, for four consecutive nights. "I didn't like it in the States," Ira observed after we'd seen it for the third time, "but it looks pretty good here."

New York, after our return, looked even better. The *Ziegfeld Follies* was doing great business, being in the midst of a five-month run. It closed for the summer, then reopened in a reprise edition which ran another five months . . . still another example of the Shuberts' up-yours philosophy. If there was any danger that the seats wouldn't be completely filled with asses, better take a hiatus and take performers and crew off salary.

I wasn't involved in the reprise show, for I went right into *The Show*

Is On when we returned from Trinidad. The Gershwins, George included, packed up and moved to Hollywood for a film assignment.

Minnelli had arrived, completely. *Vanity Fair* had, during our trip, featured me in their "We nominate for the Hall of Fame" department. Their reasons: ". . . because he designed both scenery and costumes for the two talked-about Shubert musicals, *At Home Abroad* and Billie Burke's *Ziegfeld Follies;* because for two years he was Art Director of Radio City Music Hall, creating a new stage spectacle each week; because he was an actor at three with the Minnelli Brothers Dramatic Company, which barnstormed Ohio in the early 1900s with suburbanized versions of Broadway hits; lastly, because his New York studio, just now a maze of miniature stage sets and costume sketches, was once the drawing room of Peggy Hopkins Joyce."

This Shubert revue was going to be the one to end them all . . . that statement proved ambiguously prophetic . . . and it would have my name above the title.

Given carte blanche, I filled it in as if it were a Southern belle's dance program.

I'd always had an affinity for Tin Pan Alley, and now I could afford to hire all my friends. They were a great fraternity, and many of them hung out at Harms Music Co., across 53rd Street from my studio. I happily got the overflow.

They were almost as gleeful about their compatriots' successes as they were about their failures. I'd seen their constant telephoning to each other. "Have you heard?" one of them would delightedly ask. "So and so is on the road. The show's in trouble. They may not reach New York." When one of them had a great hit, the comments were a touch more reserved. "It's okay, but—"

Now they were going to hang together. I bought songs from them all. Ted Fetter and Vernon Duke supplied "Now" and "Casanova," Lorenz Hart and Richard Rodgers wrote "Rhythm," Yip Harburg and Harold Arlen wrote "Song of the Woodman," Stanley Adams and Hoagy Carmichael wrote "Little Old Lady."

Ira Gershwin in *Lyrics on Several Occasions,* the book I didn't get to work on, described how one of his songs came to be in the show:

"In New York one night in the spring of '36, stage director Vincente Minnelli was present when my brother and I were musically kidding around by exaggerating the lifts and plunges and *luftpauses* of the Viennese waltz. We had written only about half of this piece when we dropped it for

83

something more usable. In August of that year we checked in at the Beverly Wilshire Hotel in Beverly Hills to start work on *Shall We Dance*. We were there but a few days when a telegram arrived from Vincente. In it he stated he was preparing a new Broadway revue and asked us please to work on the Straussian take-off, which he felt he could use. So we took off a day from the film for the stage take-off, finished the waltz, and air-mailed it. We never saw the show, but I understand the song was acceptably presented and received."

"By Strauss," as sung by Grace Barrie and Robert Shafter, and danced by Mitzi Mayfair, certainly was, for it was full of the many stage clichés that the show was meant to spoof.

Harold Arlen was very much evident during rehearsal time. We'd been great friends since our days with Earl Carroll. I, in fact, had been a chaperon of sorts when he was courting a showgirl named Annie, who later became his wife.

A charming fellow, Harold worshipped Gershwin and Kern, the latter especially, affecting huge knots on his ties like the master. His humor, impudent and contagious, was at odds with the plaintive melodrama of many of his songs. It was the wail of his father, a rabbi, combined with the blues of Harlem . . . he'd already written "Stormy Weather" for Ethel Waters.

Harold took special delight in baiting Harry Kaufman, Lee Shubert's associate. Kaufman acted like an evangelist, and with his celluloid collars and conservative suits, he also looked like one. Everything to him was beautiful and wonderful.

Kaufman was after Harold to write a "jingle" for the show. "It'll be the hit of the show," he told Harold. "We need a jingle . . . a jingle!"

It got so that Harold dreaded seeing Kaufman around. "Here comes High Collar Harry," he'd say with considerable distaste.

One of these times, we'd been through a set-to . . . the anger and screams that come when you're trying to get something right. We were all quietly seething, storing up more steam to be shortly let out, when Kaufman arrived on the scene. "Go on ahead," he cheerfully called out. "Keep working. You're all looking good. Everything's fine."

Though no one ever found out what Kaufman meant by a "jingle," and he was generally considered a figure of fun, he also had the instinct of getting talented people together . . . which J. J. Shubert almost succeeded in tearing apart. Lee became very ill during rehearsal, and Jake filled in for a few weeks. He called me to his office as soon as he became involved. "There's too much money being spent," he bellowed.

"Cut it down! Get rid of some of the chorus. Use cheaper materials. Less money all around!"

I looked through him. "Mr. Shubert," I said, "you're going to die of apoplexy." He calmed down and I went back to rehearsals, ignoring his orders. I wasn't going to be cowed.

Freddie de Cordova, just out of college and eager to please, told me he was totally conditioned to Jake's fierceness. He once yelled at Freddie, "You get your hat and coat, and go over and tell them I want 750 yards of material, tomorrow and no later!" Freddie went running out. Then he suddenly stopped short. He didn't know where he was going, who he was to talk to, what he was talking about. When Freddie began doing well in Hollywood, he went back to visit the Shuberts. I think the reaction of the two brothers is indicative of their characters. "We must have taught you right," Lee told him. Jake pretended not to know Freddie had been away.

Moss Hart was working with David Freedman on the sketches, which Beatrice Lillie, Bert Lahr, and Reginald Gardiner would be performing.

One was a wonderful satire on John Gielgud's *Hamlet,* with Gardiner in a prologue sensing disaster in his performance that evening. It came in the form of Bea, with her outrageous asides from the audience interrupting the Prince. Gardiner ends up in the audience with her, a quivering mess.

Another was based on an author reading his play to the cast. The sketch was based on *The Royal Family* by Edna Ferber and George S. Kaufman, with Bea playing a *Folies-Bergère* star accompanied by her manager, husband, and lover to the reading, and Gardiner as a seedy Barrymore. I'd seen a picture of such a reading, and I tried to re-create it. In it, one actor was stretched on a bearskin rug, the others lolling around him. I would light it as a still tableau that would come to life.

Hart and Freedman, in writing the sketch, had inserted one piece of instruction: "Actor enters through door at stage left, provided Minnelli hasn't placed red velvet sofa in front of it." That sounded more like Moss than Freedman, actually.

After the author has finished reading the play, there is silence. He asks, "What did you think of the play, madame?" She answered, "I did not understand a god damned word!"

Bert Lahr's great number was "Song of the Woodman." His rendition was a Nelson Eddy baritone. In the middle came Bert's recitation: "What do we chop when we chop a tree . . . a thousand things that we often see." Then he starts enumerating all the things that are made of wood, stage hands throwing chips in his face as he chopped.

85

His funniest sketch revolved around a one-hundred-dollar tax rebate. He enters the tax man's office, furious because he's been overcharged. "Sit down," the tax man says, "and we'll discuss it. By the way, who is Nina Lahr?"

"She's my grandmother," Bert answered, "a darling lady. She's almost eighty." The tax man responded, "Oh, I see. You have her here as a gag man at two hundred dollars a week." The tax man goes over the tax return point by point, and Bert winds up owing the government $200,000.

When the show opened, a newcomer to the Broadway scene was in the pit as conductor. I'd often been critical of the brassy quality in theater orchestras, as well as arrangements that primarily carried the melody. I'd heard some marvelous André Kostelanetz arrangements on the radio, and I called the young man responsible to come in for an interview. His name was Gordon Jenkins, and I hired him to conduct and arrange.

Other New York arrangers ganged up on him. They went to Lee Shubert and said his arrangements were impossible to play. He'd introduced guitars and vocal backgrounds as part of his work. It hadn't been done before, according to the arrangers, because it couldn't be done.

It was time to put a stop to such nonsense. I called an orchestra rehearsal, paying for it myself, and invited Bea Lillie to come over to a meeting with Lee Shubert and me. She was absolutely enchanted, as we all were, and that was that.

The show opened on Christmas Day of 1936. It went on to play 237 performances, a reprise version opening the following September and playing two weeks before being sent on the road.

Brooks Atkinson's New York *Times* review continued in his past laudatory vein: "Although Vincente Minnelli's previous revues have been stunning and original, this is the finest of the lot, and Beatrice Lillie and Bert Lahr are in their top form as the chief performers. Perhaps this is no time to begin talking of intelligence and beauty in relation to a spacious show at the Winter Garden, but Mr. Minnelli and his merry-andrews have reformed that old arcade of song-and-dance pleasures. 'The Show Is On' skims gaily through an evening of radiant high jinks."

John Mason Brown in the *Evening Post* followed the same line, calling it "a sumptuous revue that Vincente Minnelli has 'conceived, staged and designed'; a revue with great effectiveness and rare good taste." Jack Gaver, of the *United Press,* noted in passing that the revue was "a Minnelli production conceived, staged and designed by this young artist who has had a sensational rise to theatrical fame."

6 | Going Hollywood

When you're trying to get your career underway, you take your blazing talent and ambition to the market place. You marshal your forces, never doubting your destiny. You're alternately ingratiating, energetic, amusing . . . and just a bit pushy. You're also vulnerable, and if appealingly so, that too can be one of the forces to fall back on. You expend all your wiles and ploys . . . you shoot your wad, in other inelegant words. And, as most often happens, you find no takers. You can't even give it away.

So you persist, breaking in the same act with the next person and the next, and if your head stays unbowed and your hide becomes thicker than leather, you might eventually latch on to a quite insignificant position . . . at the expense of some of the sensitivity and idealism with which you started out. Then you start that long climb.

When your career is in full and successful swing, and you can seemingly do no wrong in the eyes of the public, you find yourself halfway believing extravagant praiseful words. You begin to think all things are possible . . . and probable. And why not, since you're the greatest thing since the internal combustion engine and peanut butter? The frustration then is that the timing is wrong and there isn't enough you to spread around.

It happened to me. I was a winner. The offers started pouring in. The re-creation of the War of the Roses, using real roses? In time. A musical version of *Medusa,* starring Merman and the inmates of the New York Herpetological Gardens? Maybe next year. A Hollywood contract? Come now.

Lillian Hellman had taken me along a couple of years previously, soon after *At Home Abroad* opened, to call on Samuel Goldwyn at the Waldorf. She'd been singing his praises, telling of his great integrity in their business relationship. I found him the model movie mogul, except that he spoke in perfectly good English. He hadn't perfected his mangled language shtick as yet. I liked him, but I found him unduly aggressive and presumptuous. He assumed I wanted a job. "You'll find the quality of Goldwyn pictures is much better than anyone else's," he said, as if I was already on the train to Hollywood. I interrupted before he could continue. "Well, that's very nice, Mr. Goldwyn. In fact, I already do. But I plan to stay in New York. I like the theater very much." He looked at me as if my IQ was minus three, and our conversation rapidly deteriorated into uncomfortable silence.

I was surprised when a few months later *Variety* reported that I was going to Metro-Goldwyn-Mayer as associate producer of musicals. My first picture would be *The Goldwyn Follies,* with music by George and Ira Gershwin. Somebody may have been talking to my agent, but no one talked to me. I still had no plans to move to Hollywood.

Friends kept saying I shouldn't fight what was preordained. They pointed out that virtually every major American writer, with the possible exception of Ernest Hemingway, was going Hollywood. The names they bandied about were an eye opener: William Faulkner, F. Scott Fitzgerald, Ogden Nash, Dorothy Parker, S. J. Perelman, George Oppenheimer.

Some writers had returned to New York, weighted down with buckets of money and full of snappy sarcasms aimed at the sun-tanned Philistines out there. Most had chosen to stay in California, however, the war between aesthetics and the mightly dollar having been fought and lost. I was later to discover that their attitudes were much more devastating than those who took the money and ran.

Many of my song-writer friends had gone back and forth with no visible effect on their output or careers. Harold Arlen, Yip Harburg, Irving Berlin, the Gershwins, Cole Porter, Jerome Kern, and Dorothy Fields—among many others—had been writing for films since the early Thirties. Perhaps there might be something out there for me after all. I instructed my agents to follow up some of those movie offers.

89

Though I liked the idea of musical films, I wasn't impressed by the quality of the early ones. I suppose one's thoughts get so ingrained that you tend to forget the exceptions. Years later, for example, an interviewer commented that I brought sophistication to musical films. "Thank you," I responded modestly. So kind of him to notice. Then from the reaches of my memory came a contradiction. I'd found the 1932 Paramount production of Rouben Mamoulian's *Love Me Tonight* a marvel of sophistication. The Rodgers and Hart songs were cleverly woven into the story of the film, which starred Maurice Chevalier and Jeanette MacDonald. I'd particularly liked the way Mamoulian took one number, "The Son of a Gun Is Nothing But a Tailor," and neatly created the most effective plot denouement I'd ever seen in a film musical. The song bounced from one character to another as each discovers that Chevalier is an impostor posing as a nobleman. So I corrected myself to the reporter.

As for other Hollywood musicals, I found them not too far removed from the age of the nickelodeon. They lacked taste, substance, and style. Perhaps I felt this way about most American films up to that time, with the exception of course of the too few classics. We still had a lot of growing up to do.

European films were more to my liking, and I'd seen great treasures in the many art houses studded around New York's Upper East Side. Buñuel, Gabin, Eisenstein, Dreyer, Cocteau. They, to me, had grasped the full potential of film. Few Americans could match their body of work.

If there was one picture that embodied my fascination in art and my attitude toward style it was Jacques Feyder's *Carnival in Flanders*. He'd taken the story of a Spanish general bringing his troops north and told it with the artful detail and luminosity of the Flemish masters. It was illuminating in more ways than one. Perhaps I could bring a similar perspective to American films.

I didn't know anything about the studios, so I left the matter pretty much up to my agents. After all the machiavellian intrigues, the playing off of one studio against the other, they settled on the highest offer. Paramount beat out bids by Samuel Goldwyn and Metro-Goldwyn-Mayer. I would be getting $2,500 a week as a producer—director and my staff—secretary Marian Herwood and technician Al Coppock—would be brought out with me.

I arrived at the Pasadena train station to a hero's welcome. Studio brass were eager to shake my hand, and to offer every co-operation. There must have been another hero due any minute, however, judging by the speed with which pictures of the historic event were taken. Dorothy Lamour didn't wear her sarong to welcome me to Hollywood, but I was glad she'd come nevertheless. No sooner were the photographers satisfied than Dorothy and I were whisked away . . . in different cars.

We arrived at the Beverly Wilshire Hotel, to go through more photo-taking, Virginia Bruce filling in where Dorothy left off.

A telegram awaited me at the front desk. It was from Eleanor Lambert: STOP PERELMAN PIECE IMMEDIATELY. PEOPLE BELIEVE SUCH THINGS. IT WILL RUIN YOU. COPY FOLLOWS.

Sid Perelman had written a profile on me for *Stage* magazine. That much I knew. How bad could it be?

The next morning, I reported to William LeBaron, the head of production, for my formal orientation. He was highly optimistic about my future at the studio. Paramount planned to break out of the Big Broadcast mold and the small Bing Crosby musicals into great things, for which I was to be responsible. I was assigned a writer, and started work.

A few days later, the Perelman manuscript arrived. He told of our first meeting in the New York Public Library: "I was deep in Bulfinch's *Age of Fable,* busily shading the illustrations of Greek and Roman divinities with a hard pencil and getting some truly splendid effects, when I became aware that a strange individual had entered the room. He was apparently a foreigner, for he bore in his lapel a green immigrant tag reading 'Ellis Island—*Rush.*' His clothes were flapping hand-me-downs greasy with travel, and his look of low cunning belied the praying-shawl and phylacteries he sported. Altogether, as extraordinary an unhung horse-thief as existed outside a Roumanian ghetto. Before him this fantastic creature propelled an ancient hurdy-gurdy, and as he ground out a wheezy catchpenny tune, made a rapid circuit of the tables, offering highest cash prices for old bones, rubber, bottles, and newspapers. Failing to stir up any interest among the few high school boys furtively hunting for dirty words in the dictionary, this bird of ill-omen managed to secrete a set of Ridpath's *History of the World* under his rusty caftan and disappeared, obviously to rifle the coatroom. The languid librarian to whom I addressed my query contented himself with a curt 'Vincente Minnelli' and resumed buffing his nails.

"I had forgotten his rapacious face when one morning several weeks later he fell into step with me on Forty-fifth Street. He proposed to sell me a set of amusing postcards and a recondite pamphlet called *The Enigmatic Miss Floggy*, but when he suggested that I follow him into an alley for an inspection of these wares, I refused shortly. With no resentment, he offered me a deck of cocaine for fifty cents. I crossed the street hoping to shake him off, but he clung like a leech. Through his connections in the South American export trade he could obtain young Polish virgins for a hundred and fifty dollars. Screaming, I fled into a cab, only to discover that he had purloined my watch-fob, a cheap German silver affair I had won in a debating contest. Outside of the sick headache I experienced, I found that I had contracted no disease from the encounter."

The article continued in a similar vein. I sent a telegram back to Eleanor: PIECE STANDS AS IS. ALL MY LIFE I'VE BEEN TRYING TO ACHIEVE THAT REPUTATION.

And now, I was preparing to become another pejorative Eastern term: Californian. Taking a house on Camden Drive, I was ready to develop a taste for the lotuses I would be eating.

Driving an automobile hadn't been necessary in New York, but the wider open spaces in the West made it a requirement. Someone at the studio advised me to buy a car, then advertise for some young fellow to take me each day to the studio and back. He could teach me to drive along the way.

We set out the first day. The very first words the kid uttered, as a car swerved in front of us, were, "Hey, look out, you son of a bitch!" He scared me to death. His tactics were those of a kamikaze pilot.

One Saturday he brought me home, parked the car in my garage, and said, "Now don't touch the car until I get here Monday morning." Then he got into his own car and tooled off.

It was dinner hour. I looked up and down the street. The neighborhood was quiet. "To hell with him," I thought, "I'll drive the car around the block."

I backed out of the driveway, going straight as an arrow, and probably almost as fast. *WHAM!*

I drove the car back into the garage, and hurriedly got out. The rear end was demolished. Had I pressed a button somewhere that explodes the back of the car? I walked to the street. Nothing, not even a blade of grass, was amiss. I was befuddled.

As I turned to step into the house, a woman came running up. "Was your car damaged?" she asked.

"Well, it didn't do it any good," I responded.

"Are you insured?"

"Well, yes, but . . . what happened?"

The woman lived across the street, she explained, and we'd both backed out of driveways at the same time, rear-ending each other's rear ends, before each of us drove back quickly into our respective garages. Needless to say, the car stayed in the garage for the rest of the weekend, until the kid came back to drive me to work.

I had an idea for a mystery chase film, incorporating scenes from current Broadway productions. The project was called *Times Square*. Leo Birinski, the writer assigned me, captured the spirit of the endeavor immediately. He was imaginative and good, a jolly exponent of the Molnar school of ideas. Leo was an enormous cigar-smoking Russian who trailed ashes wherever he went. The chase we devised was a race against time, jumping from one theater to another to piece together vital clues. Creating an all-star film of Broadway names in scenes from their hit productions was a catchy way, I felt, of introducing stage players to a far greater audience.

I briefly discussed the concept with Adolph Zukor, who was then head of the studio, but most other discussions were held with LeBaron. I found him optimistic, abstract, and vague. "Keep up the good work," LeBaron said, "wonderful having you with us." But nothing happened.

Perhaps we were proceeding too rapidly for Paramount to absorb our ideas. Marian and Al were already sitting at the studio twiddling their thumbs. Now Leo and I would also have to slow down. I didn't like it.

But I did appreciate Leo's ready way with a story. One sticks in my mind.

"There was a holy man," Leo said, "who lived in the desert on locusts and wild honey. His life was totally ascetic. People would come from miles around for absolution. One day the holy man heard the sound of silver bells. He looked up to see a young man walking toward him, bells tied to each toe. 'I've come to confess,' the young man said, 'because I'm a miserable sinner.'

"The holy man looked at him. 'But why the bells, my son?' The young man answered, 'I wear them to warn the insects that I'm coming. That way I won't step on them and kill them. We are all murderers, you know.' To which the holy man answered, 'You're not a sinner. You're a saint. I should be confessing to you.'

"The young man disagreed. 'No, I'm a terrible sinner. Before I married my wife, we lived in sin for several years.'

" 'That's very bad,' the old man said. 'But you did make an honest woman of her. As your penance, say five Our Fathers and five Hail Marys.'

" 'Wait, Father,' the young man cried, 'there's more. She had a sister. One day we were working together in the fields. She was so zaftig and seductive. I persuaded her to sit with me under a tree—'

" '—and you seduced her?' the holy man asked. The young man closed his eyes and nodded. 'That's very bad,' the holy man said, 'very bad.' He pondered awhile. 'But anyone who wears silver bells on his toes to warn the insects can't be all bad. You must take a pilgrimage to the shrine of St. Jude. Go, my son, and sin no more.'

"The young man sighed. 'There's more, Father. My wife also has a brother and—'

" 'May I interrupt?' the holy man asked. 'I have a suggestion. Take those silver bells off your toes and hang them SOMEWHERE ELSE.' "

Why did I remember that particular story? I must have been thinking that Paramount executives had hung their bells in the wrong place too. They were doing quite well before I got there, and they had no serious intention of experimenting with an unknown quantity.

Paramount had many stars at the time: Bing Crosby, Gary Cooper, Claudette Colbert, Paulette Goddard, Ray Milland, Marlene Dietrich. They had two of the biggest stars behind the camera too. Cecil B. De-Mille was the king of kings, autocratically heading his own unit. Ernst Lubitsch was on the lot directing a Dietrich picture. We were casually introduced. I didn't get to know him better.

I did meet another émigré from New York, and points east. Kurt Weill. I don't know what he was doing at Paramount . . . as he probably didn't know about me. We talked about working together in the future. He thought my fascination with surrealism and his intense interest in psychiatry would work well together. *Lady in the Dark,* which he wrote with Ira Gershwin in 1941, was the culmination of his interest, but I wasn't involved in the production.

I was beginning to feel guilty about taking all that money. I'd walk through the lot on my way to the commissary and imagine that other producers would look at me through Venetian blinds as I walked by their offices . . . and wonder who I was and what I was doing there.

My most happy times were at the house Ira and Lee Gershwin had taken with George on Roxbury Drive. We'd spend weekends around their pool with many of the same friends from New York, and an occasional visit from Paulette Goddard, who George was then romancing.

94

Ira and I had long been close friends, of course, sharing a love for word games and light verse with Yip Harburg. We also had a similar cockeyed view of human foibles. Now I was also getting to know George better.

We talked about working together, possibly my directing a Spanish gypsy opera or a Hebrew opera based on a dybbuk. George was planning to turn more to the classics, including the composing of several orchestral pieces.

He and Ira were working on a Fred Astaire-Ginger Rogers musical at RKO. Its title changed from *Watch Your Step* to *Stepping Stones* to *Stepping High*. None of the suggestions pleased the studio. I was saving a title for my own future use. How about *Shall We Dance?* George and Ira wanted it, so they called producer Pandro Berman in New York and got his approval. They set out to write a title song. They'd already written "Let's Call the Whole Thing Off," "They Can't Take That Away From Me," and "They All Laughed."

The two most often worked at home, occasionally going to the studio when a problem needed an immediate solution. I went with them to RKO one day. A theme was needed for a shipboard sequence. George sat down to the piano fifteen minutes before lunch, and put together a wonderful piece of music. He handed it to the arranger and we went off to eat.

When in later years I mentioned how impressed I'd been by the short time taken composing the "Walking the Dog" sequence, Ira snapped, "What do you mean, short time? It took a lifetime." He was quite right.

George's genius was so perfected that the difficult looked easy on him, and the long agony of creation was considerably shortened. He could find time for an enormous social life of tennis and golf and Sundays around the pool.

But he wasn't happy in California. None of us were. George had been idolized all his life. He was put off by the casualness with which the Hollywood crowd treated him. It wasn't like New York, where people had made special trips from Europe to meet him. None of us spoke of these frustrations. It would have been a cheap shot to accept the money and grouse at the people who gave it to us. But I quietly instructed my agents to get me out of that gold-plated strait jacket.

George and Ira then started working on *The Goldwyn Follies,* which George Marshall was to direct and United Artists was to release. That old *Variety* item was wrong in reporting both director and studio. I turned my attention to *Artists and Models,* in an advisory capacity, putting *Times Square* on a back burner and realizing that's where it would probably stay.

George and Ira were writing a beautiful score for the picture. Two of the songs—"Love Is Here to Stay" and "Love Walked In"—were nearly completed when I invited George to join me and a couple of girls about town for Saturday dinner. He arrived in his usual high spirits. "This is George Gershwin," I told the girls. They stared blankly back. Neither had ever heard of him. George pretended not to notice. His spirits remained ebullient. He played the piano for us, and sang, seemingly without a worry in the world on that night in late June. The fact the girls didn't know his name depressed me more than it did him.

The next day, I reported for my regular Sunday duty at the Gershwins. George wasn't feeling well. He didn't join us.

A couple of days later, Lee told me that George was suffering from violent headaches and the light was extremely painful to his eyes. They'd called a doctor, but he could find nothing wrong. Another doctor was consulted, but he also couldn't diagnose the problem.

I went to the Gershwins' for dinner a few nights later. George joined us accompanied by a male nurse who'd been hired to care for him. George and I were sitting alone in the living room for a few minutes. He turned to me. "Don't let them get to you, Vince, and complicate you." I was stunned. This was so unlike George, who was always vital and cheerful. It was as if he'd given up. The dinner over, the male nurse took George back to the darkened room where his eyes didn't pain him as much.

The doctors still couldn't locate the problem. Long hours were spent with Ira and Lee as the shock of George's incapacity hit them. Ira had the studio take them off the picture . . . temporarily, it was hoped.

After many false diagnoses, the trouble was determined. George had a brain tumor, and an immediate operation was needed. A group of us went to the hospital. Some of the Gershwins' friends went to the operating theater to watch what was happening. I stayed downstairs with Ira and Lee. One of the group would periodically come down with optimistic reports. Toward dawn, the surgeon himself came down, reporting that the operation was successful and George was resting comfortably. Relieved, we all went home.

Lee called me the midmorning of July 11, 1937. The operation had come too late. George never regained consciousness.

Ira, who worshipped his younger brother, was inconsolable. There

96

was no way he could return to work. Vernon Duke and Kurt Weill finished the assignment.

It was a sad and sobering time. George, cut down at the age of thirty-eight, had accomplished so much, but he died with so many ambitions left unfulfilled. What about the rest of us? What was I doing in Hollywood when there were so many things I'd rather be doing in New York? I *had* to get out of the contract.

It was some consolation that Harold Arlen would be doing the music for *Artists and Models*.

We conceived one number together—"Public Melody Number One" —a spoof of the gangster era featuring Louis Armstrong and Martha Raye. Harold dedicated the sheet music to me. As filmed, I found the involved production number a full scale mess, missing all the nuances we'd supplied.

I kept plugging away. Why not do a surrealist ballet involving the stars? I prepared a detailed concept. It was rejected.

Lee Shubert had just offered me a show in New York. I wanted to do it. After much give and take, I was allowed to buy myself out of the contract. I returned East, wiser, but not the least bit sadder.

7 | New York Reprised

The Broadway scene during the first year of Franklin D. Roosevelt's second term had a most definite pinkish cast . . . that, at any rate, was what right-wing conservatives felt. Its dominating influence was a proletarian movement of muscle and sweat, purveying harsh and painful truths. Message was the medium.

The government was as responsible for this blue-collar theater as any other single influence. The Federal Theater of the Works Progress Administration was founded in 1935 primarily as a Depression measure and coincidentally as an endowment to culture. A most welcome sinewy vitality came to the fabulous invalid, and breathed new life into her. She was lean and hungry, and infinitely more exciting.

I'd laughed at Moss Hart's tale when, two years previously, he'd gone on a world cruise with Cole Porter and Monty Woolley to write a musical called *Jubilee*. They'd check on New York happenings as their yacht docked at occasional ports. First they heard about a riveting surrealistic opera by Virgil Thomson and Gertrude Stein—*Four Saints in Three Acts*—based in Spain but performed by an all-Negro cast. Then a drama about lesbianism—*The Children's Hour*—opened at the Maxine Elliott Theater. Moss then heard of Orson Welles's plan to mount a *Voodoo Macbeth*. What had happened to stylish comedies and musicals? "There won't be any place for us in the theater when we get back," he told his friends. He was quite wrong, for *Jubilee* was a hit.

I'd been away seven months in Hollywood and, though I had no fears about my own place in the theater, it was apparent that the artistic New Deal had crystallized during my absence. Superficial fripperies had to go. The most obvious casualty was the musical revue. Where little more than a year ago I was enjoying the greatest success of my career with *The Show Is On,* the feeling around Shubert Alley was that a revue just couldn't make it in this new climate. The book show was the solution, and the project the Shuberts offered me was *Hooray for What!*

When I accepted the assignment, I knew I'd only have three months to put the show together if it was going to make its scheduled December first opening. (Paradoxically, a show which was to open four days earlier contradicted all current theory and broke all long run records for a musical show . . . and it was a revue. *Pins and Needles* was produced by the International Ladies' Garment Workers' Union Players. It was strictly amateur night, but oh what amateurs. They brought social significance to the genre, and the show ran 1,108 performances during a time when 175 playings was considered a successful run.)

Yip Harburg had supplied the idea for *Hooray for What!* and he would be writing the score with Harold Arlen. The story was very much of its time, though the message wasn't as strident as most. It told of a Schweitzer-like owner of an orchard constantly experimenting with chemicals that would repel but not kill insects. He was a talented bumbler who succeeded in concocting the most dangerous explosives known to man. He becomes an international pawn, as countries of various ideologies offer to set him up in his own laboratory so that he can continue his experiments.

Harold had taken over my apartment while I was away, so I stayed in the Lombardy Hotel for a couple of weeks until he could find new lodging. My old studio was now rented to the Theatre Guild as a rehearsal hall. I found a place a block over on East 54th. Hara had defected to new employers and wouldn't be lured back. I settled on a woman to come in by the day to take care of my modest needs. For there weren't any ambitious social plans in my near future. My sleeves were rolled up, and I was ready to get back to work.

I would direct the show and design the sets. Raoul Pène Du Bois, who'd assisted me in the *Ziegfeld Follies,* would do the costumes.

The specter of Nazism was being felt in America. I naively felt that fascism could be laughed away, and the direction was slanted to this premise. Howard Lindsay and Russel Crouse supplied a very good book. It was lovely working with professionals—and perfectionists—again. They would write and rewrite until it pleased us all.

I approached my first book show as if it were a revue. The only difference to me was that one set of characters carried through from beginning to end.

The action opened with the title song, townspeople at a Fourth of July celebration. Ed Wynn, as the farmer, is then introduced in his laboratory, mostly a painted backdrop. The first act rapidly unwinds into a finale, a Geneva peace conference where opposing powers are trying to get their hands on Ed's formula. I designed a pink set with a baroque Peace figure set in the middle of the fountain, where the cast threw in all the items mentioned in the song, "Down with Love," into a huge bonfire: flowers, rice, shoes, Valentines. It was a dandy finale, the vital good nature of the chorus the responsibility of Kay Thompson, a radio singer I'd hired to do the vocal arrangements.

The second act ridiculed Nazis, one number having each member of the chorus raise his arm in a Nazi salute, five prop arms attached to his body and being raised at the same time.

Putting the show together, a frantic race against time to begin with, became even more nerve-wracking when we reached Boston. The previous show took its sweet time getting out of the theater. The week we planned on for raising the sets dwindled to only three days. But it could be done. I just wouldn't sleep.

I got through three twenty-four-hour days. One of my colleagues feared the pace would break me. "You should get a few hours sleep," he told me. He took out two pills. "Take this one to go to sleep. When you wake up, take the other one."

I went to the hotel, and spent a few hours in chemically induced sleep. When I awoke, I took the other pill. My friend was right. I flew through rehearsal, getting everything working in record time. Nothing was beyond me, I took it all in my rapidly accelerated stride. Then with no warning, this super human collapsed. That was warning enough. My system couldn't absorb such drugs, and I'd be very careful about taking them in the future.

Working with Ed Wynn was a delight. He was returning to the stage after six years as the Texaco Fire Chief on radio. His methods were very similar to Bea Lillie's, for Ed was equally as serious about his work. He could probably intellectualize about the cause and effect of audience laughter if called upon to do so. He was more secure in his talent than Bert Lahr, a button-twisting, people-fearing worrier without parallel.

Ed was one of the rare comics who could ad lib on written material and not destroy the spirit of the dialogue. His voice was that of an eternal adolescent, with a distinctive affected lisp. He would speak the lines in a normal adult voice, the ad libs coming in a high-pitched croak. He might be telling a tale about being in the woods alone and suddenly coming upon a big black bear. "A stunning animal," he'd parenthetically state. The Perfect Fool was perfect indeed. He knew exactly what he was doing, and his reading of lines was unvarying. Every comic nuance was repeated, even in the ad libs he kept in the show.

The show opened in New York on December 1, 1937. "Sometimes the plot shuffled dully between old-fashioned musicomedy and pretentious satire," the December 13 review in *Time* magazine read, "but it ceases to matter when Ed Wynn comes on wringing his hands as if he thought man would be better off without them. Like Chaplin, he has always been a little fellow, lost in an insane world of slickers. In that role he is both funny and sympathetic and never better than in the scene where he runs to a park bench to rest and read only to be badgered and bullied by some extraordinary performing dogs.

"Sharing credit with Wynn for the show's success is able Vincente Minnelli, trained in the hard school of movie stage-shows, who directed it and designed the scenery."

More reflective analyses of Ed's singular talent were written during the show's 200-performance run.

The Stage, in January 1938, described Ed's role as "an amateur chemist whose gas for killing apple-worms becomes the football in a dippy international struggle involving some spies (Local No. 81), the League of Nations, and a man with rubber bones who won't stand up. The Winter Garden rocks with laughter. The customers mop away tears of joy.

"How the lovable fool does this, nobody really knows. Partly, of course, with gadgets, secret panels, trained dogs and his lisp. The authors have given him the finest material he has ever had, including some comments about the world situation that make sense, in their demented way. The trouble with Europe, he says, is that Italy'th in Ethiopia, Japan'th in China, Ruthia'th in Thpain—nobody's home!"

"He has never been so blissfully funny before," Gilbert W. Gabriel wrote in the February issue of *Stage* magazine.

"He proves himself not only all over again but as never in any prank-fest in the past, sublimely ridiculous. His outrageously silly costumes and bonnets are only the trimmings of goose-feathers flying around his monumental helplessness and imbecility. Everything he cackles, every sweetly agonized stage he bestows on his laughers, is the utmost of personal communication. Surround him with trick dogs or trick spies, shoot smoke out of his ears, do any of the crazy things which *Hooray for What!* does to him, and he always comes out of it peculiarly triumphant . . . a Parsifal of the circus, a Santa Claus caught without his beard in the boudoir of the grown-up world."

The success of *Pins and Needles* and *Four Saints in Three Acts* convinced me that a surrealist revue would be viable. My contractural obligation to the Shuberts was ended, I could now move on to new things.

Would Bea Lillie, I wondered, be interested in working with me on still another show? She would, she indicated, so I put together a rough presentation for her. Lee Shubert said he might be interested in producing.

"The show is called *The Light Fantastic,*" I wrote Bea. "It sets out to prove that the world today is completely screwy. A surrealist fantasy set to jig time.

"The poor average guy stands in the middle of a three-ring circus with everybody screaming at him. Fascists—anti-Fascists—Royalists—Loyalists—Communists—Democrats.

"Everybody is selling him something in a loud voice—reforestation—the housing bill—Benny Goodman—bust developer—bust reducer—hair restorer—hair remover—annuities—Wheaties.

"The pages of his magazine scream out at him. 'Why don't you put your head into a bag of gold net or pin paper roses and egg shells on your cherry-colored evening jacket?' . . . 'Why don't you wear an old mustache cup around your neck?' . . . 'Why don't you give yourself up?' . . . 'Why don't you let yourself go?' . . . While the advertisements leer at him with horrible innuendos about his metabolism, his digestive tract and his aroma.

"Does he like art exhibits? He can only see paintings of wet watches and sea lions hung out to dry or an old lung supported by a crutch.

"He finds that department stores can only display a dress to advantage on a figure who holds her own head in one hand and a live lobster in the other, as she sits on an old Franklin heater."

I suggested that in this rat race revue, Bea should have four musical numbers and four sketches. Among them: A lady-in-love-with-a-lug song, performed at Lilly Daché's, while a super-sleek saleslady fits hats on her in contradictory counterpoint to the lyrics of the song; a song about life on the open road now that gypsies were on relief; a talking picture, a glamour girl returning from lunch at the Colony and talking to her more casual image in the mirror, who has undone her hair and taken off her girdle.

Bea, in England, delayed in her answer. By this time, I'd become intrigued by an idea brought to me by Vernon Duke. How about a musical version of *Serena Blandish*, the S. N. Behrman play adapted from Enid Bagnold's *A Lady of Quality?*

My approach would be somewhat different than the original. Though I would stage the play as the same very elegant high comedy, it would be with an all-black cast. To change the concept in any way because of the cast's skin color struck me as condescension of the worst sort.

I wanted to do a sophisticated black show because I felt uneasy about the conventional stereotype of the Negro as simple, naive, and childlike.

I then went to producer Sam H. Harris with the idea. In our discussions, it was theorized that Cole Porter would be a more saleable name than Vernon's among potential backers, so Sam contacted Cole about his availability. Vernon, I felt, would have done as great a job, but these are the show business breaks. We've all suffered from them.

Sid Perelman agreed with the approach, and he began adapting the Behrman work. I brought former Cotton Club star Lena Horne from Pittsburgh, where she'd retired after marrying to raise a family, to read for the part of Serena. I hoped to interest Ethel Waters in the part of the Countess.

My concept for the sets would take note of the black characters, but only in passing. The Countess's bedroom, for example, would be papered in newspapers, as was the humble shack where she'd been born, but all the furnishings and fittings would be luxurious and elegant. I began sketching out plans for a ballet treatment of the Bluebeard legends, as though it took place in Martinique, for the first act finale.

Sid's script was delicious. The story of Serena, being loaned a diamond for a month by a jeweler and being introduced to society by an Auntie Mame countess so that she could make a good marriage, had all the cockeyed elements Sid liked to work with.

His synopsis proved it, as did one of the several scenes he got down on paper.

ACT I   Scene III

SCENE: *The bedchamber of the* COUNTESS FLOR DI FOLIO. *The massive bed and canopy at rear center dominate the room. Exits rear left and right. Large window with drapes and blinds at stage left. Downstage a chaise-longue and boudoir chair.*

At opening, the stage is in half darkness, the sleeping form of the COUNTESS *dimly discernible in the bed upstage. (Music under this portion of scene should be slow, almost turgid.) A moment later* MARTIN *enters softly rear left. An experimental glance at the* COUNTESS, *and he switches on a bedside lamp. The* COUNTESS *emits a single hollow groan, rolls over.* MARTIN *swiftly busies himself tidying up; picks up and folds a negligee thrown carelessly over foot of bed, retrieves a pair of mules from under table, etc. The* COUNTESS's *eyes open. After a moment they focus and she hoists herself heavily to a half-recumbent position.*

COUNTESS
Arh-h-h . . . Martin.

MARTIN
Yes, your Grace.

COUNTESS (*eyes close again, sepulchrally*)
. . . I've been poisoned . . .

MARTIN (*unmoved*)
Yes, Countess.

COUNTESS
Did I take any . . . brandy?

MARTIN
Only your usual decanter, my lady.

COUNTESS (*accusingly*)
I . . . remember eating several grapes. (*eyes open*) Martin, I'm sure I swallowed a seed.

MARTIN
I'm afraid they were seedless, Madame. Besides, you ate them last Friday.

COUNTESS
Grapes are treacherous, Martin. So are you.

MARTIN
Yes, madame.

COUNTESS
Stop soothing me. You're hateful in that mood . . . What kind of day is it?

MARTIN
Glorious, my lady. The pink dogwood is flowering.

COUNTESS
Must you hum under your breath like a schoolboy, Martin?

MARTIN

I believe those are bees you hear—in the garden.

COUNTESS

Well, report them to Sloane. They're positively maddening. (*as* MAID *enters with breakfast tray*) How were the newspapers this morning?

MARTIN

Unanimous. The "Morning Post" called it the most decadent party of the year. The radical papers see in you a symbol of our moral bankruptcy.

COUNTESS (*with satisfaction*)

Excellent. Remember to send them flowers. Who's awaiting to see me?

MARTIN

Four or five persons, your Grace. Mr. Entwistle of the Horse Show committee, Mr. Crispin from Cox & Ballard's, Major Tamish—

COUNTESS

Isn't my astrologer here yet?

MARTIN

Yes, madame, she—

COUNTESS

Show her in at once. You know very well I wouldn't start the day . . . (*as* MARTIN *exits,* COUNTESS *removes cover from dish on tray*) What's this—kidneys?

MAID

Yes, your Ladyship.

COUNTESS

Well, take them away. They're too depressing.

Another Perelman scene, so typical of his use of cliché situations for comic effect, was a prelude to Serena's assignation with Lord Ivor Cream, a meeting both the Countess and her butler Martin advised against. Sid's treatment no longer exists, but I remember it going something like this:

SCENE: *The chambers of* LORD IVOR CREAM. *His* BUTLER *enters.*

BUTLER

Excuse me, sir, there is a veiled lady to see you.

LORD IVOR CREAM

A veiled lady? Show her in. (*The* BUTLER *leaves and returns a moment later with a* VEILED LADY *all in black. The* BUTLER *departs.*)

VEILED LADY

I shall be brief. Tomorrow I am marrying the proudest name in England.

105

LORD IVOR CREAM

And how does that concern me, madame?

VEILED LADY

You have, I believe, certain letters in your possession. I want these letters and I mean to have them.

LORD IVOR CREAM

And if I refuse?

VEILED LADY

Then you leave me no recourse. (*She opens her reticule and takes out a small pearl-handled revolver. She cocks the trigger.*)

LORD IVOR CREAM

One moment, madame. What address did you want?

VEILED LADY

Isn't this Number Ten Mincing Lane?

LORD IVOR CREAM

No, madame. This is Number Nine. Number Ten is across the street.

VEILED LADY (*putting revolver back in reticule*)

So sorry. (*She turns around and abruptly departs*)

LORD IVOR CREAM

Not at all, madame.

Negotiations for large productions rarely run smoothly, and the wheeling and dealing for *Serena* had been rockier than most. Enid Bagnold would be getting her customary author's cut, as would Behrman. Sid would also get a percentage along with Cole. It was beginning to look as if it wouldn't be economically feasible, but I worked into 1939 trying to find a way to do the show. Unfortunately, I couldn't. Neither could anyone else. After six months on the project, I regretfully admitted defeat.

It was time to take a breather. A travel agent made all the arrangements for my first trip to Europe. I sailed alone, armed with letters of introduction. One of them was to Louis Bromfield, then staying in London. I called him at the Ritz Hotel.

"Oh, yes," he cordially answered when I identified myself. "We're having a crowd at the Ritz. Will you join us?"

I accepted the invitation and showed up at the appointed hour. Looking into the dining room, however, all I noticed was a sea of unfamiliar faces, the host's included. I was overcome by an attack of shyness and beat a hasty retreat. My telephoned apology the next morning, received by Mr. Bromfield's secretary, was readily accepted . . . though I never got another opportunity to meet the great man.

I was more comfortable with Bea Lillie, who took me under her wing and introduced me to her friends.

Too soon, I departed for Paris and points south, and the rest of the trip was a happy montage of museums and palaces, with a few extracurricular activities thrown in.

On the boat trip back, I resolved to get to know the Continent better, whenever a spare moment would allow me a more extensive stay.

Back in New York, I was debating the merits of reviving *The Light Fantastic* when Max Gordon distracted me with an offer to direct *Very Warm for May*. Oscar Hammerstein would be writing the book and lyrics, and Jerome Kern would compose the score.

The story was about putting on a show in a barn theater, and I proceeded to design principal sets, among others. One was a conventional barn, inspired by my childhood in Delaware, with dark woods and an ever-present hay loft. The theater was remodeled, and the second set transformed the old barn by stripping down the wood and maintaining the geometric lines, while building in a stage.

The first act was a marvel. Its highlight was a song Oscar didn't think would go anywhere: "All the Things You Are."

Hiram Sherman, as the pretentious producer, was to hold the show together. But even he couldn't save the second act. Its only merit, to me, was a psychiatrist ballet, Sherman narrating as the dancers went through very serious paces. He told of every phobia that afflicted him. The dancers danced it straight and somber, but it had comic effect. I was to use the same device in writing the Girl Hunt Ballet for *The Band Wagon*. Sherman would talk of his masochism, sadism, Oedipus complex, ad nauseum. The action would satirize it. "I took a hell of a beating," he'd say about his emotional health, and the dancers would bring out lighted neon rods and whack away.

We tried to rearrange the second act in several different ways. To little avail. The show opened at the Alvin Theatre on November 17, 1939, and the public was anticipating its arrival, for *Very Warm for May* was the first Kern-Hammerstein show in eight years.

"Out of respect for their immortal achievements in 'Show Boat' and 'Music in the Air,' Broadway is accustomed to bowing three times whenever their names are mentioned," Brooks Atkinson wrote in the *Times*. "But it will be impossible to enshrine 'Very Warm for May' in the same niche that does honor to their two masterpieces. For the book is a singularly haphazard invention that throws the whole show out of focus and makes an appreciation of Mr. Kern's music almost a challenge. They have mounted it lavishly; they have also populated it with beguiling young people. But there has seldom been a book that fought entertainment as successfully as the story of this musical play.

"Although Vincente Minnelli, serving as designer, has adorned it with glorious colors and some splendid costumes, Mr. Minnelli serving as director, has not resolved the confusion of the story. The direction sometimes throws away the point of the music.

"As is usually the case with aristocratic musical shows, a wealth of talent is represented backstage and on. But it seldom has a chance to put its best foot foremost. The plot scheme is against it; and the return of Mr. Kern and Mr. Hammerstein, which has long been anticipated, is not so hot in November with 'Very Warm for May.' "

"Kern's tunes were bright and strummy enough," the *Time* magazine review read, "but a raucous, epileptic plot made the show a bird that would sing but not fly.

"Not that 'Very Warm for May' lacks 'ideas.' Rather, it is swamped by them. Providing an elaborate burlesque of summer barn theaters, with their mauve-tinted playwrights, dimwit patronesses, and clod-like performers, it lunges wildly in every direction. It jazzes up Freud, mimics Dali, writhes and wriggles, gambols and glides, rains schottisches, streams gavottes, blows ballets. The atmosphere, at its thickest, is very warm for mayhem. The whole thing suggests perfectly the hysterical side of summer theaters, but doesn't turn the funny side into laughs."

Oh, my . . . and those were the *good* reviews.

Do you know how fly-by-night producers extract favorable phrases from disastrous reviews and foist them on the public in their advertising? I did much the same thing.

"Atkinson, the *Times*: '. . . does honor to their two masterpieces . . . they have mounted it lavishly . . . populated with beguiling young people . . . glorious colors and splendid costumes.'

"*Time* magazine: 'Kern's tunes . . . bright and strummy . . . an elaborate burlesque . . . suggests perfectly the hysterical side of summer theaters.' "

That's the only way I could react to my first disaster . . . it ran only 59 performances. Look at the positive elements.

It could have been worse. Consider poor Oscar. He was to have a sixteen-year dry run between *Show Boat* and *Oklahoma!* But he always reacted with rare humor and grace. After his hit show with Richard Rodgers opened in 1943, Oscar took out an ad in a trade newspaper. In it, he listed all the flops he'd been involved in since *Show Boat*, *Very*

Warm for May included. Over his signature, a message: "I did it before, and I can do it again."

A young novelist was having better luck with his first show, which opened three weeks before *Very Warm for May.* His name was William Saroyan, his show *The Time of Your Life,* and his friendship was most welcome. Someone brought us together, and we decided to do a black surrealist musical comedy, with Rodgers and Hart writing the score.

Bill at the time was a refreshing gee-whizzer, a lover of humanity and its foibles, a spontaneous and infectious guy you couldn't help having an animal liking for. He went through life finding marvelous human stories in every encounter, and wisdom in the most unexpected places. "That man is a genius!" he'd enthuse after we left a cab driver or a bootblack. Later, in Hollywood, he'd look at Baba, my black poodle, go through his paces, and echo the sentiment. "That dog is a genius too!" I don't know the forces that made Bill an embittered man in later years, but I treasure the refreshing vitality and innocence he shared with me at the outset.

I'd discuss ideas for the show, and he'd enthusiastically get to work. He would write a sketch at one sitting, then hand it over to me. I'd seen David Freedman work for hours on just one line, tightening the material so that it was as succinct as possible. This Bill was unable to do. He'd gladly sit down and write another sketch, but he couldn't rework the original one. The project fell apart, but we remained close friends. With Bill, the alternative was unthinkable.

Here I stood in the spring of 1940, at the crossroads. I was itching to move on, for there was so much more I had to offer.

While I was at liberty, I started to socialize more, to catch up with friends. Dorothy Fields had come in from California, and I invited her to the opera. We retreated to the old champagne bar at the Metropolitan between acts. We were standing together when I saw two familiar people bearing down on us. Their names . . . I couldn't remember their names. They were getting nearer. As they stepped toward us, I miraculously remembered, and smiled over at them. "Why, hello," I said, "so nice to see you. Mr. and Mrs. Schulte, I'd like you to meet—" I turned to my companion. And I drew a blank. She burst into paroxysms of laughter. The young couple looked quizzically at us. I had crawled under the carpet.

"Dorothy Fields," the lady said when she recovered, sticking out her friendly hand.

About this time, Eleanor Lambert was holding out her helpful one. She was aware of my indecision about the future.

"There's this marvelous soothsayer on the West Side," she told me. "You must see her. She's absolutely uncanny." Eleanor set up an appointment.

I reported on schedule. The lady, her pompadour in a hair net, operated out of an apartment heavy with mission oak furniture. An upright piano stood in the corner, and every soft surface in the main room seemed to be covered in chenille.

"You're in the entertainment business," she said as a matter of fact.

"Yes," I answered. Eleanor must have told her when she called.

"And you're going West to work in the movies."

"Oh?"

"You're going to have a dog, and you'll be crazy about it. And you're going to marry a star. Your first project will be very successful. I see something all black." I took this to mean black-and-white, since few pictures of the time were filmed in color.

But enough of that mumbo-jumbo. I excused myself. Eleanor later called. "What did she tell you?" she asked.

"You know," I answered, "all the usual things."

8 | The Freed Unit

If I'd known this was going to be a momentous occasion in my life, I would have remembered the most minute details of that spring day in 1940 when Yip Harburg brought Arthur Freed to my studio. Arthur probably couldn't have remembered them either. It's situations like these that convince me of the basic truth of that duet to muddled memory written by Alan Jay Lerner and Frederick Loewe for *Gigi*, the picture Arthur and I made together in 1958. Ah yes, I remember it well . . . if not the time, the weather, the occasion or what we wore.

What I do remember about Arthur is that I liked him immediately. He reminded me a great deal of Roxy, though Arthur wasn't as crude . . . as tough, perhaps, but he wasn't the rough diamond.

He wasn't a particularly imposing man . . . average looks, medium height, heavy set. He had a roundabout way of getting to the point. Alan once said Arthur started a sentence on Wednesday and finished it on Friday. But Arthur and I had a direct line of communication that wasn't always verbal. That may be why we got on so famously later.

At the outset, however, I liked him mostly for what I'd heard about him. He was a great appreciator of talent and sought out the best. His presence in my studio was obliquely flattering. I knew why he'd come.

My instinct told me Arthur was a great showman, as the rest of the world would be discovering in the next few years. Today, whenever film cultists point to my contributions in the progress of the movie musical, I plead not guilty. The true revolutionary was Arthur. He, more than any one man, made it possible. He gave his creative people extraordinary freedom, and this is the highest confidence one person can place in another.

Arthur had started out as a lyricist. He was one of the best. With composer Nacio Herb Brown, he wrote such popular classics as "You Were Meant for Me," "Temptation," and "Singin' in the Rain."

His friend Louis B. Mayer felt Arthur's talents could be effectively used in film production. He set Arthur up with his own production unit to develop musical properties and foster new talent. With the exception of *The Wizard of Oz* the previous year, the musical was one genre Metro hadn't had much success with in the 1930s. It was Arthur who bought Metro's first successful musical property from Samuel Goldwyn. And it was Arthur who, though he turned the producer reins over to Mervyn LeRoy, insisted that a song by Yip and Harold Arlen be kept in the film. Its title: "Over the Rainbow."

Arthur had just finished his first picture as a solo producer, *Babes in Arms*, starring Judy Garland and Mickey Rooney. Its huge success gave him even greater latitude with Mayer. He was now in New York to round up talent for the Freed unit.

"How would you like to work at Metro, Vincente?"

"Well, I don't know, Mr. Freed," I answered. "Things didn't go too well for me the last time I was in Hollywood."

"The job at Paramount?"

"Yes. As soon as I got there, I knew it wasn't going to work out. I spent the next eight months trying to get out of the contract."

"That happens in Hollywood," Arthur conceded. "Tell you what. Why don't you try it my way for a year. You won't have a title, but you'll be learning the business. You'll be working with me. Other producers will be able to call on you for your services. You can read scripts and make suggestions . . . direct musical numbers . . . work in the cutting room. If you don't like it after that time, and if you see that you don't have a future in pictures, then come back to New York. But if you like the work and decide to stay, I have the feeling you'll make a damn fine director."

"Well, that sounds very good," I hesitated. "But I don't know if—"

"What do you think your living expenses would be?" he interrupted. When the timing was right, Arthur could forego the verbosity and pounce.

"Oh, I could probably get by on $300 a week."

"You're on!"

Before I knew it had happened, I had already started.

People were willing to take the chance with Arthur. He soon brought out Gene Kelly, vocal coach Kay Thompson, and choreographer Robert Alton to join composer-arranger Roger Edens as the nucleus of his unit. Other producers had put together similar groups before, but this was the first to be composed of newcomers to the industry. Later, Arthur imported still more New York talents: costume designer Irene Sharaff, Alan Lerner, choreographer Charles Walters and set designer Oliver Smith. He would also be giving other directors their starts, Stanley Donen and Richard Brooks among them.

Once I made up my mind, I set off immediately for Hollywood. If I had to come to California, this was the way it had to be. Decide on a course of action and act on it quickly. My enthusiasm for films was suddenly back with me.

I didn't feel much had been done to progress the film musical since my last sojourn in Hollywood. (*The Wizard of Oz* was still too new to place in any historical perspective.) If there was any exception, it was *The Goldwyn Follies,* which United Artists had produced in 1938. My old friend George Balanchine did the choreography. Much as I respect him, I'm sorry to say that the only impression his work left on me was that this was the first time I'd seen ballet used in a film. The ballet itself, as well as the photography, was movie-conventional, Zorina entering and leaving through a diving bell device in the middle of a marble pool.

I knew from my experience at Paramount that I wasn't going to be the Great Savior of the musical film. But I had the temerity to think I still might have something different to offer.

The field seemed wide open. There weren't any musical talents before or behind the cameras which impressed me . . . except one. The Fred Astaire dance numbers were the only bright spots in musicals of the late 1930s, though I found the stories inane.

I wasn't impressed by Busby Berkeley's spectacular effects while at Warner Brothers, though I found his later work with Mickey and Judy at Metro to have great charm. His devices were ingenious, but they bore little relation to the story or to the "reality" of the piece. Like most musicals of the period, his were crudely made "backstage" stories. The songs weren't integral to the plot. Musical numbers were mounted on a stage, and no sooner was a number placed within a proscenium than it would unrealistically open up. Suddenly there'd be fifty dancing girls on the wings of a plane. The sky really was the limit. I suppose the audience accepted this brand of fantasy as a kind of license. If it still does, the reason may be because the audience is nostaligc about its first exposure to camp rather than impressed by the merits of the over-all picture.

I didn't object to fantasy per se. But fantasy should have its physical limits too, with a canvas of pre-established dimensions.

I found film versions of Broadway shows even more unsatisfying. Nowhere was the movies' poor quality of sets and costumes—despite the dollars spent—more obvious. Although one or two of the original numbers would be used, many of the other songs were dropped, songs that helped make the show a success to begin with. New songs would be written to fill in the gaps, but they didn't have the original flavor.

Such was the logic to the musical pictures of the time. Film-makers didn't seem to care what the picture was about as long as it had some splashy pyrotechnics. One or two highlights among the fatuous and banal was hardly enough for me.

These were my thoughts as the Super Chief whizzed its way West. I was also thinking of how I could apply my experience in the theater to films. The most logical application would be lighting. This was one area where films were far behind the theater. Lighting for pictures was a harsh cliché: conventional, rather flat, with everything bright. To me, *Carnival in Flanders* remained the most notable exception.

American cinematographer Harry Stradling had shot the film, and he had recently come to the United States to work. He was one man I wanted to meet.

John Ford seemed the only American director with an eye for both lighting and composition. I didn't understand why other film-makers couldn't do as well, why so few of them used lighting to establish mood.

There was no studio brass to meet me this time. I was getting a fraction of my salary at Paramount. The difference was readily apparent.

I checked in at the studio the next day. Metro still had "more stars than in the heavens." In residence were Greta Garbo, Norma Shearer, Joan Crawford, Clark Gable, Greer Garson, Rosalind Russell, Spencer Tracy, and Katharine Hepburn. But times were changing.

The enormous success of *Gone With the Wind*, which Metro had financed and distributed, coupled with the extraordinary reception given to *The Wizard of Oz*, marked a new era for the studio. The flossy women's pictures, the Norma Shearer and Joan Crawford vehicles being the most successful, were on their way out. Spectacular and nostalgic

114

films were coming into vogue. The threat of war—and it was a gloomy cloud hanging over everything we did—had much to do with this.

Arthur's desire to make musical pictures about back-home America with its homely values seemed to anticipate the public's shifting interest. Suddenly the climate at Metro was ripe for innovation, and many of us were being given the opportunity to show our stuff.

Arthur was now preparing *Strike Up the Band* with Mickey and Judy. The studio had found a vital team, whose audience was as rabidly fanatic as that of such great romantic teams as Garbo and John Gilbert.

I was bunking with Eddie Powell, a musical director I'd worked with in New York. I'd drive my jalopy to Culver City and park off the lot, since my apprentice status didn't allow me special studio privileges. I'd walk through the lobby of the administration building to my office in the writers' wing. Walking along with me, among others, would be such talents as Dorothy Parker, Lillian Hellman, and Sid Perelman. We'd often lunch together, either at the big round writers' table in the commissary or off the lot. I'd hear them grouse about the way they were being exploited. Some of them actually believed it, though I never heard them complain about the size of their pay checks.

The challenge of the job soon engulfed me. I'd get to work at nine and stay until five or five-thirty. It was a cram course in film-making, and I took to it with absolute ease. The creative climate was balmy, the administration seemingly benevolent.

There were dark undercurrents to be sure . . . the talk of the dehumanizing of the stars and the prostituting of the writers' talents. But never had I met such animated robots nor such willing whores. Some of the talk became real to me when I discovered a prevalent studio practice. Writers would prepare scripts; other writers were working right behind them on the same project. A fine writer would deliver a perfectly workable script. Three or four other writers would then have a crack at it. The process could completely demoralize a man. I liked Arthur even more when he showed his contempt for such practices.

Being new to pictures, I never recognized their physical limitations. No matter how difficult the problem, one could always find a way of solving it. My approach wasn't orthodox. I took each problem individually. Things I didn't like, I just ignored. By cutting away at such nonessentials, I could see the way it should be done.

During my first few months at Metro, the only challenges were to my imagination. Lena Horne came to the studio at the same time, and my first assignments were to direct her musical numbers. Another director would do the rest of the film. Lena complained in her autobiography that because she was black, her many numbers were never integrated into the script. They could thus be cut out of the film if Southern distributors objected. This was, of course, contemptible. Could it have been only thirty years ago that we considered it daring to cast a black actress in a non-servile role? We were raising our puny voices for social progress. They should have been louder.

I was nevertheless charged with the responsibility of delivering these pieces of film at minimum cost but with maximum style. We settled on the expedient of having a lavishly gowned Lena standing in front of a constantly changing assortment of sets. Sometimes her specialty numbers were shot on a proscenium stage. I was learning how to move the camera.

In the meantime, I was supplying ideas for other pictures.

"Come down to the set," Arthur said one day. *Strike Up the Band* was still shooting, with Busby Berkeley directing.

"Mickey, this is Vince Minnelli," Arthur said in casual introduction. "Hi ya," Mickey said. I found him as boyish and cocky as the many roles he'd played up to then. But I admired him. He was imaginative and enormously versatile. He sang, he danced, he cried.

Then Arthur took me over to the eighteen-year-old Judy. "Glad to meet you," she bubbled cheerfully. I was attracted to her open manner, as only a man who has been reserved all his life can be. Though still a teen-ager, Judy was already a big star, meeting a production assistant who someday might become a director . . . and it was becoming a bigger uncertainty by the day. I hadn't realized before I came to Hollywood that studios preferred to go with tested talents and it was near to impossible to get that first break: your own picture. This is a far cry from today, when it seems every director of a catchy television commercial moves on next to a feature film.

But introductions weren't what Arthur had in mind. A problem needed solving. He showed me the set. "We need a big production number here. Mickey and Judy are in the house, and he's telling her he wants to be a famous band leader like Paul Whiteman. Something big has to happen."

"Who else is in the house?" I asked.

"Nobody. They're alone."

I looked around, and noticed a bowl of fruit on a table in an alcove.

"Why don't you take that bowl and have Mickey set each piece of fruit as if it were a musical instrument . . . apples for fiddles, oranges for brass, bananas for woodwinds. Then have Mickey conduct with his hands. The pieces of fruit are now puppet characters of musicians."

"Good!" Arthur exclaimed. "Thank you." He turned to talk to someone, and that was that. All I did was supply the idea. I had nothing else to do with the number. The studio did the rest. Someone in the research department remembered a layout in *Life* magazine the previous year. Artist Henry Fox had created table-top musicians out of pieces of fruit, and the studio hired him to do the same for us. I received my first critical mention, of sorts, for my work in films. The critic for *Variety,* in his review of September 13, 1940, commented, "The episode is an outstanding example of imaginative entertainment."

But far greater critical notice came at the studio. Mayer later would point me out to visitors. "This is the genius who took a bowl of fruit and made a big production number out of it." I looked appropriately modest . . . as well I should. But perhaps the genius of creating something out of practically nothing was the kind Mayer most respected.

If that's the case, there must have been many geniuses at Metro. The people I worked with had fallen so in love with the medium that we were working overtime and, if aware of it, not caring. We wanted all of us to succeed, so we gladly helped each other.

That's the major thing I miss about the old studio system—the solidarity we once felt. I'd seen musicians and arrangers get together at Eddie Powell's house whenever any one of them was in a spot. Composers and arrangers assigned to a picture had to work very quickly during filming and their colleagues—many of them "at liberty"—would work all night to help out. The same held true with the craftsmen I worked with during those early days at Metro.

Call it dedication. Call it professionalism. These were qualities I hadn't associated with film-making. Certainly Mayer wasn't so appreciative that we did it for his sake. There were limits to our devotion, as he learned soon enough. His brainstorm to have a talent audition one night each week in the commissary didn't go over. He must have sensed a hint of rebellion in his captive audience, for the practice was quickly dropped.

I, for one, wasn't resentful about the auditions cutting into my evenings. I wasn't all that busy on those famous Hollywood nights . . . nor on the crazy Sundays that F. Scott Fitzgerald wrote about. Though I was fascinated by the work at the studio, I had trouble becoming acclimated to the town itself. I'd made several friends. but I still felt isolated. It was a strange brand of loneliness, one I hadn't experienced before . . . relentless and unrelieved. I could walk across town for rehearsals while in New York and see dozens of fascinating visuals along the way. The crowds of people hurrying along, the honking of traffic and the city lights gave New York a tempo Hollywood couldn't match. I'd leave the studio at dusk and look at the flatlands around me. In the distance stood a solitary oil well. I found the lonely silhouette rising out of the ground quite symbolic.

It took me a while to realize you had to have a home you liked, where you did most of your entertaining, instead of scurrying over to the Mocambo or Ciro's. Even after I moved into my own apartment at the Regency on Doheny and later to a house in the Hollywood Hills, I sensed this indifference about the town. So many of us were alone in a crowd of impassive faces.

Work continued. I was thrown several problems and solved them as best I could. More scripts to read, more numbers to stage.

I was now involved with *Babes on Broadway,* again starring Mickey and Judy, with Busby Berkeley directing. Arthur and I were sitting in his office one day when an agent walked in with a four-year-old child. (It's indicative of Arthur's nature that his office was open to everyone.) The little girl was wearing kilts. "All right, Margaret," the agent said, "do something for Mr. Freed."

The little girl, a tam at a rakish angle on her brunette head, marched directly to Arthur, sitting behind his desk. She grabbed his shirt sleeve and cried emotionally, "Don't send my brother to the chair! Don't let him fry!"

My mouth fell open. So did Arthur's.

I rushed to the office of Fred Finklehoffe, who was writing the screenplay. "I know you're writing an audition scene with a producer," I told him. "I've just seen this extraordinary little girl. You must use her —just the way she is—kilts and all." So the part was written in. Margaret O'Brien got no billing in the film, but it was her first appearance in pictures.

If this suggestion proved to work well, another one didn't: a sequence in the picture had Mickey and Judy absorbing atmosphere in an old theater. I suggested that, under the spell of the old theatrical posters on its walls, they could transform themselves into stars of the past. Mickey could imitate Sir Harry Lauder and George M. Cohan, and Judy could impersonate Sarah Bernhardt, Fay Templeton, and Blanche Ring. I suggested Elsie Janis be hired to coach them.

The director decided that Mickey and Judy would not attempt accurate imitations, doing the stars' turns in their own personalities. It wasn't very successful. I thought I knew why.

Would I ever get a chance to do it my way? The months passed quickly, and the trial marriage was almost up. I still had no indication whether Arthur and the other studio brass felt I had something to contribute.

One day, Arthur called me into his office.

"What do you think of *Cabin in the Sky?*" he asked.

"I think it's very true and very human . . . a wonderful story."

His eyes showed no emotion.

"How would you like to direct it?"

9 | Foreman at the Factory

Arthur Freed had just been through a fur-flying donnybrook in the front office. After Leo's lions inspected themselves, and determined that not much face had been lost, it was decided he could emerge as the victor. His hotshot New York stage director could have the job.

I was aware I'd checked my Broadway reputation at the studio gate, and that I'd have to prove my worth all over again in films.

To those in charge, I was just a one-year apprentice . . . and there were many more where I'd come from. Under contract at the studio with first call on the best properties were such master journeymen as Sam Wood, Victor Fleming, Clarence Brown, and George Cukor. If *Cabin in the Sky* hadn't been a small picture—and a risky one too—I would have had to wait much longer for that first break. But I interpreted the assignment, with more freedom than I'd dreamed possible, as just reward for past contributions. Arthur allowed me that conceit. I didn't learn until years later how hard he'd had to fight on my behalf.

I also didn't know of his other battles to get a decent budget, nor of the dirty work he took on himself so that my sensibilities wouldn't be offended. I wasn't as grateful for this insularity in later years, when the studio contract system virtually ended and we all had to fend for ourselves. I was the world's oldest babe in the woods; I knew nothing about, and had no stomach for, the necessary in-fighting. But how was Arthur to know? We thought the studio would last forever.

If there were any reservations about the film, they revolved around the story, which reinforced the naive, childlike stereotype of blacks. But I knew there were such people as the deeply pious Petunia and Joe, her weak gambler of a husband, and that such wives constantly prayed for the wavering souls of their men. Good and evil, however, usually fought their battle in the man's mind instead of in vivid fantasy between the devil in black and an angel in white, as we were attempting to portray. If I was going to make a picture about such people, I would approach it with great affection rather than condescension.

Arthur also had some unspoken reservations, I'm sure. He had originally wanted to film *Porgy and Bess,* but the property wasn't available. The first all-black musical since King Vidor's *Hallelujah!* in 1929 would be *Cabin in the Sky* by default.

A portion of the militant black and liberal white press was highly critical of the proposed endeavor, finding the story patronizing. But there were an equal number of publications supporting us. Lena Horne and I, on our occasional dinner dates, were doing some patronizing of our own . . . at restaurants where my prior call determined that we wouldn't be turned away. I put the question to her. "You must do it," she urged. Once we decided to go ahead with the film, we gave no thought to public reaction. We would never knowingly affront blacks . . . or anyone else for that matter.

Ethel Waters was repeating her stage role as Petunia. She'd also been in my first Broadway musical, *At Home Abroad.* She became my talisman. Lena was finally getting her big chance as Georgia Brown. I wanted Dooley Wilson to repeat as Little Joe, but his stage name wasn't as big as Eddie "Rochester" Anderson's film and radio name. I was overruled. Had we waited a couple of years, after Dooley's great success as the Sam who played it again in *Casablanca,* he surely would have gotten the part. Rochester came through nonetheless.

I wanted Petunia and Joe to look as attractive as possible, for the audience to be aware of their simple goodness. Making Lena into a beautiful siren was no problem.

When the art department showed me sketches of a dirty cabin, they discovered a temper my bland exterior usually kept hidden. How could they have missed the point? These people were poor, but not slovenly. Petunia would try to make her surroundings as pleasant as her limited funds would allow. At my suggestion, handsome but inexpensive wicker furniture was used to transform the cabin. One set more to my liking was a street in the southern ghetto, with a warm golden look, created from a permanent studio version of a New York street.

My first exposure to the art department as a director was the first in a running series of battles. It was a medieval fiefdom, its overlord accustomed to doing things in a certain way . . . his own. Few directors took exception to this. I did. We eventually adjusted to each other's styles, and our differences were worked out.

I decided to create a realistic framework for the fantasy, using the homely, everyday objects around the characters as points of reference. Petunia would blow out the coal-oil lamp, leaving the room where Joe is fighting for his life after being shot by a local tinhorn. The fantasy sequence would begin with the lamp inexplicably glowing again and the sinister shadow of Lucifer being projected against the wall. The battle for Joe's soul would be waged around the bed and under the sheets where Joe lay cowering.

The emphasis of the mundane was extended to Lena's role. She was an economy class siren, and her seductive artifices reflect that. I introduced her as an agent of the devil taking a bubble bath in a very old bathroom . . . bubble bath, after all, can be bought at the five-and-dime. The censors at the Hays office, in their infinite wisdom, made me drop the scene, however. I also had her cut a huge magnolia off a tree to replace a less becoming hat as she prepared to visit Joe at home.

The touches I'm proudest of—though neither audience nor critics took note of them—involved an inquisitive, restless camera. Sydney Wagner proved extremely adaptable in implementing the effects I had in mind.

My spare time hadn't been idle since coming to Hollywood. I haunted studio projection rooms and commercial theaters, wanting to learn everything about film. Though I was struck by the sophisticated subject matter of many pictures in the Thirties, I wasn't impressed by the stationary cameras with which they were shot. The mobility of silent pictures was lost with the advent of the microphone and the sound booth. But technology had advanced in these fifteen years. Why hadn't camera movement returned?

Of course it had never gone away in Max Ophuls's work. His films swirled with movement, dancing about the deep-toned décors along with his waltzing actors. He'd become my spiritual leader. I soon learned, however, that no one can teach you how to move a camera. It's innate in the director.

Plotting the movement of the camera is a form of choreography. Perhaps that's why the shot taken from a crane had been largely limited to musical numbers in the past. The audience wasn't aware of its use because the movement glided along with the singer or dancer.

But a moving camera can heighten the dramatic effect too. Many directors make a big thing of determining the master shot, alternating it with shots from different angles. I found this unimaginative and repetitious. Most scripts are too wordy, and much dialogue can be eliminated by quickly showing what's happening instead of having the actors verbalize it. As the movement sweeps toward or away from the action, a wealth of atmosphere-creating detail can be shown. But even with today's perfection of the zoom lens, which saves precious hours spent on laying track on which the camera unit will move, motion is used too little. I planned it for my first picture, and I've used the moving camera ever since.

There was another device too often used in motion pictures which I felt tended to slow up the action: the fade-out of one scene to black as a means of transition to the following scene. I was determined not to use it. There was, in fact, no situation in film-making which I felt called for fade-outs. I've never used them in any of my pictures, preferring to use dissolves of different lengths as a smoother way of progressing the action.

In dissecting the stage play, we discovered several production numbers put in for showy effect, but having nothing to do with the simple story. We decided to drop them, and to interpolate additional numbers which would better progress the plot.

The original composers weren't available. Vernon Duke was in the service, and John Latouche was working on another show. We turned to Harold Arlen and Yip Harburg.

Harold had started his career in Harlem's Cotton Club, and he had a special empathy for blacks. Yip was as fine a lyric writer as any, and he was close to Arthur and me. They wrote "Happiness Is a Thing Called Joe" for Ethel to sing while her husband is convalescing, and "Life's Full of Consequences" for Rochester in the scene where he's tempted by Georgia Brown. Roger Edens, as musical supervisor, easily integrated the songs into the production.

We started shooting the summer of 1942.

The first rush of patriotic volunteers had left Metro by then, eager to join the war. (I'd been rejected when it was discovered I suffered from severe anemia.)

Gene Kelly was starting out in films on an adjoining soundstage as Judy Garland's co-star in *For Me and My Gal*. The word was out on him. Studio executives thought he was a mistake, not the movie star type. Gene later told me this lack of enthusiasm may have been due to an angry letter he'd sent Mayer after a screen test promised by the studio head failed to materialize. It got the Kelly Irish up. "I wouldn't work for you even if I had to dance in the street for pennies," he wrote. Gene signed instead with David Selznick, and Arthur had innocently borrowed him for the Garland film.

In a writer's cubicle in the Thalberg building, my friend Bill Saroyan was writing a screenplay called *The Human Comedy*. I'd brought Bill to the studio one day. Knowing how susceptible Arthur was to talented people, I wasn't surprised when Bill was hired. He later delivered a script over 300 pages long, twice the length of the average script. It had visual elements and gentle charm nonetheless and Arthur thought it could be filmed if rewritten. He took it to Mayer, who agreed. Bill was called to Mayer's office.

"What do you want for your script?" Mayer asked.

"Oh, nothing," Bill answered airily.

"No, the laborer is worthy of his hire," Mayer said.

"Well, whatever you feel is right."

"Come now, young man," Mayer said, beginning to show his impatience. "What is your price?"

"Oh, I don't know," Bill said. "How about a hundred thousand?"

Bill suddenly found himself in the anteroom outside.

He went on to use the script—which Metro finally did buy at less than the quoted price—as the basis for a novel. And he found himself in the unenviable position of having both film and book introduced to the public in the same month, and competing with each other for the entertainment dollar.

Ira Gershwin was back in Hollywood. He was working on the film adaptation of *Lady in the Dark* with composer Kurt Weill, their show having been produced the previous year in New York. And he was now collaborating with Jerome Kern on *Cover Girl*, which Columbia was to make the following year starring Rita Hayworth and the hottest male dancer since Astaire, a guy named Gene Kelly. Small world, this show business.

Nowhere did it seem smaller than at the Metro factory where I was getting my start as a foreman. We knew it was the best studio; we kept telling ourselves that at the writer's table in the commissary where I was still lunching. But I didn't feel comfortable in the executive dining room with the studio heads who made it so, whenever I ate there with Arthur. I preferred the outer room—Siberia—which I continued to frequent for some time. As my directing career got going, time became such a problem that I only had time to grab a sandwich in the director's office assigned to me.

Metro was full of Peyton Place intrigue in those days, for those who wallow in that sort of thing. Enough gossip was circulated to fill several books . . . and it has.

Gene Kelly occasionally talks about plotting on a far greater scale. There was unspoken competition between the three musical production units headed by Arthur, Joe Pasternak, and Mayer's nephew, Jack Cummings. Yet, as Gene observes, the units should have considered their real threat those units specializing in dramatic films. A Greer Garson or Katharine Hepburn picture could be made at half the cost of a musical and grossed twice as much.

The only touchstone of the studio was success at the box office. Times haven't changed, nor are they likely to in that regard. A director was given almost total freedom while the picture was being made. It was only after the sneak previews and the first look at audience reaction cards that changes were suggested.

Even I, my first time out, was given that consideration. The studio put on an extra man to teach me the simple techniques of the camera, primarily when to look left or right. Once that simple lesson was learned, I could dispense with the consultant's advice. My instincts saw me through.

Arthur also hired Al Lewis, one of the producers of the stage play, to discuss ways of making the play cinematic. We hit it off immediately, and I found his ideas quite sound.

Some of the stage elements adapted well to film: the way the characters would look up to the sky to pray to God just as children do; the frenetic jitterbug sequences; the outstanding musical score, the biggest hits being the title song and "Taking a Chance on Love."

Al was enthusiastic about my cinematic contributions to the work. The moving camera followed both dramatic and musical interludes. One of the earliest was the scene in the church, with the soloist center screen, a gossiping parishioner in the foreground. The camera on a long boom follows the talk as it progresses from the front of the church to the rear, another soloist being picked up behind the buzzing foreground action.

125

It finally rests on the subject of all that scandalized talk, Little Joe sitting in a rear pew with Petunia.

Shortly thereafter the camera followed the action on the street as Petunia runs toward the sound of a gunshot, fearing that Little Joe is involved. The motorized camera couldn't keep up with the running Ethel. "Should I slow down?" she asked, after the first rehearsal.

"Absolutely not," I answered. "We'll have to keep up with you." I had members of the crew push the camera instead, and we got the scene shortly after.

The camera stuck its nose into other dramatic action. It picked up every nuance when Petunia comes home and finds Little Joe apparently in Georgia Brown's clutches. It continued through the next scene, with Ethel slowly making her way into the cabin, sinking heavily into a rocker to reprise in an ironic way, "Happiness Is a Thing Called Joe." Earlier she'd been hanging laundry on the line as she sang the song to her husband, rocking beside her in the yard. As the song ended, she took down a sheet to reveal the ominous sight of two gamblers coming to collect the money Joe owes them.

I also used a boom in a night club number, the camera following the customers inside, observing their dancing and finally resting on Duke Ellington leading the band.

Stock film footage of a tornado, which culminates the action, was first used in *The Wizard of Oz*. It was rear projected so that it could be seen through the night club window. Petunia and Joe are killed by the same tinhorn who'd previously wounded Joe. The night club falls around them. Shovel-shaped devices were tripped to bring down the plaster, being timed to fall just after Lena flees each well-plotted area. A staircase and mirror on the landing were left standing, so that the stairs to heaven (built as an extension of the night club stairs) could be shot through the mirror's reflection.

The shooting went quickly, the picture being finished below schedule. My good luck charm came through. Ethel translated her bravura, outsize stage performance into a more naturalistic film portrayal. She owed it to her very expressive face and eyes. Ethel, however, claimed she owed it all to God. She has a direct pipeline to Him, you know.

Arthur and I were looking at a finished print of the picture one day. I don't know which one of us suggested the possibility of reprocessing the black and white film in a sepia tint. We experimented with a portion of it. The film was transformed. It seemed more magical. Sepia created

126

a soft, velvety patina more flattering to the actors' skin tones. The picture was released that way.

I was pleased when, at the preview, Arthur told me how proud he was that his name was associated with the movie. I was just as proud when the picture was released in May of 1943. The anticipated brouhaha never materialized. It was accepted by the audience as the loving look we intended. The critics saw it the same way.

"*Cabin in the Sky* is a bountiful entertainment," Thomas M. Pryor wrote in the New York *Times*. "The Metro picturization, which settled down at Loew's Criterion yesterday for what should prove to be a long tenancy, is every inch as sparkling and completely satisfying as was the original stage production in 1940. In short, this first all-Negro screen musical in many a year is a most welcome treat."

Doing a comic potboiler like *I Dood It* wasn't my idea of logical progression after such an auspicious start. Call it my sophomore jinx.

My discussions with studio executives ostensibly left the decision to me, but it wouldn't have been politic for me to refuse the assignment. The studio was stuck with footage and sets of a project that wasn't working. I was flattered that they turned to me for help. An added inducement was the assigning of Sid Herzog and Fred Saidy to rewrite the slipshod script, a story based on a Buster Keaton silent picture. They were a delight and great fun to work with. I found myself drawn into the project.

Some footage had to be maintained, I was instructed. They were two irrelevant musical numbers shot previously, one of them an Eleanor Powell production number on a battleship and the other an exercise in twirling ropes.

Might as well throw them into that kitchen sink of a story: a moony fan played by Red Skelton adores a star, Eleanor, and attends her every performance of a Civil War melodrama in which she's appearing. Her true love has taken up with another woman, and she impulsively marries Red on the rebound. They are of course in love at the end, after Red has foiled a saboteur plot . . . saboteur plots were very big in those days . . . and gets to replace the actor who's the villain of the piece when he's dragged off to his just desserts.

We all did the best we could, and managed to do a creditable job. Producer Jack Cummings was pleased. "It's a joy to see the rushes," he told us. "I never know what's going to happen."

If nothing else, the picture taught me that I could function in an uninteresting exercise if I had to. It marginally gave me a look at the comedian's psyche, Hollywood style. It wasn't much different from the Broadway version. Red's humor revolved around one-liners and he was unsure of his effectiveness in comedy of the situation. "I'm not funny," he complained to Edna, then his wife and manager. She and Red's agent came to look at the rushes. "You're crazy," she told him. "You've never been funnier." Red proceeded to agonize over all his previous performances. It was a wonder to him that he'd ever gotten this far.

When the film was released, I received a letter from an outraged fan. He'd taken exception to the scene where Red, very confused about his predicament, is sitting on a park bench. Butterfly McQueen, Eleanor's maid, joins him. Her little black dog (played by Baba, my then pet poodle) sits on the other side. Red, in his bewilderment, first talks to Butterfly, then turns to talk to the dog. I thought it was a mildly amusing bit. "How dare you make fun of black people by equating them to a dog?" the moviegoer wrote. I was surprised by such an interpretation. Like my general attitude to the picture, this was the farthest thing from my mind. My thoughts were too filled with the carrot Arthur was dangling before me in the form of our next project.

10 | Judy

Arthur wasn't consciously aware, I'm sure, that with our next picture, he would be giving me that final boost into the major leagues. But he did nevertheless. The film he had in mind was based on a series of nostalgic pieces Sally Benson had written for *The New Yorker*, which were later published in book form as *Meet Me in St. Louis*. Her childhood reminiscences were praised as a wonderful evocation of a past era, and Arthur felt a sentimental mood piece could be created.

I found the book affecting, humorous, and warm. One sequence, where the children fantasize Halloween as blood and thunder and get involved in all sorts of malicious mischief, was the convincer for me. The burning of feet and slashing of throats they envisioned, almost a wistful longing for horror, wasn't the sweet and treacly approach so characteristic of Hollywood. This was the type of fantasy that real children, raised on the grimmest of Grimm's fairy tales, would have. Yes, I told Arthur, I would gladly direct the picture.

Two screen writers had put together a script while I was working on the Skelton film. Since they saw no plot in the book, they concocted a tale of the blackmail of Esther Smith, the part Judy Garland eventually played. This is hardly the stuff of which lyrical evocations of an era are made, so I suggested we get another version.

129

Arthur then hired Fred Finklehoffe, who'd made a great success a few seasons back with *Brother Rat* on the stage, and Irving Brecher, a former comedy writer now trying his hand in films. He instructed them to write a script with Judy in mind for the starring part.

They took the very human values of the Benson work—the simple goodness of the time, the earnestness and purity of its people, the gentle humor and the laughs of recognition at their universality—and constructed a story out of an episode in the book. Though fragile, it had great charm. It revolved around the imminent transfer of the husband to New York and the effect the prospective move has on his family—his wife, his father, four daughters, son, and a cook.

Arthur showed Judy the script. Now twenty-one and recently separated from David Rose, she intended to move to the more adult roles. From her now mature viewpoint, she thought it would be a mistake to play a seventeen-year-old. She'd just starred in *Presenting Lily Mars,* a picture about a stage-struck girl, and felt it was the first step in her transition from child to adult. The picture wasn't as good as she thought it was. But at its end, Judy whirled in black tulle as the star of a grown-up production number. To revert to a teen-aged girl in her next film would be a mistake.

Most of her advisers agreed. "This picture will set your career back twenty years," Judy later quoted one of them as saying. There had been so much conflict in the advice given her by studio executives, all of whom had a special fatherly feeling for Judy, that it must have been a welcome novelty to find most of them agreeing with her for a change.

I wasn't aware of her feelings when I first discussed the role with her. She looked at me as if we were planning an armed robbery against the American public. She later told me that she'd come to see me thinking I would see it her way.

"It's not very good, is it?" she asked.

"I think it's fine," I answered. "I see a lot of great things in it. In fact, it's magical."

Judy couldn't see the magic, neither in my approach nor, I suppose, in me. She tried to get the point across, but I was too dense to perceive it.

I learned soon enough. The next day, Mayer called Freed. "Judy says she doesn't want to do the picture. For once I have to agree with her. I've read it and there's no plot."

Arthur stood firm. His track record was so good that Mayer backtracked. After Arthur's string of successes, the studio owed him a failure. The picture would be made and its star would be Judy Garland.

I now had a leading lady, no matter how reluctant. Time to really get going.

Ralph Blane and Hugh Martin were hired to write most of the songs for the picture. Both had been part of Kay Thompson's chorus in *Hooray for What!* and gone on to write *Best Foot Forward*, the 1941 hit musical. A friend touted their talents to theatrical producer Max Gordon, who wasn't familiar with their work.

"In five years, they'll be the next Rodgers and Hart," the friend said. "Bring them back in five years," Gordon drily answered. Arthur had brought them to Hollywood instead. They'd written songs interpolated in several of his musicals. Three of those five years were almost up when they began to work on the picture. They turned out three of the most melodic songs ever used in films and all deservedly became standards: "The Boy Next Door," "The Trolley Song," and "Have Yourself a Merry Little Christmas."

I felt the whole picture should have the look of Thomas Eakins's paintings, though not to the point of imitation. Set decorator Lemuel Ayres, recently brought out from New York by Arthur, and art director Preston Ames captured just the right nostalgic mood in the 1903 St. Louis sets they created on a back lot. Irene Sharaff also came from New York to design the costumes.

The picture was divided into four seasons. I decided to introduce each segment of the film by using the Smiths' American Gothic house at 5135 Kensington Avenue as a lovely filigreed illustration, like the greeting cards of that era. Each card would dissolve into the live action of the Smith family.

Summer introduced the family and explained the situation; fall had the Halloween sequence and further developed the problem; winter showed the bittersweet final Christmas in St. Louis; the film ended in spring, the family having stayed in St. Louis after all and going to the opening of the World Exposition.

This was my first picture to be shot in Technicolor. I was advised to rely heavily on the advice of Natalie Kalmus, the studio's color consultant. She came over regularly to check on our progress.

"You've heard the truth about Natalie Kalmus," someone on the set told me.

"No, I haven't," I answered, not sure I really wanted to know.

"She's color blind."

A laugh was very much needed at that point. My juxtaposition of color had been highly praised on the stage, but I couldn't do anything right in Mrs. Kalmus's eyes. "You can't have one sister in a bright red gown and another in a bright green," she said. "The colors together are wrong. The camera will pick them up as rust and greenish black." She was basing her judgment on the trial color shot of swatches of the material.

I had enough faith in the technology of the time to assume the camera wouldn't distort the colors, as it picked up the movement of the costumes under the constantly changing lights. Her advice was probably right—and safe—but I depended on my own instincts from then on.

We started shooting.

Judy at first was kept busy with the make-up tests—her hair for the picture was rinsed an auburn color and some experimentation was needed—and on costume fittings.

Her first work in the picture was in the scene with the two elder sisters standing in front of a mirror, nervously primping before a party. Judy, in the reading of her lines, was making fun of the script. Her intelligence showed through, and she didn't come off as an impressionable young girl.

Lucille Bremer had been cast by Arthur to play the oldest sister. She'd been a Rockette, but Arthur later discovered her at the Club Versailles where she was doing a specialty dance act. He felt she had the makings of a big star. She was wonderful in her approach, believing every word she said. Lucille was doing a far better job than Judy.

"I want you to read your lines as if you mean every word," I told Judy. I might have added, "like Lucille does," but I didn't.

We shot the scene several times that morning. None of them were right. I called the lunch break. "We'll shoot it again after lunch," I informed everyone.

A short time later, Arthur came down to the set. He told me he'd just come from Judy's dressing room.

"She said she doesn't know what you want . . . she doesn't feel she can act any more."

I was naturally disturbed, but Arthur assured me. "Don't worry. It'll work out. I told Judy you know what you're doing and to trust in you."

We eventually shot the scene to my satisfaction.

The next day, Judy began to come around. Our relationship remained polite, and the entire cast began to mesh into the ensemble it had to become if the picture was to succeed.

Margaret O'Brien was a huge success as Tootie, the youngest child.

132

I found her performance—and the lengths one had to go to achieve it —engrossing but enervating.

She'd played a war orphan desperately in need of psychiatric help in her first starring film, *Journey for Margaret,* and the roles in her next four pictures were equally neurotic. Now she was playing a child. A seven-year-old Bernhardt or Réjane was no longer needed. It took some doing to capture a more natural performance, though she was exceptional in the emotionally charged scenes in the picture.

Her mother and aunt would whisper to her just before we shot the dramatic sequences and, like the salivating of Pavlov's dog, Margaret would get highly emotional and cry. I often wondered what they said to her to get that reaction. I was soon to learn.

We were preparing to shoot the scene toward the end of the picture where Margaret hysterically knocks down the snow men. Her mother came to me. "Margaret's angry at me tonight. She doesn't want me to work her up for the scene. You'll have to do it."

"But how?" I asked.

"She has a little dog," her mother replied. "You'll have to say someone is going to kill that dog."

"Well, I don't know—"

I could see Margaret sitting inside the house, a blanket wrapped around her shoulders. It was a bitterly cold night. She looked expectantly at me. I braced myself, then walked over to her.

"Margaret—"

She looked at me through enormous brown eyes.

"There's this little dog . . . and somebody is going to take a gun . . . and shoot it."

Her eyes got even larger. "Is there going to be lots of blood?"

"Yes," I answered. Her face retained its stunned expression . . . but no tears. Out of the corner of my eye, I could see her mother and aunt looking curiously at us.

I was on the spot, and I knew I'd have to do more.

"And the dog is going to suffer terribly," I heard my sinister voice saying. "It's going to yelp and stumble around." I was working myself up to a feverish pitch.

"AND THE DOG IS GOING TO DIE!"

"Oh, no," Margaret said in a tiny voice. Her tears started flowing. I turned to the assistant director. "Turn them!"

She did the scene in one take . . . mercifully for me . . . and went skipping happily off the set. I went home feeling like a monster.

Today I marvel that Margaret didn't turn out to be one too. That sort of preparation struck me as most unhealthy.

But, I'd had earlier indications of Margaret's "normality." She was spontaneous and delightful in the cakewalk number with Judy, and it turned out to be one of the highlights of the picture. I like to think it wasn't acting entirely.

I was beginning to feel that Judy was coming around . . . until we had to shoot the dinner scene where the older sister gets the long-distance phone call from her boy friend. It had to be played like a fugue, and it involved much cutting from one actor to another to get the proper reactions. I felt it needed a lot of preparation, so I scheduled rehearsals whenever we had a short shooting day.

Judy hated them. She'd get in her car and zoom off before I had a chance to call a run-through; I'd phone to the studio gate to intercept her.

She went grousing one of these times to Mary Astor, who was playing the mother. To her surprise, the veteran actress turned on her. "He knows what he's doing. Just go along with it, because it means something." Judy informed me of this much later.

I didn't give up trying to reach her. I eventually could tell Judy what I wanted her to do with just a look, but at first I had to find the key words to get her to react. What seemed obvious to me was perplexing to her. Though the lines seemed silly to her, she had to believe in them. Each of Esther's crises, no matter how minor, had to be treated like the 1929 crash.

Finally, the message got to her . . . I still don't know how. Once she grasped the motivation, she was as brilliant in the dramatic scenes as she'd been in the musical numbers. She was alternately wistful and exuberant, but always endearing.

Since Judy was the singing star of the picture, she was the much-needed continuing thread in the integration of the songs to the story. If she hadn't valued the enterprise, the film would have failed. So when she threw her heart into it, I knew we had something great going.

For I never underestimated the range of her talent.

In an early scene, after the going-away party for Esther's brother, the relationship between the girl and the boy next door is established. It was very conventional, the dialogue realistic but banal. I felt it could only interest the individuals involved, not the audience.

I supplied camera movement to eliminate these five pages of dialogue. Esther asks John Truett to turn out the lights for her. She wants to get him to kiss her, but her only reward for her trouble is a series of friendly handshakes. The action followed the two from room to room. It flowed smoothly, but it took considerable preparation. Lighting had to change as each of the dozen gas burners was extinguished by Judy. We took one full day for rehearsal—we probably could have shot those five pages in that time—but we got the scene the first thing the next morning.

It couldn't have been done without George Folsey's fluid and mobile work. He proved that my thoughts on the choreography of the camera weren't half baked. He'd followed the couple through the intricacies of the "Skip to My Lou" number, as well as Judy weaving her way from one end of the trolley to another. His work, to me, was just as lilting as "The Trolley Song" which accompanied the action.

George had already established his genius in "The Boy Next Door." He spent an enormous amount of time setting up little lights and masking them off, capturing the highlights of Judy's face.

He had very able co-operation from Judy's make-up artist, Dotty Ponedel, a jolly eccentric. Her gear was always in a mess. But little matter. If there was no water available, she'd dip her make-up brush in a paper cup of cold coffee.

Dotty was responsible for Marlene Dietrich's look while at Paramount, and now she was working with an actress whose features weren't as classically symmetrical.

Judy reported to Dotty's department with her own gear: rubber discs which were inserted to change the shape of her nose and caps to disguise her slightly irregular teeth. "What are these?" Dotty asked. Judy explained.

"You don't need all this junk," Dotty said. "You're a pretty girl. Let's see what we can do."

She didn't do all that much, Dotty recalls. "I raised her eyebrows a bit, and gave her a fuller lower lip. I put on a make-up base that was pretty to the eye. I knew it would be pretty to the camera too. I tweezed out some of the hairline." And that was that. A make-up artist simply has to know what she's doing.

"You can't just apply make-up. You have to feel the whole face, then apply the make-up very sparingly. It's like painting the face, and you apply it in a translucent way, almost as if it were bone china."

Judy never looked as beautiful, her expressive eyes becoming more so because of the white eye liner applied to her lower lids. From that moment on, her make-up artist was always Dotty. Later, as Judy's weight fluctuated from day to day, Dotty would shade under her cheeks when her face was gaunt or on the sides when her face was full. "But weight wasn't a problem in *Meet Me in St. Louis,*" Dotty recalls. "Judy was happy then."

We all were. Everything was falling into place. Even the predictable snags were smoothed out. One of them was Fred Finklehoffe's departure in the middle of shooting to try his luck as a Broadway producer. I worked with Irving Brecher from then on to tighten up the script wherever I felt was needed.

Judy, as a girl about to enter her senior year in high school, was too young to marry. Yet, she and the boy next door, played by Tom Drake, were in love, and their relationship would end with her move to New York. The problem: How to do a love scene that couldn't be consummated? Irving and I kicked a few ideas around. None of them worked.

Then, I thought of something and wrote the scene almost as rapidly as it took to speak it. The lines might seem banal, but with the actors' hesitant and insecure pauses, the extravagant professions of love alternated by shy withdrawal, every word was just right. Esther was crying, as we came in on the snow-covered scene outside the Smith house. Judy's singing voice had a distinctive emotional throb—some call it the Caruso note—and she called upon it in her reading of the lines.

JOHN

I wouldn't have said it, Esther, if I thought it would make you cry.

ESTHER

I imagined your saying it thousands of times . . . and I always planned exactly how I'd act . . . but I never planned to cry.

JOHN

Well at least you didn't laugh.

ESTHER

Laugh?

JOHN

I never asked a girl to marry me before. I guess maybe I was kind of—

ESTHER

John—no one could have done it more beautifully. I'm very proud.

JOHN

Esther, will you? Will you, Esther?

ESTHER

Of course I will, John.

(*The two embrace, as the music swells.*)

136

JOHN

Gosh, the time we wasted—say—do you realize I might have lost you? Three more days and you would have been gone.

ESTHER

Let's not even think about it.

JOHN

We might never see each other again.

ESTHER

I kept telling myself that even if I did go away we'd find some way to be together. But I never really believed it.

JOHN

When you go to New York it'll be with your husband. And your folks can show us the town. Let's go and tell them now.

ESTHER

Oh no. Not tonight. I'd rather just the two of us knew about it tonight.

JOHN

Esther, you're not changing your— You do think it's the right thing to do, don't you?

ESTHER

Oh yes! Yes!

JOHN

I don't have to be an engineer. College takes too long anyway. I can get a job right away and support you in style.

ESTHER

Of course you can, darling.

JOHN

Now we're not going to let them talk us out of it. After all we are of age . . . practically.

ESTHER

John, even if I did go to New York—we could still work something out somehow, couldn't we?

JOHN

Do you think so?

The town clock strikes midnight. Esther and John kiss, whisper "Merry Christmas" to each other, and Esther runs into the house. All their plans have blown themselves apart.

The following scene has Esther trying to comfort Tootie, who is sitting in her room crying about the forthcoming move. I'd found a music box with a monkey on it in an early American toy store in New York.

It accompanied Esther's singing of the song, which was supposed to comfort her as much as it did Tootie.

The original lyrics started, "Have yourself a merry little Christmas . . . it may be your last." They obviously wouldn't do. Judy should be trying to cheer her little sister up. The lyrics were changed . . . "Have yourself a merry little Christmas . . . make the yuletide bright." With this rewritten hopeful message, the song became a classic carol.

Toward the end of the shooting, Don Loper decided Judy and I should get to know each other better on more neutral territory. He was the great organizer, as I'd discovered when I first met him in New York (Don did a specialty dance number in *Very Warm for May*). He arranged a double date for Judy and me with his lady friend, Ruth Brady. The four of us hit it off immediately.

We were held together by Judy's delicious wit, which went so well with Don's sardonic outlook. Ruth and I were content to act as audience for their routines. I laughed at the time, not wondering why Judy invariably turned the humor on herself. In her stories, she was always the slightly stupid butt of the situation. But at the same time, she also zeroed in on the other person involved . . . as she did when she started talking about the people at the studio.

She told of the times Mayer would bring visitors on the set. "Do you see this little girl?" he'd ask. "Look what I've made her into. She used to be a hunchback."

The visitors gasped.

"Yes, a hunchback. Isn't that true, Judy?"

Judy would think about it for a while. "Why yes, Mr. Mayer, I suppose it is."

Talking about that famous schoolhouse at Metro where Mickey Rooney and Lana Turner were classmates, she described how scandalized she'd been by their behavior. "Did you know that between classes they used to sneak behind the building for a smoke?" she asked. "For that matter, so did I."

I found Judy's self-deprecating wit disarming, and the vulnerability she disguised with it all the more touching. Like everyone else at the studio, I wanted to protect and love her. And Judy was affectionate and loving right back.

The four of us continued going out together, a merry but somewhat platonic group. Then Don called me prior to one of those scheduled evenings. He'd been taken ill. I called Judy.

"Don is sick," I said, "so I guess we'll have to postpone the evening."

A low throaty chuckle came from the other end of the line.

"We don't have to go out with Don and Ruth every time, do we? We can go alone."

Her point was wholly logical and from that time on we didn't see as much of Don and Ruth as we had in the past. We were learning how to make two lovers of friends.

I'd evaded marriage up to then and, since Judy was still married, I didn't know where our relationship would go. It was presumptuous to latch onto her, as I'd seen so many fellows around town do with established stars, and I wasn't about to be accused of doing the same thing. I wanted Judy to be sure and, until she was, I'd keep a tight rein on my own emotions.

One night we were having dinner at the Villa Nova on the Sunset Strip. We were contrasting our days as children in the theater. The talk logically turned to Judy's early days in pictures.

"I always have to be my best in front of the camera," she said. "You should know that. You expect it of me too. Well, sometimes I don't feel my best. It's a struggle to get through the day."

What was she driving at?

"I use these pills. They carry me through."

"Well," I said, "as long as you don't overdo it, I guess it's all right."

Judy smiled. Our talk shifted easily to other subjects.

Monstrous stories have been told, accusing some Lucifer at the studio of starting Judy on this tragic, gradually accelerated treadmill. I don't believe them. Why would anyone want to make a non-functioning player out of a very important star?

The way it happened wasn't nearly as nefarious. The unions, during Judy's early days at the studio, weren't as powerful as they later became. Everyone put in long hours. Some fellow actor, trying to be helpful, probably offered some amphetamines to Judy during one of those especially long days. It probably wasn't long before she herself was seeking them out to see her through her many fourteen-hour work days. The pills probably left her wide awake, unable to sleep, so somebody else probably offered her sedatives. Few people knew about the long-range effects of such drugs at the time.

By the time of *Meet Me in St. Louis,* the working conditions at Metro were more humane and Judy shouldn't have needed them any longer. But she continued using them.

We finished shooting the movie in April of 1944. Judy and I started living together about the time I started cutting. The film was too long, and a group of us got together to see how it could be shortened. Someone suggested the Halloween sequence be cut. "It's the only scene that doesn't have anything to do with the plot," he said. The film without the scene was run for us. I was dying. If it hadn't come off effectively, I could understand. But it had. We'd taken the kids to the studio costume department and spent a whole day collecting a wild assortment of clothes, looking for our idea of what St. Louis in 1903 would be storing in its attics and closets. These, after all, were the places the children would find their costumes. Then we outfitted the kids. Margaret's costume, for example, was a man's coat worn inside out, pajama bottoms, and a derby. Her face was smeared with burnt cork so that she wouldn't be as visible in the dark night. With such costumes the kids came through beautifully. The scene was the reason I wanted to do the picture to begin with. I said nothing.

The lights in the projection room came back on. "It's not the same picture," Arthur said. "Let's put it back." Relieved and happy, I looked for other places to cut.

"Boys and Girls Like You and Me" had been dropped by Rodgers and Hart from *Oklahoma!* I thought it would work well in the scene where the young people are at the muddy fairground construction site. It would further develop the courtship of Esther and John. But their romance came through much better with the family used for counterpoint. The song, as well as the scene, was eliminated.

Judy celebrated her twenty-second birthday while I was still cutting. I gave her a metallic evening bag. She wrote me a thank you note.

VINCENTE DEAR,

Your beautiful birthday gift has changed my outlook on life. It used to be a difficult task for me to walk into a room full of people with any self-assurance. But not any more. Now I merely hold my handbag at the proper angle, descend upon the group and dazzle each individual.

Thank you for one of the loveliest gifts I've ever received.

Love,
JUDY

The picture was now ready for release. I felt it was quite good. The story had sentiment without stooping to sentimentality. It told of real people and had many subsidiary human touches: the crusty grandfather, the cook with the no-nonsense manner, the affectations of the oldest sister. One of the most personally enjoyable was the scene with the husband and wife singing. I didn't want a pure singer's voice for the Freed-Brown number, "You and I." I asked Arthur if he would dub the singing for Leon Ames. His sweet croak was perfect. He started to sing in too high a key, so he had to start all over again. Arthur loved doing the song. He also loved the picture.

It was my coming of age. Mayer was overjoyed. The executives who'd been against it from the start admitted they were wrong.

The reviews were ecstatic. "The real love story is between a happy family and a way of living," the critique in *Time* read. "Technicolor has seldom been more affectionately used than in its registrations of the sober mahoganies and tender muslins and benign gaslight of the period. Now and then too, the film gets well beyond the charm of mere tableau for short flights in the empyrean of genuine domestic poetry."

Bosley Crowther wrote in his New York *Times* review: "Vincente Minnelli, in his direction, has got all the period charm out of ladies dressed in flowing creations, gentlemen in straw 'boaters' and ice-cream pants, rooms lush with golden-oak wainscoting, ermolu decorations and red-plush chairs. As a comparable screen companion to *Life With Father*, we would confidently predict that *Meet Me in St. Louis* has a future that is equally bright. In the words of one of the gentlemen, it is a ginger-peachy show."

The public took to the picture as well. It became the studio's second highest grosser (after *Gone With the Wind*) up to that time.

On my last day of work on the picture, Arthur arranged a meeting.

I knew he'd been working on a film version of the *Ziegfeld Follies*. It was to be the biggest all-star production ever attempted in films, with a three-million-dollar budget for its twenty sketches and sixty-five scenes. Arthur had collected all known material about Ziegfeld. Several classic comedy sketches had been dusted off, and every writer at the studio was being called on to supply additional material. Every M-G-M star was notified to make himself available if called. The production was buzzing along.

Arthur asked me to direct it.

Perhaps he was waiting to see how *Meet Me in St. Louis* turned out before offering me the job. But this seemed to be his pattern. I wasn't given time to ponder the matter. If he was looking for an impulsive answer as a reliable indicator of my enthusiasm for the picture, it must have worked. I later found the projects that didn't immediately interest me were those I didn't handle as well.

I was eager to plow into more hard work. The picture was to feature

Fred Astaire, Lucille Ball, Lucille Bremer, Fanny Brice, Lena Horne, Gene Kelly, Victor Moore, Red Skelton, Esther Williams, and William Powell. It would be a showy assignment . . . and a distraction from a broken romance. Judy had left me.

She'd been seeing another man before we started going together. He was tortured and complicated, and very much the intellectual. She simply gravitated back to him just as she had toward me at the start of our affair. I theorized that Judy must have been flattered by the attentions of such a brilliant man, and intrigued by the fact he was in analysis. It didn't alleviate my pain.

The plan was for me to direct all the numbers. We would shoot numbers whenever the stars became available from their full-time film projects. Handling it in this way would save considerable money. As we got underway, it was discovered that some stars were free at the same time and some numbers were reassigned to other studio directors. The picture would take some time. In addition to the lavish set construction, and rehearsal time for complicated production numbers, shooting of the picture would take a minimum of five months, and probably as long to process and edit. Doubling up on the shooting schedule might cut down on the time needed to get the picture before the public.

I directed ten of the fourteen final sequences, with Robert Lewis, George Sidney, and Lemuel Ayres handling most of the others.

Four sequences, for a variety of reasons, still stand out in my mind. Two were dance numbers with Fred Astaire and Lucille Bremer.

The first was "This Heart of Mine," in which Lucille proved to be a wonderful dancer and equal to the test of dancing with the master. I created a slight story of a jewel thief attending a ball, homing in on a lovely, diamond-encrusted young girl. Robert Alton did the choreography for the number. All stops were out: treadmills running in opposite directions, a turntable where dancers carrying white trees suddenly materialized, an opulent circular ballroom with Tony Duquette statuary in the background. It was a sumptuous mounting, but it didn't distract from the poetic movements of Fred and Lucille.

The second was "Limehouse Blues." The precision Chinese fan dance around which the sequence was built had already been choreographed and the music recorded. It had little in common with the song, which had originally been written in the early twenties for Gertrude Lawrence to sing in *Charlot's Revue,* and which was inspired by *Broken Blossoms,* the D. W. Griffith silent movie.

To have any integrity, I felt the sequence should respect the tradition of the song. I decided to do the prologue and epilogue in a style combining musical melodrama and the techniques of silent movies. A setting of a London Street, standing on one of the sound stages which had been used in *The Picture of Dorian Gray,* seemed right for the number. I set up headquarters on the stage, sent out a call for people who might suggest characteristic types, had racks of stock costumes sent down from wardrobe, fitted them on the spot, and worked out the pantomime story. I limited the colors of the costumes and set to black, brown, and shades of yellow, filled the stage with fog and lit it with yellow light to suggest the quality of an old English mezzotint. The number was theatrical, it could be lit as theater. Later we did the dream sequence with chinoiserie costumes designed by Irene Sharaff. The art department, in looking over her sketches, noticed the eighteenth-century chinoiserie artifacts which Irene had drawn in the background. She always did this sort of thing with her costume sketches. Her suggestion was so right that it was adopted; thus Irene wound up doing the sets as well.

The action of the fantasy section opens with the lit figure of Fred, all in red, surrounded by blackness. It gradually picks up another lit figure, Lucille's, in the distance. Fred moves toward her, the lighting following him through the darkness. His hand reaches out and they touch. Suddenly the whole set is ablaze with light, a stunning device which captured their interrelationship. We accomplished this by first lighting the set. Then black shields, what the industry knows as gobos, were placed in front of the lights. At a synchronized count, the shields were removed to unveil the lighted set.

The number was a total triumph. Howard Thompson's overview twenty-five years after the fact, in *Fred Astaire: A Pictorial History of His Films,* explained why:

"For visual impact, staging (again Minnelli, with choreography by the studio's Robert Alton), atmosphere and extraordinary use of technicolor, blending a wisp of story and, of course, the superb footwork of two dancers, here was the finest production number ever poured into a screen revue. It still is. And credit should certainly go to the Metro orchestra, for seldom has such a popular song arrangement ripened a sound track.

"This was sheer movie poetry, thrillingly evocative in its use of exotic costumes and background crowds, and triggered, it should be remembered, by four people from the Broadway stage, yet fulfilling the potential of the musical screen. It was a 'Limehouse Blues' to end them all and a far cry, with all due respect, to the tatty little mounting of the number that Gertrude Lawrence had poignantly introduced on the boards in *Charlot's Revue* (1919)."

There was another number with historical significance. Gene Kelly, in retrospect, feels that since "The Babbitt and the Bromide" number was the only time he and Fred Astaire worked together, it shouldn't have been as light and unchallenging. I disagree. This was a revue, they should have been kidding their rightly exalted stations. The dancing might have come easily to Fred and Gene, but it was impressive nevertheless. Fred had done the George and Ira Gershwin number with his sister Adele in *Funny Face* in 1927, but their approach was different. The plot line I devised for the picture followed the music, the two men meeting each other at twenty-year intervals, ending in heaven. Their conversation is depressingly, platitudinously the same.

Fred and Gene devised their own choreography. "We were so polite and generous and nice to each other it was almost boring," Gene recalls.

When they did get down to work, each was hesitant to make the first suggestion. Neither wanted to be accused of foisting his quite different dancing style on the other. Everything was put in the form of a suggestion . . . "What if we did so and so?" . . . no reaction . . . "Well, I guess that isn't a good idea" . . . "Oh, no," the other would protest, "it's fine. Maybe we can take a bit of it, and then we can—" . . . no reaction from the other to that suggestion . . . the same protests repeated, the compromises finally worked out.

What we finally shot was a high-spirited romp in which Fred and Gene traded off steps, each of them given specific musical interludes to show his stuff.

When I told Fred what Gene thought about the number, he cracked back, "What does Gene mean by unchallenging? Didn't we beat hell out of the floor together? We were supposed to be a popular team. We weren't trying, after all, to do *L'Après-Midi d'un Faune.*"

That Fred and Gene never worked together again is the movie-goer's loss. Arthur and I tried to interest them in a project or two later, but they didn't work out.

We were planning on having Greer Garson sportingly poke fun of her Mrs. Miniver/Madam Curie image in "The Great Lady Has an Interview" number written by Kay Thompson and Roger Edens. But as Kay and Roger got deeper into the satiric piece, and the music became more challenging, it became obvious that a singing performer would have to play Madame Crematon. Kay suggested Judy.

It was a singing tour de force preceded by devastating commentary,

144

the sort of number Kay did herself with such great high style. Judy was capable of the biting lines, if her way with a story was any indication. Yes, I agreed, Judy would be perfect.

Any pain I might have been dreading in seeing Judy again simply didn't come to pass. We were no longer lovers, but we could be friends. Shooting the number was great fun. Judy came off extremely well. Her singing was as vibrant as ever, and she revealed a satirical style which owed a great deal to her terrific version of Kay's performance.

Shooting was finally completed, and the processing and editing which would take well over a year started. Then I got involved in the trial and error of putting the sketches in a proper sequence, alternating a musical number with a comedy bit, attempting to make each of them separate entities that didn't encroach on the effects of the sequences around them, then meshing them into a whole. There was no formula to follow, other than my past experience directing the *Follies* on the stage. When I felt it was finally right, I was ready to take a breather.

It was interrupted by a call from Judy one day, inviting me to lunch. Curiosity consumed me. We met at the Players Club, settling easily into comfortable talk. "What picture are you doing next?" I asked.

"Well, you know *The Clock* has been canceled," Judy said. "But I've told Arthur how much I believe in it."

Now I was beginning to understand. Our meeting could well have been Arthur's idea.

"Would you consider doing it?" she asked.

"I guess I can look into it," I answered. "I'll look at the script and see the footage." If I decided it could be made, I would have to talk to the fired director first, I decided. And Judy would have to agree to leave the picture completely in my hands.

The script by Robert Nathan and Joseph Schrank was sensitive, and the dialogue had interesting shadings. It captured the romantic mood of the original story written by Paul and Pauline Gallico. But it wouldn't play. Each scene from the two weeks of footage shot thus far looked as if it came from a different picture. It was very confusing. I could see why Metro's executive committee had canceled the project.

I thought there might be a way to make it workable, but I wouldn't go into it without the past director's approval. I dropped him a note. He was quite put out at Judy, but he gave me his blessings.

Three days after our lunch date, in September of 1944, I was on the new picture. All the filming, with the exception of exteriors shot by a second unit in New York, was scrapped. We would start over. There was no time to write a new script, however. We'd have to go with this one.

Except for stars Judy Garland and Robert Walker, the only other carryover from the first venture was the Pennsylvania Station set. It is here where the couple meet and embark on an accelerated weekend courtship, and here where they part as the young man goes off to war. The studio decided it would be too impractical to try to manage the thousands of people who daily used Pennsylvania Station, so it was re-created on a sound stage. It must have been a costly reminder, and was probably as instrumental in reviving the project as anything.

Nobody asked why a musical director was now being entrusted with a drama. Most people were more curious about Judy's reasons for wanting to do a dramatic, non-singing role.

We tackled the script. We kept all the parts we felt were good, and tried to alter the rest. My plan was to develop the city of New York as a third major character.

Though New York's many landmarks were essential to the picture, it was decided to shoot everything on the lot. The war was still being fought on several fronts. The mass deployment of our troupe didn't seem proper. Since it had to be a small picture, the money spent on the Pennsylvania Station set already having cut a big chunk out of the budget, economy went hand in hand with patriotism.

I tried to remember everything about New York. I set out to create an unexpected gallery of people whose lives might conceivably touch that of the boy and girl.

New York was created through the use of photographic plates. They served as backdrops via rear projection, with the live action in front. Sometimes more than one plate was used in a scene, the dividing line between them disguised by a tree in the foreground. Or we would suggest a New York street through the reflection of the photographic plate in a window. In one scene we even blew up a small picture of Rodin's *The Thinker* and placed it on the edge of a photographic plate. The rest of the background suggested a museum where the young couple have gone to absorb culture. The effects created by this simple device were ingenious . . . and inexpensive. The audience might have noticed that the backgrounds, being second generation pictures, weren't as vivid or sharply focused as the actors in the foreground. But no one—neither audience, critic nor studio head—mentioned the discrepancy. Perhaps their involvement with the story caused them to overlook the fact.

Judy felt insecure about her acting ability, so she began working with

146

a drama coach. She'd come back from these sessions with a new bag of surface tricks. I felt her native ability should carry her through. We were preparing to shoot the scene where she and Robert Walker meet in Pennsylvania Station. It was your typical cute movie meeting, one of Judy's high heels having snapped off and Bob coming gallantly to the rescue. She went through the drama coach's paces prior to shooting, limping along as if one leg were shorter than the other. I found that ridiculous. A girl would walk on her toes in order to keep her balance. No more coaching for Judy. I insisted. She'd already proven to me she was an actress. She would need to believe it herself.

If she needed any further help, I would supply it. I hit upon the device of writing an essay that answered many questions about her character. What was the girl like? What magazines did she read? What were her sexual hangups? Who were her favorite movie stars?

I devised the same questions for the ordinary, small-town boy played by Robert Walker. I didn't share these questions with either of them, but with this history of the characters in front of me, each sequence took care of itself.

The picture opens with a crane shot of Pennsylvania Station, hundreds of people scurrying along. It picks up the young soldier, dazzled by his first visit to the city, making his way through the crowd. At the end, when the girl sees the boy off, the process is reversed, following Judy, then panning back on the boom until her figure is lost in the crowd.

In between it develops a sweet story, people meeting and falling quickly in love in wartime New York, where all emotions were heightened. I tried to show their story as tenderly as possible without necessarily having them articulate their love. We settled on much pantomime as a way of doing this.

There were still too many sticky spots in the screenplay, and this device neatly side-stepped them. One was near the opening. The script called on the soldier and girl to come across a young boy sailing his toy boat in a pond. The soldier tousles the boy's hair, with the little boy smiling sweetly back. I found this excessive. I instructed the little boy to get angry and kick Bob in the shins. The little joke was repeated at the museum a short while later, where a child bursts out crying when he sees Bob walk toward him.

A scene I particularly liked was in the Italian restaurant modeled after a real second floor one in New York's theater district, where the couple has a temporary misunderstanding. The pair looked calm as the camera moved in through the small confined set to pick them up. Behind the scene, all hell was breaking loose, children being grabbed by parents and members of the crew moving swiftly if the action was to be smoothly followed. The couple have their fight and make up, the camera tracking back again to give an over-all view of the restaurant and that attractive young couple in the corner.

The scene that truly established Judy as an adult was in the park. She and Bob are talking about the sounds of the city, and the way people tend to blot them out of their minds. They become silent as they listen. I'd heard a Saroyan radio play—*New York Wears a Slouch Hat*—shortly before that time, and been very impressed by a symphonic piece made up solely of the city's noises. I suggested to George Bassman something similar might be done here, but the idea didn't fascinate him . . . nor anyone else at the studio for that matter. An attempt to create it myself didn't quite work, since there was a jarring effect when George's music changed over to the sound effects.

The scene was lovely otherwise. Bob is standing at the far right edge of the park set, lobbing stones into the water. His appealing character was well established by now, a reading with quiet dignity which I found more believable than his too precious touches in *See Here, Private Hargrove*.

They are listening to the city's sounds, and they automatically walk toward each other. Suddenly they are very close. Judy has to be the instigator, the soldier isn't the type to push it, regardless of how he feels. It's her irresistible impulse to kiss him.

We had a short closeup of Bob, lingering much longer on Judy's face. Some people who see the picture today say it was obvious that I was deeply in love with Judy because of this scene. I must have had a rival in cinematographer George Folsey, who captured Judy's face so lovingly.

My feelings for Judy *did* show, as hers about me also did. The script dictated the action, however, and this is one spot where it was followed. Another actress may not have had that special glow, but with me as director, the reading would have been the same.

In a later scene, an exchange with a bully proved too much for me. I changed him into a drunk played by Keenan Wynn who gets belligerent and accidentally hits the milkman they've befriended. The couple takes the injured man home and meet his wife. Originally, the dialogue of the older couple was so cloying that it would have been laughed out of the theater. "Mother and I have been married for thirty years," was one of the lines that made you want to strangle instead of embrace them.

148

I captured their loving relationship in a different way. They would constantly bicker, but in such a way that they built each other up. The wife chastizes her husband for fighting, then asks, "What happened to the other man? Is he dead?"

After separating and miraculously finding each other again, the pair decide to get married immediately. They are soon involved in a frantic rush against time as they meet with every delay. They're shunted from one sordid office to the other fulfilling the requirements of the license, and are finally married in an ugly ceremony that depresses instead of exalts.

Their wedding dinner in a cafeteria underscores the feeling. I devised the character of a man eating pie à la mode and listening openly to their conversation. Their wedding lacked dignity; their starting out of married life lacked privacy.

They finally feel married when they pass a church and see a departing wedding party, the groom in uniform and his bridal-gowned bride a sharp contrast to their pathetic ceremony. The script had the couple express their bitterness, but I had Judy and Bob smile at the tableau instead. They go into the church and sit in a pew. With quiet sincerity they repeat their vows in this more fitting setting.

The next morning—this was the time of the discrete movie code—we find the pair having breakfast in their bridal suite. It's shortly before their parting.

I placed this scene toward the end of the shooting schedule. It was six or eight pages of dialogue which, any way you approach it, seemed to add up to nothing but mock heroics. It negated the gallantry you'd felt in the boy and the girl in the rest of the picture. The one valid thing in the scene was a short and appealing speech by the soldier telling the girl not to worry and giving his reasons why he felt he would come back.

The scene knocked around in my head. The day finally came when it couldn't be postponed any longer. I made the decision on the morning of the shooting. Bob's short speech would be given to Judy. It seemed nobler for her to say it. Then I staged the rest of the scene in pantomime, hoping their comfortable gestures would imply after their first married night together that theirs was a good marriage and would endure.

The picture ends with their parting at the station. They know it will be all right. They haven't a care in the world, and they can smile their goodbyes. (Bob didn't smile, however, when he discovered he would have to descend via unexisting stairs to the train below. In the middle of this emotional scene, he had to play the old vaudevillian's trick, lowering his body as he descended so that only his head was visible. He never forgave me.)

The picture was good, I knew. Everything meshed well, including the Bassman music and his use of "If I Had You" as a recurring theme.

The actors delivered one hundred and ten per cent. I'd heard that Bob Walker, suffering the heartache of a broken marriage, was looking at life through the bottom of a liquor bottle. But he was always cheerful and on time. I wasn't aware of the toll the picture was taking on his nervous system at the time. But Judy knew. Dotty Ponedel recalls one night when Judy was supposed to be having a hen party with the girls, her publicity woman and stand-in included. The two of them actually went through West Side bars looking for Bob. They finally found him and took him to Dotty's to dry him out for the next morning's shooting. Judy never told me of this. Yes, there was much that was noble in her character.

She believed in Bob and she believed in the picture. She also believed in me.

Judy came off extremely well, and she was grateful. A desk clock arrived for me one day. With it, a note.

DARLING,

Whenever you look to see what time it is—I hope you'll remember 'the Clock.' You knew how much the picture meant to me—and only *you* could give me the confidence I so badly needed. If the picture is a success (and I think it's a cinch) my darling Vincente is responsible for the whole god damned thing.

Thank you for everything, angel. If I could only say what is in my heart—but that's impossible. So I'll say God bless you and I love you!

JUDY

We were back together again. Judy gave up her rented house in Beverly Hills to move in with me. I was ecstatic when Judy told me she wanted to marry me as soon as her divorce was final. I let go of my emotions, feeling so needed for the first time in my life that there was no alternative. We would face all problems together.

Judy and I were already sharing the joys. Arthur Freed treated a group of us to a trip to New York. Officially, the tour was designed to meet national critics, but it was primarily a pleasure junket.

I showed Judy the spots in Central Park we'd re-created in Culver City: the plots of grass, the park benches, the lake where kids sailed their

150

boats. We took in the Metropolitan, as well as that second-floor Italian restaurant I'd remembered and copied for *The Clock*.

New York, to her, was a giant theater, and Judy was a rapt audience. I was exposing it all to her. We went to see *Oklahoma!* and Judy was thrilled with its innovations. It was the first Broadway play she'd ever seen.

We went up one night to Richard and Dorothy Rodgers's house. They were delighted to meet Judy, for they'd been bowled over by her super talent. Judy asked Dick to play the piano, and he eagerly did, going through every song of his Judy had ever sung.

The theatrical high point of our trip was Billy Rose's circus-like opening for *The Seven Lively Arts*. The war was being won on both fronts during that December of 1944, and the celebrity-studded audience needed little excuse to depart from the austerity program. There was much popping of champagne corks and crystal laughter, accompanied by the usual publicity-conscious gimmicks associated with Rose's name. Salvador Dali had even lent his name to the enterprise by painting works on the seven lively arts, which were being displayed in the lobby of the Ziegfeld Theater.

Judy was amazed at all the hoopla. Oh yes, I led her to believe, just another Broadway opening.

The gala evening was dampened only slightly by the pedestrian production, which the talents of Beatrice Lillie and Bert Lahr couldn't quite save. Cole Porter's music wasn't up to his excellent standard. I remember only one. Could its title have something to do with my personal feelings at the time? It was "If I Thought I Could Live Without You, I'd Die."

Judy had now been exposed to the great sophistication, as well as the hedonistic fun of New York. California provincial was now not quite good enough. She was eager to learn much more.

When we returned to Hollywood, she became an eager student. Judy developed an interest in antique furniture and jewelry, and we began traipsing through showrooms and galleries as she started educating herself. There was no concentrated effort on my part to teach her. I was simply there to share any knowledge I might have whenever she asked for it, and she absorbed it like a sponge.

We were happy with each other. There were the sad times, to be sure, but they were so minor compared to what we usually had. I'd learned to accept those aspects of Judy's makeup that couldn't be changed. She was a Gemini, so her frequent swings from exuberance to moodiness were understandable as part of her sun sign's twin personality. She was left-handed, and folklore had told me this usually meant a hot temper. And she was an actress, plagued by the temperament and insecurity which affects every great one. She simply couldn't help being what she was, and what she was simply was much more than I ever felt I'd merited. She gave me so much. I could well learn to live with her occasional moments of despair.

It was after one of these episodes that Judy confessed, "I think I might be taking too many of those pills."

"I know," I answered.

She waited for me to go on.

"I can't put my foot down and tell you to stop," I said. "I know there are times when you're tired and when things don't go well at the studio. There are several actresses around who are doing the same thing. And I can always tell when they're on benzedrine. Just as I can with you. You think you're doing wonderfully, that this is the best performance you've given. But you're not nearly as effective as you think you are."

Judy had become a great star, like many others, by manufacturing her own adrenalin and filtering it through a relaxed approach toward performing. But she'd made twenty-three pictures in her nine years in films. The demands on her natural vitality were excessive.

Judy didn't answer. "Promise you'll stop taking them," I said. "Please try."

"You know I try," she answered softly.

And she did. There were many days when nothing went wrong, when she didn't need the crutch to prop up her insecurity. But they were invariably followed by those other days. Her mother, who must have been the model for Mama Rose in *Gypsy*, was a strong-willed woman who attempted to dominate Judy, and who tended to agree with everything Mayer wanted Judy to do. She felt betrayed by Mrs. Gilmore . . . she loved her mother . . . she hated her. I felt that Judy still had a lot of growing up to do. I'd be there to help her.

Judy continued trying, and there were long periods where she took no drugs at all. Then life would get too much for her, and I'd come home to find her speech and gestures going double time. "I'll quit," she often said. "I promise."

She'd recovered from the periodic spells to become her natural sweet and considerate self. Judy's instincts were to do the right thing, and she was capable of the most profound good behavior.

152

As soon as we decided to marry, she wrote my parents in Florida. "We haven't met," she wrote, "but Vincente has told me such wonderful stories about his parents and the tent theater, that I feel I know you and also love you."

Mother and Dad were absolutely charmed. The letters were followed by frequent telephone calls, and Judy unfailingly said just the right thing to them.

Though I often tried, I wasn't capable of saying similar right things to Judy. The lover was not a poet, and she simply had to understand the depth of my feeling for her. She must have been discussing my inarticulate ways with Betty Asher, her publicity woman, one day. I walked into the room to see Judy adjusting her stockings. "Darling," I said, "you have great-looking legs."

Betty burst into laughter and, though Judy tried not to, she couldn't control herself either.

I wasn't one to verbalize my feelings. That would have to serve as my sonnet to her, and Judy would have to understand how beautiful she was in my eyes.

She became even more so after we shared an exhausting traumatic night. We received a phone call from Bob Walker. He drunkenly informed us he was going to kill himself.

We both got on the phone, alternately talking to him, trying to get him to tell us where he was. He steadfastly refused to say. After much cajoling, he agreed to come over to our house.

He showed up half an hour later.

"Give me a drink," he commanded belligerently, "and make it snappy." I fixed him a drink and sat down with him and Judy. We were prepared to offer Bob all the concern and understanding that he would allow, but he wasn't having any.

He hated the town, he hated the people in it . . . but most of all Bob hated himself. And then he zeroed in on Judy and me. We heard a lot of ugly things. Judy reacted with super-human patience. She was loving. She wanted to show that someone cared.

All the while, I was busy on the phone calling Bob's other friends, trying to find out who his doctor was. I couldn't reach anyone. Finally, I called my own physician and he said he'd come over.

Bob's mood hadn't altered. I was given more brusque orders, most of them demands for more drinks. I tried watering them down, but Bob would have none of that. He knew what I was doing. The resentments he must have been storing up during filming came spilling out. I chose to endure them.

Finally, around dawn, the doctor arrived. Bob took one look at him, let out a stream of profanity, and the doctor indignantly walked out.

At about this time, I realized the only solution would be to keep giving him drinks until he passed out.

I reached Bob's doctor at last, and he came right over. He called the hospital. "I'll be bringing in Mr. Walker," he said. "We'll use the rear entrance and register him under another name. Please make all the arrangements." The doctor had obviously been through all this before.

I tell of the incident now, not to reflect on Bob's short and tragic life, but to show how Judy would reach out to people.

Bob was hospitalized for a long period after this, and when we saw him again, none of us chose to remember the incident.

When *The Clock* was released in May of 1945, I was overcome by the reaction. *Time* magazine, in particular, heaped hozannas. "Vincente Minnelli's talents are so many sided and generous that he turns even the most overcontrived romanticism into something memorable. He has brought the budding dramatic talents of his betrothed, Judy Garland, into unmistakable bloom. He has helped give Robert Walker an honest, touching dignity in place of the shucks-fellers cuteness he has sometimes seemed doomed to. It is Director Minnelli who gives a passage like the silent breakfast scene its radiance. He has used most of his bit players and extras and crowds and streets so well that time and again you wonder whether some swarming, multitudinous human scenes were made in the actual city, with only a few actors aware of the concealed camera.

"*The Clock* is a pleasant, well-told romance rather than the great, true picture it might have been; but few films in recent years have managed so movingly to combine first-grade truth with second-rate fiction."

When I later met with the editors of the magazine they told me the picture was so visually arresting and complete that it stood up very well without sound. They'd run it that way. I was pleased that the film was as good as a silent picture . . . without the subtitles.

I was even more pleased when, in an article on my work, they praised my use of the boom shot. This was the first time my use of the moving camera had been noticed in print. They described it as "snooping and sailing and drifting and drooping."

Comments of other critics, one in particular, bemused me. Lee Mortimer's review concluded: "If the Garland-Minnelli team works out in

154

life as it has in make-believe, that will set a new standard." He never said for what.

But I wasn't concerned. I was such a name that even the people in the trade were taking notice. I received an enthusiastic wire praising my work from an executive at *Box Office Digest*. It was addressed to Vincenti Mellini.

Judy and I were eager to get married. She suggested we elope to Mexico, but her divorce from David Rose wasn't final. Though he was a very nice man and wouldn't cause any difficulty, I suggested we wait it out.

Judy's mother wasn't pleased. She'd written me a long letter in which she expressed her unhappiness about our living together. She said I should know better, and that I didn't have Judy's best interests at heart. I immediately answered the letter as respectfully as I could, saying I would never do anything to hurt Judy and we would get married when we could.

Judy and I went on to different projects. She started filming *The Harvey Girls* with George Sidney and I started preparing *Yolanda and the Thief*.

Judy was in the midst of her wake-up-at-five, studio-at-six schedule when I received a call from Aunt Amy. Mother had died suddenly. Her damaged heart had just given out.

I made that sad plane trip alone. With Judy's picture costing some $20,000 a day to produce, and her presence on the set constantly needed, it would be unthinkable for her to accompany me. It was a long journey, first to New Orleans, then on to Miami and St. Petersburg, but I arrived in time for Mother's funeral.

Dad bore up nicely. He was nearly an invalid himself, but he insisted on paying homage to Mother by going through the whole dismal proceedings of rosary, wake, and High Church burial.

I returned to California and to Judy's comforting arms. Work again proved to be a healthy distraction from the sadness, sweet because it conjured up so many happy memories of Mother, but understandably sad nevertheless.

"Yolanda" couldn't be kept waiting any longer, obviously.

The picture made money, but those who look at my career categorize *Yolanda* as my first interesting failure. It was based on a sophisticated fable by Ludwig Bemelmans and Jacques Thery. The story was naive, however, and much of the public couldn't accept a simple story in an avant garde setting.

155

I tried to get the quality of Bemelmans's books and illustrations, a curious mixture of worldliness in high places and a primitive naiveté, using his sometimes crude prism colors right out of a child's paint box and combining them with beautifully subtle monotones.

The screenplay was written by Irving Brecher. It incorporated all the outrageous elements of the original story. Fred Astaire and Frank Morgan, two American con men hiding from extradition in South America, hear of a young girl, heiress to a vast fortune, and decide to clip her. The girl has led a sheltered life in a convent. Coming home to take charge of her estates, she's shocked to find that everyone around her is after a slice of the fortune. As Astaire climbs her garden wall one night, he hears her praying to a figure of her guardian angel, asking for guidance. He materializes as if he were the angel responding to her call.

There was one joke in the script which I found hilarious. After Astaire tells Morgan of his plan, the older man tries to dissuade him from the idea.

"Do you know the penalty for impersonating an angel?"

Fred turns toward Morgan and answers, somewhat belligerently, "No, what is it?"

Morgan fumbles. "Well . . . it's very severe."

For some reason the line never got a laugh. I still think it's funny.

Astaire proceeds with his plan and manages to secure the girl's power of attorney. He moves in for the kill, when his partner accuses him of falling in love with the girl.

Since Astaire has a horror of legitimacy and marriage, the fantasy ballet sequence evolves as greed fights it out with the mating instinct. It was the first surrealist ballet ever used in pictures.

His background haunts him—we see suggestions of the sporting set, the grafters, the jockeys, the fast women in his past; the newspaperboys and Latin people of his present.

The main setting of the ballet is an abstraction. I wanted to suggest South American baroque without actual architectural forms, and used a series of rock formations in fantastic shapes. These were on rollers and could be grouped in different compositions for each shot. Irene Sharaff's stylized costumes complemented the action. South American touches are used in the ballet, combined with the surreal. Peruvian llamas walk by, South American women are washing their laundry at the edge of a pond, the sidewalks of Rio de Janeiro are suggested by curving black and white stripes on the ground. The laundry women trap Astaire in between white sheets, a gauze-wrapped figure comes walking out of a smaller dank pond, totally dry, and as each veil is undone, we gradually are aware that it's Lucille Bremer as Yolanda. (The effect was created by having her double walk backward into the pond, then reversing the film so that she seems to be walking out of it.)

The ballet ended with a bitter laugh. At the wedding, Astaire attempts to steal away with a box filled with gold coins. But he gets hopelessly enmeshed in the train of Yolanda's wedding veil. The dream ends. He wakens, all tied up in his bedsheets, Frank Morgan holding a pitcher of water over his head, about to bring him back from his tortured sleep.

Over-all, my design was a simple attempt to show the interplay between the dream and reality. Every dream is an arrangement of some real aspects. Ideals, aspirations, and desires consciously or subconsciously color the thoughts, actions, and relationships with other people. Only in the dream does all this become real, do we get to the truth of it all.

Film buffs say the picture was ahead of its time. I like to think so.

The picture had great style. The reputations of those associated with it was enhanced. If there was one casualty it conceivably could have been Lucille. The studio gave her every opportunity to deliver. Nothing was spared to show off her extraordinary dancing ability. However, she lacked star quality. But then, Lucille never wanted to be a star, and it probably showed. She got married as quickly as she could, leaving pictures shortly thereafter. Her "defection" is sad in a way, for I consider her one of the finest dancers I've ever worked with.

The picture was completed, and I could now devote more time to my personal life. I was going to make good on my promise to Mrs. Gilmore, Judy's mother.

A week after her divorce was final, on June 15, 1945, Judy and I were married at her mother's house in Beverly Hills. It was a small wedding for the immediate family and a few friends. Father was too ill to make the trip from Florida.

Ira Gershwin was my best man. Betty Asher, Judy's publicist and best friend, was maid of honor.

Arthur Freed was there, studio publicity head Howard Strickling was there, Louis B. Mayer was there to give the bride away.

I don't remember much about the ceremony, being nervous to the point of palsy.

Ira swears that at the end of the ceremony, the minister brought out a symbolic wooden staff. He asked Betty to grasp it first, then Ira, followed by Judy and me. Then, out of nowhere came an alien hand and grasped the staff by the knob on the top. It was Louie B. establishing his territorial imperative. We were now man and wife in the eyes of God. But what's more, we also had the blessing of a man upstairs who in many instilled far greater dread.

We went to New York for our honeymoon, taking an apartment on Sutton Place. We were deeply in love. This marriage would last.

A few days after we arrived, Judy gave me a cherished gift—a silent promise. We were walking in a park by the river. "Hold my hand," she said softly. I did. It was then that I noticed a vial of pills in her other hand. She threw it into the river.

11 | And Liza Makes Three

Of recent years, the latter day Grover Whalens have been saying that New York is a summer festival.

It already was for Judy and me that summer of 1945, for our friends had scheduled a busy pace of parties, theater, and more parties. Judy was quite taken with the excitement of such impromptu evenings, a marked contrast to the predictability of Hollywood social life, where evenings with friends are arranged weeks in advance and programmed to the minute.

No actress' reactions were as visually arresting and contagious as Judy's. I saw New York through her eyes, and we shared the joy of discovery together.

We were too in love and too caught up in the buzz of the city to allow apprehensions to gnaw at our innards. Problems? There simply weren't any.

I like to think it was as perfect for Judy as it was for me. If she expressed any slight irritations during our honeymoon, they revolved largely around her child-star image, which was being held over for another decade, it seems. She, who yearned for sleek satins and upswept hairdos, had to be held down while the studio forcibly dressed her in blue gingham pinafores and red patent leather Mary Janes. "I'll probably qualify for Social Security and play my first love scene in the same week," she would joke. Then, in New York, Judy saw the way she affected people. Though she bridled, she became aware that the studio brass might have had a point in trying to keep her the world's oldest adolescent.

We'd take long walks on those humid summer evenings when we weren't planning to go out. The people we met on the street mostly treated her with loving familiarity.

"Hi ya, Judy!" a truck driver called out on one of our outings. "Howza kid?" A young man across the street heard the commotion, and he too called out. "Judy, baby!" Approaching us was a stooped figure. "Is that you, Judy?" the old woman asked, just as if the girl she was running into was someone from the neighborhood she hadn't seen in several years.

"Yes," Judy giggled. "And this is my husband. His name is Vincente Minnelli and he's a very fine movie director."

Judy could have played the imperious grande dame with these people. But why would she want to, when they approached her with such well-meaning warmth? She responded in kind, transmitting back the same friendly waves.

She was well aware of her special standing, for Judy was quick to fall back on it during the one emergency that marred our honeymoon. When we'd taken the cross-country train East, we decided that Gobo, the more neurotic of my two standard black poodles, would have to come with us. He and Judy had a special kinship, and it would have been unnecessarily cruel to part them.

We were out with friends for an evening on the town. Our car was parked outside a night club, with Gobo in the back seat and our driver in front. It was a hot night, and all the windows of the car were open. Some fans, hearing this was Judy's car, gathered around it. They frightened the sensitive and shy Gobo, and he bolted.

When we were informed what happened, we came running. The fans spread out, running and searching. But Gobo was not to be found. As the car inched its way through the streets, people would come up and report they'd seen Gobo at such and such a place. Some of the reports were manufactured by fans who merely wanted an opportunity to talk to Judy. But periodic reports from a nearby police car kept us straight. Gobo had first made a beeline for a tree in Central Park, then he was seen in the East 90s, finally making his way downtown.

By this time, we were back at our apartment after two hours of

160

fruitless search. Judy was nearly hysterical. Yet even in moments when she seemed to lack control, she still had the situation in hand. She was too upset to think of sleep. Something *had* to be done. She picked up the phone and called the police department, the city pound . . . in fact, anyone she felt could be of help.

"This is Judy Garland," she said. The thought was allowed to sink in on the other end of the line before she continued, and the difficulty was explained. Everyone responded, stopping all activity to search for "Judy's dog."

Dawn was nearing when we heard that Gobo had been cornered on the docks. But he wouldn't give up without a fight. He jumped into the river. He was quickly fished out and delivered back to us, looking like a contaminated bird, his coat covered with tar.

No return of the prodigal son could have been as emotional as the reuniting of Judy and Gobo. Once they'd both given vent to their feelings—Judy's cries of relief and Gobo's high-pitched whines—they were ready to retire. But Gobo had to be cleaned up first. I told Judy I would wash off the tar, and Judy trudged off, exhausted, to bed. I took off my clothes and jumped into the tub with Gobo. Any tar I got off him managed to stick to me. It was a lost cause. The sun was up by this time, and the groomer would be open in a couple of hours. The cleanup duty could be better handled there.

I wonder how successful we would have been in finding Gobo if my wife wasn't Judy Garland. I was thankful, of course, that the public thought so much of her that they would drop everything to help her in time of need.

She encountered, after some preliminary skirmishing, the same avuncular attitude among the more sophisticated people from the theater I introduced her to. They had their own brand of savage humor, and they were determined not to be easily impressed. They expected the sugar of her movie image; they found spice instead. Her attractive self-effacing wit captivated them. Obviously she had a healthy disrespect for the movie business. So did many of them, who'd been victimized by the studio system during their brief professional stays in California. But the cause for their unconditional surrender was Judy's hint of malice. She showed it by being as perceptive about the theater as they were. Her estimation of what was excellent and mediocre jibed with theirs. By dismissing a current offering with a short aside or a cocked eyebrow, she proved herself. She would even go along with the prevailing attitude, though she might not agree with it, if it afforded an opportunity for a witty line. Some sophisticates found the wholesale wholesomeness of *Oklahoma!* too much for their jaded viewpoint. Judy took a line from one of the show's songs as her pseudo-opinion. "The corn *is* as high," she said, "as an elephant's eye."

Also, if the situation demanded, she could trade the most convoluted, high level sarcasms with the best—and worst—of them. Looking back at those early days through the wrong end of a telescope, I can't recall what they were. But their tenor was similar to her devastating appraisal years later of Robert Goulet and his shiny good looks. "He's an eight by ten glossy," she said, a label Goulet will carry to his dying day.

Judy had the makings of the greatest rogue and vagabond of them all. Consequently, our friends—scamps too—sought to protect her.

With them, as with everyone, she more often summoned forth her effusive charm. It was all-encompassing, bowling you over through the force of her personality. For Judy, if she chose to, could will people into adoring her. It wasn't even a particular challenge with a room full of people, no matter how sophisticated. She'd been doing it all her life with far larger audiences. When all else failed—the wit, the self-efface-ment, the warmth and the genuine concern for others—she fell back on her greatest weapon. How can you resist a woman when she shows you her vulnerability?

This art of swaying emotions, both in her professional and personal life, left her largely unimpressed by the theater we took in during our three months in New York . . . as our friends had already discovered.

There were two exceptions. She knew all the tricks used by the players in *Carousel,* but she was so transported by the affecting story that she blubbered all the way home. I might have teased her about being such an easy mark if I hadn't been blubbering too.

There was also *The Glass Menagerie.* Laurette Taylor's was one of the great performances in theater history. Judy's eyes brimmed with tears, not only because of the drama itself—the most lyrical of Tennessee Williams's works—but because she was inspired by Miss Taylor's genius. To her, this was what acting was all about, a height to aspire to.

When a celebrity is in the audience, protocol requires a visit back-stage after the performance. Such visits can be deadly, especially when there is little cause for praise. But Judy was eager to tell Miss Taylor of the way she'd been struck by her brilliant portrayal. Judy came pre-pared to kneel at the feet of the legendary Laurette, but Miss Taylor would have been more pleased if Judy had sat in her lap. Her instincts were those of any other fan who devoured the movie magazines. She wanted to know all about this talented girl.

From so close a vantage point, I was shocked to see that the years of Miss Taylor's alcoholism had taken a ravaging toll. As a result, her performance as a faded Southern belle living with the memory of her many gentlemen callers became even more poignant.

She was averse to talking about her art, dismissing it as yet another cross the black Irish must bear. We refused to settle for that, wanting to know more about her approach to the part. "Well," she finally responded, "the mother, you see, may be very shrewd but she isn't intelligent. That's why I'm wearing bangs. I have a high intelligent forehead and I have to cover it."

"Is the character patterned after Tennessee Williams's mother?" I asked.

"I've met his mother," she answered, "and if it is, she's completely unaware of it. She talks about the character as if it has nothing to do with her."

I wish I could report some symbolic passing of the torch between the two during this meeting . . . some indication each was aware of extraordinary common bonds. Both brought a highly individual tragic quality to their dramatic roles, and both were victims of excesses which nearly destroyed their enormous talents. But that would be speaking from hindsight. Miss Taylor's troubles were behind her; most of Judy's hadn't begun.

We just felt enormously thrilled to have met this singular woman. We didn't realize how fortunate we'd actually been, however. Laurette Taylor would be dead within a year.

If Judy's natural exhilaration needed artificial stimuli, I wasn't aware of it. We had our friends and the theater to distract us, but more often we were wrapped up in each other. It's either highly indicative of my personality or a tribute to Judy's charms that, though I can remember our awed reaction to the dropping of the atomic bomb on Hiroshima, I can't recall where we were or how we reacted to the Japanese surrender and the end of the war.

If there was dancing on the streets, as I've read, and hundreds of thousands congregated in Times Square, it may have been just another symptom of New York's summer madness, which we chose to bypass in order to spend more private times with each other.

But our friends didn't allow us to hibernate for long. Eleanor Lambert, among them, took Judy under her wing, taking her to fashion showings and generally introducing her around. They traded hot tips, Eleanor cueing Judy on fashion, and Judy passing on some of Dotty Ponedel's make-up hints. Judy would never be able to emulate Eleanor's genius for organization. We both envied Eleanor's ability to get to her office early in the morning, put in a full day, then come home to prepare a sit-down dinner for sixteen . . . all the while looking fabulous.

Judy's efforts to play the hostess copied some of Eleanor's easy grace. We'd have a few people in from time to time, but the culmination of our entertaining was a dinner party we had for all our New York friends.

The guest list included Eleanor, Moss Hart and Kitty Carlisle, Sam Behrman, Oscar and Dorothy Hammerstein, Bea Lillie and Harold Arlen.

Judy organized every detail, down to the votive candles in big red snifters which were placed on the tables on the two terraces. Once the caterers arrived, Judy had the great good sense to become a guest at her own party, and a highly entertaining one. I was understandably proud.

"I think I'll keep you," I told her after the guests had left.

"My dear sir, you do me such great honor," she answered extravagantly, and not a bit mockingly. And thus the germination of an idea . . . which I had in the back of my mind all along.

I told Judy she reminded me of *The Pirate*, the opéra bouffe by Sam Behrman which Alfred Lunt and Lynn Fontanne had starred in. It was a marvelously concocted plot, I felt, a musical without music. The Lunts, in the 1943 Theatre Guild production, played the improbable farce in a probable way . . . the only way farce should be played. It was great camp, an element that hadn't been intentionally used in films up to now . . . I say intentionally.

Judy read the play and loved it too. "Let's make it into a musical," she suggested, thinking it was her idea all along.

Absolutely. I got on the phone to Arthur Freed in California. He resisted the idea at first. Judy had never played such a role. He and studio executive Sam Katz read the property and, after some discussion, grudgingly agreed to buy it.

We were looking forward to doing this as our next picture together, after Judy completed her cameo role as Marilyn Miller in *Till the Clouds Roll By,* the musical very roughly based on Jerome Kern's life.

About ten days before we were due to return to California, I took

164

Judy to a doctor on Park Avenue. He confirmed her suspicion. She was pregnant.

We decided not to tell the studio just yet . . . plenty of time for that when we returned to California. We would have the three days on the train to decide how to tell them the awkward news. Million dollar productions might be kept waiting, and the studio had proven notoriously impatient and unsympathetic to Judy in the past.

When we finally informed Arthur, the anticipated blowup didn't materialize. He was genuinely happy for us. In a trice, though, he began mentally figuring out how Judy could still be used in their Kern picture.

Pre-production planning for *Till the Clouds Roll By* was accelerated, so that Judy could complete filming before her pregnancy started showing. Though Richard Whorf directed the picture, I handled Judy's three song numbers and the few dramatic scenes she had with Bob Walker and Lucille Bremer, playing Kern and his niece respectively.

The picture was planned as still another all-star extravaganza, with June Allyson, Kathryn Grayson, Lena Horne, Van Johnson, Dinah Shore, and Frank Sinatra contributing musical interludes. This was the formula that had been developed in past film biographies of composers, and rightly so, I think. The times didn't permit film-makers to do composers' actual lives . . . they probably still don't. How could they be both entertaining and real, when so much of the composer's life is static? It hardly makes for inspired movie-making to have a composer sitting at a piano, saying, "And then I wrote . . ."

Judy's three songs didn't—and couldn't—take long to shoot, for she was four months pregnant when we finally were able to start filming in October. We wrapped up our part of the enterprise in a little more than two weeks.

I'm proudest of "Sunny," the number which crammed all facets of circus life in three and half minutes. One circus ring was set up, for it had to look as if the number was being done on the stage, and a boom camera swept in to cover the action . . . baby elephants, riders, clowns, and tigers . . . its movements designed so that it would be at just the right spot when the most interesting action was going on.

Judy sang the number, then ran behind a group of people. When next you saw her (actually Judy's double), she'd jumped on a horse and the two of them were off and performing all sorts of riders' tricks.

Her second number was "Look for the Silver Lining," in which Judy was seen washing dishes, as Marilyn Miller had originally introduced the song on the stage.

Judy felt her pregnancy showed in the last number. It was a full-scale glamour mounting, with a chorus of sixty and spiral stairway in support. Judy later talked about the ridiculous figure she felt she'd cut in that scene. "There I was, sticking out to here. I keep running up to each man in the scene, singing the question: 'Who?'"

Her numbers completed, Judy temporarily retired to await our child's birth. Those few months were the longest she'd been professionally inactive since she signed on at Metro more than eleven years previously at the age of thirteen.

The confinement wasn't idled away. Since I had to report to the studio every day, much of the responsibility for supervising the building of a nursery, enlarged kitchen and dressing room for Judy fell on her shoulders.

These were our happiest times. Our life together was atypically golden even for Hollywood. Judy and I weren't falling prey to the Hollywood syndrome where one mate is up and the other is down, the situation in *A Star Is Born,* tragically repeated with many couples I could name . . . but won't.

With the remodeling completed, we were now ensconced in our rambling house on the hill, the kind songs are written about, with a view of the city below us. It was decorated in lavish style, conveying the impression that its inhabitants were professional successes. With Judy pregnant, we were well on our way to raising our allotted brood of 2.3 children.

Money was streaming in weekly from the studio, there was no worry about tomorrow and no indulgence too extravagant. We'd begun acquiring fine furniture in our house. Though I noticed friends building up impressive collections of French impressionist art, I had no desire for fine paintings, for I felt unworthy possessing things that rightfully belonged to the whole world. I was enormously fortunate to be able to indulge my obsession in art books, for I was able to own the world's great paintings in this way.

Judy had been introduced to designer clothes by Eleanor Lambert, and she began to frequent fashion showings in California. She would want a new wardrobe after the baby's birth. I would go with her to jewelry auctions, for I was just as interested in the antique collection she was beginning to acquire as she.

Only after we'd settled into this truly spoiled existence did we attempt to mesh our markedly different personalities and present them to the world as a unified entity.

Judy and I hadn't thought of our mismatched interests when we married. Actually, she wasn't as unschooled nor I as intellectual as the sob sisters would have it. Neither one of us had to travel all that far for our inevitable meeting somewhere in-between. I took it for granted that as Judy matured, her knowledge would broaden, just as she assumed that my reserved demeanor would become more outgoing. If she stumbled along the way, I would always be there . . . that is, whenever she asked for assistance. For I was determined not to foist my attitudes on her. Why would I want to play Svengali to one of nature's already adorable creatures?

I knew that Judy wanted to grow to her full potential, and I wanted her to. My hopes for her weren't noble, however, for they were based on the most selfish of motives. I deeply loved the girl, and whatever was best for her was best for me. Together we would be sensible; together we would be adult.

Judy set out to become the complete housewife. Being a child of whim and short attention span, her efforts came in not too steady spurts. But this wasn't cause for alarm. If I'd wanted a super-domestic wife, I'd have married Betty Crocker.

What pleased me most about Judy's homemaking was not that she did it well, but that she bothered to do it at all.

She'd get these periodic compulsions. One day she might get down on her hands and knees to scrub the kitchen floor, ignoring the fact we had a staff to do it. The next day, she would try out a recipe for chicken fricassee. On another occasion, she might bring home an assortment of needlepoint canvases to work on. Our friend Sylvia Sidney had long been urging her to take up the hobby. "It calms the jangled nerves," she advised.

It was momentous whenever Judy decided to bake a cake. The effort, whether fallen in the middle or with gooey frosting running off the plate, required a minimum of ten compliments.

"Terrific, sweetheart," I'd say, as she set up the ingredients on a kitchen counter. Our cook stood beside her, cleaning up after Judy, possessed of a bottomless reservoir of patience. Every pan in the kitchen would be used, and every surface would be coated with flour once Judy was finished baking.

After dinner, the cake would be brought out. Another compliment on its appearance. "No, I don't think it's lopsided. I'm sure it's delicious." With one bite, my next line was, "This is without doubt the best cake I've ever eaten."

167

Judy might not have noticed that I wasn't eating it all up. Of course, when it came to compliments, that's exactly what *she* was doing.

Her desire for constant approval was pathological. If she soon became bored with the kitchen floor or the needlepoint canvas had only half a dozen stitches, then I quickly assured her that was the cleanest half of a kitchen floor in existence and those few stitches were the most uniform ever executed.

The finishing up would be delegated to the servants . . . if one can call them that. Never was there a more casual household. Judy became pals with the cook, the nurse, the housekeeper, the driver. I'd come home from work and find her in the midst of some sweet conspiracy, the muffled laughter and shifting of eyes telling me they were trying to keep something from the old man. She consequently had no stomach for creating discipline and order among them. Why, they would have thought she was putting on airs! I became the ogre in the setup, the force to be reckoned with when things went wrong. And though she'd cast me as the heavy, Judy wouldn't let me function on my side of the battle line she'd drawn up. I'd try to speak to the servants in an authoritative way. Judy's giggles informed me how ineffective I was being at it, and we both inevitably collapsed with laughter at my efforts to play lord and master.

It was in her dressing room and bath that Judy felt the most comfortable playing lady of the manor. I'd designed the room—its walls covered in antique glass and furnished in Victorian papier-mâché pieces—and it became her hideaway. Plopped on the fur-covered chaise, she would spend hours there primping or reading.

Her tastes were becoming as catholic and eclectic as mine . . . she had graduated from the movie magazines and the true romances to light fiction and theatrical biographies. And she also began reading the national periodicals. For the first time, she began following the writings of film critics. Here again Judy discovered that her instincts and insights were just as valid as they'd been with our friends from the theater in New York. She often found herself in agreement with critics, though she claimed she couldn't have worded her thoughts as well. But when Judy disagreed, she became highly articulate . . . particularly when it was her husband whose work was being found lacking. What did those critics know, anyway?

About a month after she took the hiatus from the studio, *Yolanda and the Thief* was released nationally. We'd heard while in New York that a couple of previews in California had gone over well. But now that it was in national release, critical reaction was underwhelming. Most reviews either didn't like the script or were offended by the idea of a con man impersonating the angel. I didn't understand their reaction. Fred Astaire did it so raffishly, and audiences have a long tradition of embracing con men, from "Get-Rich-Quick" Wallingford to Tatum O'Neal. Why wasn't this version accepted? I liked the picture. I still do. But the critics didn't.

Bosley Crowther's assessment in the New York *Times* was the most flattering pan I'd ever received: "Taste and imagination are so rare these days in musical films that a good bit of both is sufficient to offset a peck of obvious faults. So that's why this corner is cheering for Metro's *Yolanda and the Thief,* which came to the Capitol with all the gusto of the Macy parade.

"Fetched from a mischievous fable by Jacques Thery and Ludwig Bemelmans, and mounted with charm and magnificence by Vincente Minnelli and Arthur Freed, it is a pleasing compound of sparkling mummery and glistening allure for eye and ear, hampered throughout by a flat script which doesn't match the visual elegance with wit."

I thought the script *was* witty, or otherwise I wouldn't have done it. But it just didn't play for some moviegoers, "a higgledy-piggledy and pretentious bore," as Howard Barnes described it in his New York *Herald Tribune* review. If there was any danger of losing my humility, that picture obviated it.

The pans depressed me, but it was pointed out that with the industry's weekly audience of eighty million, no sensibly budgeted film like Yolanda could fail.

The rationale freed me to concentrate on more pressing matters: the expected child, the remodeling at home, and my first try at a melodrama.

With my past successes in musicals, it was offbeat casting for producer Pandro Berman to approach me with *Undercurrent,* an Edward Chodorov screenplay based on a story by Thelma Strabel. He already had Katharine Hepburn as the star and, I'm sure, she had approval of both director and leading man.

"I had no rules on how to cast," Pan recalls today, "but I probably decided on you because you were the best man available at the time." Nice words, but rather insignificant, since I was an unknown quantity with this type of story. It was probably Pan's showman instincts that contributed to his decision to hire me.

Pan is a rough, ready guy. He doesn't claim to be an artist. He has absolutely no intellectual pretensions, saying it's all business with him. His violent temper most often explodes around actors, for he has no patience with their whims. I frankly don't think he likes the breed very much, although he's put wonderful things together for them during his more than forty years in the business.

Though I paint him as gruff and irascible, he's a marvelous guy despite this, possessed of good manners . . . most of the time. Little wonder that Kate adores him.

He produced several of my favorite Hepburn pictures while at RKO, *Morning Glory, Alice Adams,* and *Stage Door* among them. He noticed the impact a new dance team had in *Flying Down to Rio,* a picture made in 1933, and teamed them together in nine more films to make Fred Astaire and Ginger Rogers the foremost film musical team up to that time.

Pan, oddly enough, didn't want to make any more musical films when he came to Metro a few years previously. And since that was my métier early in my career, I had little contact with him until the day he offered me *Undercurrent.*

The story was about the daughter of a small-town college professor who marries a brilliant young industrialist and moves with him to the city. The girl is socially insecure, as is evident in the gauche and dowdy impression she creates at their first big party together. The husband then takes her in tow, transforming her into a stylish young matron. In the background is a brother the husband despises, whom the wife has never seen. Their acquaintances tell conflicting stories about his disappearance, and the suggestion is subtly made that her husband might be responsible for the brother's murder. This is the dark undercurrent that threatens to destroy their marriage.

The wife feels she must get to the bottom of the matter. She begins to accumulate as much knowledge as possible about the missing brother, and in so doing discovers she shares his tastes in music, literature, painting, and art. She is irresistibly drawn to his gentle character. The doubt about her husband can no longer be suppressed. Is he the psychopath some people suggest?

Robert Taylor was cast as the husband, his first picture since the war. Robert Mitchum had received an Academy Award nomination for Best Supporting Actor for *The Story of G.I. Joe* the previous year. Pan and I decided he would play the brother.

Bob Mitchum feels it was fiscal collusion between the studio and David Selznick, to whom he was under contract, that brought him the part. For he admits he was never comfortable in the role of the sensitive Michael.

But Bob didn't need the later-developed Mitchum swagger to convey his innate strength. He's always underestimated his ability.

I can't deny that Selznick was being paid $25,000 a week to loan out Bob for my picture, and getting the same amount for a second Metro picture, *Desire Me,* which Bob was shooting in the afternoon. On top of this, Bob was working at night on *The Locket* at RKO. "I worked the three pictures for twenty-six straight days," Bob remembers. "We'd shoot all night at RKO, then I'd report for *Undercurrent* from seven in the morning until noon, when I'd be flown to Monterey to work all afternoon on the picture with Greer Garson." No wonder he became famous for his sleepy eyes.

He reported for our first meeting, and we discussed concepts and approach. He would work very well, I thought. "Bring something tweedy," I instructed. (He would have to supply his own wardrobe for the picture.)

But at the time, Bob recalls, he had only two suits, and both of them were still being made. "I show up on the set with my clothes stuck together with pins. Minnelli notices that I don't look too elegant. 'Are those your own clothes?' he asks. I'm sure he didn't understand that an important player could be tapped out and have no money for clothes." (Bob's contract with Selznick, regardless of the number of pictures he was making all at the same time, paid him a weekly salary of $350 . . . tops.)

I'd met Kate many times at the studio, but didn't get to know her well until we made the picture.

"I'm sure we'll get along," she said. It sounded like both an order and a threat. Never had I met anyone with such self-assurance. She made me nervous. And here was I, theoretically the captain of the ship, being made to tiptoe through my assignment.

The script needed work. I felt the young woman's first party in Washington after their marriage should be treated more significantly. It would show how inadequate she felt in this milieu of politically oriented people. She'd try to ingratiate herself to her husband's friends, but she couldn't break through the outer fringes of the group. She found herself laughing senselessly at jokes she didn't understand about people she didn't know. She felt deserted whenever her husband wasn't at her side. My friend George Oppenheimer gladly supplied additional dialogue for the party-goers, consisting mostly of sophisticated political jokes, receiving no credit for his contribution.

I also worked extensively with set decorator Jack Moore in designing the Maryland ranch house from which Michael had disappeared, his possessions and mementoes intact. The house had to suggest Michael's serene character. It would draw the young wife to a person she'd never seen. It worked quite well, I thought, as did the musical score of Herbert Stothart, particularly his selection of a Brahms theme to suggest the nobility of the brother's character.

We began shooting at about the same time Judy's physician advised that, due to her narrow pelvis, a Caesarean birth would be advisable. There was no hysteria at the news, no turning to barbiturates or amphetamines. Judy was so desirous of a perfect child that she tried to keep totally away from them during her pregnancy. Her actions proved it. The problem, however, was still not discussed.

A more happy quandary was deciding what to name the baby. We'd decided on Vincente Junior if it was a boy, but the name for a girl was a stickler. Not every female name went well with Minnelli.

Judy nudged me awake one night. "How about Liza?" she asked. I loved the Gershwin song, she knew, and in a way it would be a tribute to Ira to use one of his song titles for our child's name. I agreed readily. "But, you know," I told Judy. "I've always wanted to name a child after my mother. Could we call her Liza May?"

"Perfect!" Judy said. And with that, we both drifted off to sleep.

Back at the studio, it was business as usual . . . but with a welcome twist.

Though I later learned that Kate wasn't struck with the idea of using Mitchum, at the time she wasn't proving to be the ogre I thought she'd be. Perhaps her role had something to do with that. She could probably beat most guys Indian wrestling three out of five, but in the film she was a fragile girl unsure of herself, a fish out of water. She may have been unsure before the cameras, but the goings on between takes were another matter.

Kate's humor doesn't turn inward. She has a capacity for striking out, and she's one of the rare people who can do it with charm. For if she's irreverent to the person she's playing those verbal games with, she's even more disrespectful of herself.

Early in the proceedings we locked horns over one scene, which Kate felt was too hearts and flowers even for her subdued movie character. She wanted it rewritten. It eventually made sense to me, so I agreed. When we shot it, however, Kate did it the old way.

"Katie, what is this?" I asked. "It's so much better the new way."

"Well," she growled defensively. "I've gotten used to the old way. You know, you can get used to anything. I got used to *you,* didn't I?"

172

Eventually, I got used to *her*. That sort of baiting can get wearing if it isn't your type of humor, but Kate relished it. She'd arrive on the set with her shirttail hanging out, match insults with the crew, go into her dressing room to prepare for filming and come out with even more good-natured barbs.

The turning point in our relationship, however, was the result of a momentary impulse on my part . . . and I learned a valuable insight into Kate's character.

We were shooting her hysterical scene in the picture, where she confronts the husband, telling of her suspicions. He wanted her to look dowdy and unsure of herself, she accuses, so that his friends could see her later transformation and credit him for the change. What other betrayals were in store for her? Kate ended the scene in honest tears.

I couldn't control myself. Running up to her, I threw my arms around Kate and kissed her. "That was absolutely beautiful," I said.

Well! From that moment on, she became ultrafeminine. The questions and requests from this clinging female came tumbling forth. "Do you think I should do this? . . . How do you like that? . . . How would you approach this?" It was her flaw, but it lasted for only a day. Kate, being Kate, returned to her brittle bits of business the next day. But it taught me what I should know. All she wanted was to be told how marvelous she was . . . and still is.

I also had something pretty marvelous going for me at home that late winter of 1946. Judy and I decided soon after our marriage that I wouldn't bring my work problems home with me, since I felt analyzing them was largely ineffective and usually left me depressed. I was so much more productive each morning, many studio problems being solved in my sleep.

We had instead the typical conversations of all parents-to-be. How many billions of times has one spouse turned to another and said, "I don't care if it's a boy or a girl, so long as it's healthy?" With all the love stored up, Judy and I were sure ours would be a happy child.

Judy was making last-minute arrangements for the Caesarean, scheduled for March 12. The remodeling was completed, the layette installed and the godparents selected. They would be Kay Thompson, who'd been my friend for ten years and who was now also very close to Judy, and her husband, Bill Spear.

Judy and I drove to the hospital that Tuesday. She may have had some of the momentary fears inevitable in all first-time mothers, but she was happy with anticipation.

I settled in for the few hours' wait, but before I knew it, I was informed I was the father of a baby girl.

Soon after, I was allowed to see Liza. She was, of course, the most beautiful baby in the nursery. As for those other wrinkled babies around her, all they needed was a cigar in their mouths to look like Eddie Mannix at the studio. There, alone on a table, was a perfect child, with absolutely no wrinkles, letting out a healthy cry . . . projecting!

The Minnellis were all back in residence a few days later. I flew through the work days, eager to get home at night to my small family.

People at the studio, of course, asked after Judy and the new baby. I tried to answer in a matter-of-fact way . . . and usually failed.

Kate didn't know Judy well at that time, though they'd often sat next to each other under the hair dryer in the make-up department, on those inhumanly early mornings before the start of the day's filming.

But being an unregenerate softie, Kate was interested in the baby's progress. I shamelessly fixed her with my soulful young-father-trying-to-bring-up-a-family look, and I swear she was an even closer ally than before.

Yet, as Kate and I were becoming good friends, I discovered that my cordial relations with Bob Taylor were in danger of deteriorating. He'd taken my chronic vagueness as disinterest, I suppose, and though he never voiced any complaints, I was aware of his dissatisfaction. Bob's wariness, that I was throwing scenes to Kate, ended when he discovered how effective he was being in the picture.

His performance helped us prolong the denouement. Though Bob had gotten over his pretty boy reputation, you still couldn't disguise his charm. The audience simply wouldn't take him for a murderer . . . until that climactic scene with his brother.

The mask was stripped, and his psychopathic character was finally revealed. I started mulling over the scene, to see if I could supply it with a new approach.

In the meantime, Bob Mitchum recalls that he and Bob Taylor were passing the time away in small talk.

"How tall are you?" Taylor asked.

"Oh, I don't know, probably six feet," Mitchum answered.

"That can't be," Taylor said, looking up to the taller Mitchum. "I'm six-one. You have to be six-three or -four." ("In those days," Mitchum recalls, "every actor was supposed to be six-one . . . including Alan Ladd. And in this scene, we're supposed to be eyeball to eyeball. So, okay, he

174

was six-one, but I know I'm about six feet and he had to look up at least an inch at me.")

To get the mad dog expression from Taylor, I suggested he do the long scene in the stable without blinking. I figured his eyes would get wider and have a teary, fanatic look. Bob did it beautifully. (The effort so reddened his eyes, that he had to be sent to dispensary for medication.)

I decided to use a lantern swinging in the wind to accompany the action, its hypnotic movement compelling Taylor to reveal himself. I think it was one of my most effective devices in the picture.

The following sequence between Taylor and Kate was the harrowing horse chase where he tries to kill her. Taylor in the process is trampled to death by the unruly horse he's been riding. The only challenge to Kate in the entire film was getting the right horrified reaction from her. It was finally worked out.

The film ends with Kate, recovering from the experience, being pushed in a wheel chair to the piano, where Mitchum is playing the melodic theme from Brahms Fourth Symphony, which had been used as recurring background music throughout the picture.

"I don't want to see that you're in love with Michael," I instructed Kate, "just the apparent hope that one day you may be."

"Isn't that cutting it a bit thin, Vincente?" she asked.

"Absolutely not." We prepared to do it my way.

The lighting men were working around Kate, getting everything just so. Mitchum noticed their equipment was blocking the line of vision between the two.

"Can you see me, Miss Hepburn?" he asked.

She turned to him with a sweet smile. "Not for dust."

Bob Mitchum may be a tough guy, but Kate's comment nearly decimated him. But once he got adjusted to the idea she apparently didn't like him, he was determined to go though the scene with dimpled chin held high.

The lighting men continued setting up. Kate, who knows *everything* about movie-making, knew she would be perfectly lit. She also noticed that Bob would be lucky to cast a shadow in the scene.

"I didn't know anything about key lights, or things like that," Bob says. "And here was Hepburn. Not only could she act rings around me, but she knew as much about the technical things as the experts."

Kate took pity, apparently, on Bob. "Mr. Mitchum," Bob remembers Kate saying, "don't let them screw you like that." And then she generously instructed the technicians to give Bob a better break. The result was that Bob now found Kate even more maddening . . . and fascinating. To this day, he still doesn't know what Kate thinks of him. Their paths never crossed after completion of the picture.

Bob never spoke of the slight friction with Kate until years later. And I, wrapped up in other phases of production, was too preoccupied to notice.

Yet there was one consolation for Bob . . . one last word . . . though neither he nor Kate had it.

Shortly after the scene was shot, Kate was wandering around the lot. She passed by Bob's dressing room and through the open door she noticed a young man, stripped to the waist, sketching. Her curiosity piqued, she went over. It was Boyd Cabeen, Bob's stand-in, drawing a quite creditable fashion sketch. Tyrone—that's what Bob called him—was designing some dresses for Jane Russell . . . his wife Carmen was her stand-in.

"You know, young man," Kate said, "you have obvious talent. You really should do something with it instead of working for some cheap flash actor like Mr. Mitchum."

Tyrone, fiercely loyal, politely turned to Kate. "Thanks for the advice, Miss Hepburn. Now may I make a request?"

Kate nodded.

"Should I survive you, would you bequeath me that lovely collection of bones?" And with that he shut the door, leaving Kate outside, mouth open, suddenly standing next to Bob. Kate, Bob recalls, giggled and walked off. She'd been very neatly put down for her presumption, and with the nicest of compliments. That she could appreciate. That was style!

12 | The Pirate

The tantrums, the feuds, the contrast emergencies, the race against time, and—most importantly—the sudden salvation of high humor which comes on and has you pounding the floor . . . there's nothing as exhilarating and challenging as getting a film or theater project off the ground. You struggle to get your idea over, first with the backers and finally with the audience. And in so doing, you work in close quarters with many disparate temperaments. The pressures are such that you get to know their weaknesses and strengths better than their wives and lovers do. You lose days of sleep to pull together the contributions of many into a unified whole. But who wants to sleep when stimulation surrounds you so? Anyone who hasn't suffered for his art in this way not only hasn't suffered, he hasn't lived.

Judy was also ready to give *The Pirate* her all. The picture would show her comedic range. It would be mounted with such sophistication and wit that she would now be in the same league as Greer Garson and Katharine Hepburn, the great and grand fillies of the Metro stable of stars.

She was quite certain she'd fly through the filming. It was going to be such a lovely labor that there'd be no need for amphetamines and barbiturates to see her through the "ordeal." Nor would she need to consult with the stream of psychiatrists the studio had been periodically sending her to since she was still a girl in her teens.

She'd show the people at the studio who were buzzing—within earshot —that she was difficult and unreliable. Judy bought the great selling job . . . both mine and hers. She would deliver. I was also confident that she would.

It didn't take Arthur Freed long to throw himself into the project. He caught our contagion . . . how could his enthusiastic nature help it? . . . and we set forth to put the pieces together.

The high comedy had to be changed considerably if it were to play for movie audiences and, more importantly, the Breen office. For Manuela, as Lynn Fontanne had played her on the stage, was already married to Don Pedro, the dull mayor of a West Indies village. She daydreams a romance with Estramundo, a notorious pirate. Serafin the actor, played by Alfred Lunt, learns of her fantasy and poses as Estramundo to win her. At the end, Don Pedro reveals himself as the real Estramundo, but Manuela leaves him nevertheless for Serafin and his theatrical troupe.

Judy's portrayal, since she was considerably younger than Fontanne, would be more naive. She couldn't be married to Don Pedro, obviously, for her elopement with Serafin would be considered inadmissible by the censors.

I never thought of anyone but Gene Kelly for the part of Serafin. Fred Astaire, even if he weren't currently retired, was too introspective to play the flamboyant swashbuckler, a pastiche—as Gene and I envisioned— of Douglas Fairbanks gymnastics and John Barrymore canned ham.

The writers tackled the project. "We have an idea," one of them said. "It's marvelous. You'll love it!" She wouldn't give any particulars. "Trust us. We won't tell you what it is until we finish the whole script."

Since they were highly respected talents, I left them to their muses, for I knew how destructive constant overseeing can be to the writer's psyche. My attention shifted elsewhere.

I'd worked on several New York shows with Karinska, the great costume designer who'd started out with Diaghilev and the Russian Ballet. She had the uncanny talent of transforming the elements of Braque and Picasso sketches into magnificent costumes. It would be no great challenge for her to suggest the many cosmopolitan influences—East Indian, Chinese, and European—of Martinique in the 1830s. She brought out a young artist—Tom Keogh—with her. When he later moved to Paris, he became a most important international painter.

I showed them my collection of prints and drawings of the period, and they proceeded to execute a very muted look, which I felt would counterbalance the more outlandish elements of the story.

Arthur and I then hired painter Doris Lee to create the pirate sketches Judy would be poring over at the start of the picture, their romantic nature suggesting why the young girl would be so taken with the legend of the black pirate.

Jack Martin Smith, who had done the art direction for *Yolanda and the Thief,* was assigned similar duties on *The Pirate,* and he set out to create the exotic atmosphere of Martinique.

Arthur and I then discussed the possibility of getting Cole Porter to write the score.

Judy and I knew working with Cole would be thrilling, should he decide to join us. It was in fact one of Judy's great ambitions to have him write a film for her, since Cole had been one of her earliest discoverers. He'd engaged her to sing at his parties when she was still a chubby unheard of adolescent.

Arthur called Cole. "Come on over," Cole said. "We'll have lunch . . . nothing fancy." Cole, wearing swim trunks and a flowered shirt, received Arthur at poolside. The luncheon table had been immaculately set, and a liveried footman stood behind each chair.

As Arthur sat down, the footman behind him flourished a handwritten menu. "I'm very anxious to have you try the entree," Cole said. "See if you like it."

The main dish was hamburger, Arthur later recalled, but it was the best he'd ever tasted. "Who's your chef?" he asked.

Cole started laughing. When Arthur pressed on, he explained why.

"I went to Chasen's for lunch the other day," he told Arthur, "and I ordered a hamburger. It was so good that I asked Dave Chasen for the recipe. He was very polite, but he refused to give it to me. I sent my butler in the following day. He ordered the same dish. When it came, he scooped it into a paper sack. Then I sent it over to a laboratory to have it chemically analyzed. You should be asking who's my chemist, not who's my chef!"

When the two discussed the film project, Cole agreed to do it if Arthur would agree to two conditions. First, he must have the completed script before he began composing. Also, could we change the name of Estramundo the pirate to Macoco? Cole had a friend by that name, whose nickname was Mack the Black, and he'd always wanted to write a comic song about him. Arthur anticipated no problem and agreed.

Cole began talking about the project. "I want it to have a lot of hits," he said . . . to pile dazzling success upon dazzling success was his greatest motivating force.

Several weeks had now gone by. The writers now had their first draft ready. Arthur Freed had us all to dinner at his house. Judy and I arrived after Cole, Gene, music supervisor Roger Edens, and the two writers.

We were having coffee and brandy when the writers rose. This was it, the formal reading of the script.

"We've made one simple change," one of the writers said. "Instead of an actor posing as a pirate, we've switched it around. The pirate is trying to pass as an actor. It'll be hysterical, this clumsy, inadequate fool trying to pretend to be a performer and showing how terrible he is at it."

On to the reading. Though the writers weren't actors, even the most transcendent talents couldn't save their approach. The reading over, they looked up expectantly.

Our silence was appalling . . . but then so was the idea. If we did it their way, Gene would have to submerge his talent to play an amateurish incompetent. It was a one-joke premise that would have to sustain the whole film. The great entertainment values would be lost, not to mention the piquant Behrman story.

Cole Porter, ever kindly, felt something must be said. "It must have taken a lot of work," he remarked. Yes, we all eagerly piped up, a lot of work. No one could look anyone else in the eye.

The evening limped along to its conclusion, and we went home—the writers included—with our private, identical thoughts.

The next day, we assigned Albert Hackett and his wife, Frances Goodrich—who should have been our original choices—to write the script.

We continued working on the physical details of the production, as the Hacketts were writing the first draft. When it was delivered, I found it a solid, workmanlike job, but still lacking much of the outrageous flavor of the stage play. In a voluminous series of notes, I suggested they go back to the Behrman work, for it had many phrases—both florid and arch—that would create the right mood for our own enterprise. These suggestions were the start of extensive reworking, which the Hacketts accomplished with great patience and no displays of artistic temperament. I at the same time had supplied some of the facets and nuances for the approach to the film, which were later to be share with the cast. Judy, in particular, was to find these explanations helpful, putting on these motivational layers like so many petticoats. And it was especially important for her to grasp them, for the establishing of the picture's emotional reality as well as the suggested sensuality would largely fall on her.

180

"We wish to show that the legendary figure of Macoco, the Pirate, has seized the imagination of Manuela and that he represents a real and deep longing in her for romance, color, and adventure," I wrote the Hacketts. "The credulity of the entire story depends upon this."

She would compare the pirate's glamour to the dullness of her boorish fiancé, the complete opposite to her dream hero in every way . . . even to his hatred of the sea. And Manuela has longed for adventure and romance. She asks to be taken to the nearby port of San Sebastian, to be fitted for her trousseau which was due there from Paris and to give her an opportunity to view the sea. "Otherwise I never will see it," she says, referring to that time in the near future when she will settle down to a dull marriage in her small village.

Her aunt is suspicious, for she knows Manuela too well to be taken in like this. "Who is it now and what has the sea to do with it?" I wrote the Hacketts, supplying Aunt Inez's perspective. "Is she planning a romantic attachment with Lord Nelson, or perhaps some scurvy buccaneer like Lafitte or Macoco?"

Then, in Port Sebastian, she meets—and rebuffs—Serafin. The chain of events during her stay there captivate the egomaniacal actor.

"He has become romantically excited by Manuela," one memorandum of mine read. "He is intrigued because she resisted what he believes to be his irresistible charm. She brushed him off—told him she was marrying someone else. And then, under hypnotism, with her defenses down, she responded to his awakening kiss in a way that he can't forget."

One of Serafin's gifts is mesmerism. Harry Lazarre, who I later came to know as the Cellini of all prop men, was already creating a four-sided magic mirror, its frame suggesting a religious chalice, which revolved when a spring in the handle was activated. Serafin hypnotizes Manuela to sing of her infatuation with Macoco in the town square of Port Sebastian, where his traveling troupe has set up its tent.

"The actor in him was excited by the way she sang and danced with him in the show," the note continued. "Together they were a minor sensation. The audience cheered, the coffers bulged. He has visions of them becoming a sort of Caribbean Lunt and Fontanne."

Back in her native village, Manuela is making her last minute preparations for the wedding. I advised the Hacketts to include a sequence where Manuela's silhouette, being thrown from the light of a magic type of lantern, is being sketched by an artist. For this was the 1830 equivalent of a bridal portrait.

Serafin follows Manuela to the village, to persuade her to call off her

marriage and to join his theatrical troupe. He discovers that her fiancé
is the real Macoco, but he blackmails "Don Pedro" into silence and
passes himself off as the villainous pirate. Serafin knows of Manuela's
adoration of the legend.

He tells the cowering townspeople that his men have the village under
siege. But no harm will come to them. All he asks is that the lovely
Manuela be delivered to him.

A comic scene in which Manuela, behind closed doors, is bewailing
her fate and resisting the pleas of the townspeople, even as she is dressing
in her finest gown and jewels to meet Macoco, followed.

Manuela makes her stately way through the crowd of townspeople,
on her way to her dire future. One of her young girl friends runs up to
her in tears.

"Manuela, I can't bear to have you sacrifice yourself. I'll do it! I'll
go in your place!"

To which the sacrificial lamb responds, rather airily, "He asked for
me!"

Manuela arrives for her rendezvous with Macoco. She first encounters
one of Serafin's men, who inadvertently reveals the ruse. Manuela's fury
brims right beneath the surface.

The Hacketts' next scene, incorporating the delicious element of the
actor's ego which we'd introduced throughout the script, was one of the
highlights of the picture.

Manuela now knows he's nothing but a cheap actor, and she's going
to rub his nose in it. Her reaction to Serafin as Macoco is extravagant,
her references to the acting profession scornful.

MANUELA (*worshipfully*)
Why did you think you had to do all this to get me here? Didn't you
know that you had only to stretch out your hand?
*Serafin is uncomfortable as Manuela circles around him, taking physical
inventory.*
MANUELA (*as she looks raptly at him*)
That sinister brow . . . the hawk-like glance of your eye . . . those
savage shoulders . . . that ferocious nape of your neck. I can see you
now in battle . . . the clash of swords, the roar of angry cannon . . .
and you, you Macoco! standing there, with lightning breaking around
you . . . You dominating everything!
(*She won't allow him the chance to reveal his true identity.*)

MANUELA

And to think that I believed you were just a silly little actor. How could I have been so gullible? I should have known, the minute I saw you on the stage, that you didn't know anything about acting.

(*Serafin winces at this blow to his pride.*)

MANUELA (*going on, ecstatically*)

Oh Macoco, my fabulous Macoco, take me away with you . . . take me away on your mighty ship.

SERAFIN

Just a minute . . .

MANUELA

I can see us now . . . you with your cutlass in one hand and your compass in another, shouting orders to your Pirate crew . . . and I at your side, spurring you on to greater and greater achievements. Wouldn't it be magnificent?

SERAFIN

Tell me . . . just what was the matter with my acting?

MANUELA (*interrupting*)

Don't speak of anything so disgusting . . . so degrading. I despise actors.

(*then looking up at him adoringly*)

You don't have to pretend before me. I love you for what you are . . . ruthless, cruel. Taking what you want! Fearing no one!

SERAFIN

Listen, you didn't see a good show. I was a little off that night but ordinarily my acting . . . why I can show you notices from the Trinidad *Clarion* . . . they compare my acting to David Garrick!

MANUELA (*interrupting, ecstatically*)

The man I love is the man who said, "Send me Manuela or I'll put a torch to the town!"

SERAFIN (*uncomfortably*)

Manuela, I have a confession to make . . .

MANUELA (*cutting him short*)

You don't have to confess anything to me. The record of your deeds is written on my heart. A murder or two might be something to confess. But when killing is done on such a magnificent scale, it becomes epic!

Manuela makes her way to the bedroom, from which she alluringly calls to Serafin, her voice and coquettish manner promising immediate delights. As he enters the chamber, he's beaned by a vase. He knows the jig is up. A hell of a fight erupts.

183

Serafin is no match for Manuela. Even when he finally attempts to respond in kind, he can't overcome her pent-up fury, which is being thrown at him in very tangible forms: vases and swords and clubs and any other object Manuela can lay hands on. Eventually, the donnybrook ends. A flying ax breaks the cord by which a painting is hanging. The picture falls to the floor, being interrupted in its descent by Serafin's head. He's knocked out.

Now Manuela comes forward. She's afraid she's killed Serafin, but even more terrifying is the thought that she's in love with him. All attempts to revive him fail. She throws her arms around him, trying to make him respond.

"I didn't mean what I said about your acting," she cries. "You're a *wonderful* actor."

Serafin's eyes open. He smiles contentedly, then passes out again, as she sings "Love of My Life."

With the script taking shape, I sought to preserve my overview, which I described to an interviewer at the time as "a fantasy, highly colored, theatrical as possible, flamboyant, swirling and larger than life." And now to make these words come true. It was to take more than a year for all pre-production activities to be worked out.

I had an approximate idea of what I wanted to accomplish visually in the picture, but it took the later cineastes to verbalize on it. *"The Pirate* is wildly, wonderfully eclectic," Joel Siegel wrote in the Fall, 1971 edition of *Film Heritage*. "One gets the feeling that the director is trying to combine and set in motion everything that has ever delighted him in the visual arts. A 19th Century Caribbean girl's room is furnished and lighted by Vermeer. A Manet woman and her black serving-girl lounge against a pillar in a port town. Conceived as a modern giggle at archaic dramatic and literary conventions, *The Pirate* is formally open enough to absorb any number of visual anachronisms."

At the time, however, I was fearful the picture couldn't fulfill all the ambitions I had for it. All the cinematographers I'd previously worked with were busy on other projects, and I would have to make do with a fellow named Harry Stradling. At last.

We set up for the first day of shooting. Aside from a brief "Good morning," there was no give-and-take with him. I described what I wanted, and he nodded his head. I didn't know if I was talking to a blank wall. He was playing cards with other crew members, and I was hesitant to interrupt it. But, of his own volition, he would periodically come over to watch our rehearsals. When time for the first shooting came, I went over to the poker game in progress.

184

Stradling looked up. "You ready for me?"

I nodded.

With a look to the others that said, "This shouldn't take too long," he went with me to look at the setup.

"Let's see," Stradling said. "You say she's walking from here to there? And there's a dark spot in the corner. Probably needs more light."

I didn't know what to expect, for I'd never worked with someone whose approach was so casual. The rushes next day dispelled all fears. They were magnificent. As far as I was concerned, Harry Stradling could play as much poker as he wanted to.

The free, cosmopolitan setting of the West Indies port contributed to the making of a very stylish picture. It was a novel twist from other adventure films, with a mixture of baroque elements, colorful costumes and my own brand of craziness at the time.

Judy and Gene knew the material quite well. There were only slight costuming problems to be solved. We had to devise something for Judy in her "Mack the Black" number. Serafin has hypnotized her into performing. The setting suggested it was a hot night, and Judy got out of her hotel room bed—under the actor's spell—and makes her way to the town square. I suggested she put a skirt over her nightgown and take bangles from the traveling actors' prop box. She looked wild and sensual, the hidden subconscious revealed in her song. I also devised Gene's costume for his opening scene. It was similar to several I'd done on the stage, a tapered—actually Irish—hat; full-sleeved shirt under his vest which he wore without a coat; and form-fitting trousers. The costume underscored his devil-may-care character.

Though Gene and Judy had both appeared in several all-star films in the interim, this was their first co-starring picture since *For Me and My Gal* seven years earlier.

Gene found her much more secure in the earlier picture. "Judy was charming to work with. There were no complications to her. If she had the beginning of a problem at that time, I don't think anyone knew it. I suppose hindsight would tell me there were signs even then. But no one was looking for them.

"The joy of working with Judy was her great capacity for laughter. She laughed . . . and she wanted to laugh. All I had to do was snap my fingers. When I made a goof, this made her laugh too. She had the movie-wise kid's knowledge that a scene could be taken over again. Coming from the theater I didn't know. I used to die when I made a mistake. This to Judy—and everyone else—was very funny."

But now, during filming of *The Pirate,* pressures were starting to build up.

"Judy had periods when she didn't show up on the set," Gene recalls. "This was my first indication that something was wrong."

She began to feel she wasn't functioning and turned again to the pills that had sustained her during past crises. I stood helplessly by, knowing she had started taking them again but unable to determine who was supplying them to her.

I'd been very proud that Judy had been temperate in their use since our marriage. Yet, Judy's tolerance was lessened, and the periodic spells of illness began. There might have been a history of squabbles with the studio and fears by executives that she would be in no shape to perform, but her indomitable spirit always came through. It was as if she could sense the exact number of days the studio could shoot around her. She would report at the last possible moment, so that her pictures usually ended within both the allotted shooting schedule and the budget. Now, for the first time, she had failed her substitute fathers, the men at the studio. The shooting schedule had to be extended. She'd been sent to psychiatrists in the past. It was again suggested that she turn to them for help.

I yearned to strike out at this monster coming between us, but I was persuaded to keep calm. If there was to be one constant in Judy's life, it should be her husband. I look back today and think that if I'd loved her less, I could have been dispassionate enough to laugh her out of the moods that led to her taking of pills. Sympathy that came too readily just didn't seem to help.

I would drive her over to the psychiatrist's every day after shooting and wait for her in the car. Judy would leave these sessions, her mood unaltered by these fifty-minute hours.

The pent-up anger found its likely outlet, the spats and bickerings becoming more magnified. I tried to control my own volatility, but occasionally failed. Harsh words were exchanged, the lashing out leaving raw scar tissue. That much hostility couldn't be held under one roof.

The Gershwins, in an upstairs sitting room, had a sofa which had belonged to Lee's mother.

When Judy and I had to be apart, Lee was the symbolic mother we went home to. I might call and ask Lee, "May I use your mother's couch tonight?"

"Of course, darling," she'd answer, her tone unruffled, never prying.

As I'd be packing my toilet case, more often than not, Judy would

186

already be walking out the door. *"I'll* go," she'd snap. "After all, this is your house."

We might go about our business for a couple of days, then have reconciliations that were as stormy as our partings. She'd be contrite, and I'd feel guilty because I hadn't been more understanding.

Toward the end of filming, she'd be gone from the set for three days at a time. I was caught in the middle. As director, I should have insisted on her fulfilling her assignment. As concerned husband, I couldn't. So I made excuses. She had a cold, or was running a fever. Then she'd be back, performing as well as ever and her mood as ebullient as before. And I would be a total wreck.

These were agonizing times. Was I responsible for her regression? How had I failed, and what could I do to improve? Submerging the private doubts while presenting an untroubled manner to the world was now a permanent way of life.

I couldn't reach Judy, to tell her that I truly cared. She still preferred to treat these periodic upheavals as solitary, lonely battles. They were, of course, always uppermost in our minds. Just one anxious look or an awkward inflection gave my thoughts away. One side of her twin personality must have appreciated my concern. Her darker side, though, resented my lack of faith, mentally storing up ammunition for future use.

I threw myself into the work with renewed determination.

Gene and I, in putting together the musical numbers with choreographer Robert Alton, had fallen into the most intense professional association I'd ever had with an actor. One idea would meld into another, and little difference who started the train of thought. I wondered aloud why our talents complemented each other's to such an extraordinary degree. "It's because my approach is less esoteric and more gutsy," Gene said, "while yours is evanescent and ethereal."

He'd been choreographing his own numbers. But as shooting progressed, Gene became involved in all facets of production. His apprenticeship was later repeated with a tyro named Stanley Donen when Gene as journeyman director proceeded to his own films, such as *On the Town* and *Singin' in the Rain.*

Judy, in her paranoia, became jealous of the time Gene and I were spending together. We'd been so concerned with getting the choreography right and of broadening the Serafin character that we excluded her from our discussions. I'd felt it wasn't necessary for Judy to have to deal with such problems, but she felt neglected.

"You and Vincente are having a lot of fun," she pouted at Gene. "You're both ignoring me. Well, how about doing something for me? Will you stage my numbers?"

"How about Vincente?" he asked.

"No, I want *you* to do it."

Gene helped as much as he could. He was caught up in a domestic squabble, and tried not to offend either one of us. The problem worked itself out. Without anything else being said, Judy realized she was being unreasonable, and her negative mood abruptly changed.

Yet an unspoken barrier remained between us. How had we come to this state of affairs where suddenly I could do nothing right in Judy's eyes? And how could I return from this impersonal limbo where she'd relegated me?

We continued working, Judy's cool behavior toward me a damning accusation. I was too much in a turmoil, and too hurt, to talk it out.

Life seemed even blacker when Aunt Amy called from Florida to tell me that my father had died. The trip East to bury him was taken alone. I left my parents' house for the last time, passing on its ownership to Aunt Amy.

Judy was sympathetic when I returned, and our life together took an upward turn. Liza, perhaps sensing this, blossomed.

The sounds of life from the adult level of the house drew her to us. Liza was a darling baby, a great beauty, and much loved. We couldn't wait to get home each night to tell her.

Her seriousness and highly determined spirit were funny and touching in one so young. Liza was only a few months old when she learned to climb the stairs of the nursery, and she'd make her arduous way to the upper level to join Judy and me while we had our pre-dinner martini.

She was still crawling at the age of two. Liza would navigate her way so rapidly that you'd swear she was moving on wheels. She'd probably still be crawling today had it not been for her first awkward scene.

All the Minnellis were at a kiddies' party. Liza was on the floor, scrambling on all fours. A guest scooped her up. "Look at Johnny, Liza," she said. "He's six months younger than you and see how well he walks. Aren't you ashamed that you haven't even started?"

Liza fixed the lady with a not-too-friendly stare, and restlessly squirmed off her lap. She walked for the first time the following day. But then no one had advised her to do so before now. "That kid has more drive than you and me put together," Judy observed.

Though her comment wasn't obvious in its self-pity, lurking beneath the surface was Judy's indictment of her mother's tyrannical efforts to instill an ambition in Judy she didn't naturally possess.

I got on well with Mrs. Gilmore, but there was constant inexplicable friction between her and Judy. She hadn't adjusted to her daughter's coming of age, and Judy's yearning to stand on her own as wife, mother, and actress. Judy resented her mother's attempt to continue to dominate her. It reminded her too much of the many advisers in the studio who also persisted in treating her like a not-too-bright child. Their relationship was alternately calm and stormy, and when the final accusations and resentments were voiced, Judy made it very clear that she felt betrayed. Her mother hadn't been there when she was needed nor backed Judy in her most drastically important clinches.

Mrs. Gilmore would often come over from her nearby house to join us for dinner. Some evenings were passed in unbridged silence. Her mother was incapable of saying those loving words that Judy so desperately wanted to hear, nor had she taught Judy to say them to her in return. The relationship deteriorated beyond salvation, and their proud spirits would never allow either of them to admit it was a tragedy.

Judy implied that had her father lived—he died of spinal meningitis when she was twelve—things would have been different. I doubt it, for it wasn't his influence which had Judy touring with her two sisters at the age of five.

Yet much as she resented this robbing of her childhood, Judy conceded that her early years in vaudeville gave her performance in *The Pirate* an added dimension. She knew what the knockabout travels of the theatrical troupe were all about.

For Judy's childhood was still with her. Her earliest demons were the same ones plaguing her today.

When she was sufficiently challenged, Judy would get outside herself and work like a draft horse. Her last sequence in the film was "Be a Clown." I worked out the costumes for Judy and Gene, and did their make-up. Though they would look like clowns, they also had to look like themselves in this, the last scene of the movie. We shot both day and night, and the two of them went through their paces like the troupers they were portraying.

Filming, except for Gene's pirate ballet, was completed when, on July 10, 1947, Judy and I hosted a cast and crew party on Soundstage Ten at the studio. Represented on the studio hierarchy were Louis B. Mayer, Ben Thau, Sam Katz, and Arthur Freed. All the people involved in the production were represented, down to, but not the least,

189

Sam the Tailor. Irving Berlin, composing the music for *Easter Parade*, the next picture Judy, Gene, and I were planning to do together, was present along with Cole and other guests from outside the studio. Judy was the radiant hostess. She and Gene entertained for the guests, as did the other members of the cast.

A few days later, the psychiatrist currently seeing Judy suggested her mental health would best be served if she removed herself from her studio and home environments.

Judy quietly agreed. She was too tired and too frightened to resist. Neither could I. Her condition was deteriorating before my eyes, and I could do nothing to help her. The only area where I felt I was being effective was in keeping the problem from Liza and—always to be considered—the press. The only mention of Judy's current difficulties was an item in Louella Parsons's column stating that she'd suffered a nervous collapse. And that was such an umbrella term, it could be describing overwork as much as anything else.

The psychiatrist thought it would be better if he drove Judy to the sanitarium in Compton. "She'll be quieter this way," he told me. "We'll give her something so that she'll fall asleep as soon as she gets there." I bade Judy goodbye at our front door. She looked plaintively back as the car drove off. When would we be together again?

"Mama went away for a little while," I told Liza the next day, "but she'll be back very soon." She couldn't begin to understand, but I felt a steady tone in my voice would assuage those fears about being deserted that plague every child. I was thankful that a very capable nurse protected Liza during these formative years. Between the two of us, we shielded the unhappy truth from her until Liza was old enough to cope with it.

I often went to visit Judy at the sanitarium, a lovely place with rolling grounds and homey bungalows, and was delighted to see how well she was responding. She was soon well enough to talk about her feelings the night she was committed. It was to become a favorite party tale.

"It was very dark that night," she told me. "Well, maybe it wasn't, but I was so out of it, that I couldn't make out anything. These two burly attendants met us at the car. They walked with me across the grounds. Suddenly, I tripped. They picked me up. I couldn't seem to control my feet. I tried to walk, but I kept stumbling. They held me up the rest of the way. 'This has to be the end of me,' I thought. They got me inside, and somehow I fell asleep. I woke up the next day . . . didn't

190

feel too bad . . . and I looked out the window. I noticed this nice green lawn. Then I saw why I kept stumbling. I'd been tripping over the croquet wickets!"

The slant of the story was so typically Judy. Though the experience had been dreadful for us both, who couldn't laugh at her macabre humor about it all?

Judy's reaction shots to the pirate fantasy had already been previously shot. The wind up of the filming would be Gene's ballet.

There were many complicated lighting effects, but Harry Stradling took them in stride. Not only was he responsible for one of my best lighted and most beautifully photographed pictures, Harry's serenity also helped calm my own turbulence during the time.

The sweep of light in the ballet went from black to reveal groups of men, the first in yellow and the second in green. The huge mounting was to represent the way Manuela would envision her pirate hero, the scourge of the seas.

Gene insisted on doing his own stunts in the number. They had to be impressive ones, for they were all figments of the girl's mind. The most dangerous was his scaling an enormous mast of a ship, from which he threw light torches which exploded as they hit the ground. Then he swung from a rope toward the camera. That sweep of action ended with a closeup of Gene's face. It was apparent to the audience that no one but Gene could have been doing the previous stunts.

With the filming of the ballet, the picture was over, except for post-production cutting, dubbing, and scoring. I felt we'd all shown ourselves to very good advantage.

Cole Porter, however, wasn't happy with his contributions. He had a presentiment that the picture wouldn't offer up any commercial song hits. He'd come to the studio to play each number as it was completed, and was often around when the cast was pre-recording the music.

I liked his work, finding it melodic and much suited to the story. Though he accepted the audience's judgment philosophically, I wish I could have assured him in a more articulate way.

But I never felt close enough to Cole to tell him. Neither did Judy, though he greatly respected her talent and was still fascinated by what he called "this little girl's prodigal voice." He was extremely polite and affable, but his demeanor made you feel he never heard what you said. He seemed to embrace people at arm's length, for he so jealously guarded his privacy that there were certain barriers one didn't presume to go beyond.

When the film was finally released in May of 1948, critics patted us on the head instead of throwing their arms around us.

Thomas M. Pryor of the New York *Times* called the picture "a dazzling, spectacular extravaganza, shot through with all the colors of the rainbow and then some that are Technicolor patented.

"It takes this mammoth show some time to generate steam, but when it gets rolling it's thoroughly delightful. However, the momentum is far from steady and the result is lopsided entertainment that is wonderfully flamboyant in its high spots and bordering on tedium elsewhere. But Vincente Minnelli, the director, doesn't permit the show to drag too much, for most of the scenes are crowded with people and—should we mention it again?—color."

Howard Barnes concluded in his review for the New York *Herald Tribune:* "Scrambled entertainment, but it has so much vitality and polish that it is a delight."

The box office reaction echoed the critical view, for the picture turned a modest profit. Though the audience was quite taken with Gene's rakish performance, they didn't know what to make of Judy in her adult role of farceuse. Arthur Freed said the film was twenty years ahead of its time.

The longer view of the picture was more to the critics' liking . . . and mine. It's typical of my conceit, I suppose, to think that they just might have grown up to it.

Joel Siegel's analysis in *Film Heritage* found *The Pirate* "above all, an exuberant parody of operetta conventions with dividend winks at Victorian melodrama and swashbuckler romance. It's a glorious and sophisticated entertainment, an immense, lavish production yet as enchantingly weightless as a daydream. The Garland and Kelly performances are extremely ambitious attempts at extending their usual ranges and are arguably the most satisfying of their respective careers. The screenplay is uncommonly witty in its satiric thrusts at theatrical and literary conventions and unexpectedly insightful in its underlying assumptions about the redemptive power of the artistic imagination. The huge, lovingly detailed production is, I'm certain, the closest Vincente Minnelli has ever come to realizing the abstract, deeply personal world of whirling forms and colors which seem to haunt the best and worst of his films. *The Pirate* has its flaws—some of which were caused by studio tampering with Minnelli's negative—but these hardly dim its lustre."

13 | The Bitter and the Sweet

Gene and I were in the thick of it again, working with Irving Berlin on *Easter Parade.*

Judy, home from the sanitarium, was gathering strength for her co-starring role in the picture. Her resentment over the time Gene and I spent together had long since dissipated. She liked what we'd all accomplished in *The Pirate*. She felt reassured. "I know you two have something great going," she told me.

Even if she'd felt otherwise, Judy couldn't have made an issue of my teaming up again with Gene. She was too busy trying to keep her own head above water . . . despite any outward indications to the contrary.

Though she'd left the sanitarium looking marvelous and in high spirits, and she was as giving and loving as in our early days of married life, she required constant attention and reassurance. The only way of allaying her fears—the same deep-rooted and open wounds of her childhood—was to give her as much love and consideration as I had in me. I thought I had a bottomless reservoir to offer, but sometimes Judy found me lacking. Sleep was ever elusive for her, and she sometimes resented that it came easily for me. She'd nudge me awake in mid-snore. "Be with me," she'd entreat. I'd put my arms around her, comforting Judy until sleep finally came upon her.

Sometimes, as I bustled around our bedroom getting ready for my day in Culver City, Judy—still in bed—would teasingly hold her arms out toward me. "Stay with me. Don't go to work today." But much as I wanted to, she knew it was impossible. There were hundreds of people waiting at the studio. She'd pout for a while, but as I'd be leaving, she'd be busy making plans with the nurse on how they should spend the day with Liza. She'd absently offer her cheek for a goodbye kiss, her attention now riveted on a day in the park or a visit to Maureen O'Sullivan and John Farrow, whose daughter Mia was one of Liza's earliest childhood friends.

The psychiatric sessions continued. I dolefully discovered that the status game was played here too. One fashionable analyst offering current theory was supplanted by another with even later concepts, later to give way to another . . . and another. I looked to each one with blind faith. The miracle cure was being dangled just beyond Judy's reach. But I prayed to a god I'd lost contact with over the years that someday she would get hold of it.

If I couldn't help Judy as much as I wanted to in the reality of our often sweet, occasionally bitter, life, I was determined she wouldn't find me lacking in my area of expertise: the business of make-believe. *Easter Parade* would have to be a great triumph.

Irving Berlin's music suited the talents of Gene and Judy exceedingly well. The title song had its own successful history, but the new numbers Irving had composed also showed great promise: "When the Midnight Choo-Choo Leaves for Alabam'"; "Better Luck Next Time"; "A Fella with an Umbrella"; "A Couple of Swells." The latter song was to be the spiritual successor to "Be a Clown," with Gene and Judy going through elegant paces, though dressed in tramp costumes. All the numbers were ready to go. Roger Edens had done his usual excellent job of adapting the Berlin songs into singable arrangements for Gene's admittedly limited voice. With Judy, Roger could open the songs up. Her voice was as staggering as ever.

I was getting ready to start casting the other parts when Arthur Freed called me into his office. His manner was extremely serious. Something was wrong.

"Vincente," he started. Arthur seemed ill at ease. I looked inquiringly back. "I don't know how to tell you this."

"Well, do," I urged. He was silent. I began thinking that perhaps the front office, for some reason, had decided to scrap the picture.

194

His words then came tumbling out. "Judy's psychiatrist thinks it would be better all around if you didn't direct the picture."

I was stunned.

"Why not?"

"He feels Judy doesn't really want you as the director . . . that you symbolize all her troubles with the studio."

Arthur's tone was kindly. "It would be better," he continued, "if you didn't do it." He, more than anyone else, should know. For we confided in him, and he'd protected Judy as long as he could.

What was there to say? The matter was settled. Of course, I understood. I had to. If our working together would create emotional problems for Judy, the solution was obvious. We simply wouldn't work together. There was now no reason why I couldn't stay home with Judy to give her as much attention as she demanded, and required.

I left work for the day, trying my damnedest not to feel betrayed. Why hadn't Judy told me directly? Why did it have to go through two other people? Weren't married couples supposed to openly discuss such things with each other?

Judy met me at the front door with a kiss. "Hello, sweetheart," I said. The evening paper was by my easy chair, and I sat down to read it. Liza came toddling in, and Judy and I had a few giggles over her antics. Any onlooker wouldn't have guessed anything was amiss, though he might have found the conversation at the dinner table unduly formal and stilted. After dinner, I read some scripts and Judy settled in with a book.

We were both in bed quite early. Even then, in the darkness and together in bed, where so many of life's differences are ironed out, no mention was made of the catastrophic happenings of the day. The reasons for my departure from the picture were like the wart on the end of a person's nose . . . too obvious to ignore, too tactless to mention.

Gene continued rehearsals with the new director, Charles Walters. He'd been at it for six weeks when the unthinkable also happened to him. He broke his ankle. The executives at the studio began thinking the picture was ill-fated. But those still involved were determined to see it through. Gene immediately suggested Fred Astaire as his replacement. Fred was still in retirement. "Why don't you wait until your ankle mends?" he asked Gene. "I really don't want to take this away from you."

But Gene was adamant, and the studio was also being highly persuasive. Judy—getting top billing in the picture—was in one of her up periods. The studio wanted to benefit from this mood while it could, to go as soon as possible. Fred generously agreed to step in.

Judy and I would drive together to the studio each morning. She'd go to a rehearsal stage to block out steps with Fred, while I went to my office to mull over my next project. I could see none in the offing.

I ran into Fred soon after they'd started filming. He was doing the choreography for the picture. "How's it going, Fred?" I asked. "How's my girl doing?"

"Just great!" he answered. "Judy's really got it. I go through these very intricate dance steps. She asks me to go through them again. That's all the instruction she needs. She picks it all up so quickly."

Much as she enjoyed working with Fred, Judy was plagued by illness during the filming. Most of the times she delivered for the studio, but at enormous personal toll. For the first time in her career, her weight began fluctuating dramatically. I welcomed her slight chubbiness as a sign that she wasn't taking amphetamines. But then she'd lose many pounds in a few short days, and I had to admit she was back on them again. I was frustrated in not knowing where she was getting them. She had to be taking them at the studio, because I couldn't find any signs of them at home. I couldn't ask Judy directly. She became highly offended when I brought the matter up.

Yet, with the unspoken terror engulfing us, Judy and I continued outwardly functioning as happily married husband and wife.

Kay Thompson and Bill Spear, Sylvia Sidney and Carleton Alsop, Humphrey Bogart and Betty Bacall: these were the married couples we spent most time with. Warm and sophisticated people, they loved Judy almost as much as I did.

When we'd get together with them, I was content to let Judy take the spotlight. She was great at trading stories, but hers had the macabre twist of being horrendous stories about herself. She could discuss our most nerve-wracking and tragic experiences and make them sound funny, having me laughing too. But that was an adjustment I had to learn to make.

"Did I ever tell you about the first time I went to the nut house?" she piped up at a dinner party. I, who'd always had a sense of decorum, winced.

She would tell the story often. If this book were a film, the lines would progress through a montage of scenes in which I'm the central character. As the anecdote is told at party after party, I gradually loosen up. The anecdote comes to an end: ". . . and the reason I kept stumbling was that I was tripping over the croquet wickets!" I join in the laughter, relieved that I am able to enjoy the story Judy told on herself, it being vastly more tolerable than the anguish of living it.

There was another form of anguish going around Hollywood at the time. I was reminded of it when I saw *The Way We Were*, the 1973 Barbra Streisand-Robert Redford film. The Red menace. Arthur Laurents, who wrote the screenplay for that picture, must have been at the same masquerade party hosted by Groucho Marx at the height of the witch hunt. It obviously left him in the same grimly gray mood as it did Judy and me.

She wore her clown outfit from *The Pirate*, and I wore Gene Kelly's. Groucho's party never got off the ground. We sat around talking about the Unfriendly Ten, some of them being quite friendly in that same room, and the implications the House Un-American Activities Committee held for the rest of us. Here we all were, dressed in clown costumes, talking of our imminent death. What if we'd unconsciously included Communist dogma in our pictures? How would this affect our careers? It was a bizarre evening.

But Judy needn't have worried. Her pictures always fostered the American way.

Her latest one, *Easter Parade,* turned out to be such a huge hit that the studio insisted on re-teaming Judy and Fred. If delays and added expense had resulted from Judy's erratic behavior, they were forgotten. The millions being grossed at the box office saw to that.

The new project was to be another story about a theatrical team, as *Easter Parade* had been, this time in a contemporary setting. It was to be called *The Barkleys of Broadway.* There was never even a remote possibility that I would direct. It wasn't thought wise to have Judy and me working together. Besides, Charles Walters had done such a terrific job with *Easter Parade* that he deserved the new assignment. In that respect—rewarding employees for their successes by giving them more opportunities—Metro was exceedingly generous.

Judy found it impossible to go through the filming. She was mentally and physically exhausted, and dangerously thin. Ginger Rogers stepped in, to be re-teamed with Fred for the first time in years.

I stayed home a few days to console Judy, for her failure to do the picture came as a bitter blow. The studio had always waited. Now it chose not to.

Gradually, Judy had come to feel that all she represented in the studio's mind was top grosses. The paternal feeling Metro executives

197

held for her, she now felt, was all tied in with how much money she could bring in. Their genuine displays of affection for her were seen as a contrivance to get her to perform. Again she was betrayed, she insisted, and nothing I could say could dissuade her from that notion. In the back of her mind, she was concocting schemes of revenge for such treachery. She proceeded to get even not by lashing out, though those who were the targets of her caustic tongue felt otherwise. The anger turned inward, seething uncontrollably, threatening to destroy Judy herself . . . the sweetest and most perverse revenge of them all.

These were my most ineffectual times. Judy was unreasonable, refusing to listen to common sense. But there was still one father figure left who hadn't failed her: Carleton Alsop.

He and Sylvia had taken us both under their wings. They were immensely sane, and unselfishly giving.

Carleton had forever endeared himself to Judy during her last birthday celebration.

"What do you want for a present?" he asked her.

"Well, I've never met Ronald Colman. I'd like Ronald Colman."

Sure enough, Ronnie was just as eager to meet Judy, and he was carried into the party by the Alsops, enclosed in cellophane and tied up with a huge ribbon. Ronnie's sense of humor so captivated Judy and me that he and his wife Benita became good friends too.

On occasions when Judy felt she could cope with neither studio nor home, she would spend a few days as a guest of the Alsops. Sylvia would offer her gentle care, determined to fatten her up. When Judy felt she could again cope with life, she'd be back with us.

By this time, Judy was professing to hate our house on Evanview. She wanted much larger quarters. Her current psychiatrist felt it would be best if she could occasionally get away by herself. We proceeded to take a year's lease on a house at 10000 Sunset Boulevard. For the next few months, we would alternate living in the two houses. When we'd periodically separate, Judy would go over to the Sunset house and I'd stay at Evanview. Carleton would good-naturedly act as our intermediary. I was performing the same service whenever he was bickering with Sylvia.

He found himself conscripted for the same role in Judy's relations with Metro. Though she had an agency to represent her, they'd thrown their hands up in frustration, and there'd been no one to represent Judy's interests until Carleton temporarily sidetracked his own film producing career to help Judy.

It was a selfless act, for Carleton, if he got any money at all for his efforts, must have been ridiculously underpaid for his months and years of work.

He singlehandedly took on the studio, as well as ironing out our hopelessly tangled finances. Judy was now down to eighty pounds. Most days she couldn't get out of bed. She was perilously close to losing the battle.

Mayer was holding up $100,000 of Judy's salary, claiming this was the amount her chronic lateness and absence had added to her last film, as well as for the wasted pre-production expenses for *The Barkleys of Broadway*.

"I don't believe you have any legal claim for taking that penalty," Carleton told Mayer. "And I feel strongly enough about it that we may just have to establish that point in a law court."

Mayer was pensive. He wouldn't backtrack from his position. However, he offered an alternative.

"If you can get Judy to do one number in *Words and Music*," he told Carleton, "we'll pay her $50,000."

Carleton came over to tell us what Mayer had said.

"Yeah," Judy said. "I'll do it. Get me up, Pa."

"And so," Carleton says, "we took the glucose needle out of that thin little girl. It didn't take her long to pick up a song and learn a dance routine. She went in and belted the hell out of it. And then she had to go back to our house to collapse."

The picture, loosely based on the lives of Rodgers and Hart, continued shooting. Judy, thrilled that she'd again delivered, was optimistic again. Everything would work out, she knew. The drugs were pushed away, and she set out to catch up on the eating and drinking she'd been missing during her illness. In a few weeks, she gained almost thirty pounds.

Mayer called Alsop into his office again. "It's ridiculous for Judy to go off to this enormous applause and not come back," he said. "We'll give her another $50,000 if she'll do a second number."

And so Judy, who'd already done "Johnny One Note" for the picture, teamed up with Mickey Rooney for a duet, "I Wish I Were in Love Again."

"It's ridiculous when you see the picture," Carleton observes. "In the first song, Judy hardly casts a shadow. Then she comes back looking like Kate Smith."

Weight problems were to plague Judy from then on. Whenever she was at her ideal weight, she was most emotionally stable.

She started her next picture, *In the Good Old Summertime,* in good shape. But as the pressures of filming began mounting, she dropped weight, then gained it, her figure changing from near emaciation to Rubens-like roundness.

With so many problems at home, I probably couldn't have functioned at top efficiency in directing a major film. But I badly needed the distraction of work, and so I grasped at any minor assignments thrown my way. I seem to have directed every screen test filmed at Metro during 1948. I read piles of scripts, and sent off detailed observations on their strengths and weaknesses to producers and other directors who requested them.

I had no paranoid feelings that the studio was out to get me, that I was being kept idle because I was now anathema to many. Never was I made to feel that the studio had written me off as a director and had relegated me to being Judy's caretaker . . . and since I wasn't doing too good a job at it, I shouldn't expect anything more from them. Never was I made to feel that, and though I disclaim any symptoms of paranoia, I admit the possibility crossed my mind more than once.

If the decision rested with Judy, that I should sacrifice my career for hers, it was a step I was prepared to take. For as Judy's illness took hold, and her rationality took leave, it seemed a small price to pay. If only she could function again.

I attempted to preserve enough strength for both Judy and me to draw on, but I was often found lacking. My own self-assurance was at its lowest ebb. A treadmill was transporting us to disaster, and we were running double time in the opposite direction just to keep stationary.

With Judy's future in jeopardy and mine at a standstill, there seemed no solution. I was still drawing my weekly salary from Metro, but how long would that keep up?

Then, with no fanfare, the tide changed. The phone in my office rang one morning. It was Pan Berman. "Are you interested in directing *Madame Bovary?*" he asked.

"God, yes! When can we start?"

Pan was aware that I hadn't done anything for a year, but he didn't find that unusual. "It happens to everyone," he says today. "I don't think there were any real problems for you at the studio. I certainly wasn't instructed not to use you."

Thinking back to those days, Pan says he has no idea why he wanted to make *Madame Bovary* as a film. It didn't have the epic sweep of such

ever made her up was under the impression that Emma Bovary is a Javanese. Jennifer's whole face is brought out to a point by this make-up; the mouth is extremely bad—in shape, in color, and in extent of make-up—to such an extent that the mouth becomes her most predominant feature as in the case of Joan Crawford; the quality of her eyes, her most important attribute, is minimized; and all of the character is taken out of her face. I urge that whoever made her up *not* be used, because I cannot tell you how strongly I feel that this make-up is just awful, and precisely what is not indicated, either for Miss Jones or the role."

We bowed to his pleadings and brought in a new make-up artist.

David also discussed the advisability of writing the dialogue in such a way that, though Jennifer was American, her word patterns were influenced by the French. He also suggested that Rodolphe's part, played by Louis Jordan, be built up. He was thinking of the box office value for Louis in his next picture, I'm sure.

We started filming on December 16, the same day that Pan and I received a 25-page memorandum from David, in which he developed his long promised thoughts on motivations. He took the pro position, then the con, meeting himself somewhere in between. His arguments were lucid and logical on all counts, and totally impossible to implement. Pan and I decided to go with what we had. I accepted all of David's proposals that I agreed with, and discarded the rest. As Pan remembers, "We didn't do anything for Selznick we didn't want to do."

David had opposed the casting of Van Heflin as Charles Bovary, for he felt Van's offbeat good looks were romantic looking enough to keep Emma Bovary home. Knowing Van for the fine character actor that he was, I had no qualms in casting him for the role.

Charles deeply loves his wife, and he indulges her desire for fine things within the limitations of his finances. She sets out to redecorate their house, and she initiates a salon for the reading of poetry. When he cannot afford some of these indulgences, Emma turns to L'Heureux for help. He fawns over her, supporting all her grand designs, as she goes deeper into debt to him. At the end she is faced with ruin, and he takes almost a sexual pleasure in being the one to finally bring her down.

Emma Bovary has great aspirations for her husband. She hears of a revolutionary operation for curing club feet which she feels her husband can master, and inveighs upon him to perform the surgery on a dull village boy. The mayor of the town and the druggist also urge the operation, claiming that it will bring great honor to their town.

The novel described the failed operation, and the subsequent amputation of the boy's leg when gangrene set in. We thought this sequence would be too gory to be shown. The ensuing shame and sense of failure Emma felt could still be shown if Charles, realizing his limitations, refuses to perform the operation at the last moment.

The debacle is Emma's rationale for her first affair. The motion of events would proceed almost of their own volition.

I hit upon several devices to suggest the narcissism of Emma's character. The most obvious one was the use of mirrors. She first looks at herself in a plain mirror in the farmhouse, while making herself up for her doctor husband. Then at the ball she sees herself in a huge oval gilded mirror, surrounded by men, the romantic vision she imagines herself as being. Then, as she proceeds to her ruin, there is a cracked mirror in a room at Rouen in which she meets Léon.

The standout scene of the picture was the waltz. The dance was new to the period, and the sequence conveyed all the giddiness that enveloped Emma at the ball.

I told composer Miklos Rozsa what I wanted to create for the scene, and he wrote a neurotic waltz with an accelerating tempo that would work well with what we had in mind. All the action of the scene was shot to his pre-recorded music.

As Emma swirled around, the baroque mirror and chandeliers swung around with her. The camera movement suggested her dizziness and breathlessness, and explained why the host ordered the breaking of the windows, an action we retained from the book. At the same time, the husband is in the billiard room, getting cordially drunk. The sequence, shot in February 1949, was among the most difficult I'd ever directed.

We were in the midst of putting it together when we were informed that *Look* magazine was going to photograph all the stars currently working at the studio on Metro's largest sound stage. Jennifer, Van, and Louis took some time off to sit for the historic occasion. It was M-G-M's Silver Anniversary, and over one thousand film salesmen had come from all over the world to celebrate. Judy took special pains to look well for the shooting. She came home brimming with the adventures of the day.

"I was there with all the others, standing around, waiting to be told what to do," Judy told me. She noticed Kate Hepburn, in her de riguer shirt and slacks, coming over to her. Kate, taking in Judy's fussy flounces, drily observed, "I knew I'd be badly dressed, and I knew you'd be badly dressed. The only difference between us is that you took the time."

206

"And if that weren't enough to do me in," Judy chortled, "then the photographer told us we'd be sitting on these tiered platforms, in alphabetical order. So who do I have to sit next to? Ava Gardner. And that's enough to make any girl feel like Primo Carnera. Clark Gable was on Ava's other side. I think he was trying to make some time."

When Judy was very new at Metro, Roger Edens had written the "Dear Mr. Gable" introduction to "You Made Me Love You." It was one of Judy's earliest hits. Consequently, whenever Judy and Gable were at a studio function, she'd have to sing the song.

"I'd sing it time and again, so that I was sick of it," she said, "and each time I did Gable would try to squeeze out a tear. I guess he felt he had to show his appreciation, so he gave me a small gold bracelet . . . a *very* small gold bracelet. So here we were, tapping our toes, waiting for everything to be set up, and Gable showing off for Ava. He leaned across her and hissed . . . he actually hissed!

"Naturally I looked at him. 'God damn brat,' he said. 'You've ruined every one of my birthdays. They bring you out from behind the wallpaper to sing that song, and it's a pain in the ass.' Do you know, I've only begun to like him today . . . now that he's leveled with me?"

(Betty Comden and Adolph Green were writing the screenplay for *On the Town* at the time, and they offer their own memories of that momentous day. "There was an air of impending disaster," Adolph recalls. "Something was very wrong. We all sat down to this luncheon. I remember Kate and Judy were laughing about being a couple of misfits there. Judy was particularly funny about it. She had this way about her when an occasion was not coming off of getting off in a corner and having private laughs. We'd laugh too, and we were glad we were on the same wave length. Then the speeches started. Mayer got up and introduced all the people who'd been through thick and thin with him over the years . . . men like Benny Thau and Eddie Mannix. Then he had to introduce Dore Schary. He gave this very involved talk, trying to rationalize why Dore was now there. I don't remember what he said, but whatever it was, none of us were convinced."

("We probably felt the handwriting was on the wall," Betty continued. "There was something very thick in the air. I think the dessert became the symbol of it."

(Adolph describes it as ice cream molded in the shape of the M-G-M lion. "We sat through the long speeches, looking at all these lions melting.")

Jennifer, during filming, was getting deeper into the character. Some may have found her voice too thin for the part, but I felt she was the perfect Emma Bovary.

I felt this even more strongly after an incident at the studio. We were shooting the scene with Emma's daughter and the nurse. Emma sweeps in after her first adultery, and as a means of atoning for her sin, smothers the little girl with attention. But the child, sensing something different in her mother, wants nothing to do with her. The maid takes over, leaving Emma alone with her guilt.

To get the right reaction from the little girl, she was not permitted to meet Jennifer, being kept totally away. The nurse rehearsed the scene with her.

I instructed Jennifer, when it came time to film, to take away the little girl's favorite pair of red shoes. The action came as a total surprise to the child, and we got the required reaction. The little girl, however, hadn't distinguished between the real and the make believe, and continued turning her back on Jennifer. This wouldn't do in Emma's death scene, after her taking poison. The child was supposed to extend her arms to Emma. Now Jennifer had to court the little girl. She had her to lunch in her dressing room; she brought her little presents. Came time for rehearsal. The little girl still refused to have anything to do with Jennifer. "She took my red shoes," she glared accusingly. It was more than Jennifer could bear. She fled the set in tears. I set out in pursuit.

"She doesn't like me," Jennifer cried. "She thinks I'm terrible. Nobody likes me."

"Jennifer," I said soothingly, "we planned it this way. You have to work with her and have a little patience." She came around, but her first instinct had been the slightly neurotic reaction to run and cry.

We finished the picture with no more incidents at the studio. I couldn't say the same thing about the goings on at home.

I'm appalled by my naiveté at the time. I thought love would show us the way out of the quagmire. My most serious mistake was misinterpreting Judy's intense infatuations and violent swinging of moods as an exuberance for life. I was blind to the compulsiveness of her behavior for too long a time.

And so was the studio. Her failure to report on time and her absences from the set were interpreted as the willful tantrums of a spoiled child.

I was similarly innocent about drugs. Barbiturates and Benzedrine were, after all, a cure for the stresses of white collar life. They were "respectable." Too late, I learned they were more addictive and more toxic than the opiates used by the low-life junkies.

Her hysterical cries for help in the midst of her periodic traumas were answered. But Judy's need was just as desperate during the time she wasn't taking drugs. She'd been raised on fear and the threat of imminent desertion if she didn't dance to her mother's bidding. Wherever she turned, Judy felt betrayed.

It took me some time to find out that the emergencies—her screams of pain and shortness of breath—were due to a very obvious cause. No doctor ever told me why. She was suffering the agonies of withdrawal, and sadly she didn't tell me . . . Judy probably didn't know herself. I had taken her tangible demons for mental phantoms. She would come through the ordeal, with the help of a combination sedative and analgesic administered by a physician who came to our house. Judy would awake from the siege, renewed, and with invigoration and anticipation. Life for her was beautiful on those mornings when she awoke from the nightmares of the previous days. For me, it was a sweet but exhausting victory, the round the clock vigil, leaving me red-eyed and with nerves shot. But my optimism was guarded, for I knew pills were hidden around the house for use during future emergencies.

Metro had recently bought *Annie Get Your Gun* for Judy, paying the highest amount ever spent on a film property. Busby Berkeley, who'd worked on many of Judy's early pictures, was to direct. But Judy refused to work with him. She imagined past affronts, and she could be enormously malevolent with other people. (She couldn't understand, in return, the animosity of others, that jobs had been lost and pictures left asunder because of her.)

Charles Walters was brought in to direct. He and Judy always got on well together.

The pre-production, which was to total well over one million dollars, proceeded.

By this time, *Madame Bovary* was edited, scored, and dubbed, and ready for preview reaction. I was now in the midst of discussion with Arthur Freed on his latest project, a popular entertainment based on the music of George and Ira Gershwin, to be called *An American in Paris*.

The *Madame Bovary* previews in Santa Monica and Pasadena were enormously satisfying. Audience reaction cards rated the picture and Jennifer's performance as outstanding or excellent. But Pan wasn't impressed.

"I've never found preview cards very effective," he says today. "They're less important to me than the audience reaction. I'm not interested in what a person writes on a card afterwards. I don't believe much in the audience becoming critics. I want to know how they're reacting while the picture's running. I'll sit down in front with them, and I try to base my own awareness on them. If I get terribly depressed, it's because the audience is too. If I enjoy myself, it's because the audience is doing it to me. I have to react to the picture apart from the script and my involvement in it. Sitting with the audience becomes my first viewing of the picture."

We relied on Pan's reactions for many of the changes made before the picture was released in late summer. For I hadn't been able to take in the previews. There were problems at home, and I couldn't get away.

Judy had completed the pre-recording of her songs for *Annie Get Your Gun,* and had started filming. But she was in terrible condition. Her weight was down to ninety pounds, and her days were spent in an irrational haze.

And yet, in this groggy desperation, she continued taking more pills. I caught her using them, and took them away from her. Her reaction was enormously angry, and for the next few days her treatment of me was cold and contemptuous.

There was no way she could keep up with the production schedule which, with the threatening inroads of television, had to be minutely programmed. She was physically unable to appear. The studio suspended Judy, borrowing Betty Hutton from Paramount to replace her. George Sidney was brought in to direct, and Charles Walters too found himself out of a job.

Judy's mother, who'd been making a career of her own of "keeping Judy in line," found that her salary as a studio consultant ended with her daughter's suspension. It was only then that she was told her handsome income had never been paid by the studio. It came from Judy's generosity, for her mother's salary was withheld from her own. I never knew how Mrs. Gilmore reacted to the disclosure, but being a proud woman, she must have been furious to discover what the studio felt was her true worth.

The suspension wasn't a callous action. Too much money was at stake for the picture to rest on Judy's wobbly shoulders. Mayer was as concerned about her as we all were.

"What do you think should be done?" he asked Carleton Alsop.

210

"Why don't you get her away from all the sycophants and the doctors who give her these pills?" Carleton asked.

"Next thing I knew," he remembers, "I was on the train with a very sick girl, taking her to a hospital in Boston."

The head psychiatrist at Peter Bent Brigham Hospital met with them when Carleton and Judy arrived on that late spring day.

Carleton offered him some very sensible advice while Judy was checking in. "I think it would be better if you told Judy you were a neurosurgeon and not a psychiatrist. She's wily and can outcraft you. Judy has this jungle intelligence, this animal cunning. It's like trying to help a drunk across the street. He stumbles and weaves, and as soon as he's on the other side, he straightens up and laughs at you."

The psychiatrist nodded his head.

"Did you ever treat a star?" Carleton continued.

"No," the psychiatrist answered.

"Well, you'd better think about it a little bit. Because you can't work on the premise as so many of you do that you're going to change her personality and make her Mrs. Vincente Minnelli, Housewife. You're dealing with a girl who is sick . . . and while sick she's making half a million dollars a year. You're going to gamble on losing that, plus all those millions of people who will hate you for destroying her talent."

"I never thought of it that way," the psychiatrist answered.

Carleton visited Judy several times every day.

"Pop, get me out of here!" she cried in desperation as she began suffering the pangs of withdrawal.

"Listen," he said. "It isn't your money, and it isn't mine. It's the studio's. Let them spend it."

Judy could appreciate putting something over on the studio. She was temporarily mollified . . . she could bear the pain.

The next visit, Carleton found Judy under the bed in her hospital room, screaming in agony.

He forced himself to speak cold-heartedly. "If you need pills, this hospital is full of them. But if you can get over it, fine. If you can't, I'm going out to buy Christmas carols. We'd better start rehearsing now."

Gradually, Judy's will brought her through. She began to see the world around her. Carleton told her he wanted to take her to visit at Children's Hospital, a center in Boston for rheumatic children. "I can't go," Judy protested. "It's too soon." Carleton nearly dragged her there. As soon as they arrived and Judy noticed how thrilled the children were to see her, she melted. "I loved feeling I could help somebody else for a change," she later told me.

Judy was so recovered that it was felt that Liza could fly to Boston to spend some time with her. The visit coincided with Judy's birthday, and she was thrilled to have Liza with her. Soon after, I made a couple of trips to visit Judy. We didn't do anything exciting, just going to a couple of night ball games. But Judy was ebullient, and looking forward to coming home. A visit by Arthur Freed was partially responsible. He told Judy the studio wanted her to star in *Summer Stock*.

It was now August. *Madame Bovary* was in national release, and critical reaction was enthusiastic.

Time magazine, in its review of August 15, 1949, found the picture "a fascinating close-up of provincial manners and morals in 19th Century France. By the same device (court proceedings against Flaubert) it deftly short-circuits the Johnston office, incorporating its apologia into its action.

"One memorable scene—a whirling, overheated ball at a local château—is a wonderfully skillful projection of Emma's half-swooning sense of her own seductiveness.

"Miss Jones, in her best picture to date, manipulates Emma's moods and caprices with sensitive dexterity. Hardly ever out of sight of the cameras, she gives a performance that is hardly ever out of focus, a feat that even the finicky Flaubert could admire."

Bosley Crowther in the New York *Times* on August 26 wrote: "Robert Ardrey has put it together into a literate and playable script and Vincente Minnelli has kept it moving with a smooth and refined directorial touch. The high point of his achievement, indeed, is a ballroom scene which spins in a whirl of rapture and crashes in a shatter of shame. In this one sequence, the director has fully visualized his theme."

To add to the triumph, Judy was back from Boston. Metro had paid nearly $40,000 for her treatment, and had brought Dr. George Thorn, the physician in chief at the hospital, to help Judy adjust again to Hollywood life. Carleton kept repeating he felt she was returning too soon, but he was paid little attention. Dr. Thorn thought it was all right. The studio wanted her for a new picture. And I wanted to be together again with my wife.

If it was true we'd been separated before her trip to Boston, as the columnists maintained, it was equally true that we were now reconciled and ready to face the world, as well as each other, as husband and wife. Judy's condition was as normal as it would ever be. Her only medication

212

was a series of glucose injections prescribed by her physician to keep up her energy.

She'd returned just in time for the studio's celebration of Ethel Barrymore's seventieth birthday. Louis B. Mayer gave his usual maudlin talk at the studio luncheon. Miss Barrymore tolerated the ordeal with her usual dignity.

That night, George Cukor hosted the *true* birthday party for Miss Barrymore and her chosen friends. Judy and I were honored to be included.

Constance Collier, Billie Burke, Kate Hepburn, Lionel Barrymore, Spencer Tracy, and Sammy Colt—Miss Barrymore's son—were in the group.

George, justly famous as a host, had gone all out for Miss Barrymore. He'd set up a big U-shaped table in his dining room to accommodate all the guests.

He asked Judy to sing "Happy Birthday." She hadn't sung in months, and I was struck by a momentary fear that her voice might be gone. Judy read my thoughts, and smiled over at me. Her *a capella* version was suffused with emotion. There was no need for concern. Her voice was indestructible. The song ended and Miss Barrymore looked lovingly at Judy. She placed her hand in front of her mouth and blew a kiss over to Judy. It was a lovely evening, and a perfect way to renew our life together.

The public also had to know that all was well with the studio. Mayer and his wife invited Judy and me to accompany them for an evening at the Hollywood Bowl. It took on the trappings of a state occasion.

Mayer came to our house a few days later to check on Judy's progress. Judy, as usual, wound him around her finger. She could explain away any transgression. He emerged from their meeting, his eyes tearful.

"The cure is very simple," he told me. "All this girl needs is to be needed and loved." He'd be tearing out his hair in a couple of weeks, after a few phone calls from Judy at four in the morning.

He could only blame himself when Judy took him at his word. "I love you like a father, Judy," he said. "You know you can turn to me whenever things go wrong."

14   An American in Paris

ARTHUR FREED (Producer)*: Well, pictures start in strange ways. Ira Gershwin is one of my closest friends, and I grew up with George Gershwin in New York when I was first writing songs. I used to spend a lot of time over at the Gershwins'. I still spend every Saturday night with Ira at his house, and we either play poker or pool. So one night I was with Ira Gershwin playing pool and afterwards, it was about two in the morning, we sat talking about pictures and I said, "Ira, I've always wanted to make a picture about Paris. How about selling me the title *An American in Paris?*" He said, "Yes, if you use all Gershwin music." I said, "I wouldn't use anything else, that's the object." This was the start of the idea. Now I didn't know what I wanted to do. The only thing I said to Ira was I wanted to use George's compositions and his title *An American in Paris* and maybe do a ballet. I didn't even know who was going to be in it, but I knew it would have to be a dancer, either Fred Astaire or Gene Kelly.

We started a deal for the music with Ira and the Gershwin estate. The main thing, first, was to find characters. I remembered seeing a layout in *Life* magazine of the GIs studying in Paris on the GI Bill. I thought that would be a great character for our leading role because George Gershwin studied art in Paris. That made the character that Kelly would eventually play a little bit of Gershwin. So I had that character. Then, for the character played by Oscar Levant, who was, as you know, always very closely as-

* Donald Knox, *The Magic Factory,* Praeger Publishers, New York, 1973.

214

sociated with George, I took David Diamond. Dave was a musician I know who always got scholarships and went to Europe but never had enough money to come back. He knew the Gershwins too. So that's the character we made Levant.

Now was the time to find a writer for the project. I talked to Vincente Minnelli about it and mentioned Alan Jay Lerner. Vincente was crazy about the idea, so I tackled Alan. I didn't think I'd get him, because Alan likes to write the songs. But, when I told him the idea and the characters, he said, "I'd love to do it," and he did. Then we decided on doing the ballet. Now, Gene Kelly is more of a ballet dancer than Fred, so that decided that. So we had all those initial elements. I told Mayer what I was doing. I'd have lunch or dinner with him every Sunday at his house. He loved the title.

Arthur's reminiscences in *The Magic Factory,* which was published shortly after his death in 1973, support my feeling that, as no one sets out to make a bad picture, rarely under the old studio system did anyone set out to make a classic. *An American in Paris* certainly wasn't designed as such. Arthur and I, in our earliest discussions about the proposed picture, were planning a solid commercial entertainment aimed at a mass audience. Yet all the elements meshed so perfectly that what was originally planned as another slick musical became a standard by which all other such pictures are measured.

Mayer also had no concept what could be accomplished by the film. Judy and I would be among the group in compulsory attendance at his Santa Monica beach house on Sundays. Most of us would sit around outside cracking sarcasms while Mayer and his cronies played cards inside.

Occasionally his wife Lorena would persuade Mayer to come out and mix with his other guests. These were the times he'd share nuggets of wisdom with us . . . as he did on one Sunday when *An American in Paris* was still in the planning stages.

"You should copy the color in *Coney Island,* Vincente," he told me. "In fact, all our color pictures should have that look." (And they should all be as profitable, it went without saying, as that Betty Grable film had been for Twentieth Century-Fox.)

Pan Berman was nearby, and as Mayer continued reviewing the troops, he whispered to me, "That picture has the most garish and vivid and ugly color in the history of the movie business." I laughed in agreement.

215

Pan's antipathy toward Mayer started when he came to the studio. Before then, they'd shared mutual respect.

"What can you do with him?" Pan complained to me one day. "He calls you into his office and starts telling you the kind of stories you ought to make. He writes them on the spot and acts them out for you . . . getting down on his hands and knees and praying and crying . . . there are only so many pictures you can make about mother love. He's the biggest ham in America. If he sees he's not getting over to you, he gets sick or complains of shortness of breath or falls on the floor clutching his heart. If he still hasn't won the point, he'll call for the doctor. In the meantime, you've wasted half the day. You just can't get out of his office without hurting his feelings." Consequently, Pan worked through general manager Eddie Mannix as much as possible.

We might have been more tolerant of Mayer if we'd known he'd soon be out as head of the studio. For if he lacked innate taste, he had the ability to entrust a picture to his underlings and keep his nose out of it. Later events showed us how rare this talent was.

Alan Lerner was already in Hollywood, under the same loose arrangement that brought me to the studio, giving the business a try. If he liked it, he'd stay. Alan had already written the screenplay for *Royal Wedding* when Arthur approached him with the idea for *An American in Paris*.

He proceeded to work on the screenplay. Until it was ready, my attentions shifted elsewhere.

Judy has spent three months recuperating before starting *Summer Stock* in November 1949. We were getting to know each other, and Liza was getting to know Judy, all over again.

The dual residences continued. Most of our time was now spent in the house on Sunset. We entertained often, and Judy's weight began inching upward . . . happily I felt.

When it came time to report to Charles Walters and producer Joe Pasternak, she was fifteen pounds overweight. She slimmed down as shooting progressed, but her difficulties were still much with her. It would take six months before the movie was completed. There would often be days when she had to stay in bed. I'd receive a phone call from our housekeeper in the midst of a business conference, and off I'd tear to handle the emergency. My colleagues at the studio were enormously patient and tactful, and I was grateful.

Judy knew that with Gene Kelly as her co-star, the picture would be stylish and pleasant. But she still had a hard time swallowing the chestnut

216

of a story, about putting on a show in a barn, and its conventionality depressed her.

We discussed her approach to the picture. "If I can just get one great number across, I won't mind the story too much," she said.

I suggested she try a bit of costuming I'd seen Tamara Geva wear on the stage. Judy fell in love with the idea. She sang "Get Happy" wearing a man's black fedora tipped rakishly over one eye, a man's tuxedo jacket altered to fit her form and a leotard beneath which revealed her great-looking legs. The number was a smash, and Judy was ecstatic.

On the heels of our last collaboration, Pan Berman came to me with another picture, a comedy called *Father of the Bride*. The Edward Streeter novel was a current best seller, and Pan picked up the film rights. Frances Goodrich and Albert Hackett, who'd written *The Pirate,* were already working on the script.

The idea of doing a comedy based on a real situation appealed to me very much. The picture could be finished long before we started production on the Gershwin picture. I gladly agreed to do it.

By this time, Dore Schary, as vice-president in charge of production, was taking on more of Mayer's responsibilities. He was also assuming prerogatives Mayer had never presumed to take.

Pan Berman recalls the day that Dore called him into his office. "I ran into Jack Benny at a party last night," Dore told Pan. "He told me he'd like to do *Father of the Bride.* I said, 'Great! Marvelous! We'd love to have you. You've got the part.' "

"Dore," Pan said, "Jack Benny is a wonderful personality, but he simply won't do. I know we don't even have to ask Minnelli, but go ahead if you want to."

"Why not?" Dore asked.

"Because it's a comedy drama about a man whose heart breaks because he loves his daughter and is about to lose her. It's not a joke. It's not a funny thing. The laughs come out of sadness and reality. We could never do it with Jack."

"Then you've got to get me out of this," Dore answered. "You've got to make a test of Jack Benny to show my good faith."

"But that's a terrible thing to do," Pan countered. "To ask us to make a test we know won't end in anything is very cruel to us. And it would be very unkind to Jack to work to no avail without knowing it."

"Well, you've got to make a test of Jack," Dore answered. "I feel confident once you do it you'll change your minds."

"Look, Dore," Pan said, "we're not going to change our minds. If you insist we make the test, we'll make the test. But if you insist we use Mr. Benny, you can tear up my contract right now."

"Naturally," Dore answered, "the way you want it is the way it's going to go."

Pan was placated, but he still had to do the test. Or rather I did.

When I was so informed, I told Pan, "That's a terrible thing. I'll have to make a good test, and I'll have to work very hard on it. Jack is my friend."

Both Jack and I worked our hardest on the scene. I kept his comic reactions and double takes down to a minimum, and he came through very well. It was a fine test and technically correct. It had only one failing. His reading lacked the conviction underneath, that only a highly gifted actor like Spencer Tracy could supply.

We then went to Ben Thau.

"Who do you have in mind?" he asked.

"Spencer Tracy."

"That's out of the question. He's absolutely refused to do the picture, and has gone to New York."

"Is there any reason why I can't talk to him about it?" I asked.

"Certainly not," Thau answered, "if you want to talk to him as a friend."

I called Kate, and told her what I had in mind. She invited me over to dinner after Spencer returned to California.

"With you," I told him, "this picture could be a little classic of a comedy. Without you, it's nothing."

Spencer was delighted. He'd heard other people were being tested for the part, and he thought we weren't interested in him. That's why he'd refused to do it. All he'd wanted was to be wanted.

Once Spencer accepted, the rest of the cast fell into place. It took no great imagination to cast a beautiful young Elizabeth Taylor as the bride. Joan Bennett, with the same coloring as Elizabeth, seemed a logical choice to play the mother.

We started filming in January of 1950. Judy was still working on *Summer Stock*.

Occasionally we'd drive to the studio together. More often, a driver would pick up Judy while I was still in bed. Times were difficult for the ladies of the M-G-M Stock Company. They'd have to be at the studio by five or six in the morning for make-up and hair dressing. Preliminary work started in their dressing rooms, but all would meet up in the hair styling department headed by Sidney Guilarof. Judy might arrive there to find Greer Garson, Hedy Lamarr, Lana Turner, and Ava Gardner sitting under their respective dryers. One of them might feel that Sidney or his associates were spending more time on another actress' hair, but rarely was any resentment voiced. How could one actress pull rank on another, who was just as rich and talented? At that ungodly hour, it's a wonder there was so little friction among all those diverse temperaments.

There wasn't any on our set either. *Father of the Bride* was the shortest and sweetest experience I'd ever encountered. Working for the first time with a brilliant cinematographer named John Alton and a cast that flew through its paces, the picture was shot in twenty-eight days.

Spencer was an inspiration. His instincts were infallible. He knew how to throw the unimportant things away, and he knew how to create the illusion of throwing the important things away too, so that they were inscribed in your mind. His way of speaking made you feel you'd stumbled on a great truth. You saw real life reflected in his face . . . and also strength.

There wasn't a better man at comedy. He wasn't a mugger, at least never in scenes with other actors. The facial contortions came when he was alone and unobserved.

One scene in particular revealed his brilliant comic flair. His daughter and her fiancé have had a fight. The boy friend comes to the house, but the daughter won't see him. The father takes over. He knows exactly how the situation should be handled. He patronizingly suggests the young man come back another time, speaking with the quiet authority of a man who, after all, should know his own daughter better than anyone. She simply cannot see him now. But before the young man can take leave, the girl accidentally enters the room. That's all they need. They rush into each other's arms. The father is left standing there, the unwanted third man, trying to figure out a way to gracefully exit.

The brilliant way Spencer played the scene convinced Thau and the other executives. Jack had done the same scene for his test, and the contrast between the two performances was easily discernible to even the most uneducated eye. Spencer's reading was the essence of comedy, because it was achingly true. And he knew how well he'd done it, for no one had greater reason to feel secure about his ability than Spencer.

His genius had been acquired at enormous cost, and unfortunately without a mellowing serenity in his later years. His Irish foreboding and sense of doom were deeply instilled.

Spencer often talked of the theater in the 1920s, when it was a badge of honor for an actor to be a drunk. He must have been one of the most meritorious. "I used to check into a hotel room with a case of booze and barricade myself inside," he told me. "I'd stay there alone until I drank the case up. Then I'd go back to work."

"Didn't you get together for drinks with friends?" I asked, thinking he should have had the Irish gift of conviviality.

"Couldn't risk it," he answered. "Too many of my cronies had been thrown out windows for me to take the chance again." Spencer's bag apparently wasn't quiet conversation.

But those days had pretty much ended and Spencer was living the lonely life in his rented house, going home to his semi-estranged wife and children on weekends. It was a well-known arrangement no one would presume to ask him about.

He, Kate, and I went one night to a screening at the studio, where *The Pearl* was run for us. The picture was about a Mexican fisherman who discovers a pearl, which he believes will release his wife and son from poverty and ignorance. It didn't seem as great a classic to us as had been touted.

Spencer, in particular, couldn't identify with the story. "It's a simple tale," he said, "a *very* simple tale." And too simple for a man of his complex nature.

Father of the Bride was edited and dubbed long before Judy finished *Summer Stock*. It was ready for release just as she was finishing her film, and it took off like a rocket. Pan immediately started talking of making a sequel.

"Easily the funniest picture in town," Thomas Pryor wrote in the New York *Times* on June 4, 1950. "The customary exaggeration that is necessary in most comedies is almost completely absent in *Father of the Bride*. There was no need for it here because there is a vast amount of latent comedy in family life, provided one has the capacity to recognize it.

"There have been other pictures of similar nature, but none that we can recall at the moment which possessed the authority of *Father of the Bride*. Authority is a rather formidable word to use in discussing a comedy, but in our opinion the success of *Father of the Bride* is due in some considerable measure to the reasonable manner in which the subject is treated."

I was exhilarated with the reaction, as was Judy. We'd finally developed a career pattern—separate though it was—under which we thought we both could function.

220

Judy was now getting ready to report for *Royal Wedding* with Fred Astaire. One of the screen tests I'd directed during my one-year leave from picture-making was Sarah Churchill's, and she'd been cast as the royal half of the romantic team opposite Fred.

Judy seemed to be testing herself and her endurance, determined to keep busy. The studio was going to find its financing of her treatment in Boston well justified.

Filming was to start the first week of June 1950. But the rigors of the last picture were too much for Judy. She didn't show up as scheduled.

Judy and I were both at Carleton's house when a call came from Mayer.

"What," Mayer wanted to know, "is the meaning of this?"

"You're treating this girl like a draft horse," Carleton told Mayer.

"That's right, the sons of bitches," Judy exclaimed. "You tell him, Pa." Carleton put his hand over the mouthpiece. "Shut up," he told Judy, "they're paying you $300,000 a year to perform. Don't believe what I say."

Carleton was instructed to report the next day to Mayer's office. When he arrived, he was given an official warning to deliver to Judy.

He got on the telephone and informed us. Judy was on one extension, I on the other. She couldn't understand the studio's action. She'd tried so hard to show her good intentions. But it wasn't cause for undue concern. It would be ironed out.

We arranged to meet Carleton for lunch at the studio. Judy's last words to him before hanging up were words of instruction. "Make them treat me like they do Greer Garson," Judy told him, "instead of like the hunchback little girl Mr. Mayer discovered at Cal-Neva."

Carleton hadn't told us the warning had been delivered by messenger, instead of by Ben Thau, as was the usual procedure. He took the paper to Mayer's office. Carleton had been ushered right in to see the head man in the past. This time, he was sent downstairs to the office of the corporate attorney.

"I am the legal representative of Metro-Goldwyn-Mayer and you are the representative of Miss Garland," the lawyer said. "I hereby hand you her suspension."

Carleton was thinking of what he would tell us now that he had two slips of paper to present to Judy instead of one.

"I wouldn't be much of a man or much of a friend of Miss Garland's," he told the attorney, "if I didn't tell you what I thought." And then he was stuck . . . he didn't know *what* he thought.

The attorney didn't give him long to think of the right words. "Before you go into that," he said sarcastically, "I'd like to show you a set of books where it can show that Miss Garland's inability to get into wardrobe and make-up on time has added at least twenty percent to the cost of her pictures."

"I'd love to see that set," Carleton answered angrily, "if you show me that other set, where I can prove this girl has earned the studio thirty-six million dollars since she was twelve years old. God willing, if I raise a delinquent, she should bring me in that kind of a bankroll."

Carleton let that thought sink in before continuing.

"I don't need to tell you that her sole education has been in your gentle hands. I don't need to remind you of the suicides of John Gilbert and other people who worked here. I don't have to tell you of several people you now have under contract who have become alcoholics or mental cases under your protection.

"But I can remind you that Mr. Mayer has race horses, and if one of them pulls up lame, it gets the finest veterinarian in the world. I want to find out if you will do as much for a human being as he does for a goddamn race horse."

Carleton stalked out of the office, slamming the door.

Naturally, I sided with Judy. But I could see both sides. The suspension was the start of days of crisis.

The studio gave every indication it had washed its hands of her. Mayer was unavailable. His power had dwindled, and Judy was probably an embarrassment, one he couldn't protect any longer.

Ten days after her suspension, on June 20, Judy and I, at home on Evanview, were quietly discussing the change in our fortunes. She was cogent and sensible in her opinions, which we were sharing with Judy's secretary, Myrtle Tully. We were weighing some of the options open to her—personal appearances, Broadway shows, a contract with another studio—but none of them interested her much. "Don't worry," she said wearily, "I'll think of something."

She matter-of-factly rose to go to the bathroom. I continued chatting with Myrtle. Suddenly a scream filled the air. I went rushing to the bathroom. The door was locked from the inside. Judy screamed, "Leave me alone! I want to die!" I tried breaking down the door, but I wasn't strong enough. Finally, I picked up a heavy chair and broke through. The mirror on the other side of the door shattered as I charged in.

Judy was holding a broken water glass. Blood glistened on her neck. I took the glass from her, and Myrtle tearfully put her arms around Judy.

222

One of the staff called a doctor, then Carleton, who came running over from his house.

I was in shock, yelling hysterically. What had I done? How had I failed her?

Carleton did the only thing he could do. He slugged me. That brought me out of it. There was no time to indulge my own sorry feelings. We had to help Judy.

In our panic we decided that Judy should not be discovered in the Evanview house. She was officially a resident of the house on Sunset, and we would have to move her there immediately. I don't know why we thought this was necessary at the time.

Carleton went running down the hill to call an ambulance for Judy. He didn't want to tie up our phones. He entered the Mocambo on Sunset. A gossip columnist accosted him. "It's on every news desk in town that Judy tried to kill herself," he said. "Is it true?"

"Not that I know of," Carleton said evenly. How could they have found out so soon, when it had only happened five minutes before? The puzzle was never explained.

He headed uphill to our house after making the call. Reporters were already surrounding the building. The ambulance idea wouldn't work. We bundled Judy up and put her on the floor of the car, and drove her to the house on Sunset, where the doctor was waiting. He looked at the injury. "It's only a scratch," he said. "But suicide attempts are desperate cries for help. You must realize that." We, of course, did.

A publicity man came from the studio as soon as the news was out. In the early reports I denied the incident, for I wanted to protect Judy at all costs. The publicist talked to us, then walked outside with Carleton. A reporter, standing in the driveway, asked, "What happened?"

The publicist made a cutting gesture across his throat. Carleton pulled him into the house. "You stupid son-of-a-bitch! All that's done is put them on twenty-four-hour duty." The man became offended and walked out. From here on, Carleton would be functioning as our intermediary with the press as well.

The newspapers forever destroyed Judy's wholesome image the following day, their black banners revealing to the world that she was, in truth, a tortured and complicated creature. Though their viewpoint was sympathetic, they reveled in details, supplying them even when they had no way of knowing them.

Florabel Muir, in the New York *Daily News,* was particularly omniscient and lugubrious: "Judy Garland, despondent over being suspended by her studio, attempted suicide last night by slashing her throat with the shattered edge of a waterglass in the bathroom of her pink alabaster mansion.

"The wound was superficial. No stitches were required.

"The 29-year-old actress, hollow-eyed, highly nervous and suffering from physical and mental exhaustion, was resting under a doctor's care today . . ." Ad nauseum.

Suddenly Metro was being accused of being responsible for Judy's attempted suicide. They were forced to issue a statement. It told of her suspension from *Annie Get Your Gun,* and of their subsequent financing of medical treatment in Boston.

"Following completion of *Summer Stock,*" the statement continued, "and after consultation with the doctors in Boston, the studio placed her on vacation status. After a rest of two months, Miss Garland reported that she was feeling fine, and physicians of her own choosing considered her all over her difficulties.

"Some time thereafter, we learned that June Allyson, who was to appear in *Royal Wedding,* was to have a baby. With assurances from Miss Garland that she was in top physical condition, we submitted the script to her and she appeared most eager in accepting the role, promising there would be no difficulties.

"Within a matter of a few days, delays already had begun, and these delays increased as time went on during rehearsals. She was then told by the producer that a warning letter was to be sent to her, but that he would ask to have it stopped if she would promise to co-operate. But the delays continued.

"With the responsibility and in justice to other artists, the studio had only one recourse, which was to take Miss Garland out of the picture, assume whatever losses were involved, recast it and go ahead.

"The substitution of an artist in any picture is never made on an arbitrary basis, and certainly a person of Miss Garland's talent is not easily replaced.

"The replacement is not a hasty move, prompted by pique or irritation. It is the last resort, arrived at with great regret after all other means have failed."

Carleton received a call from a wire service reporter in the middle of the night, asking if there would be a counterstatement. (He called him Mr. All-slop, Carleton remembers.)

"I haven't read it," Carleton answered. "Would you read it to me?"

The reporter did. "Now will you comment?" he asked when he

finished. What could Carleton say? The facts as the studio had accurately painted them were black and indefensible. But he wanted to protect Judy's reputation, as we all did.

"Well, no," Carleton thoughtfully responded. "I wasn't paying too much attention."

There was a pause on the other end of the line. Carleton filled it in. "But if you get a chance, reread that statement," he suggested. "And see if you can find anything that extends any sympathy or concern for Miss Garland."

"By God!" the reporter exclaimed. "The sons-of-bitches!" The resulting story blasted the studio—it had broader shoulders and could better carry the blame—and balanced the picture somewhat.

The Sunset house was still surrounded by reporters. We decided that as the hundreds of flowers and packages began arriving, they would be sent over to the Evanview house. Most of the reporters followed the delivery trucks there, but they weren't fooled by the ruse for long.

Carleton, noting my continued agitation, put me to work. "They're going to be outside for a long time. You want them to go easy on Judy, right?"

Of course.

"Better set up a bar and a buffet table in the driveway." I found myself catering what must have been the next thing to a wake.

The reporters stayed forever. Among them was a woman who wasn't going to leave until Judy told her directly—and exclusively—why she'd done such a terrible thing. She was backing Carleton against a wall one morning when he counter-attacked. He'd always wondered why the woman wore long-sleeved blouses. He grabbed one arm, jerked up the sleeve. He discovered several scars on the reporter's wrist. He looked meaningfully at her. She walked away, and from that point on her treatment of Judy was also sympathetic.

Kate Hepburn ran the gauntlet of the newspaper people, arriving to visit Judy as soon as she found out what happened. She walked defiantly through the crowd of reporters. "Don't you dare take my picture!" she commanded. The reporters drew back. "Don't you have anything better to do? Why don't you get back to work?"

She came into the bedroom, swept past me, and lit into Judy. "Now listen," she said. "You're one of the three greatest talents in the world. And your ass has hit the gutter. There's no place to go but up. Now, goddammit. Do it!" Judy smiled weakly back. Now that Kate had her attention, all her solicitude came pouring out.

"Your only trouble is your talent," Kate continued. "You can't cope with it, and others don't know how to treat it. It's difficult all the way around."

Throughout the day, Kate was there to offer comfort and advice. She and Judy discussed every conceivable subject . . . including Kate's own ups and downs.

"It was a bitter blow," she told us, "a very bitter blow, when the exhibitors labeled me Box Office Poison. I had to show them."

Her pictures in the late 1930s had been uniformly bad, and the tide didn't seem to be changing, so Kate decided to go back to the theater. Singlehandedly she put *The Philadelphia Story* together, hiring Philip Barry to write the play and negotiating with Lawrence Langner of the Theatre Guild to produce it.

"Philip's first two acts were marvelous, but we were still waiting for the final act. We were getting close to rehearsal time. Larry finally said he was going to have to call Philip. 'Don't you dare,' I told him. 'I'll walk right out if you do.' I made Larry wait. And I waited too . . . for days. Finally Philip called. I sensed that he felt guilty about not delivering on time.

"'How are things going?' he asked. I answered, 'Oh, Philip, it's terrible. We can't get the right casting. We're having trouble getting the Shubert Theatre. Nothing's going right.' Well, he perked right up . . . perked right up! For he found out we were in trouble too, and he wasn't responsible. I guess this was the right psychology, because he seemed to gather strength from that. The onus was off him, you see, and we got the last act within a week. Nothing to it, really. Just have to know how to treat creative people. God knows most people have never known how to treat me!" And with that, Kate let out with her distinctive chortle.

She left by the back door, jumping over a fence to avoid the reporters. Once they discovered what she'd done, they set out in pursuit. It must have cut a comic scene, Kate walking rapidly down Sunset Boulevard, with a carful of newsmen inching along behind her, calling out questions about Judy's condition and state of mind. Kate ignored them and kept walking. She turned down a side street, and before the reporters knew what she'd done, she scaled the wall of a house—Greta Garbo's—who fortunately was not in residence. She waited until the reporters drove on before walking back to her own house.

One never knew what courage Kate must have summoned up to go through that line of piranhas to begin with. She's a most contradictory creature, a woman whose many displays of personal courage are legendary, but who falls apart whenever she has to appear in public.

Judy could only be cheered by her visit, Kate's concern profound but largely unspoken. So much better than the lugubrious approach Judy detested.

She was also cheered up by a wire from Fred Finklehoffe and his wife, Ella Logan, which Carleton brought in. DEAR JUDY, it read. SO GLAD YOU CUT YOUR THROAT. ALL THE OTHER GIRL SINGERS NEEDED THIS KIND OF BREAK.

Her eyes filled with tears. "God, Pop," she said to Carleton, "isn't that sweet?"

There was no mistaking it. The sob sisters were out in force, offering knowing analyses and suggestions. Even the pseudo-sciences were having their say. A handwriting analyst in her newspaper column compared Judy's writing at the beginning of her career with a sample when she completed filming *The Harvey Girls*.

"As you can see from her writing," she wrote about the first sample, "she wasn't afraid of anything. Note the self-assured script of her girlhood with the flamboyant capitals and lines that slant vigorously uphill."

About the second sample: "Note the narrow tall letters. Lines of writing run sadly downhill on the right side. The capitals in her signature look wilted."

The columnist, commenting on the assurance and buoyant showmanship in the first sample, asked: "What happened to those gay, balloon-like capitals? What or who punctured them? Did someone think Judy should be 'put in her place' and no longer consider herself princess of the screen? Could it have been overwork that crushed her confidence?

"When she lost what envious ones might have considered 'conceit' she lost her wings. Come on, Judy! All you need is a little more of that old 'I-can-do-anything' spirit you had when you first wrote that note to me. Remember? Maybe that writing does reveal a lot of traits a schoolteacher or an office worker shouldn't have for success, but you are different. To soar again as you will, you've got to get up someday and say to yourself, 'Why, I'm Judy Garland.' Let those capitals bulge all they want. Swirl that gay underscore beneath your name again. Be you!"

But the fatuous observations weren't confined to the press. Colleagues at the studio, when they offered their well-meaning advice, had me tearing my hair, "Tell her to snap out of it," was the gist of their counsel. No one offered any constructive ideas on how this could be accomplished.

During the next few weeks, we fought to regain our bearings. Judy took permanent leave of the house on Sunset, with its many ugly memories, and we were all together again at the Evanview house. Miraculously, Liza was spared the hell we'd been through. Judy's days in bed were interpreted as being just another of Mama's periodic illnesses. Then she was up and around, snapping back with her innate resilience, again in control of herself.

There were no remonstrations, no censoring, by either Judy or me. With the open disclosure of her problems to the world—what people in Hollywood had long known about—we found ourselves better able to function.

Judy's mood was tinged with bitter humor, but she was also philosophical. Yes, I was sure it would be something she'd joke about when the dark cloud lifted.

My days at the studio, where we were rushing to begin the filming of *An American in Paris,* were spent in as deep a concentration as my confused nature would allow. There was now added reason for that distraction. Judy was coming along well, her doctor said, but I always took an involuntary jump whenever the telephone rang.

I'll forever be grateful that the studio kept the press away. It would take volumes to describe the situation, and I had neither the talent nor the stomach to condense it into a thousand-word Sunday feature.

The picture started shooting in August. Judy was resigned to the fact her tenure at Metro was at an end, and she went her enterprising way as I got deeper into *An American in Paris.*

Though the picture was designed as a highly commercial entertainment, I didn't feel at the time that I should talk down to the audience. I was determined to use as much ingenuity as I had in creating the picture. And I was going to shamelessly borrow as much ingenuity from my associates as they could spare. It was an embarrassment of riches. The stimulation of all these talents—the best of their kind— lightened my mood. My personal life might be on the road to hell, but I must be doing something right professionally to have so many enthusiastic people to work with. Work again became such an obsession that it came near to being my tragic flaw.

Some erudite types point to *An American in Paris* as the perfect example of the studio-as-auteur theory. I disagree, and I don't feel there's any need for Gaston-and-Alphonsing. Though I don't minimize anyone's contributions, one man was responsible for bringing it all together. That man was me.

Before I was finished, I was sweating blood. But the experience was such a giddy joy that I hardly noticed. I'd drag myself to bed each night so exhausted that I fell asleep before my head hit the pillow. I'd wake at an hour as early as it was uncivilized, and charge down to Culver City to get on with it. That sweetly masochistic experience was being repeated each day by dozens of others.

When we'd first started thinking of casting the picture, Gene Kelly was our original choice for the young expatriate, Jerry Mulligan. We thought of no one but Oscar Levant for the part of Jerry's sidekick, Adam Cook. He was the definitive interpreter of Gershwin. Including Oscar in the film lent the enterprise a sort of legitimacy . . . though he would have blanched if I'd told him that.

We agreed to cast a French girl in the part of Lise. Gene was spending some time in London when Arthur and I wired him to make a test of a French music hall star we'd heard of. Gene remembered a young girl he'd seen in a Roland Petit ballet, *The Sphynx,* and included a second test of her. When we saw both tests, we were struck by the younger girl's gamine quality. She wasn't conventional looking, but her waif's appearance grew on you. The more you saw her, the more beautiful she became. And she had a built-in advantage. She could dance. We decided to take a chance with this seventeen-year-old, whose name was Leslie Caron.

Originally, we'd wanted Maurice Chevalier as the French entertainer affianced to Lise. He was unavailable. We settled on Georges Guetary, an entertainer largely unknown to American audiences but with a considerable following abroad.

Arthur and I had discussed Celeste Holm for the American heiress who becomes Jerry's patroness, which would round out the major players. Nina Foch read for us first, and we made our minds up immediately. Celeste might have been as good for the part, but we didn't see how she could be better.

I then sent out a call for French people around Southern California, to cast the lesser roles and fill in the crowds. This picture was going to look as authentically French as possible, even though it was being filmed in the United States.

While we were casting, Alan was finishing the screenplay. It was like a Chinese puzzle, for he had to work backwards. The elements of the script and the song were pre-supplied. So was the approach. The script had to be tailored to Gene Kelly's ingratiating personality, as well as reflect his love of Paris. The story served its purpose beautifully. I always resent criticisms of the screenplay, and the occasional negative comments about Alan's work. It was a simple story beautifully told, and it accomplished its purpose, telling a charming story about a charming period.

Working with Alan was one of the most enjoyable collaborations of my life. He's an artist, but with none of the artist's pretensions. He doesn't feel his words are inscribed on marble. He's susceptible to suggestions, and doesn't mind changing anything, if his colleagues believe it will improve the work. Of course, he has to believe it too.

When we first talked about doing the picture, Arthur and I thought it might be shot in France. We were advised this wouldn't be feasible, so we settled on shooting only the ballet segment there.

Ira and Lee Gershwin had taken their first trip to Europe in many years, to reacquaint themselves with the setting of the story. It was as close as we ever got to France, for we were also unable to shoot the ballet in Paris. The timetable would have us filming exteriors in the middle of winter. What's more, we wouldn't have the optimum control of soundstage conditions. Consequently, we decided to attack the sequence in the same way a painter would, with bold and imaginative splashes of color.

Ira wrote me several letters at the time, bemoaning the fact we weren't there with him and Lee. I regretted it too, having every confidence that such a trip wouldn't be the fiasco our West Indies vacation had been so many years before.

If the ballet couldn't be filmed on the actual location, we would have to develop a new premise. It didn't take us long to decide on using stylized settings of Paris, as influenced by French Impressionist painters. George Gibson promptly created a contest in his art department, to see which contributions would most closely approximate scenes of Paris as they might have been painted by Rousseau, Lautrec, Utrillo, Renoir, Dufy, and other painters.

Since there were so many great songs to choose from, we had to pick them through trial and error. Some were easy choices. Gene wanted to dance with a little old lady, and we felt their doing a waltz would add a lovely touch. "By Strauss," which had been introduced in *The Show Is On,* was an obvious choice. Gene's partner was actually a middle-aged dancer made up to look older.

Gene also wanted to do a number with children, and he came upon an idea for "I Got Rhythm" which would work well, the song being used as an English lesson, with the children yelling "I Got" while Gene finished each line.

Working with little old ladies and children can be cloying, but Gene achieved just the right balance, maintaining the charm without stooping to sentimentality. His irrepressible personality can't be upstaged, and he's one of the rare people who can get away with such cute touches.

Gene wouldn't need much direction. It was a role he was born to play. In later years, he joked about my words of instruction. "Now, Gene," I would say, "make it jaunty." Gene, of course, was born jaunty.

Shooting began in August of 1950. I approached the film as a culmination of all the influences I'd been experimenting with during the 1940s. Everything I knew about Paris, or had heard about Paris, would be incorporated wherever possible. I pored over thousands of pictures with set decorator Preston Ames. Together we created a Paris so authentic that Frenchmen are amazed to discover the picture was filmed in the United States. This was Preston's first musical, but his five years spent in Paris during the postwar period was a great help to us all.

There was one problem that had to be overcome: how to make the transition from the Artists' Ball, with all its splashy revelry, to the ballet fantasy in the hero's mind. I didn't like the idea of a masquerade, and so I began thinking out the problem.

Then the idea struck me. Why not make it a Black and White Ball? The action would be as boisterous, but the use of black and white would direct the eye to the riot of color in the ballet that followed. Walter Plunkett was brought in to design the costumes, a bewildering and dazzling assortment of checks, stripes, and spirals. (When I saw the stage production of *My Fair Lady*, I recognized the influence of our ball on the Royal Enclosure scene.)

When I think back on the making of pictures, I tend to forget the day-to-day drudgery of it all. *An American in Paris* offered none that I remember, for it was a lovely labor for those involved. Everyone delivered, graciously and unselfishly. No request was too outlandish.

We would be needing black and white confetti for the ball, as an example. Harry Lazarre, the head prop man, found enough for one day's shooting. "We'll be needing more confetti tomorrow," I told him. We'd cornered the market on black and white confetti, and there was no more available in the city. Harry, of his own volition, stayed up all night punching out tiny rounds from black sheets of paper so that the confetti would be available for shooting the following day.

These wholehearted contributions fostered a creative climate that invigorated us all. I was working with people I loved and admired. These were busy times, a period of great professional joy.

With so much dancing involved, the work of Gene and his assistants, Carol Haney and Jeanne Coyne, was a vital part of the picture's success.

My way of photographing the dance hadn't changed such since *Cabin in the Sky*. Many short takes using several cameras from different angles tended to interrupt the flow of movement. I always composed the dance with the central figure in mind, with an establishing long shot to take in the head and feet. Sometimes I might use as many as twenty different stops on the camera to accommodate different details. But it was always done with one camera moving all over the place. If it was done right, the audience would be conscious of only the dancers' movements, and not the camera's.

There were still greater challenges to the filming. One of the first tests a director must meet is the ability to sustain mood from one scene to another. Few pictures are shot in sequence. Shooting doesn't usually move from one set to another, then back to the original one. When all the sequences in one location are shot, the set is dismantled and filming moves elsewhere. The director must pigeonhole all these disjointed parts in his brain and bring them together later so that they come cohesively together. I notice that many young directors today seem to lack this ability.

Another challenge is to make the exposition entertaining. Every picture has its low and high spots. They must all be entertaining. One picture that achieved this admirably was Garson Kanin's *My Favorite Wife* in 1940. A man who'd been incommunicado for fifteen years returned to find his wife married to another man. The rather complicated premise had to be explained at the outset. Kanin used several devices . . . a judge misunderstanding the situation and trying to assimilate the idea, the consequent mixup of other people. It was high comedy that proved plot exposition needn't be dull . . . another lesson young filmmakers might learn.

I tried to break up the many long scenes by supplying the attractions of Paris, as they would naturally occur.

The opening sequences of the picture introduced all the characters. Gene is seen in his tiny room, rising for the day, his movements of raising

232

the bed and preparing for breakfast choreographed like a ballet. "It should look like you're swimming under water," I told Gene. The hilly streets of Montmartre are concurrently revealed, with Sacré Coeur in the background. The camera wends its way through the Quarter, fixing momentarily on the back of a Sunday painter, who looks suspiciously like Winston Churchill. A passing boom shot reveals the concierge feeding a cat, and a mirror introduces a primping Georges Guetary before he meets his old friend, Oscar Levant.

They get together in the sidewalk cafe, and Georges extols the virtues of his intended.

This was the sequence that introduced Leslie to film audiences. She had to be showcased with great splash. As Guetary describes each facet to her extraordinary personality, Oscar misinterprets each time. We devised a different background, using the same poster color in both the backdrop and the furnishings, for each mood . . . yellow for Jacobean and red for the Twenties, for example. Leslie is costumed in a contrasting color. She ranged from studious to fun-loving; she dances the ballet as well as the Charleston. It was a most auspicious introduction in films.

Such interplay required great preparation, and I took all the time necessary. Studio policy required the assistant director to report to the front office when the first setup of the day was shot. Some directors would shoot anything to give the impression that filming was proceeding smoothly. I refused to stoop to that, to take a shot I didn't need. If it took all day to prepare and not even one setup was filmed, then that was a problem the front office should worry about. I was too involved elsewhere.

Leslie was delivering a beautifully modulated performance. In only one scene was there a false note. In retrospect, I feel she relented too easily in agreeing to have a first date with Gene. He's pursued her all over Paris, and she's matched every compliment of his with an insult. Suddenly she does an about face, and agrees to see him. Her coming around should have been more gradual. Blame the director.

Not being one to take his players' temperatures every other minute, I didn't learn of Leslie's insecurities until years later. She was adapting to a new medium, and in a new language to boot, so her anxiety was understandable. But all I could see was the way she was delivering for us, a natural movie talent if there ever was one, and I didn't think to reassure her more.

It was more difficult getting a performance out of Georges Guetary, an entertainer with far greater experience. Carol Haney took him in hand, and worked until they both dropped from exhaustion. The biggest difficulty was getting Georges "American" enough so that he could be understood in his song number, "I'll Build a Stairway to Paradise." At the same time, he had to maintain his Gallic charm, for the number was designed as a satire of the *Folies-Bergère,* with as much nudity as the movie code would allow.

I came upon the idea of lighting each step as he moved up and down the stairway.

"Can't do it," the studio electrician said.

"Yes you can," I insisted.

A console with buttons controlling the lighting of each step was set up. Jeanne Coyne counted cadence while Georges went through his movements, and the electrician pressed the appropriate buttons. It took a great deal of time to perfect the lighting, but the effort was well worth our while.

Oscar Levant? Well, Oscar was Oscar. He played his wise-cracking self with his usual brilliance, and his command of the piano wasn't bad either.

Arthur wanted him to perform a Gershwin medley. Oscar insisted on doing "Concerto in F."

"I've always wanted to perform the concerto in a picture," he told me late one afternoon, "and now Freed won't let me. Is there anything you can do?"

I thought a while. Then came a brainstorm . . . from Oscar.

"Why can't I be not only the pianist, but everyone else too: the other musicians and the conductor?"

Terrific! I called Arthur's office but he'd just left for home. We ran to intercept him in the parking lot. Oscar and I caught up with him just outside the Thalberg Building. We explained the idea. Arthur was skeptical. "I'll shoot it in one day," I assured him. He agreed.

We quickly rigged up a set. The concert hall was painted to resemble yellow marble, and lighted in yellow fog to suggest the dreamy quality of the sequence. The over-all effect suggested Dufy's paintings of orchestras.

Oscar played the Renaissance Man. First he performed at the piano, then he conducted the orchestra, followed by his image being repeated five times or more to suggest whole sections of the orchestra. At the end of the one-man show, a solitary man rises from the darkened audience, moved to the point of tears. He starts applauding, and as the brilliance

234

of the interpretation gets to him, he yells "Bravo!" at the top of his voice. It was Oscar again, naturally. Though I thought his reactions were just a touch excessive, that's what made them so delicious.

Oscar loved the segment.

Unfortunately, he didn't like the ballet. A scene near the end of the picture was to round out his character, suggesting that Nina would go on to sponsor him after Gene's defection. They would both be slightly drunk in the scene, feeling sorry for themselves. But the segment detracted from the main story between Leslie and Gene and interrupted the flow of action leading into the ballet. It was cut. Some may believe Oscar was a personality and not an actor, but you couldn't have proved it by his vanity-wounded roar.

As shooting of the bulk of the picture neared completion, we discovered we were well over budget. There wasn't enough money left to film the ballet. We'd have to go back to Dore Schary, now the undisputed head of the studio, for more money.

Our selling job wasn't made easier by such people as Irving Berlin or Comden and Green. Irving had been brought on the set before we started filming. He looked doubtfully around him.

"You say you're going to film a ballet?" he asked.

I nodded.

"And it's going to last seventeen minutes?"

I nodded again.

"And it's going to come at the end of the picture?"

Yes.

"I sure hope you fellows know what you're doing."

Arthur had run a rough cut of the picture shot thus far for Betty and Adolph. They raved. "This picture is perfect as it is," Betty said.

"Wait," I told her. "The best is yet to come."

"But do you think you really need a ballet?" she asked.

"Yes, I think so."

"I don't," she insisted. "Release it now."

Adolph agreed with Betty.

But on this point, Arthur, Gene, and I were adamant. I'm not a fighter, in that I don't do battle over non-essentials. Often in the past I'd used actors who didn't excite me and had agreed to cuts that weren't to my liking. These were perils of the trade I'd learned to abide, and to surmount. But this struck at our vitals.

A meeting was called with Dore Schary. Arthur, Gene, costume designer Irene Sharaff, and members of the art department were present. It was up to me to sell him.

"The ballet is constructed in terms the audience can understand," I said. "The hero is at the lowest point of his life. It's an emotional nightmare which alternates with moments of great joy. Then he returns to the sad reality. He thinks of life without the girl. He searches for her throughout Paris. He finds her for a moment, then he loses her again. All of Paris has lost its color and excitement. The ballet doesn't review what's happened in the picture so far. It shows instead the conflict within the hero."

I went on to describe the visual devices we would be using, as well as the choreographic effects Gene had in mind. Then I put it right into Dore's lap.

"How much did you say it'll cost?" he asked.

"Three hundred thousand tops," I assured him, referring to the estimate the budget department had drawn up.

"Well, I think it's enchanting. Go ahead and do it."

(By the time the sequence was completed, it cost a cool half million, but the ballet was the high spot of the film. Some feel it is the high spot of all musical pictures.)

Now that we had the go-ahead, we had to come up with a scene to replace the one with Oscar and Nina. It should explain all the emotions Gene would be feeling during the ballet.

Alan Lerner had returned to New York. I called him and described all the complicated ideas that would have to be included in Gene's speech. What he supplied was perfect.

The scene opens with Jerry sketching on the back of a dance program while he talks to Lise. She is marrying someone else and going away. This is to be their parting.

LISE

Oh, Jerry, it's dreadful standing next to you like this and not having your arms around me.

JERRY (*simply*)

You'll always be standing next to me, Lise.

LISE (*looking out at city*)

Maybe not always. Paris has ways of making people forget.

JERRY

Paris! Not this city! It's too real and too beautiful. It never lets you forget a thing. It reaches in and opens you wide and you stay that way.

236

I came to Paris to study and to paint it . . . because Utrillo did . . . and Lautrec did . . . and Roualt did . . . and I loved what they created . . . and I thought that something would happen to me, too . . . Well, it happened all right! And now what have I got left? Paris!
(*He tears the sketch in half and throws the two pieces over the railing.*)
Maybe that's enough for some, but it isn't any more for me. The more beautiful everything is, the more it will hurt without you.
    LISE (*looking quickly into ballroom*)
Jerry, don't let me leave you this way.
(*They embrace tearfully. She turns and walks into the ballroom.*)

The scene is now set for Gene's emotional turmoil, caused by the parting from Leslie . . . the ballet itself.

But when were Gene and I going to find the time to create the story for the sequence? We'd been kept so busy with the rest of the picture that we couldn't get together to plot out the movements.

We were shooting the final scenes when Nina Foch came down with a case of chicken pox. We couldn't shoot around her, so production ground to a halt. I would have kissed her had Nina not been contagious. The standstill gave Gene and me an opportunity to implement Phase Two of our battle plan. Gene, Irene, and I locked ourselves in my office. When we came out three days later, we had a complete ballet. Nina should be given a Purple Heart for making it all possible.

Arthur Freed had suggested that, as a young and vital American, Gene should use a George M. Cohan strut.

"What does he mean by that?" Gene asked me.

"I don't know," I answered.

We continued working, trying to figure out a way to implement Arthur's idea if at all possible. A few days later, Gene told me, "I think I know what Arthur means by that Cohan strut idea." As it was worked out by Gene, the hero, surrounded by Paris, should be readily identifiable as an American. The most American dance was that jaunty Cohan walk, which Gene adapted to his own talent.

The ballet evolved to our satisfaction.

Yet, as Gene and I were plotting the effects of the parting on the young lovers, the scene for another parting was being set.

In September, Metro announced that Judy had asked for, and been granted, a release from her contract.

She'd spent fifteen years at M-G-M. "My life sentence was commuted," she described to friends later, adding ironically, "for good behavior." She was now ready to explore new areas of expression.

I was going back to a slightly used one. The time being spent to construct the sets for the ballet gave me an opportunity to direct the sequel to *Father of the Bride*.

Spencer knew that virtually all sequels are never as good as the original. Besides, he didn't want to repeat the same role, when there were so many other facets to his talent he wanted to explore.

Kate again stepped in. In her practical way, she convinced Spencer that he owed it to the studio to do the film. Movies were a business, after all, and the first picture had been such a huge success that this one couldn't fail either.

It took us twenty-two days to film *Father's Little Dividend,* the continuing story of Stanley Banks and his married daughter, Kay.

The sets were still up, all the players were under contract. We breezed through the shooting with great humor. At the same time, I was completing post-production for the Gershwin picture.

Father's Little Dividend, with the Hacketts creating the story of the birth of the first grandchild, was almost as great a commercial success as its predecessor, and was warmly received by the critics.

"Admirers of *Father of the Bride* will not be let down," *Time* magazine's review concluded. "All they have to fear now is that M-G-M will be tempted to go on working its father lode until the ore thins out."

Newsweek concluded that "once again Spencer Tracy wraps the picture up with a grand comedy performance as an innocent bystander turned baby-sitter."

Judy and I had a few days together, with no distractions, before I was to return to filming the *American in Paris* ballet.

We were as affectionate as ever with each other. But we were also taking long, appraising looks. Our life was calm for the first time; reflection was now possible.

I'd obviously failed Judy. Those periods in her life when she'd been least able to cope with the world coincided with the years of our marriage. It was an indictment I couldn't ignore.

But Judy had failed me too. She would never be able, nor willing, to create a home with me. Our future would always be marred by her indulgences and compulsions. I'd either humored them or fought them for almost six years. Events had been so cataclysmic that we were forced to cling to each other.

I was still saying to Judy that I loved her, after that love had given

238

way to the empathy that one concerned person can have for the troubles of another. My feelings could never turn to hate or indifference, but my affection for Judy was now colored by a harsh realistic view. As for her, I don't know what she felt. Perhaps I never did.

I could only analyze my own feelings and failings. I'd been too sympathetic, too ready to see it her way, when I should have been more assertive. Rather than lose my temper in front of her, I'd leave the house to cool off. I suppose it was just as obvious to her that I was bottling up the explosion. "You think Vincente's a doll," she told Dotty Ponedel, "but you should see him when that dago temper of his gets going." She took this strength for weakness, and she was right, for that's what it had become. Our relationship was drastically damaged.

A shocking confession from Judy made me realize that much as I'd loved her, in the final analysis I loved Liza and myself more.

Someone at the studio had counted up the number of psychiatrists she'd been sent to. They totaled sixteen, Judy was told.

"So what?" she retorted. "I never told any of them the truth. There's more than one way to get even with you people."

Her admission deepened my depression. The months of near nervous collapse we'd both suffered had been for naught. She hadn't even tried . . . at least not as much as she should have. It was damn near impossible for me to forgive Judy for this. I opted for sanity. Liza's well being would be better served if she had one stable parent living apart from his mate rather than having two emotionally wounded parents living together.

The tumult died down with the confession. Judy was surprisingly placid. She survived again. As for me . . .

Gone were the sleepless nights, the long watches, the self doubts, the strain of work, the unending lies to protect her. Ended were the constant calls from the press, coming at odd hours, checking out the latest rumor . . . which was too often true.

We'd functioned quite well without each other whenever we'd separated . . . perhaps even better.

"I think I'll go to New York for a few weeks," Judy told me one day early in December.

"Why don't you?" I responded. "Might do you some good. Why don't you take Dotty?"

Judy started making plans for the trip. Liza would stay with me while she was gone.

Judy kissed Liza goodbye as the driver came to take her to the train station. She gave me a friendly hug, and walked out.

It was three days before Christmas, the day when families renew their loving bonds. But we needn't pretend any longer.

We also wouldn't be going to Harry Cohn's annual New Year's party, where most Hollywood couples showed to the world they'd made it through another year together.

Our life together was over . . . including the shouting . . . our recycled and separate lives began.

Mine took up with a donnybrook at the studio. I felt so strongly about the ensuing dispute that, despite the cordiality up to now, I would walk off the picture if I lost the battle.

Our Place de la Concorde in the Dufy style was the setting our hero would keep returning to during the ballet. It would suggest his moods, through use of several light changes.

In the midst was a fountain, on which Gene and Leslie would dance the only erotic segment of the ballet. Henry Greutert, the studio's sculptor, designed a marvelous fountain in miniature, using cutouts rather than solid forms, so that it would look like Dufy in any light.

Cedric Gibbons, the head of the art department, insisted it should be done differently. "That isn't in the style of Dufy," he said. "Dufy is all lines. Therefore, the fountain should be solid and the lines should be painted in."

Gibbons didn't know my plans for light changes, but he remained steadfast in his opinion.

"Cedric," I told him, "the solid fountain won't work. It will look just like a Henry Moore, you know, those doughlike figures. It'll be nothing."

Gibbons still couldn't see my point. "But it doesn't look like Dufy," he insisted.

A meeting of the entire production unit was called. When I explained why I wanted the original design, which would allow an interplay of light to suggest different emotions, Gibbons reluctantly gave in.

Saul Chaplin agreed with me that the music of the ballet shouldn't be unfamiliar to the mass audience, and themes from "An American in Paris" were subtly injected in the background score of earlier sequences.

Saul's orchestration was so skillful that no one noticed the Gershwin themes were changed around to better tell the story of the ballet which Gene and I had concocted. Themes were repeated to expand the twelve-minute suite into a seventeen-minute ballet score.

Ira's devotion to his brother's memory is a thing of beauty. He could

240

have voiced strong objections to what the purists might consider sacrilege. But he didn't. The ballet served the music well.

If there had been one reservation during the filming, it was the work of the cameraman. He'd been highly recommended because he was so skillful at shooting day for night. I don't know what relation that bore to our picture, but he was assigned to shoot it nevertheless.

His absence of mood wouldn't do for the ballet. John Alton had done such a terrific job on the two Tracy pictures that I requested he be assigned to handle the ballet. It created some turmoil among the cinematographers. They interpreted John's continental poise as effete and arrogant. And for rough-and-ready American film crews that can be the greatest affront of all. But I got my way . . . I knew he'd approach the light changes in the ballet with the boldness—and the madness—that was needed.

He had both the soul and the gift of the artist, and I was pleased when he took up my suggestion to seriously take up painting, which John was to do a few years later.

We decided the red rose Leslie has given Gene should act as the symbol for the ballet.

It opens with Gene gazing down at Paris from the balcony in Montmartre. His mind is dead and empty and as devoid of color as the black and white sketch he's absent-mindedly drawn on the back of a program. A maelstrom of confused thoughts and angers crowds his consciousness, creating a kaleidoscopic pattern of images, symbols of wishful thinking, of hope and despair.

Paris appears, but all its color has been drained. It's a fickle city that will falsely enchant, then mock you. Suddenly the color is harshly splashed into the image and the spirit of the city is evoked. We used two identical sketches—except that one is in black and white and the other in color—placed at an angle so that they're reflected in the center black glass mirror through which we were shooting. The black and white sketch was first lighted, then gradually the color sketch comes into existence—Gene standing in front of it—as each segment of color is splashed onto the image to suggest the spirit of the city.

It's a crowded and shrill carnival . . . strange crowds in the Place de la Concorde . . . revelers from Maxim's, the pleasure seekers, the midinettes, the officers, the exotic Eastern potentates . . . a beautiful city but, for all that, one that is cruel and impersonal. The American tries to mingle with the crowds, to touch and to be heard. But he's ignored.

Suddenly he imagines that he glimpses the face of the French girl,

241

separated by the traffic and the crowds. He dodges through cars and pedestrians to reach her, only to discover she's disappeared.

A new image is then imposed, a quiet place, the flower market at dawn, as suggested by Renoir . . . beautiful, but lifeless and sad. The girl appears, but she's an illusion. There is no feeling of contact. They move together like two automatons. Her being is as tenuous and fragile as the flowers around them. He gives way to the feeling of emptiness.

He next chances upon a deserted street reminiscent of Utrillo. Hope stirs in him. The memory of something to cling to is symbolized by the appearance of the American servicemen . . . his own people . . . his own roots and rhythms . . . something that may recapture the desire to live.

This mood elaborates itself in his mind. He's with Americans, and Paris becomes naive and gay.

The scene becomes the Zoological Gardens in the manner of Rousseau. Purged of sadness and resentment, he meets the girl as for the first time in her own environment, the embodiment of all that is young and lovely about Paris. They dance together, carefree, the Americans and the French.

The suppressed physical yearning blots out every other emotion and his mind feverishly indulges in a dream of a great and reciprocated love. He is drugged with the thought, the dream expands. Paris is again alive, but now it is part of him and he is a part of Paris . . . the Paris that loves a lover. The gay crowds in the Place de l'Opèra come to life and he and his love dance with them. They imagine themselves as characters in a Toulouse-Lautrec poster. Their hysteria becomes an orgy of fulfill-ment when, without warning, the nothingness returns. People disappear and the color drains out of everything. He's left again, as he started, hopeless and alone.

There was a happy coda attached to the end of the picture, the lovers reunited because the older French entertainer has overheard their part-ing words to each other, and will not stand in their way.

The great strain of filming left us all enervated but giddy. We knew something great had been achieved.

Judy called from New York to see how things were going. Liza, I told her, was thriving . . . and so was I. *An American in Paris* was going to be a huge success, I predicted.

A few days later, she called again. "Well, I've seen your little picture," she said. "Not bad. Only a masterpiece."

"Do you really think so, Judy?"

242

"I loved it! I'm very glad for you."

I thanked Judy, and that was that.

Came the time for the first preview, somewhere in Pasadena. A group of us made our anonymous way to the back of the theater . . . as anonymous, at any rate, as studio limousines and roped off sections can be. As soon as the picture started, I began thinking of using some of that rope for a noose. The sound was awful, as if everyone was gurgling under water. No one had sense to stop the picture, and we suffered through the dismal proceedings. Somehow, we got back to Ira's house. We were absolutely desolate. It was the most terrible experience of my career.

But the sound was fixed for the next preview, and the picture was on its way to its unparalleled commercial and critical success, as well as developing its singular place in film history.

When the picture was first released, the critics knew it was something special, but didn't know how to gauge it. The reaction of the commercial audience would crystallize their thoughts.

In the meantime, we had to make do with reviews that were curiously dispirited. Bosley Crowther's in the New York *Times* was a case in point:

"Count a bewitching French lassie by the name of Leslie Caron and a whoop-de-do ballet number, one of the finest ever put on the screen, as the most commendable enchantments of the big, lavish musical that Metro obligingly delivered to the Music Hall yesterday. 'An American in Paris,' which is the title of the picture, likewise the ballet, is spangled with pleasant little patches of amusement and George Gershwin tunes. It also is blessed with Gene Kelly, dancing and singing his way through a minor romantic complication in the usual gaudy Hollywood gay Paree. But it is the wondrously youthful Miss Caron and that grandly pictorial ballet that place the marks of distinction upon this lush technicolored escapade."

Crowther's review continued in a similar vein. The only excitement he could muster was over the ballet, "and a ballet it is, beyond question— a truly cinematic ballet—with dancers describing vivid patterns against changing colors, designs, costumes and scenes. The whole story of a poignant romance within a fanciful panorama of Paree is conceived and performed with taste and talent. It is the uncontested high point of the film."

It was also, according to the French film cultists, the greatest movie ballet ever filmed.

15 | The Minnelli Touch

I always find it a hoot when film buffs turn directors' names into adjectives . . . the Lubitsch touch, Hitchcockian suspense, a Fellini situation. I'd never presume, God knows, to use the word Minnellian to describe anything I've done, as some current writers on film are doing. It's an embarrassment, a pomposity I don't relate to and an intellectuality I don't espouse. I'd rather be out being it than waste endless hours analyzing what the term means.

Admittedly, a director can be type cast. Both the public and his colleagues associate him with a particular kind of story, or see recurring effects in his work. That assessment isn't always a compliment, however, for it implies there are certain limitations to overcome.

I look, for example, at the films of directors who specialize in violence and machismo. They equate the gun with the phallus . . . the greater the explosion the more profuse the symbolic ejaculation. It suggests the deep-seated aberrations of people one wouldn't want to know better. I concede their bloody stories are gripping and, in their own way, rather catchy. You can appreciate the gimmickry, if not the humanity. I have, nevertheless, detected in some of their films a suggestion of tenderness that suggests a most-welcome versatility. But I'd want to reserve judgment on whether these people are great directors until they tried their hand at a comedy or a drama or—perish the thought—a musical.

If my métier wasn't established in the public's mind, it certainly was at the studio by now. I was the resident specialist in sophisticated musicals, in adapting visual influences from the higher world of art, in using a realistic framework for fantasy.

But did anyone call it the Minnelli touch? Come now. We all realized we were cogs in the business machine and, as such, we weren't allowed the luxury of such affectations. More importantly, my immediate past successes now gave me greater latitude in deciding future projects, and that was a victory far sweeter than any posturings of the great artiste I might assume.

It afforded me the opportunity to reach back to down-home values, as I had in *Meet Me in St. Louis,* with a proposed musical version of *Huckleberry Finn.* Alan Lerner and Burton Lane would write the score. Gene Kelly, riding the wave of his huge success in *An American in Paris,* would star along with Danny Kaye, a free agent who'd signed on at Metro just to take that particular river cruise.

Gene had just started co-directing and starring in *Singin' in the Rain.* Metro, trying to get as much mileage as possible out of him, devised a schedule where he would rehearse with Danny in the morning and work on his own picture in the afternoon.

The two would be playing the Duke and the Dauphin, with William Warfield enacting Jim the Negro.

Marvelous bits of business were being concocted for Danny and Gene in their roles as itinerant con men who, upon meeting, size each other up as prospective pigeons. In private they prepare their identical mechanical devices as crooked gamblers preparing to hoodwink the other. Dressed in the height of fashion, as envisioned by Irene Sharaff, they meet in an elaborately casual way. They soon sense their true character, however, and team up to prey on the innocents of the river towns.

I'd started rehearsing Danny in a sequence right before he embarks on the river boat where, as the owner of a dancing school in the Arkansas mountains, he either has to make dancers of his monstrous students or bear the wrath of their shotgun-toting mothers.

Then the production hit a snag.

Gene recalls that the strain of working on two productions at the same time was so great that he asked the production be postponed for six weeks.

245

"Danny quit the picture," he says, "because he wasn't very enthusiastic about it. He saw that the two vagabonds were not as important as Huck and Jim, the slave. He was delighted to leave it. Being part of the M-G-M staff, I couldn't quit. But I wouldn't anyway, because I loved what was being done with it.

"But they scheduled the picture much too close to *Singin' in the Rain.* This is the only time in my career that I got sick from overwork.

"When we were ready to pick up again, Kaye wouldn't come back. The studio shied away from it. They couldn't see it without Kaye. It's a crime, because this was probably the best score ever written for films."

I remember the happenings in a quite different way.

As I recall, Arthur Freed called me into his office. He said that Gene's agent, Lew Wasserman of MCA, had succeeded in re-negotiating Gene's contract with the studio. A provision in the Federal tax law then permitted an American to avoid paying taxes if he spent eighteen calendar months working outside the country. Gene would be allowed to take advantage of this provision for his contributions to *An American in Paris* and the upcoming *Singin' in the Rain,* already being touted as a smash picture.

If this wasn't the actual reason for the cancellation of the picture, I've been laboring under a misapprehension for more than twenty years. Gene *did* leave for Europe almost immediately to start work on his own *Invitation to the Dance.*

Any thoughts I might have had about my exalted station at the studio were somewhat tempered by the development. But these were the breaks of the profession, and not worth moping over. There were more important adjustments necessary at home.

Liza found it easier to accept my new status of bachelor father than I did. But how could she help it? I gave her everything she asked for, and then some.

Lee Gershwin, playing the surrogate mother during Judy's absence, finally felt compelled to speak out.

"Vincente," she said. "I love her dearly, but Liza is very spoiled. It's your fault, you know. Judy's the disciplinarian with her, and tries to instill some character in her. But you . . . you give her everything . . . you're nothing but a puddle of love. For her own sake, Liza should be disciplined. If she's not, you mark my words. She's going to grow up to be a commuter to an institution."

"I know I should," I told her, "but you see . . . I just can't help myself."

246

Lee shook her head at me and laughed. I would try to do better.

And now that she had made her feelings known, she was just as ready to participate in some of that spoiling herself.

Liza's birthdays were always celebrated at the Gershwins'. Our own house wasn't conducive to children's parties . . . it was too small for the large-scale celebrations which these parties entailed.

Lee and I were planning Liza's fifth birthday party when the Academy Award nominations were announced. A couple of them surprised the executives at the studio and delighted me, giving me added cause for celebration.

Spencer's nomination for Best Actor, though he eventually lost to José Ferrer in *Cyrano de Bergerac,* was very satisfying to Pan and me, since it supported our contention that only a veteran actor could play *Father of the Bride.* The Hacketts were nominated for Best Screenplay, an honor they so well deserved. They lost, however, to *Sunset Boulevard* and writers Charles Brackett, Billy Wilder, and D. M. Marshman, Jr. The picture was classified as a minor effort by the studio, and it had been parlayed into a major box office success as well as a critical one. My stock was climbing higher.

Liza, of course, was too involved in her own world to pay more than passing notice to mine. It was going to be her turn to offer an afternoon's entertainment to her little friends. Their life consisted of one party after another, each one laying claim to being the most diverting, and each one offering a fillip of its own.

It was at this party that Lee pointed out the undue attention a solemn little redheaded boy was paying Liza. He was, in fact, her first beau.

"Who is he?" I asked.

"He's the son of Jean Paul Getty," Lee answered.

I had fantastic visions that, following their marriage, we would all retire to the South of France . . . courtesy of Mr. Getty, of course.

But the presence of the son of the world's richest man implies that such parties were the latest in status and opulence, when such was not the case. Lee Gershwin, in particular, resents such implications.

"In those days everyone had the same kind of parties for their children. But the object wasn't to see how much money could be spent. It was to find things that would delight the children. There was a choo-choo train outside. The Beverly Hills police had blocked off the street, and the kiddies would get in the five or six cars and ride from one end of the block to another and back. Then there might be pony rides, and a magic lady, a drunken clown, a Punch and Judy show, Disney shorts in the projection room, a taffy pull in the corner. There were almost one hundred children. Their nannies would sit guard by the pool. The children never talked to each other, you know. They'd just go through all the attractions and come back for their ice cream and cake."

The number of guests would be even greater inflated when both parents would show up. Humphrey and Betty Bogart were present for Liza's fifth birthday, as were several other parents. One well-known actress was conspicuously absent, and so, soon after, was her daughter. The little girl had been thoroughly enjoying the afternoon. We were getting ready to serve ice cream and cake when her mother's driver appeared to take the child home. She was carried, crying and screaming, to the car. It was imperative she should get home in time to watch her mother on television.

The incident upset the adults much more than it did the kids, the little girl excepted. They were eager for Liza to tear into her pile of presents. There was an unwritten rule that none of the gifts should cost more than three or four dollars, but the mystery of what each package contained was a source of constant fascination. Which present would the birthday girl like most? That, to them, was the mystery of the universe.

It recalled a viewpoint of their special world which my friend, cartoonist Percy Crosby, shared with me. His comic strip, "Skippy," was the "Peanuts" of its day.

"I have total recall," he told me. "When people grow up they forget what it was like to be a child. Life is full of so many tragedies for children. A kid is invited to a birthday party. His mother says, 'You go to the house and tell Mary that I didn't have time to buy her a present. I'll send one later.' The child goes to the party, and Mary doesn't mind, but to that child it is a tragedy and a humiliation. He's the only one who showed up without a present."

On the other hand, there are some children's perspectives which reflect on the complexes of the parents.

Lee gave Liza a make-up box one Christmas. Liza became very angry. "Don't you know my daddy doesn't allow me to use make-up?" she asked. In the back of her mind were my stern words, a carryover from my own childhood. One of the actors in the tent theater had given me a box, filled with used make-up and props, and I dirtied an antimacassar in the rooming house where we were staying. My parents punished me, and so I inevitably passed on the stricture to Liza. She must have looked at Lee's gift as the temptation of the devil incarnate.

Judy was now back from New York. Our separation was official. She took another house in Beverly Hills and began throwing small parties to introduce her friends to a fellow she'd met while away: Sid Luft.

We agreed that, with her own life so up in the air, Liza should continue to stay with me for a while.

When we got together to discuss the divorce, I told Judy I'd go along with whatever she wanted. I was glad she was happy and functioning, and would do nothing to cause her a moment's concern. Peace and freedom was something we both wanted.

We remained friendly, not just for Liza's sake, but because we also respected each other. Judy told me of her plans to do concerts. She was so excited at the prospect that I knew she'd be an enormous hit. She was now leaning on Sid, who'd seemingly discovered the secret to keeping Judy sane and healthy.

She called me one day. "Do you have some time to spare?" she asked.

"Of course, Judy. What can I do for you?"

"I want to come over and show you my act."

Judy arrived with her accompanist, and went into her one-woman show for this one-man audience. Her voice was better than ever, for it had a new-found maturity. The heartache in the sad songs and the frenetic drive of the upbeat numbers created an extraordinary impact. She'd developed marvelous gestures which put the stresses on the most unexpected words. The effect was awkward and occasionally graceless, but strangely, it was right. The gestures she was developing were to become standard for other singers in a few years.

Judy completed the act, and turned to me.

"What do you think?"

"You're great! What can I tell you?"

"Well . . . any suggestions?"

I thought about it for a while. "Well," I said tentatively, "there's one thing maybe. People have always said you're the greatest entertainer since Jolson. Why don't you sing one of his songs? It'll give them some basis for comparison."

I came up with one song idea: "Rock-a-Bye Your Baby With a Dixie Melody." Judy thanked me, and went on to include the song in her act. It was the final bit of professional advice I gave her.

The divorce hearing was held in March of 1951. We'd earned millions of dollars during the years, but the money had slipped through our fingers. Hundreds of thousands were spent on doctors and psychiatrists, but much more went to finance every conceivable indulgence. We were broke.

As part of the property settlement, I agreed to give up any claim to the house on Evanview.

I went home and packed my clothes, leaving everything else for Judy to dispose of. For the last time, I left the house on the hill and moved into a smaller rented house.

Judy left for England, where she had a date at the Palladium and a destiny with theater history. Once she was settled, Liza would fly over to join her. I would take her to New York and put her on the plane to England. They'd been apart far too long. Though I'd selfishly wanted Liza to myself, now was the time she should be with Judy, during the period of one of her mother's greatest triumphs. Only then could Liza, who'd lived through so many of Judy's down periods, begin to understand her mother's staggering talent . . . and the enormous personal cost by which it had been achieved. Liza would also know that, though her parents couldn't live together any longer, her father would always remain a Judy Garland fan.

If she could never belong to one man, Judy would always belong to the people. She might exasperate them or try their patience, but she would remain the national addiction.

One could analyze her phrasing and timing and her distinctive emotional throb, and still not capture Judy's essence. She believed every word, and her sincerity made believers of us all. She could take the rigid structure of a song and improvise it into something uniquely her own . . . not necessarily sad, but always vulnerable.

Audiences would be moved to tears whenever she sang "Over the Rainbow." They may have been crying over their lost innocence, but they also realized that—whatever her personal tragedies—Judy's essential purity always remained. Her whole being was suffused with emotion, and we her public were fortunate that she generously shared it with us. Her kind of talent comes along only once in a generation. Would it appear unseemly to suggest that Liza now wears that mantle? And how many men can lay claim to being loved by the most extraordinary talents of not one, but two generations? And who loved, not always wisely, in return?

But love is what life is all about, I suppose . . . love of wife, love of family, love of work. There's always enough love around. You just have to be on the lookout for it.

Sometimes, it seeks you out. It next came in the guise of Mervyn LeRoy, who was directing *Lovely to Look At,* the remake of *Roberta.*

For some reason Mervyn had to leave the picture before the filming of the fashion show finale.

"Could you handle it for me?" he casually asked. "It's just a little show. Shouldn't take you longer than three days."

I was between pictures, and it sounded like a nothing assignment, but I was willing to help out a friend.

Once I got into it, however, I decided that if the sequence had to be done, it should be done well. My three-day assignment was to stretch into three weeks.

Adrian had designed over forty costumes, at a cost of $100,000. They deserved as extravagant a mounting as we could give them.

The production department had many sumptuous sets to choose from. I decided against any of them. The fashion show should be held in the courtyard of the couturier's building. I'd been to some fashion shows in Paris, and I particularly remembered one being held in the courtyard of the Georges Cinq in Paris, which was normally used as an outdoor cafe. Handsome archways abounded on the permanent set, and I requisitioned one of them for creating a tunnel of louvers, as I'd first done in *At Home Abroad* on the stage.

Four different settings would be created as a backdrop for the costumes, as well as the solo numbers of the picture's stars: Kathryn Grayson, Howard Keel, Red Skelton, Ann Miller, and Marge and Gower Champion.

Tony Duquette designed the costumes for the chorus, in addition to the props they carried to change the settings. First came street clothes, modeled against a green background, with the chorus in costumes from Italian comedy; then came bathing suits against a blue backdrop. The red sequence was largely devoted to the Champions' dance. The last segment had the chorus in gold armor, wheeling in opera boxes, against which the formal fashions were shown.

The fashion show did credit to the picture, I feel. It was the first time—to my knowledge—that a permanent set was so adapted. I didn't receive billing for my contributions, nor did I ask for any.

I was itching to start on my own projects. The studio had come to me with the idea of directing *Lili,* the fragile story of an orphaned French girl. The sentiment wasn't that far removed from *An American in Paris,* and I wanted to take another creative path. What I was offered turned out to be a superhighway.

John Houseman, after a brilliant career in the theater and films as an associate of Orson Welles, was now a contract producer at Metro. He'd already made a small film, *Holiday for Sinners,* when he approached me with an idea for a film.

Tribute to a Bad Man, a short story by George Bradshaw, traced the rise of a charming heel in the world of the theater. John suggested to studio head Dore Schary that the setting be changed to Hollywood. Charles Schnee was assigned to write the script.

When the first draft of the screenplay was finished, John invited me to lunch at Romanoff's. I didn't know him well, though his reputation as a theater and film associate of Orson Welles spoke reams about him.

Few producers could claim to be both tasteful and avant garde as John could. I found him to be honest and sensitive, and more creative than any producer had any right being.

When he described the story to me, I was intrigued. "Will you read it?" he asked.

I assured him that I would.

The screenplay fascinated me. It told of a film producer who uses everyone in his rise to the top: the actress he deceives by professing his love; the young director whose picture he expropriates; the screenwriter who loses his wife because the producer maneuvers her into an affair. Yet, at the end, all those who have been exploited are better off for having worked with him, their reputations established and their careers flourishing as never before. The cruelties they've suffered at his hands are unforgivable, yet they must grudgingly admit he's largely responsible for their success. His own career is now at low ebb and their curiosity is piqued enough to consider a new project he has in mind as a comeback.

It was a harsh and cynical story, yet strangely romantic. All that one hated and loved about Hollywood was distilled in the screenplay . . . the ambition, the opportunism, and the power . . . the philosophy of "get me a talented son-of-a-bitch." But it also told of triumphs against great odds, and the respect people in the industry had for other talents.

There was a pitfall to avoid, I felt. The actors could become caricatures if not properly controlled. It was a challenge. I was hooked. Forty-eight hours later, I called John to tell him I would love to direct *Tribute to a Bad Man.*

With its budget of little over one million dollars, it was designed as a small picture. Dore was surprised I wanted to do it. But not for long, when he noticed how eagerly the cast fell into place.

John and I first approached Kirk Douglas. He eagerly accepted the role. Then Lana Turner volunteered her services.

The part of the B-movie producer was being dangled before a character actor at the studio when Walter Pidgeon informed us he wanted to do it. His suave image didn't jibe with our concept of the slightly seedy character, but Walter was adamant. He turned up one day at my office, his gray hair disguised by a crew cut wig and in an ill-fitting suit, to show me how he would look in the part. He convinced me, so he too was cast.

We'd planned to hire two actors not under contract to Metro: Dick Powell to play the young director and Gloria Grahame as the flighty Southern wife of the screen writer. Dick had a better idea. "Don't I look like a writer?" he asked when he came to see me. The part of the Southern novelist brought to Hollywood by Jonathan Shields was much more to his liking. Dick didn't relate to the part of the director who loses control of his picture to the ravenous ambitions of the producer. We saw it his way, and assigned contract player Barry Sullivan to play the director.

Gloria quickly agreed to the flirtatious portrayal of the wife of the writer who elopes with a Latin movie star and dies in a plane crash for her efforts.

Even as we were casting, we were revising the script, incorporating the legends of Hollywood we knew about. The hero would be based on David Selznick and others, the heroine would remind the audience of Diana Barrymore. The director of the cat people film and other small budget pictures would be patterned on Val Lewton.

With Robert Surtees manning the camera, we started to film.

Arthur Freed seemed somewhat ambivalent about a musical director taking on such a serious melodrama, particularly when he had some projects of his own in mind. He decided, I suppose, to let me get it out of my system. A note just prior to filming wished me well:

DEAR VINCENTE:
Good luck! I hope that your "Tribute to a Bad Man" ballet turns out to be as exciting as the "Father of the Bride" ballet. So, until we do our ballet, good luck!

Love
ARTHUR

So on with the dance.

When Kirk and I discussed his portrayal I suggested he approach the part in a different way.

"Your strength is always there ready to explode," I told him, "so you don't have to stress it. The audience understands that. You should play it for charm."

He accepted the suggestion. Kirk repeatedly turned to me during filming to observe, "I was very charming in that scene, wasn't I?"

He required very little directing, for he grasped the Jonathan Shields character immediately. We'd both met many such people during our years in Hollywood.

In one scene, I suggested an offbeat approach. Kirk hasn't yet made it as a major producer, and he is bankrolled in a poker game by his young cronies. He leaves a palatial house after an evening of gambling and walks toward the jalopy where his friends wait to pick him up. He smiles all the way to the car. His friends, anticipating great news, smile back at him.

"How much did you win?" one of them asks. Kirk smiles back, "I lost." I thought their comprehension should be delayed. "Keep those smiles on your faces," I instructed the actors. I felt the disillusion should gradually sink in, for it would make the scene more powerful. And with Kirk's suggestion of bravado, it would seem oddly more real.

Sometime during the course of filming, wiser heads suggested a title change. Since Lana Turner was getting star billing, the name of the picture seemed inadequate. An alliterative title, *The Bad and the Beautiful,* was settled on.

Lana was at the height of her career, one of the top sex symbols in films. Those who made easy judgments said that in being manufactured into a personality, one very important cog had been left out: a consuming talent. This to me was unfair.

I agreed with John Houseman's assessment of Lana's acting ability. "On a long curve, she's never been capable of sustaining a whole picture as an actress," he told me. "But on the short curve she's very good."

My challenge was to make her portrayal a series of short curves. I wouldn't allow her to indulge her insecurities as an actress, and I called on many ruses and subterfuges to extract a performance from her.

Lana's face was never shown in her first scene. It was nevertheless as challenging a bit of acting for her as any other scene in the picture.

Kirk Douglas and Barry Sullivan break into the deserted house of her late father, a famous movie profile of the past. Their mission is a sort of homage to the late actor's spirit. Only Lana's legs were visible as they dangled through the railing of an upper level of the main room. Her slurred speech would have to suggest that the character was drunk.

254

It was a difficult scene, and Lana approached it with justifiable nervousness. The reading had to be an absolutely true one. Otherwise the picture would start on a ludicrous note from which it might never recover.

Louis Calhern supplied the narration for the excerpt from Shakespeare in the scene, in the voice of the young woman's late father, as played on a phonograph. He received no billing for his contribution.

Lana was to suggest the unhealthy bond she still feels, though according to the movie code of the time it was considerably short of incestuous.

Her first efforts were respectable, but not quite what I wanted. She would have to establish the torment of living with her father's exalted reputation in addition to suggesting the lush and the tramp she has turned into.

"That was good, Lana," I told her after one of the early takes, "but the sound men said they didn't quite pick up the last part of your speech. Let's try it again. This time, try to speak the lines with less emotion . . . more matter of fact . . . and of course you'll have to slur them again."

Another take was required due to "trouble" with the lighting. In fact, every retake was needed because it was somebody else's fault but Lana's. I finally got what I wanted, a brilliant reading by Lana.

As she got more into the picture, her nervousness disappeared. She effectively made the character's transition from tramp to glamour queen, and proved what a fine actress she was along the way.

Lana's portrayal in the film within the film of a character loosely resembling Anna Karenina was also satisfactory.

I devised a scene with a dying lover, very much of the Russian court and in the Garbo tradition. John Houseman took one look at all the pyrotechnics involved and asked, "What kind of a picture are they trying to make anyway?" Frankly, I think only Kirk Douglas knew.

The sequence gave me an opportunity to use a boom camera, zeroing in on the scene and drawing up high to show the technicians involved in the filming. Their reactions, unlike those of the stage hands in *Citizen Kane* to the singing of Kane's beloved, was respectful. This was the right assessment of the acting talent of the movie actress Lana was playing. Those actually involved in the shooting also were showing new respect for her ability.

It was never more evident than in the scene where she leaves Kirk's house on the night of her greatest professional triumph, after finding him there with another woman.

255

He has courted her into becoming a star, and she has delivered for him out of the love she bears for him. She discovers his betrayal and the reason for it.

The following sequence was probably as cinematic a piece of business as I've ever been associated with. The script called for Lana to get into the car and drive off into the night. That was all right, but how much better it would be if her hysteria could be contained in the car, the claustrophobia underscoring her feelings. I plotted out a scene as if we were photographing a ballet.

The car was on a turntable. I devised the camera's in and out movement, first zooming in on Lana's face, then on her foot as it pressed down on the accelerator, then on the back of her head so that the blurred image of the rain she had to drive through was suggested. When it was all laid out, I explained the scene to Lana. Her hysteria was to increase as the car speeded along, until that point where the car skids and Lana presses the brake, her whole being dissolved—and somehow cleansed—by an avalanche of tears.

It was going to be a long take, and I was prepared to spend the whole day to get the scene right. The cameras rolled, and Lana went through the tortured scene with the technique and instinct of the consummate actress. I was astounded, and thrilled that she had come along so far in the picture. She was a hungry kitten lapping up milk and she proved she was a very good actress . . . if only a director would take the time with her.

We were still shooting when Academy Award nominations for the previous year were announced. *An American in Paris* was nominated in eight categories.

The people at Metro, myself included, were stunned. There'd been a smattering of nominations for musicals in the past, but it was a Hollywood truism that the genre simply wasn't taken seriously. Only once, in 1944, did Best Picture and Best Director go to a musical, *Going My Way*. But that picture was essentially a comedy-drama with interpolation of musical segments to accommodate the talents of its stars, Bing Crosby and Risë Stevens. Purists didn't classify it as a traditional Hollywood musical.

The number of nominations put our picture in the same league as the multiply-nominated *Gone With the Wind* and *The Best Years of Our Lives* in previous years. *An American in Paris* had been considered merely a mass entertainment, and its financial success certainly proved that. To be further recognized in this way was the rarest of compliments.

Two dramas, *A Place in the Sun* and *A Streetcar Named Desire,* were the early favorites for Best Picture. Metro had two nominations for the category and, frankly, it would have been preferable for the studio if *Quo Vadis* had won, since considerably more money was tied up in that picture than in ours. The studio, however, would have been quite happy to concede the many technical awards to our picture, though they were being avidly contested with nominations from other studios.

I didn't expect to win as Best Director, for the other nominations had gone to giants of the industry, all of them working in dramas: John Huston for *The African Queen;* Elia Kazan for *A Streetcar Named Desire;* George Stevens for *A Place in the Sun;* and William Wyler for *Detective Story.* Kazan and *Streetcar* had already won New York Film Critics Awards, so they were probably the favorites.

But March 20, 1952, was to be a night of upsets. Humphrey Bogart in *African Queen* nosed out Marlon Brando in *Streetcar* for Best Actor. Stevens beat Kazan as Best Director. The assumption from then on was that *A Place in the Sun* would be named Best Picture. Then, the Academy, in another example of cutting up the pie, gave the Best Picture to *An American in Paris.* It was probably the most triumphant night in Arthur Freed's life, for he was also the recipient of the Irving Thalberg Award for exemplary creative standards. Gene Kelly won a special award for his choreography. The picture won in all but two nominations: Best Director and Best Film Editing (Adrienne Fazan).

One by one, colleagues went up to the stage of the Pantages Theatre to accept their well-deserved awards: Alan Lerner for Best Story and Screenplay; Alfred Gilks and John Alton for Best Color Cinematography; Cedric Gibbons, Preston Ames, Edwin B. Willis and Keogh Gleason for Color Art Direction and Set Decoration; Johnny Green and Saul Chaplin for Scoring; Orry-Kelly, Walter Plunkett and Irene Sharaff for Color Costume Design.

With so many awards, I wasn't too disappointed in my loss. I was glad to get back to the reality of film-making the following day, and to the conclusion of work on *The Bad and the Beautiful.*

John today says *The Bad and the Beautiful* was his most painless picture.

It was for me in a way too. Toward the end of the shooting, however, my divorce from Judy was final. I suffered a temporary pang over things that were never meant to be, but the picture intruded itself again on my attention.

Filming ended on June 4, at about the same time Judy and Sid were married. I looked at what had been accomplished, and marveled at the many contributions of others.

Kirk certainly deserved a Best Actor nomination. The mannerisms mimics love to imitate weren't evident, and his performance was quietly powerful . . . and charming. Lana's performance was equally as riveting, and I hoped the members of the Academy would discern that. Gloria's Southern belle was a highly accurate impersonation, with just a touch of humor and malice.

The work of the crew was equally as inspired. The whole Hollywood milieu was exactingly re-created in Edward Carfagno's art direction, Keogh Gleason's set decoration and Helen Rose's costume design. Surtees's photography was brilliant. To this day, I think it's the best photographed black and white picture I ever directed. The camerawork was a contrast in lush and velvety blacks and intense whites. It was as slick as other Metro productions, but without Surtees we could never have captured the alternately affectionate and cynical moods which we needed.

Our colleagues in the industry found the picture to be true, apparently, for Gloria won an Academy Award for Best Supporting Actress, along with the creative talents who captured the feel and look of Hollywood: Surtees for cinematography; Carfagno for art direction; Gleason for set decoration and Helen Rose for costume design.

Enough writers on film have cited *The Bad and the Beautiful* as the best drama about Hollywood. The shorter view of the critics when the picture was released was a slightly different matter.

Crowther in the New York *Times* found the film "a vivid and devastating portrait of a hard and perfidious man who rules and rides roughshod over people in his career as a producer of films.

"The details of Hollywood's machinery—the executive offices, the sound stages, the screening rooms, the make-up chambers, the residential equipment, the facilities of bars and beds—are unmistakably authentic.

"For the script of Charles Schnee, for all its movement and accumulation of vivid episodes, does not comprehend the Hollywood fever or what makes its tortured people run. Nor does Mr. Minnelli's direction provide insights in sharp pictorial terms."

I didn't understand Crowther's vacillation on the film, particularly the way he drew a slightly negative conclusion without offering any concrete reasons for it. I surmised that somewhere along the way my message stopped getting to him.

Hollis Alpert, in a *Saturday Review* piece, said the picture "provides a more complete and sociological view of the dream factory than any movie has yet attempted." Alpert never mentioned Lana by name, but he could only be describing her as he wrote,

"When one sees acting from people who were not hitherto thought to possess any marked degree of ability, the accolade is generally fixed on the director. Vincente Minnelli has undoubtedly coaxed the best out of his players, but blood does not spring from a stone, and perhaps he has utilized to the fullest what was already there. Thus there are some opinions about certain of Hollywood's big names that are going to have to be revised. I am all for the theory that beauty need not be a hindrance to an acting career, and it would be salutary if Hollywood would show further signs of adopting the theory.

"To go on with Mr. Minnelli, he has done about all you can ask a director to do: his picture is visually exciting, strikingly photographed, and now and then reminds, in its lighting, of 'Citizen Kane.' (John Houseman, the producer, and once associated with Orson Welles, may have had some influence here.) Minnelli has captured the eerie quality of an empty sound stage at night, the sterilized look of a writer's office on the lot, the dull meaninglessness of a noisy cocktail party attended by picture people. As an exhibition of know-how in picture-making 'The Bad and the Beautiful' is first rate, although every now and then Charles Schnee's screenplay goes in for dubious melodrama."

Alpert concluded his review by voicing reservations about Kirk's role. Was the heel ultimately good, since all the people whose lives he touched were better off than they'd been before?

Kirk Douglas had no such reservations about the character or the picture. He sent me a note telling me so:

Dear Vincente:

After seeing the picture the other night, I feel like saying to you all the lines that Jonathan Shields started to say about the picture that he directed; especially when it comes to what he felt about his direction —my compliments would just begin to soar.

In all honesty, Vincente, I think you did a magnificent job and made a very interesting picture. I think every part was well played. Lana, especially, came off better than I thought she would, and you know that I always thought she would be excellent in it.

259

I was very pleased with what I did, because you got out of me a much more quiet quality than I have ever been able to get in any picture.

I hope we work together again, and again many thanks for everything.

Sincerely,
KIRK

Working at Metro, with its non-stop work schedule, usually didn't leave time for such niceties. That Kirk *took* the time was highly appreciated.

I was now being asked to squeeze in the direction of one of the segments for *The Story of Three Loves* before turning to another full-scale project. Producer Sidney Franklin planned to hire different directors for the three segments. Gottfried Reinhardt wound up directing the other two.

Jan Lustig and George Froeschel wrote the script for "Mademoiselle," the segment I would be directing, an adaptation of a story by Arnold Phillips.

Leslie Caron was playing a French governess, with Ricky Nelson enacting the son of an American diplomat who objects to his nanny's demands. Ethel Barrymore portrayed an elegant witch who transforms the boy into an adult Farley Granger who, naturally, falls for Leslie. Fantasy again, but one with humor and romance.

Leslie worked closely with Ricky until they knew each other very well. He had to be so familiar with her that it would breed a normal nine-year-old's resentment, if not contempt, toward his strict nanny.

Working with Miss Barrymore was the joy I expected it to be. She had a personal charm which was complemented by her extreme professionalism, qualities she shared with Maurice Chevalier.

Her eyes were wonderfully hypnotic, growing larger to convey certain thoughts. Her portrayal was consequently totally convincing.

She knew the comparatively short part cold, and it took only a couple of days to put her performance on film. It took no great effort to show her the enormous respect to which she was entitled.

Arthur Freed had discussed the idea of doing a picture based on the songs of Howard Dietz and Arthur Schwartz, and now he was ready to move. He even had a name for the new picture.

The team's most famous stage musical, in 1931, was *The Band*

260

Wagon. Arthur thought it was still a great title. The stage production, however, had been a revue, and a plot would have to be concocted around the title.

Fred Astaire, who'd starred in the musical on Broadway with his sister Adele, was semi-committed to the project. His presence sparked an idea. It would be delicious to base the characters on actual people. Why not base his part on the Astaire of a few years back, who'd been in voluntary retirement? Why not develop the situation further by suggesting that fame has passed him by?

The subsequent brainstorm of patterning the role of a producer on such flamboyant types as Orson Welles and George S. Kaufman came easily to mind. The writers would be based on Betty Comden and Adolph Green. It was a great coup to get them to write the screenplay, and they proceeded to satirize themselves.

I'd been their great fan, as had Sid Perelman, since they and Judy Holliday were part of the Revuers, a quintet of performers at the Village Vanguard in New York in the late 1930s. Their brand of topical satire was to be emulated by many groups after the war.

By this time, Judy was a star, and Betty and Adolph were established as the brightest of the writing lights in theater and films.

Arthur had brought them to Hollywood in 1947 to write the screenplay for *Good News.* They'd stayed on to write *On the Town, Singin' in the Rain,* and *The Barkleys of Broadway.* All of them were landmark musicals. Now it was my turn to benefit from their brilliance.

"The picture had something that was different than the others," Adolph says today. "In a few spots it came very close to achieving the intimacy of a live performance. There are certain shots where people are standing and singing that creates the feeling of live theater."

"We decided to take the most ordinary story line and bring everything into it that we knew about putting on a show," Betty adds. "That's really the only world that matters to the principals."

"We wanted to show all the clichés," Adolph continues, "how the troubles out of town can happen . . . how it happens that friends can turn to you and ask, 'how can you smart people get together and turn out such a mess?'"

For Comden and Green, *The Band Wagon* was the second time they were handed someone's musical catalog and instructed to write a movie around it. This time they'd be working with the songs of Dietz and Schwartz, where in *Singin' in the Rain* they'd written around the compositions of Arthur Freed and Nacio Herb Brown.

There were certain numbers, many from the original musical, that Dietz and Schwartz wanted in the picture: "A New Sun in the Sky," "Dancing in the Dark," "I Love Louisa." But Comden and Green ferreted one out by themselves. It was "By Myself," which Jack Buchanan had originally sung in the Broadway musical *Between the Devil*.

At the time, we hadn't planned on using Jack in the part of the theater's Renaissance Man, Jeffrey Cordova, with several Broadway shows running at the same time, in one of which he was starring.

Clifton Webb was originally offered the part. He opted instead for the role of John Philip Sousa in *Stars and Stripes Forever*. Clifton suggested Jack, a great English music hall star, for the part. We took him up on the suggestion, for we sensed Jack could supply the impulsive, scatter-brained explosiveness we were looking for.

The story was indeed fragile: a has-been movie actor takes a train to New York and is met by two writer friends, who urge him to do a Broadway play. They introduce him to a brilliant producer, who casts him and a classically oriented ballerina in a production which becomes more artily pretentious as the producer's ego gets increasingly involved in it. It opens to abysmal notices, but the members of the company resolve to rework the show and bring it to Broadway as the popular entertainment originally intended. Along the way, the star and the ballerina fall in love.

I discussed every inch of the script with Betty and Adolph. Neither one of us let go of it until we were all satisfied.

We shared the same favorite moments in the picture:

Fred, worrying that Cyd Charisse as his new dancing partner is too tall, as so many male dancers do, and subtly standing next to her when they meet to determine if this is true . . . Jack Buchanan dragging Fred into a washroom during rehearsal and telling him rapidly, while allowing no interruption, "Tony, you're showing me one-eighth of the iceberg, and I want to see eight-eighths. Now go out there and give it to me" . . . Somebody idly talking about ideals, with a subsequent rejoinder: "Did you ever try spreading ideals on a cracker?" The line somehow found its way into the play the people were putting on . . . Oscar Levant, emulating Adolph's enthusiasm, and jumping up and down, yelling, "I'm so glad" when things start looking right.

In an early scene, the backer's audition in Jack Buchanan's apartment, I thought several camera angles would work best, so I suggested several anterooms to the living room be constructed. The stars, kept purposely isolated, would periodically open doors to the salon where

Jack was breathing fire and brimstone as he explained his concept for the modern day version of *Faust*.

Betty and Adolph wrote the scene to the architecture.

I'd previously brought out Lemuel Ayres from New York to supervise all the visual details on *Meet Me in St. Louis*.

Too many pictures—none of mine, I hope—had been harmed by the lack of an overseeing eye, and I was determined that it wouldn't happen on *The Band Wagon*.

The picture needed a certain look, and it had to be a theatrical one. Oliver Smith seemed the ideal choice to supervise the aspects of set decoration, art direction, and costumes. He was cast with as much fore-thought as if he'd been one of the picture's stars . . . which, in a way, he was.

Michael Kidd was brought out to choreograph the numbers. They had to be believable as theater, as well as cinematic.

We started filming.

It was a bittersweet moment when Fred Astaire got off the train in New York. No press were there to meet him, no fans to welcome him to the city.

He shrugs it off, singing "By Myself," his attitude toward fleeting fame one of easy come, easy go.

But he's forgotten the writing team of Oscar Levant and Nanette Fabray who come storming in late to the station, carrying signs reading TONY HUNTER FAN CLUB and WELCOME TO NEW YORK.

(Betty and Adolph borrowed the idea from their own life. "At one point our fortunes were low," Betty recalls, "and I'd gone back to New York before Adolph. When he was due to arrive, I went down to the station to meet him."

(Adolph picks up the story. "I was this abject defeated figure sneaking into the city. And I looked up to see Betty bearing down on me, carrying this sign which read 'Adolph Green Fan Club.' It was a tre-mendous lift psychologically. In fact you could say it was a turning point in my life.")

Twenty years later Fred was on the same train station set, supplying one of the narrations to *That's Entertainment*, Metro's anthology of its top musicals. The condition of the set spoke volumes about what had happened to the studio in the interim.

"The set was a mess," Fred says. "All the windows on the train were broken. Nobody had tried to sweep or clean up. It was just a wreck. The Twentieth Century Limited looked so black and dreary.

As I walked along, I noticed that the carpeting was torn and the seats of the train were missing. But I suppose nothing should last forever."

Of course, the song from *The Band Wagon* which Jack Haley, Jr., expropriated for the title of his later film probably will, as an anthem to the world of entertainment.

So will the the far-sung talents of Fred and Cyd as probably the greatest dancing team in films.

In an earlier scene, they'd already had their fiasco, trying to dance on a stage with explosions blasting around them. It was highly comic, and the two were so worn out by the sequence they could only laugh about it.

But could they really perform together? "Dancing in the Dark" would answer the question. The two have had dinner and they saunter over to Central Park. They pass by a dance pavilion, and some people snickered when they saw the obvious device being planned to get them to dance with each other. But they went right on past the dance floor, lost in their own thoughts. They arrive to a semi-lit area, and they feel each other out.

Their movements were even more lyrical than the way *Newsweek* magazine described them in a cover story: "As the story goes, the Charisse-Astaire feud begins to simmer down in the course of a moonlit carriage ride through Central Park, and by the time the couple has descended and walked to the public dancing place the atmosphere is definitely serene. They stroll on into a blue glade and there, to the tune of 'Dancing in the Dark,' they drift into mutual rhythms with the ease of a zephyr springing up in Bermuda. The dance continues as what might be called a Hesitation Fox Trot—long, suave patterns excitingly broken. The number is full of witchery, and Charisse is a fine foil for the Old Master."

The Old Master, by the way, didn't feel the filming glided as easily as his dances with Cyd. In his autobiography, Fred described an incident which marred the very complicated take in the hotel room, where the kids of the cast hold a wake after the opening night fiasco:

I had a strange experience during the filming of that picture.

When you work with the brilliant Vincente Minnelli as your director, you want to come through with everything he asks for and sometimes the order is a bit difficult to handle.

In this instance, the scene was a small hotel room crammed with members of our show at a party immediately after our opening-night flop.

264

We were all supposed to be trying to forget the miseries of our flop and it was a difficult scene to stage with all those people in such tight quarters. Nothing seemed to play and Vincente kept changing lines and positions.

After about an hour of this confusion I ran into a complete mental block. I couldn't think of one definite thing of any kind, including my own name, and I shouted, "That's it—kill the lights—I can't think—I've got to get out of here," and walked off the set directly to Arthur Freed, who happened to be sitting there. I can remember the astonished look on everybody's face as I left. I had never done that in my life, and there was a strained silence.

I said to Arthur, "Come on, walk around with me for a few minutes, will you—I've cracked." Arthur, amazed, looked at me. "What's the matter, kid, take it easy." I kept saying, "I can't think, I can't think," as we walked arm-in-arm. All I remember is that I wondered what Phyllis and the children would say when I was brought home a sort of maniac. Concentrate I could not.

We walked for at least fifteen minutes. Then, I called the script man over to feed me some dialogue cues. They meant nothing; I was mentally blank. After about five more minutes I sat down with my head in my hands and started to function again. I was able to resume work.

I went to Minnelli afterward and apologized, explaining my mental lapse, and Vincente said, "Oh, that's perfectly all right, Fred, I drive everybody crazy."

Fred's story actually didn't go far enough, for he didn't know that my reaction to his apology was automatic. I hadn't a clue to his discontent. I was too busy concentrating on the scene to even notice that he'd stormed off the set. I thought he'd left to answer nature's call, or something.

I actually recall only one unpleasant incident during the making of the picture. The production department fired cinematographer George Folsey. They felt his thoughtful preparation was too slow. In a way, his firing was a reflection on my own work, for I'd always taken my time in thinking out my approach. A higher-up apparently thought it would be a risk to have two such types working together, and George was let go. I immediately wrote him a note, sympathizing for the unfairness of the action, and promising that we would work together again. Which we did on *The Cobweb*.

Shooting resumed with Harry Jackson.

Howard Dietz was in Culver City during part of the filming. His irrepressible humor was now legendary within the company. Several years previously, while on another tour of duty, he was leaving work for the day at three in the afternoon. Howard ran into Mayer outside the Irving Thalberg Building. The old man looked at his watch. "Howard," he said, "you're supposed to work until six. You're leaving so early."

Howard, unflappable, answered, "Yes, Mr. Mayer, but you have to realize that I also get to work very late."

Mayer nodded, "Yes, that's true." He continued on his way to his upstairs office.

How Howard fit so much activity in twenty-four short hours was a daily wonder. Not only did he run Metro's publicity office in New York, he also had a full-time composing career and a social life equal to that of any man of leisure.

As shooting continued, I was delighted we had still another frequent visitor: Liza. She was now quite the young lady. She'd go to the rehearsal hall and watch Cyd Charisse limber up. Soon she was standing beside her at the ballet bar. "She picks things up as quickly as Judy," Cyd told me. I was delighted that Liza was taking interest in my work, and that she was showing signs of inheriting her mother's talent.

Judy and Sid were again in residence in California, beginning production on *A Star Is Born,* which George Cukor was directing. I was glad that Liza was again in California, so that I could see her maturing in those areas where life with Judy hadn't already cast her as a near-adult. She was only seven, but onerous responsibilities were already being delegated to her. In many ways, she played mother to Judy's daughter.

Judy was most often doting with Liza, but there were times when neglect was inevitable. Thankfully, I would now be around for Liza to turn to during these difficult times.

I smothered her with love. If I spoiled Liza outrageously, the fairy tale quality of our relationship achieved a balance with the starkness of her life with Judy. Much as Liza loved her mother, Judy represented duty and worry. I required nothing but love. As a result, I shared Liza's most carefree times. Judy was sadly short-changed.

Every Christmas, I would commission Adrian or Irene Sharaff to execute five different costumes for Liza. They were made up with the same exactness of detail that a star would demand. Some, in fact, were adaptions of film and stage costumes. Perhaps it was a case of overkill for Liza to do her Halloween trick-or-treating disguised as Gertrude Lawrence. She thrived on it, however.

(On a previous Halloween, I'd had a witch costume designed for Liza, something Margaret Hamilton could have worn in *Wizard of Oz.*

266

This was during her serious period, when she wouldn't be laughed at. I took her around the neighborhood. "Will I scare the people?" she asked. "You'll frighten them to death," I assured her. She'd ring the door of house after house, as I stood on the sidewalk. Whoever answered the door would look at this tiny little girl and had to laugh. Liza was getting more and more upset. "They're laughing to hide their fear," I told her. She wasn't convinced. Finally we stopped at Gene Kelly's. His was an award-winning performance. "A witch! A terrible witch! Save me!" Liza walked home with her pointed witch's chin held high.)

She knew the elaborate costumes and my desire to have her with me on the set were a symbol of love and not a symptom of sickness. Analyzing it for an interviewer years later, Liza said, "I don't think you can be spoiled by extravagant gifts from people who love you. It's when they're given to put off having to love you that the problem starts."

But much as I tried to protect Liza, some emotional scars were unavoidable.

"You know," she told me recently, "you're writing your autobiography, and I bet there's not going to be anything in it that describes you as I see you."

"What do you mean?"

"You know . . . your habits . . . your peculiarities."

"Well," I said, "be my guest. Why don't you write something?" And so she did. Though the tone was loving, it would give any divorced father pause for thought:

TIME: From my sixth to my thirteenth year . . . say a Tuesday.
PLACE: Any of my father's houses—Hollywood, natch.
6:30 A.M.
We awaken at the same time . . . I in my room, which has been decorated to accommodate a passing fairy princess . . . he in his, which smells of tobacco, warm colors and thinking of all kinds. His alarm has wakened him up . . . his turning off his alarm clock wakes me. I lie still and listen to his early morning ritual: cough . . . the crinkling of bed sheets in reluctant goodbye . . . absent-minded whistling, followed by humming, which will go on for the whole day . . . the tub water running . . . cough . . . bathroom door closes . . . muffled cough.

Soon, Jeanette will start the clattering breakfast tray music downstairs. I get up and put on my robe—the one he likes—it's yellow—and my slippers, which we went especially to Magnin's to buy—Capezios, of course—and leap into his room to wait for him. The double doors swing open and he is in pajamas and robe . . . hair wet and combed.

"Hi, daddy."

"Ah ha, darling," he sings.

That same greeting every morning makes me feel like a constantly surprising present. He picks me up in his arms and I kiss his nose and he kisses both cheeks . . . seven times . . . five on one and two on the other. We settle back and he lights a cigarette, just in time for Jeanette to come in with breakfast and tell him to put it out. He eats quickly, and lets me eat the honey from the cut glass bowl. The tray gets pushed aside. Out comes a script.

"How come you're reading that now?"

"I'm preparing."

"Preparing what?"

"What I'm going to do today."

"Oh."

I don't understand till much later that at least he took the time to answer me . . . he always does!

Then he finishes dressing . . . quickly . . . in gray or black pants and a yellow shirt—always. He kisses me goodbye and hurries to the studio. I know where he's going because I'll join him there after school.

School is dreary but the studio will be fun. I hope he is making a musical . . . "Oh please, Daddy, be making a musical" . . . why doesn't three o'clock come so I can whiz toward Culver City? The guard at the gate says, "Hi, Liza." Soon I'm helping Nanny push open the heavy soundproof studio door.

Hooray! Fred Astaire and Cyd Charisse!

Daddy moves swiftly around the stage, telling everyone what to do in a quite definite way. Fred moves quickly. Cyd moves quickly. Everyone moves quickly. Daddy then whispers something to Cyd Charisse and as she walks away, she tells her make-up man . . . and me . . . "He's the wittiest and most charming man I've ever known." Dozens of people are still moving around. Then Daddy yells, "Okay!" All action, except for that going on before the camera, stops.

To Astaire: "Okay, baby." (He calls everyone Baby) "Here we go . . . camera . . . roll it." Everyone is still holding his breath . . . "All righty! Action!" Fred dances and sings for a while. Then Daddy says, "Cut. Let's go ahead. Marvelous, Fred." "New deal," yells the assistant director. Daddy starts moving quickly. Fred moves quickly. Cyd moves quickly. Everyone is moving quickly. Except Daddy and me.

Mr. O'Hara, the cookie man, comes over to the chair where Daddy has plunked me and gives me an Oreo. Daddy sits beside me and asks me about school.

268

I leave the studio. The studio leaves Daddy. Perf.

As we drive home, I sit on his lap . . . from the ages of six to eight, that is . . . and he teaches me the lyrics of a song . . . "Love me or leave me, or let me be lonely." We sing together through Beverly Hills every time we go home together. "Say the words," he says, "like you're talking."

We have dinner alone and he tells me about a lady named Colette and a place called Paris. He tells me about it until I can smell it. "Can we go there some day?" He says yes, so I know we will.

Over the ice cream, I'm told I will have to go live with Mama after dinner.

"When can I come back to you?"

"In a few days."

"How long is a few days?"

"Not long."

"How long?"

"A few more than a couple."

"Oh."

"Your mama needs you and loves you too."

"I know. So do I. But I'd like to stay with you a little longer."

"Next time!"

"But—"

"Did you ever hear the story of *The Nightingale and the Rose,* by Oscar Wilde?"

"No."

"Oh, darling, it's wonderful. Listen."

I hold his hand and listen to his voice and wonder at how he still smells of Floric talc from this morning.

I say farewell to my slippers. Mama thinks they are bad for my feet. And I get into the car with Mama's driver.

8:30 P.M.

"Goodbye, darling."

"Goodbye, Daddy."

"Goodbye."

"Goodbye."

I've always hated that word.

Arthur had seen an enormous photo spread on the Mickey Spillane cult in *Life* magazine. He suggested the phenomenon might be ripe for satire.

I got copies of Spillane novels and took them with me on a short holiday to northern California which I took with Tony and Beegle

269

Duquette. When I was through reading them, my eyes were out on sticks. It was one of the loveliest periods of my life.

Applying the term satire to a ballet based on this school of fiction was actually a bit redundant, for in practically every page the writing contained the seeds of its own parody . . . the inevitable blonde and brunette, the vicious kicks in the stomach, the farewell kiss as the good girl—who turns out to be the bad girl—dies.

I conceived an improbably plot involving the blonde and brunette. Roger Edens adapted themes from Dietz and Schwartz songs for the ballet. Since Comden and Green had returned to New York before the ballet was fully plotted, I wrote Fred's voice-over narration to the action. It was disjointed and made little sense, but it incorporated all the Spillane clichés:

MUSIC. A woman screams, followed by the sound of whistling, then the riddling sound of a machine gun. A city street, night. Rod Riley approaches.

The city was asleep . . . the joints were closed . . . the rats, the hoods and the killers were in their holes . . . I hate killers.

My name is Rod Riley. I'm a detective.

Somewhere in a furnished room, some guy was practicing on a horn. It was a lonesome sound. It crawled on my spine. I had just finished a tough case. I was ready to hit the sack . . .

A distraught blonde enters the scene.

I can smell trouble a mile off, and this poor kid was in trouble . . . big trouble. She was scared, scared as a turkey in November.

Gunshots. The blonde collapses. A thug, who'd apparently been pursuing her, drops down on a live track. His body is blown apart by an explosion.

There was nothing left of the guy, nothing at all, except a rag and a bone and a hank o' hair. The guy had been trying to tell me something. But what?

Riley is blackjacked from behind.

So that's the way they wanted to play. All right. Somewhere in the city there was a killer, and that was bad. Bad for the killer. Because I shoot hard, and I hate hard.

Riley stands outside a couture shop. He's carrying the rag. He sees a matching piece of fabric in the display window. He enters the very

270

elegant shop. He notices an emerald ring in a case. Nearby is a brunette.

I was playing a hunch . . . she came at me in sections. More curves than a scenic railway. She was bad, she was dangerous. I wouldn't trust her any farther than I could throw her. She was selling hard, but I wasn't buying.

They go into the stockroom. Riley is set upon by three men. He kills them. The back of a fourth man, in black hat and coat, is seen running away.

This had to be Mister Big. Get him and you get 'em all. I chased him from one end of Manhattan to another.

Subway scene. The blonde enters.

There was something about this kid that made you wanna protect her for life.

Gunshots. The blonde runs away. A man falls dead, killed by the gunshot.

That bullet was meant for me!

Riley stands outside a beauty shop, the second clue—the hank of hair —in his hand.

Maybe this was a long shot, but I've seen some funny ones pay off. *He climbs up the fire escape. Inside is a masked blonde wearing the emerald ring.*

I was beginning to see daylight . . .

Riley's hit on the head again. As he comes to:

These mugs are smart, but they made one mistake: they got me mad. *Riley stands on a city street, a bone in his hand. He enters Dem Bones Cafe. Thugs rush at him, but he draws a gun and they all back up. The brunette stands at the bar. She languidly takes off a bright green coat. Underneath is a bright red dress. They dance. As the music ends, she strikes a pose. Riley notices the back of the same man in the black hat and coat, as he approaches the bandstand, He grabs the trumpet.*

Suddenly all the pieces fitted together. I knew how the crime had been done: the high note on the trumpet had shattered the glass . . . *Riley pushes the glass down the bar as the man starts to blow on the trumpet. The glass explodes.*

. . . the glass with the nitroglycerine . . . Now I knew who the killer was, but it didn't matter. Killers have to die . . .

The trumpet player pulls a gun, but Riley is faster. He shoots. The trumpet player collapses in his arms. His hat slips. It's the blonde. Before she dies, she kisses him. On her finger is the emerald ring. The scene dissolves to a city street, night.

The city was asleep . . . the joints were closed . . . the rats, the hoods and the killers were in their holes. I felt good, but something was missing . . .

Riley puts a cigarette in his mouth. A hand holds forth a lighted match. It's the brunette.

She was bad . . . she was dangerous. I wouldn't trust her any farther than I could throw her. But she was my kind of woman.

The two walk away.

The satire couldn't have come off without Oliver Smith's fanciful sets and Michael Kidd's inspired choreography.

Oliver supplied an extraordinary background for the opening scene, a photomontage of the New York skyline with the tenement district in the foreground.

Betty Comden observed that Fred seemed wary around Michael who, despite his youth, brought a more classical approach to dancing than Fred was accustomed to. "It reminded me of the lack of common ground between the movie hoofer and the ballerina, which we had in our script," she says.

But they wound up being firmly in tune, if the relatively short period of three days—in which the ballet was shot—was any indication.

The rest of the filming, in fact, went quickly. Before we knew it, the picture was ready for release.

The Band Wagon opened in New York in July of 1953.

"Take it from us," Bosley Crowther wrote in the New York *Times,* "it is a honey—a genial and comprehending snipe at the rampant egoes of theatre people, their reckless excusions and alarums and all of the manifold headaches that accompany the production of a show. It is also, by chance, a very touching appreciation of the nature of Mr. Astaire. If there is anything wrong with it as entertainment, it is too subtle about the theatre for all to get."

Howard Dietz sent a wire to Howard Strickling:

NEVER HAVE PAPERS GIVEN ANY MOTION PICTURE MORE EXTRAVAGANT PRAISE THAN THAT ACCORDED BAND WAGON TODAY. FROM TIMES WHICH

272

CALLS IT "A SHOW THAT RESPECTFULLY BIDS FOR RECOGNITION AS ONE OF THE BEST MUSICAL FILMS EVER MADE" TO TRIBUNE WHICH DESCRIBES IT AS "THE BIG LOAD OF MUSICAL PLEASURE WHICH HAS ROLLED INTO MUSIC HALL," THE MIRROR WHICH SAYS IT IS "A SURE WINNER" AND THE NEWS WHICH IN FOUR STAR REVIEW SAYS IN BOLD HEADLINE "IT IS WONDERFUL."

Howard had a doubly vested interest. As head of promotion and publicity for Metro in New York, he was delighted because this would be an easy picture to sell.

But as one of its most vital contributors, he had to be ecstatic that his work was praised by the critics. Given special mention was the one number written for the picture: "That's Entertainment."

As soon as I read the reviews, I took time off from my work on *The Long, Long Trailer* to send some wires of my own. I was especially pleased that Jack Buchanan, Michael Kidd, and Oliver Smith were singled out. All were newcomers to Hollywood pictures, and all had delivered beautifully.

JACK BUCHANAN, GARRICK THEATRE, LONDON . . . DEAR JACK . . . YOU HAD AN ENORMOUS PERSONAL TRIUMPH LAST NIGHT. I AM VERY PROUD OF YOU . . . LOVE VINCENTE.

MICHAEL KIDD, SHUBERT THEATRE, PHILADELPHIA . . . DEAR MIKE . . . YOU WERE THE HIT OF THE EVENING LAST NIGHT . . . I COULDN'T BE PROUDER OF YOU . . . CONGRATULATIONS VINCENTE.

OLIVER SMITH, NEW YORK . . . DEAR OLIVER . . . THE PREVIEW LAST NIGHT WAS THE MOST EXCITING I'VE EVER BEEN CONNECTED WITH . . . YOUR WORK DAZZLED EVERYONE. I COULDN'T HAVE BEEN PROUDER OF YOU. COME BACK IMMEDIATELY . . . VINCENTE.

I returned to work with Lucille Ball and Desi Arnaz with the assurance that I must be doing something right. The work on the picture was an added convincer. So did my meeting of a beautiful girl.

After years of marriage, I was playing the field romantically, with no compulsion to marry in the near future.

I'd started entertaining again. Though I don't recall who acted as my hostess on one of these evenings, I do remember that Vernon Duke arrived with a very beautiful brunette. Her name was Georgette Magnani, and she was newly arrived to the United States. She'd come over to act as a sort of chaperone for her younger sister, Christiane Martel, who'd just been named Miss Universe and had signed a movie contract.

Georgette was of Italian and French blood, as was I. Her parents were simple country people, she told me, and I was attracted by the open manner she must have inherited from them. It wasn't long before I was seeing her every night. Her brand of Latin temper was much to my liking, as was that of another Latin I was working with during the day.

16 | Hits and Misses

Desi Arnaz, Sr., called me the other day. "Did you know," he asked, "that *The Long, Long Trailer* was the most successful comedy in Metro's history?"

He claimed to have some special knowledge—perhaps a percentage? —which proved it was the studio's highest grossing comedy. If it's true, then Pan Berman must be doubly satisfied over the success of his brainchild. For he had to hard sell to get the studio to back the picture.

"Metro wanted no part of it," Pan says. "They subscribed to the theory that the audience wouldn't pay to see actors they could get at home for free. But I insisted these were different parts, and Lucille Ball and Desi Arnaz could make the picture hilarious. If the picture was funny enough, I had no worries that enough people wouldn't pay to see it."

Pan had bought Clinton Twiss's novel and assigned Frances Goodrich and Albert Hackett to fashion a screenplay. When he suggested my possible participation, he found a very eager accomplice. The book was based on real-life, and my past experience with *Father of the Bride* convinced me that the humor of true situations is the best possible kind. And it has to be played realistically, capturing the humor inherent in the situation. Even slapstick must have a basis in reality, as should fantasy . . . but, then, that's ground I've already covered.

If that approach is generally right for comedy, there are other aspects specifically right for me. I revel in the humor of the anticlimax, in inflated plots revealed as holding nothing but hot air, in people who hold themselves seriously without realizing the caricatures they actually are.

To me, one of the funniest pictures I've ever seen is the 1939 French production, *Bizarre, Bizarre,* starring Jean-Louis Barrault and players from classical French theatre. Based on a novel by Britain's F. Anstey, it told of a murder, involving several people. At the end it's revealed there was never any murder at all. It had been a misunderstanding.

The Halloween sequence in *Meet Me in St. Louis* is of similar humor, the children making up horror stories that don't exist. The meeting between the producer and director in *The Bad and the Beautiful* and a wardrobe man was similarly funny . . . even more so when one considers it was based on an actual incident.

They are discussing a low budget potboiler, *The Cat People,* and the wardrobe man has fit some moldy cat man costumes on some players. They are as ill-fitting as they are ill-smelling. But the wardrobe man, in all seriousness, assures the producer and director that this costume can be fixed and that one freshened up, but the third might be a bit of trouble because it's made of imported material. His enthusiasm for the most commonplace of work depresses the young film-makers. They retire to a projection room where they decide, as director Val Lewton actually did, never to show the cat people but to suggest their presence through imagination. And, as Lewton did, they succeeded in making something quite distinguished out of nothing.

I'd discussed these ideas with Pan during our previous pictures, and perhaps that's why he thought of me when he decided to produce *The Long, Long Trailer.*

Once he had sold the studio on the idea, and the picture was in production, Pan left for Europe, for his *Knights of the Round Table* was being filmed at the same time.

If I needed an overseer, he left me in the very capable hands of Jane Loring, his long-time associate. Pan had surreptitiously, he thought, brought her onto our previous pictures as a means to help me keep up with the shooting schedule. He was aware that I sometimes got so enamored of a scene that I would dwell too long on it. Decisions would

276

be needed for the filming of other sequences, and Jane was assigned the duty of prodding me into making them so that shooting could proceed.

Lucy and Desi were at the height of their television popularity. I thought the story was perfect for them. There were times when the action was broad, and those were the opportunities Lucy grabbed hold of and ran away with.

It was an inexpensive picture to make, and a painless one. All the film editor had to do was clip off the end slates of the film to make this a smoothly flowing picture. With Lucy and Desi in it, it also had to be an extremely funny one.

Lucy is one of the few comedic talents who can be broad and uniquely human at the same time. She can get away with things that less talented people wouldn't even presume to handle. On television, week after week, she's handled manufactured situations and passed them off as real.

Her slapstick interludes in the picture, however, were based on fact. She decides to get into the trailer while Desi is driving along, explaining that a gourmet dinner will be ready by the time they reach their evening's destination. It's one misadventure after another, food falling on the floor and Lucy slipping on it, until after the jerky ride Desi discovers, when he stops the car for the night, that Lucy looks as if she'd been wallowing in a pigpen. Only then is it explained to them that it's against the law for people to ride in trailers while in motion, because of the dangers involved.

But their every experience with the trailer is a misadventure. I always wondered why the American Trailer Association put its Good Trailer-keeping Seal of Approval, or whatever, on the picture.

Madge Blake, playing Lucy's aunt, was called upon to smolder after the trailer had knocked down a portico of her gingerbread house. (It was one of the houses on the old *Meet Me in St. Louis* set.)

She wrote a note thanking me for the part, then offered a perspective on what it must have meant to Liza to be the daughter of noted parents.

"I didn't get a chance to tell you," Madge wrote, "that as I walked toward the house after my 'uncontrollable rage' scene (the first time), your little Liza came up to me and asked, 'Why don't you like that trailer? I think it's a very nice trailer!'

"I adore little girls—and I think children are the most important people on earth, so I tried to explain how I, personally, thought it was a lovely trailer, but the lady in the story, who had planted the roses and owned the house, which was not a *real* house, hated it for ruining her

277

roses. She seemed satisfied and sat down. We talked about other things and I, because I have taught children, asked, 'Where do you go to school?' It was just to make conversation, of course.

"Suddenly she stiffened. She got up and said in a strained little voice, 'I have to find my daddy now!'

"I had completely forgotten she is a famous little girl and has undoubtedly been instructed not to answer personal questions. It made me a little sick for a moment. I hope she didn't identify me with the kind of people who pry into the private lives of well-known people in every possible way.

"She is adorable and I'd like to tell her that when my second grandchild arrives in September I hope it will be a little girl as lovely and talented and well-mannered as Liza."

On that picture, we were all lovely and talented and well-mannered.

I didn't use any fancy gimmickry. None seemed to be needed in the straightforward telling of the story about the misadventures of a young couple in their honeymoon trailer.

Most of my direction seemed to involve very practical matters, such as having Desi sit on a couple of pillows as the two of them drove along in their car. Though Desi and Lucy are the same height, Lucy is taller when they sit next to each other.

I supplied an in joke, as the two of them climb up a steep grade, afraid they may fall off the side of the cliff. Lucy, to calm Desi, tells the story about a movie in which the good brother is really the bad brother. She got the story all mixed up, but the reference was to *Undercurrent*.

All film-making should be as easy, if the reviews of critics are any indication. *Time* magazine called it "a wonderfully slap-happy farce. Director Vincente Minnelli, as skilled a comedy hand as Hollywood employs, has a way of letting the story babble on absently between solid banks of common sense until the audience is lulled in smiles. Then all at once the boat is rocking wildly in farcical white water."

The *Newsweek* review said I maintained "this terrifying ratio between man and machine throughout the Technicolor film with a series of crises so broad, wild, and—a good deal of the time—hilariously funny that he almost makes Mack Sennett look, in retrospect, like a reticent disciple of Ibsen's."

Though my notices were so complimentary that some people may have suspected I wrote them myself, I had no delusions about the greatest assets to the picture. It needed the foolishness of Lucy and Desi to make the proceedings take off.

278

If something was needed for *Brigadoon,* my next picture, I still don't know what it was.

Gene Kelly describes the movie version of *Brigadoon* as a singer's show on Broadway that had to be made as a dancer's show.

"My voice wasn't good enough to do the Lerner and Loewe numbers," he says. "If we could have done it off the lot like a Western, we all would have been very happy. The picture never did what it should have done. There was some talk of shooting it in Scotland, and Arthur Freed and I went there to scout locations. But the weather was so bad that we had to agree with the studio. So we came back to the United States, and started looking for locations here. We found some highlands above Monterey that looked like Scotland. But then the studio had an economy wave, and they clamped the lid on that idea. Somehow the fun went out of it."

If the picture couldn't be of the real earth, we'd have to do the next best thing. Our company took over a huge soundstage and proceeded to construct the outdoor hills around the village of Brigadoon.

Arthur must have sensed my misgivings about the project, for a lovely note arrived from him just as we began preparations for the film:

DEAR VINCENTE:
I saw Joe Pasternak coming out of a projection room and I said to myself: "There but for you go I."
I love you.

ARTHUR

How could anyone help not loving Arthur in return? We'd had our battles royal, but his constant encouragement and confidence had us all walking through fire for him. He was aware that his production unit produced the studio's most stylish musicals. Arthur was happy to share credit with others, and with me—it was done by paraphrasing the title of one of the songs of our current picture.

Brigadoon was to be my first film in Cinemascope. I disliked the shape of this widened screen. I never felt the screen was truly wider. It just tended to cut off the top and bottom of the picture. This had actually been done with *The Band Wagon,* which was released just as Cinemascope was taking hold. Some theaters used the Cinemascope mat and cut off Fred's feet in his dancing scenes. This was heresy.

The four to three ratio of the standard movie screen approximates the shape of conventional paintings. Such a configuration has stood the test of the ages, and I'm not surprised that the shape has returned in today's pictures.

At the time, however, we were stuck with Cinemascope, and we tried to live with it. The wider screen might capture the breadth of the Scottish moors, but it didn't help the more intimate aspects of the story.

The tale is an ingenious one, coming I'm sure from Alan's preoccupation since childhood with the mystic and the psychic, as did his later *On a Clear Day You Can See Forever*. It told of a village which comes to life one day every hundred years, and of two Americans who stumble upon it during a hunting trip to Scotland.

The score was melodic and haunting, its songs among the best composed by Lerner and Loewe. I'd remembered seeing Fritz Loewe on television, explaining the influences on his music. "There aren't many Scottish tunes," he said. "Actually I based the music for *Brigadoon* on Brahms. His work sounds Scottish. You can't be slavish, especially to influences that aren't that plentiful. You have to keep the freedom to compose."

In preparing the film, I rationalized more than adequate reasons for shooting on a studio soundstage. Many different kinds of terrain would be needed. We would have to travel to several locations in Scotland to capture them all, fighting the impossible weather all the way. Even if we'd shot at Big Sur, we'd have to travel to scattered spots, as we were forced to do ten years later when I was directing *The Sandpiper*. We would have better control in the studio. By working with art director Preston Ames, I was able to work out a setting that would capture a different aspect to the landscape with each camera angle.

Joe Ruttenberg, the old pro, would be manning the camera. We decided to approach the filming in such a way as to stack the cards in favor of the Gene Kelly character returning to Brigadoon.

Interiors were lighted to suggest Flemish paintings. Exteriors were enveloped in romantic mist. The modern-day segment, concentrated in a noisy bar in New York, would spell out everything that is ugly and lacking in humanity about the everyday rat race.

Cyd would be starring with Gene, and she made a most lovely Scottish lass.

The filming went as easily as it had for *The Band Wagon*, helped immeasurably by Gene's assistants, Carol Haney and Jeanne Coyne. With Gene so busy on the choreography, I depended on Carol to fill in when Gene was occupied elsewhere. This was to be her last picture as assistant choreographer. She would be leaving for New York and *Pa-*

jama Game, and from that point on, she was known as Star. Jeannie, later to marry Gene, was the perfect intermediary with the crew. She'd sit on a camera crane and count the numbers for the crew as we played back the recorded music. Her patience was inhuman.

And yet, with all this sterling assistance, something was definitely missing. Perhaps Gene was right about having lost faith in the project. I noticed that he seemed curiously remote and slightly down. He'd returned from his eighteen-month sojourn in Europe and the filming of *Invitation to the Dance,* to find that the musical genre was in the descendant.

I had many talks with him, trying to impress on him the need to show exuberance in the part. He had to light up the sky, he was so struck by the wonder of the place. Gene delivered as much as he could.

Van Johnson, on the other hand, embarrassed me with riches. His portrayal of Gene's sidekick was magnified, if not magnetic. Van was cursed with the mugger's face, and every director had to watch him to make sure he wasn't too expressive.

I felt frustrated by the picture, but I didn't know what to do to salvage it. I was sure it would be visually arresting, but I didn't know if the slender thread of a story would go over.

A more personal matter was also coming to a head.

Her sister's movie obligation was completed, Georgette informed me, and the two of them would soon be returning to France.

We talked it out, and decided we would marry.

Cyd Charisse, who'd become a good friend of Georgette's, was her matron of honor in February of 1954 when we were married in Riverside, California. Claude Dauphin was my best man.

We returned to Hollywood to start married life together. I reported back to the studio for the continued filming of *Brigadoon.*

Somehow the picture was finished. When it was released the following September my misapprehensions were confirmed.

"Despite the resurgence of good films," the *Newsweek* notice read, "Hollywood can still put its worst foot forward in the classic manner."

Crowther in the *Times* found *Brigadoon* "curiously flat and out-of-joint, rambling all over creation and seldom generating warmth or charm . . . pretty weak synthetic Scotch."

And so, like the aerialist who's just taken a bad fall, I was eager to get back on the tightrope.

Green Mansions loomed as my next project. The novel, written by William Henry Hudson and published in 1904, was an old man's fairy tale. It told of the longing for perfect feminine tenderness and loveliness, which is found in Rima, a semi-human embodiment of the spirit of the forest. She's an elfin creature living in trees and rain forests, speaking like a bird and wearing a dress woven by spiders. Her youth can never fade, her love is constant.

Arthur Freed and I agreed the movie should appeal to the senses and not the mind. Previous efforts at adapting the work had failed because they'd tried to rationalize a plot and nail down the dream. Alan Lerner was approached to write the script.

Art director Preston Ames and I then took a trip to Venezuela with a studio unit manager. Though Hudson had written about it as a never-never land, all the elements were there. The colors of the minerals in the area transformed the scenery. It was the most beautiful land-scape I'd ever seen . . . vividly green jungles broken up by high plateaus, from which flowed enormous waterfalls.

Coming back on the plane, I picked up a copy of *Life* magazine. In it was a layout of Pier Angeli as Rima. She'd wanted the part so badly that she persuaded a photographer to shoot her on the studio back lot, dressed as the character. I used her in a very elaborate test opposite Edmund Purdom, and it was as much a test of us—to see how we would approach the picture—as it was of Pier.

Alan Lerner soon became as absorbed in the project as Arthur and I were. He approached the screenplay with his usual lack of intellectual pretense.

The ethereal premise of the story would have to be developed at the outset. It was the biggest stickler in the writing of the screenplay.

"We need a gun in the drawer," Alan told me. He repeated the phrase over the next few days.

Though I didn't know what he meant, I pretended that I did. Finally, I allowed my ignorance to show. "What do you mean by that?" I asked.

"A gun in the drawer? Well, it was in one of those melodramas George Cohan used to play. Somewhere in the first act, a secretary came into his office and told him there was a man waiting to see him. The man came in and they proceeded to discuss the situation. It was all exposition. Without that scene there could be no show. But the players hated to do the scene, for the audience always got restless and coughed.

"One night Cohan asked the prop man, 'Do we have a revolver?' The prop man answered, 'No, we don't, but the prop man at the Booth Theatre does. I'll run over and get it.'

282

"Cohan said, 'Fine. Load it and put it in the desk drawer.' When his secretary came in at the next performance, Cohan said, 'Give me a minute, then show the gentleman in.' He opened the drawer and took out the gun. He checked to see if it was loaded, then cocked it and put it back. The scene played like a million dollars, though the gun was never referred to again in the play.

(Alfred Hitchcock, of course, has made a career of guns in drawers, for suspense and apprehension is the basis for all his work.)

While Alan and I tried to work out the solution, Brazilian composer Heitor Villa-Lobos was working on a symphonic piece for the picture, building a mystical score upon the actual harmonies found in the songs of tropical birds. It would be electronically composed by raising and lowering the tones of the bird calls and playing them back at varying tempos.

Try as we might, however, we were finding it nearly impossible to develop the necessary guns in drawers. We were discussing what future avenues to explore when a development made the problem a moot one. A musical version of George Bernard Shaw's *Pygmalion* was being planned for Broadway. Alan and Fritz were offered the assignment of writing the music. Alan returned to New York, and we temporarily suspended our plans for *Green Mansions*. The project shifted to other hands, just as my next picture was falling into mine.

John Houseman had sent me a copy of a current novel, *The Cobweb,* the story of the goings on in a mental clinic apparently patterned after Menninger's, embroiled in a staff dispute over the type of new draperies to be installed in the library of the clinic.

Woven throughout were separate stories of members of the staff and patients. It was so rich in possibilities that I volunteered to direct.

John Paxton was fashioning a script under Houseman's direction. What was finally submitted, though well structured, didn't have the flavor of the book. I suggested Bill Gibson, the author of the novel, be hired to write additional dialogue for the screenplay. (Bill would later write *Two for the Seesaw.*)

In the meantime, we began putting the cast together. Houseman thought using James Dean as the young patient, a talented young artist who may be allowed to design the curtains if the staff member in charge of the art group has her way. The deal was almost set, but it fell through because Metro and Warner Brothers, Dean's studio, couldn't agree on money for the loanout. We looked around for a replacement and found him in John Kerr, who had attracted favorable notice in the Broadway production of *Tea and Sympathy* with Deborah Kerr.

Another newcomer, Susan Strasberg, would be playing a young patient at the sanitarium.

Richard Widmark, Gloria Grahame, Lauren Bacall, and Lillian Gish, were easy choices for the respective roles of the head of the clinic, his wife, the staff member with whom he has an affair, and the controller with whom he locks horns.

Houseman and I differed on the casting of the charlatan doctor. I thought Charles Boyer would be an offbeat choice, but John didn't see it. He found the casting not within the structure of the picture. I held my ground, and John came around.

One of the patients was originally written as a homosexual. Since I wanted to use Oscar Levant, I suggested the part be rewritten according to Oscar's neuroses and complexes. He would be more or less playing himself.

We used several standing sets at the studio. Preston Ames and Keogh Gleason adapted them to the small-town setting.

The film veered from the book in one very important regard. After stacking the deck against the Gloria Grahame character, at the end of the picture Richard Widmark returns to her instead of leaving her for Lauren Bacall. It seemed dishonest, since we'd established extraordinary bonds between the doctor and the staff member, but the conclusion was very much within the existing movie code.

Getting the many detailed stories on film gave us an overlong picture. I'd fallen so in love with some of the sequences that I hesitated to cut the picture, which now ran almost two-and-a-half hours.

"It isn't an epic picture," John kept telling me. "It doesn't warrant that much time." I still vacillated.

Finally, John got tough. We somehow managed to bring it down to more manageable size. We all felt it was a respectable effort.

"The picture seemed to have the same fate as the novel," John says. "It took off quickly, but it didn't sustain interest to become a huge hit. It's more highly esteemed today among film buffs than when it was made."

The reviews, nevertheless, were quite favorable when the picture came out in July of 1955. "There are several things about 'The Cobweb' which makes me feel it is one of the most rewarding films I have recently seen come out of Hollywood," Lee Rogow wrote in *Saturday Review*. "It appears to me a completely new story, which is headline material in itself.

284

More, it's a mature story of the most exciting kind, in which the interior dramas of the individuals are brought together in outward dramatic events which have revelation and consequence. I have quibbles about the casting which seem to have introduced some coldness, but I wish to tell you that this is quite a motion picture."

A few days after I'd finished editing the picture, Dore Schary called me into his office for a discussion. "Are there any projects you're interested in?" he asked.

"Yes," I informed him. "The studio has had a property under option for several years, and I think it should be done."

"Which property?"

"*Lust for Life.*"

Dore was intrigued. John Huston's *Moulin Rouge,* based on the life of Toulouse-Lautrec, had been a huge success for United Artists in 1953. Perhaps Metro could do an artist's biography too. Irving Stone's biography of Van Gogh could make for wonderful cinema.

The legal department discovered that Metro's option on the property would end in December. It was now almost March. Metro asked for an extension on the option. Stone refused. He wanted to film the picture himself.

Would it be possible to complete filming of such a major film before December 31? John Houseman and I swore we would try.

While we were speeding through pre-production, Dore again called me to his office. He very politely twisted my arm.

"We need you desperately for *Kismet,*" he told me. "You could direct it before you go to Europe for *Lust for Life.*"

Arthur had already asked me to direct the picture, but I didn't relate to it, and declined. Now I was being asked again, and the implication was that I wouldn't get the Van Gogh picture if I didn't direct *Kismet.* I capitulated.

There's an old saw about some theatrical musicals: The audience left the theater humming the sets. Though the Borodin-inspired music was richly melodic, the same could have been said about our picture. Art director Edward Carfagno and set decorator Keogh Gleason again delivered.

The cast—Howard Keel, Ann Blyth, Vic Damone, and Dolores Gray —tried hard. The whole enterprise sank. The experience taught me never again to accept an assignment when I lacked enthusiasm for it.

The end of filming nearly coincided with a more momentous event. The birth in April of 1955 of Christiana Nina. Like Liza before her, I'd insisted on giving her a family middle name, this time in honor of Grandmother Le Beau. She would be known to us as Tina Nina.

She was only a couple of months old when I started making plans to fly to France. Fortunately she couldn't read the reviews a few months later of *Kismet*. Bosley Crowther pegged the proceedings rather well, I grudgingly concede. His *Times* critique said, "Charles Lederer's and Luther Davis' script has been staged by director Vincente Minnelli as though it were marching orders for the Macy parade."

My own marching orders may have had a lot to do with the leaden proceedings. *Lust for Life* beckoned. The day after shooting on *Kismet* was completed, Georgette and I flew to Europe. Georgette's parents, Mr. and Mrs. Magnani, would follow in a few weeks, making their first trip back to France since their immigration to the United States, bringing our infant Tina Nina with them.

17 | Lust for Life

Nature wasn't going to wait for Metro-Goldwyn-Mayer . . . and Metro couldn't wait for Minnelli.

It was late July of 1955, a time when flowers lost their first innocent bloom and untended wheat fields turned fallow.

In Arles, members of the company crew—on location for the past two months—were trying to fool mother nature by keeping a wheat field chemically alive until my arrival.

I would be forced to shoot Van Gogh's suicide scene first, and though few pictures are shot in sequence, starting out with the culminating action presented a problem I hoped wasn't insuperable. What if the preceding action didn't logically build? It's the director's constant nerve-wracking question.

We had five short months to complete production on the picture, otherwise title would revert to the author. Studio executives were imperturbable about our race against time. They had far greater faith in us than we ourselves had.

It was to be time turned inside out, in which we met ourselves coming when we thought we were going . . . and the most thrilling and stimulating creative period of my life.

The fights we were to have during production were kept in the family, so to speak. We'd fought our battles with the studio during pre-production, and now we were left on our own. More realistic types would say we were neglected.

When Schary first agreed to do the picture, he assigned Norman Corwin to write a screenplay. Then he called me to suggest a contract producer sign on with me.

"He's a fine man," I told Dore, "but I've recently worked with John Houseman. He has great taste, and I think he'd be a better choice."

Dore agreed.

I then talked to John.

"I've seen too many pictures about artists that have been an embarrassment," he said. "I'll only work on it if we agree that the reproduction of the paintings should be brilliantly done."

That was no condition at all, as I saw it, so John and I came to an agreement and started putting the picture together. This was being done during the filming of *The Cobweb* and *Kismet*.

We hit upon a plan, and it proved to be extraordinary. Van Gogh's paintings would be photographed on plates eight by ten inches. Then they'd be set up on a table in the studio camera department, where they'd be made up into large transparencies to be lighted from behind. In that way, they'd photograph as exact copies of Van Gogh paintings, showing all the brush strokes and even those areas where he'd squeezed paint out of the tube on the canvas.

Then, John and I began discussions on the physical details of the production.

If ever a picture shouldn't have been filmed in Cinemascope, it was *Lust for Life,* since the dimensions of the wider screen bear little relation to the conventional shape of paintings.

Arthur Loew, a studio executive, insisted otherwise. John and I tried to dissuade him, but to no avail. "Wouldn't you rather be responsible for the composition, instead of trusting it to a projectionist in a theater?" he asked.

"What do you mean?" John asked.

"No matter how you shoot it, it's going to be projected in Cinemascope, and millions of people are going to see it in Cinemascope. You can shoot it any way you want, but just remember that fact."

It was an unanswerable argument. Cinemascope it would have to be.

There was one fight we fortunately won. I'd noticed that Eastman negatives, in which Metro's color pictures were then being shot, didn't have the subdued tones that would be needed in a film about Van Gogh.

288

The color process had originally been developed for Twentieth Century-Fox's production of *The Robe* in 1953, and the palette was straight from the candy box, a brilliant mixture of blues, reds, and yellows that resembled neither life nor art. Since that time, Cinemascope and Eastman color had become as inseparable a team as, say, Dean Martin and Jerry Lewis. But events had proved how constant that association was, and perhaps there was hope for us too.

I insisted the picture be shot in Ansco film. But that company, having conceded to the popular taste that the best was the brightest, had stopped producing its line of color negatives. We badgered, cajoled, wheedled, and bullied, and Metro finally saw it our way. The studio bought 300,000 feet of Ansco film, the last remaining inventory, and persuaded Ansco to open a special laboratory to process what we shot. It was to prove to be the most important victory of the many battles John and I fought during the making of the picture.

Joe Ruttenberg was sent ahead to film the fruit trees in blossom. For on the night Van Gogh first arrived in Arles sixty years previously, he'd opened the shutters of his room and saw the trees in a blaze of color. They were the first objects he painted there. *The Great Waltz,* a picture released in 1938, had brilliantly used a montage of flowers, and I supplied Joe with diagrams suggesting how he might capture the movement of the blossoms in all their variety, while remaining true to the Van Gogh style.

Other concepts for the camera would have to wait, for I'd have to develop an approach for Cinemascope. In addition, I didn't have a cinematographer to bounce ideas off at the time, for Joe wouldn't be supervising the filming in Europe. Working with a European crew, it was considered more advisable to hire someone who knew the ways—and byways—of filming there.

I wish I could say that when the time came, the solutions I offered Frederick Young were the work of genius. They were made up of something more practical. Van Gogh's paintings were shown by panning up and down on them. Only a few of his works were in the Cinemascope shape, his last, the crows in the cornfield, among them.

We settled on other ways to show the paintings. They would hang on the walls of his brother Theo's apartment, or in his yellow house at Arles, as they surely did in real life. Van Gogh had executed so many paintings that we could periodically spread them out on the floor of the house, as any painter would do, and as we envisioned Van Gogh doing prior to Gauguin's arrival.

We also decided to use a collage of paintings during the opening and closing credits, showing more dozens of paintings at one time.

I anticipated the rest of our filming approach would be fairly conventional, for the story was so powerful that we wouldn't need to muck it up with razzle-dazzle. But I hadn't figured on Freddie Young. Once he understood that I wanted to re-create the same mood and lighting as in Van Gogh's time, Freddie proved his work started where the work of most others left off. He was tireless and inhumanly patient in getting the right effects. Little wonder that he and David Lean have worked so well together on such films as *Lawrence of Arabia* and *Ryan's Daughter*.

My plan was to re-create the subject matter of Van Gogh's paintings, not as frozen tableaux, but within an everyday context. Freddie grasped this immediately, and he was setting them up before I'd even had time to think about them. He had the uncanny ability of adopting the director's eye for his own, as has been proven by the work for such disparate filmmakers as Lean, King Vidor, and Richard Brooks.

When it came to casting, there was never any other choice but Kirk Douglas for the part of Van Gogh. His resemblance to the artist was uncanny. All we had to do was give his hair and beard a reddish rinse. He was born to play the part, as Kirk also must have believed, since he'd bought another story about Van Gogh for his own production company, with plans to star in it. Anthony Quinn was an obvious choice for Gauguin, the blustery extrovert.

The rest of the cast would be hired in Europe. I decided to pay no attention to accents of the British and American cast, and they proceeded to adjust to each other's language by meeting somewhere in between, say the mid-Atlantic.

Before Corwin's script was delivered, I was doing research on my own, so that I could approach the picture with an educated eye.

Van Gogh's five volumes of letters to his brother Theo were of enormous help. I pored over them, marking anything of significance, developing an attitude I felt the picture should convey.

The sun subconsciously represented turmoil to Van Gogh, the maelstrom he was always fighting, for it was a symbol used in many of his paintings. Streaks and whorls around the sun and lamps represented the inner core, his inherited insanity.

Never did a color palette so closely parallel an artist's life. Van Gogh was to paint for only eight of his thirty-seven tortured years.

His first drawings in the Borinage, where he worked in the mines, are all in black, as if they were covered in coal dust. They reflect his somber mood at the time.

Then he became ill, and went home to Holland, where his paintings are dominated by the dark green of the countryside, as seen in paintings of his Dutch contemporaries.

Later in Paris, dazzled by the Impressionist school, his colors are splashed in brilliant reds and blues. Painters like Gauguin, already established, considered Van Gogh just an amateur, the brother of a very successful art dealer. Van Gogh shows his admiration for them by emulating them within the limits of his own vision.

His period in Arles, and later at St. Remy, is suffused in yellows and subdued reds and greens. This period is to be his greatest and most prolific, though the time of his commitment in the sanitarium is included in those two years. Van Gogh worked like the madman that he was, sometimes painting two canvases a day, going hatless in the boiling sun, driven madder by the dry mistrals from the north.

The final period of his life at Auvers outside Paris is a combination of all his influences, the dark circles around his sun motif closing in during this last creative effusion before he ended his life.

When we arrived in Arles, I told John Houseman several spots in the script were still unsatisfactory. He agreed, and being a talented writer himself, John volunteered to do the rewriting. He didn't know how much work this would entail . . . nor did I. But as we got closer to the facts and saw the real settings of Van Gogh's life and paintings, we changed the script as we went along.

Corwin, thankfully, had already eliminated Irving Stone's use in the novel of an imaginary lady as love fantasy. The intrusion of this element was so at odds with Van Gogh's asexuality that it struck us as ludicrous.

Georgette and I were staying in the same mountain inn between Arles and St. Remy as Kirk and Ann Douglas. Le Beau, with its three-star gourmet rating, was a lovely place, but the food was too rich for our palates. Georgette discovered a charming place in Avignon, operating since the time of Napoleon III, only half an hour from our main shooting locations. The food was simply prepared and beautifully presented, and we enjoyed our stay at this inn enormously.

Georgette seemed much happier in Europe than she'd been in Hollywood. Though she'd tried to adjust to life in the United States, it was proving difficult for her. She didn't understand the Hollywood pecking order and, even if she had, Georgette wasn't outgoing and socially ambitious. In France, however, she was among her own people. She could be herself without worrying about being misunderstood.

When we went looking for the yellow house in Arles, where Van Gogh had lived during his most productive period, we were told it had been bombed out by the Americans during the war. We rebuilt it.

We spent a couple of days in the countryside around Arles, picking up shots of Kirk painting. Our van carried different costumes, so that we could take advantage of whatever vista we settled on. Carrying drawings and replicas of paintings in various stages of progress, we would compare them with the landscape, decide where Van Gogh would be at that particular time, and shoot the appropriate scene. It must have been much like the travels of a third-rate repertory company. Kirk didn't know what drama he might be playing the following day, but he was totally prepared for whatever befell him.

There was one setting, however, that couldn't be found: the toll bridge Van Gogh had painted. Hans Peters, our art director, said it would be prohibitively expensive to build one. Someone in the crew absently offered the suggestion that there might be such a bridge in the remote part of one of the many canals around Arles. We went to the location, and found it. The setting so closely matched Van Gogh's painting that it might well have been his model.

We shot for two weeks around Arles before Anthony Quinn arrived. The crew was having lunch at an outdoor location when he showed up. Tony knew we were still trying to put the picture together, but that didn't prevent him from voicing a slightly defiant observation.

"Ever since I've arrived here," he said during our first meeting, "I've been hearing nothing but how great Kirk is. I'm beginning to feel like Gauguin must have felt when *he* came to Arles."

Could I have been hearing him correctly? The thought was put in a different way, but it was virtually the same as mine.

The sequences, as written in the script, were very ordinary. Gauguin's arrival was treated as if the Rover boys had started living together. Van Gogh wanted Gauguin in Arles, for he envisioned the two of them starting a brilliant art movement there. Gauguin would be the subject of his smothering attention, for all of Van Gogh's relationships were intense. He couldn't be fond of a person, he had to envelop him with love and reverence.

Gauguin, on the other hand, came to Arles because it represented security for a while. His work hadn't gone well in Brittany. Theo hadn't liked his painting, and neither apparently did the public. Burdened with debts, he allows Theo to pay them off, and goes to join Van Gogh in

Arles. He discovers the younger man has developed into a great artist, and Gauguin is jealous.

They were, of course, the original odd couple . . . Gauguin, the libertine, who took his animal pleasures where he found them, who cared for nothing but his art . . . Van Gogh, the ascetic, with his disastrous habit of trying to get inside everyone's skin. The contradictions in their characters, their personal habits, also had them on opposite ends . . . Gauguin, with his compulsive neatness . . . Van Gogh, the slob.

Painting should have been their meeting ground, but here is where they disagreed most. It may have been *jalousie du métier*, but in the final analysis they dislike each other's work.

"It's bizarre, disordered," Gauguin says of Van Gogh's painting, "the paint slapped on. You paint too *fast!*"

"You *look* too fast," Van Gogh hotly responds. He, in turn, finds Gauguin's work curiously flat.

Matters might have been different had Gauguin not been suffering through a dry creative period, but the end result was probably inevitable. If Gauguin was jealous of Van Gogh's work, the Dutchman resented the easy way Gauguin had made friends of a village whore, who Van Gogh had been subjecting to his claustrophobic attentions.

The two men quarrel, and Van Gogh throws a glass at Gauguin. The Frenchman leaves the house, and Van Gogh sees all his dreams of a flowering art colony in Arles leaving with him.

He sets out in pursuit, inexplicably carrying a razor. When he catches up to Gauguin, the Frenchman turns around and fixes him with a cold stare. Van Gogh returns to the yellow house, both his painting and love of humanity rejected by Gauguin's action.

But he will show both Gauguin and the whore how deeply he can care. The ear he will cut off will be sent to the whore. Would Gauguin do likewise?

Everyone knew the cutting off of Van Gogh's ear would have to be incorporated in the screenplay. One thing I was sure of: I refused to be graphic about it. But how to avoid the issue?

I hit upon a solution. As Van Gogh came into the house, a lamp becomes the nucleus of the scene. It gives off light as reminiscent of Van Gogh's whorls and streaks as we could make it without being artificial.

Van Gogh, still smarting from his argument with Gauguin, goes through various stages. He stands before the mirror and looks at himself with total loathing. He makes a tortured face and grinds his nose in the mirror. He steps away, and the lamp is reflected in the mirror for a while. There is no sound. Then Van Gogh screams in pain. The scene is still reflected in the mirror. He is seen staggering by, holding his bloody hand to the side of his head.

Kirk thought the solution was marvelous. He was pretty marvelous himself.

Throughout the shooting, Kirk's intensity shown through. I don't know how the tales of a monumental ego got started, for in the pictures we've worked on together, Kirk has always been the most reactive and co-operative of actors. He got so lost in the role that he didn't care what he looked like or how he photographed, showing none of the actor's reputed vanity.

Our stay in the area would end with the shooting of a final sequence.

The sanitarium where Van Gogh had committed himself was still in operation in St. Remy. John Houseman and I went to talk to the administrator. He was an old man, very matter-of-fact, and he reacted to our visit as if we were concerned friends of a current patient.

"Oh, yes, Van Gogh," he said. He turned to his files. "Yes, there were pressures that became intolerable." He proceeded to read the case history, including vivid descriptions of the way Van Gogh's insanity manifested itself, in the most casual way, as if this were just another not very interesting case.

I couldn't wait to excuse ourselves. No sooner were we out of the building than I turned to John. "That's the way it should be written . . . as if the doctor were dictating the case to a clerk . . . speaking in a curious sort of offhand way . . . underplaying the whole tragedy of the raving maniac."

John agreed, and a whole new section, which he wrote, was added:

Dr. Peyron's official journal for the institution of St. Remy—CAMERA CLOSE on the first two columns:

NAME, AGE, ADDRESS and OCCUPATION of the party committed	: : : : :	NAME, AGE, ADDRESS, OCCUPATION AND RELATIONSHIP of the person requesting commitment
At his own request, Van Gogh, Vincent, born at	: :	Van Gogh, Theodorus, age 32, born in Holland, resident of Paris—brother of

294

Groot-Zundert in Holland,   :   patient.
now residing in Arles   :

PULL BACK to show the AIDE's hand busily writing in the fourth column as a voice dictates:

> DR. PEYRON's voice (*off screen*)

. . . exhibiting symptoms of acute mania, accompanied by hallucinations
of his sight and hearing. In the course of this attack, the patient mutilated
his left ear.

Now we see:

DR. PEYRON'S OFFICE—DAY

Dr. Peyron is dictating his official progress reports to his AIDE who sits
before a large ledger, entering them in a fine hand.

> DR. PEYRON (*to* CLERK)

You've entered Dr. Rey's report and the brother's letter of consent?

> (*the* AIDE *nods*)

Very well. ". . . mutilated his left ear . . ."

> (*consulting the notes before him*)

In view of the above, and in the light of my examination of the patient,
it is my professional opinion that it will be necessary for Mr. Van Gogh
to undergo extended observation and treatment in this institution. Signed
Dr. Peyron. Dated Saint Remy, May 9th, 1889 . . . Copy to the
Department . . . Copy to Mr. Theodore Van Gogh in Paris.

The pen scatches on for a moment. When he has finished, the AIDE
looks up.

> DR. PEYRON (*still consulting his notes*)

Second entry . . . May 25th. The patient shows signs of improvement
in his general condition. He continues to suffer, however, from a condition of chronic inertia, accompanied by symptoms of extreme terror,
particularly at night. He complains of nightmares of an alarming kind.
Treatment prescribed—complete rest. General condition of the patient
—Fair. Non-Violent.

DISSOLVE:

INT. VINCENT'S CELL—DAY

It is utterly bare. The shutters are closed and the room is in semi-darkness.
Vincent lies inert and silent on his bed. In foreground a nun, SISTER
CLOTHILDE, stands beside him, watching him in silence. After a mo-
ment—

> SISTER CLOTHILDE (*quietly*)

Would you like me to open the shutters?

> (*no movement, no answer*)

295

The sun's shining . . .

(*still no answer, no movement*)

INT. DR. PEYRON'S OFFICE—NIGHT

The AIDE now sits under the lamp. DR. PEYRON walks as he dictates.

DR. PEYRON

Van Gogh, Vincent. June 14th. The patient's condition appears satisfactory with continued improvement, though he still finds himself unable to associate with the other inmates, due to the persistence of his former terrors. He has requested that his painting equipment and other personal effects be placed in his room. Request granted.

The scene described better than any histrionics the state of Van Gogh's mind, preparing the audience for that last surge of violent action, a last outpouring on the canvas before his suicide.

We next shot a few short scenes in Paris.

Several messages awaited me upon our arrival. One was from Henri Langlois from the French Cinematheque. Would I be interested in meeting some young men from the *Cahiers du Cinema* crowd? I would, and a lunch meeting was arranged.

It was one of the greatest eye-openers of my life. The young men approached film with such furious dedication that I felt like a dilettante. They could quote chapter, verse and rhyme about my work . . . the average length of my scenes, the recurring motifs, the camera angles I used . . . even the brand name of the camera itself. They gave me back copies of their magazine, in which several major articles had been devoted to my work. There was no doubt about. To them I was a star. And they were eager to know about such other stars as John Ford, Rouben Mamoulian and 'Owaire 'Oaks.

(Liza tells the story of attending later get-togethers with the French film cultists: "One of the young Frenchmen asked a long question. 'Een 'Ze Clock' Zhoo-dy Gar-lah and anuzzer woo-man are wear-eeng ze same dress. Eet was a pair-fait seem-bol of Amerique of ze time . . . ze economique si-too-a-cion. 'Ow did zhoo arrive at zis won-dair-foool seem-bol?' To which Daddy answered, 'I did it because I thought it was funny.'")

(She didn't think it was funny till much later when, during a recent performance at the Olympia Theatre, some members of an obscure French film society who professed to be my great fans, asked if they could come to one of her performances. "Sure," she said, "be my guest."

She expected ten or twelve people to show up, but she had to pay for 256 tickets.)

The company then moved on to Holland, where we shot scenes in Van Gogh's native village, including sequences at the family house and in the tiny church where his father had officiated.

We were quartered in an old castle, complete with moat, which had been converted to an inn. It was family time. Tina was again with us, her grandparents having taken her around to meet all her French relatives before turning her over to her parents. Ann Douglas was pregnant, and every day seemed to be getting more so. These little domestic scenes were a decided contrast from the rough-and-ready of film-making.

There was no doubt about it. Despite the exhilaration and the challenge, this was the most grueling work I'd ever done. Racing to finish the job created a lot of stresses . . . and a lot of fights. John Houseman knew the job had to be finished by a certain time. I knew it should be as perfect a job as possible, and perfection took time.

We arrived in Brussels for filming in the Borinage. John and I still hadn't choked each other, so we just might come out of this ordeal still friends. The company completed the Dutch potato eaters sequence at a studio in Brussels. I'd always thought Van Gogh had distorted the subject matter, and that we would have to use false noses on any actors we might hire, but we discovered many people in Holland who resembled the painting, and we brought them over to work in the sequence.

Freddie's camerawork in this scene, his last, was typically inspired. Van Gogh is seen sitting near a fireplace drawing. A woman brings potatoes to him. She turns back and sits down, and in that instant the exact composition of "The Potato Eaters" is shown.

The rest of the picture would be shot in Culver City. Georgette, Tina Nina, and I, along with Georgette's parents, flew back to America, exhausted but happy.

Russel Harlan, an old hand at Westerns, took over as cinematographer. The bulk of the interiors were his, and his extraordinary work suggested the lighting of Vermeer.

Looking at the rough cuts during post-production was a revelation. I though we'd done well, but I didn't need any critics to tell me it was a great film. It looked and smelled right. We'd pulled it off.

Kirk's performance was his best ever, so on key that I could find nothing to fault in it. Tony's was a wonderful foil. Together, they established the epic quality of the characters.

When the picture was released the following year, all the work, we were assured, had been worth our while.

The *Time* review said "because the Hollywood story builds relentlessly to Van Gogh's ear-slicing for its climax, *Lust for Life* falls midway between being a first-rate art film and high-pitched melodrama." *Newsweek* said, "The fragmentary bits of art history which are scattered throughout the movie are treated with good sense and much knowledge. In all, an exciting and serious idea of the whole enterprise of painting is brilliantly projected." In summing up it found the picture "Hollywood's most profound exploration of the artistic life."

But the phrases of Bosley Crowther's review in the New York *Times* were the ones I kept coming back to. He found the picture "consciously made the flow of color and the interplay of compositions and lines the most forceful devices for conveying a motion picture comprehension of Van Gogh . . . color dominates the dramatization—the color of indoor sets and outdoor scenes, the color of beautifully reproduced Van Gogh paintings, even the colors of a man's tempestuous moods.

"And so, Mr. Houseman and Vincente Minnelli, the director, have wisely relied upon color and the richness and character it gives images to carry their tortured theme. The cold grayness of a mining district, the reds of a Paris café, the greens of a Provençal village or the golden yellows of a field of ripening grain—these are the stimuli that give us a sensory knowledge of the surroundings that weigh upon Van Gogh and reflect the contrasting umbers and purples of that fated man."

But then, the reviews in general were the best of my life. *Lust for Life* was variously called the finest film about painting ever shot and the best biography. But the greatest satisfaction was an entirely personal one. I knew the challenges that had been surmounted, and found it an enormous triumph for us all. It remains my favorite film, simply because it contains more of my favorite moments than any other film I've directed.

I have only two regrets about the picture. The Eastman positive of the Ansco negative has a tendency to turn brown—as I feel all Eastman film does—and didn't hold up as well as Technicolor, so that today a color-perfect print of *Lust for Life* is a rarity. This is one of my pictures I feel *should* survive, and yet the quality that made it distinctive has faded. I'm also sorry the picture wasn't more honored than it was. The Academy has always been capricious in its actions, and one must learn to live with that. Both Kirk and Tony was nominated. Tony's more flamboyant role won, but Kirk's portrayal lost to Yul Brynner's in *The King and I*. The New York Film Critics Circle, whose standards are more exacting than the Academy, offered Kirk the consolation of naming him Best Actor of the Year. I'd already privately named him Most Grateful Actor. Of all the people nominated for their work in my pictures he was the only one to write me a thank you note for my contributions. The performance itself is normally thanks enough, but a fellow still likes to feel appreciated.

Professional careers in the old Hollywood weren't marked by long intermissions. Projects overlapped, so that two films usually were "running" at the same time.

Pan Berman had talked to me about directing *Tea and Sympathy* before we left for Europe. Bert Allenberg, my agent, worked out the details. Deborah Kerr, John Kerr, and Leif Erickson would re-create their stage roles, and playwright Robert Anderson was already adapting his own work into a screenplay.

The project was perking along as we celebrated the new year of 1956.

Deborah Kerr, also represented by Bert, wrote me a letter from Toronto, where she was touring.

My dear Vincente—

Bertie told me that there was every chance that you will direct T&S, when and if it is made—and I just felt I *must* drop you a line and tell you how absolutely thrilled I was with the news. I had a very nice talk with Bob Anderson on Saturday night in Philadelphia—and he has some really quite interesting and unusual ideas about scripting it—and making it a "whole" thing if the Breen office are very difficult about the homosexual angle—which is I understand their objection—adultery is o.k.—impotence is o.k.—but perversion is their bête noir!! But as you will see when you see the play—it *really* is a play about persecution of the individual, and compassion and pity and love of one human being for another in a crisis. And as such can stand alone I think—without the added problem of homosexuality. But above all—it needs a sensitive and compassionate person to make it—and that is why I am so thrilled at the prospect of your doing it. I wish we could do it in color, and incorporate all the atmospheric feeling of spring and "things about to flower" and all that romantic and artistic nonsense!! Anyway—this may all be premature—there are hurdles I know—but in case they are all leaped —I want you to know how very excited I am—

With affection,
DEBORAH

299

Pan says that if the play had actually been about homosexuality, the motion picture code wouldn't have permitted us to do it. In retrospect, it wasn't a very shocking picture, but it might have set up a brouhaha at the time. Ostrich-wise, the censors refused to admit the problem of sexual identity was a common one.

Deborah's letter was to be the first of several received from principals involved in the stage production. The months they'd worked in the play gave them a certain proprietary interest—and expertise—so I paid their advice more than usual heed.

Bob Anderson, in a thoughtful letter to me, set down some truisms about the play. The drama told of a young man at a boys' school who's falsely accused of being homosexual because of his off-beat interests in tennis, music, and poetry instead of baseball and dormitory bull sessions. His housemaster, perhaps a latent homosexual himself, has a wife who shares these interests with the boy. In a generous gesture, she gives herself to him to prove he's not perverted.

"I have always seen the play basically as a love story," Bob wrote, "a love story which never would have had a happy ending except for the persecution of Tom. That is the irony of the story . . . that Tom is persecuted in a sense for his love for Laura, but the persecution brings about fulfillment of the love. Of course the meanings of the play are various . . . the chief one being that we must understand and respect the differences in people . . . Along with this is the whole concept of what manliness is. I attack the often movie-fostered notion that a man is only a man if he can carry Vivien Leigh up a winding staircase. I stump for essential manliness which is something internal, and consists of gentleness, consideration, and other qualities of that sort, and not just of brute strength. Another point, of course, is the tendency for any mass of individuals to gang up on anyone who differs from it . . . if there is nothing to persecute in the individual, they will invent something. That is the only way they can show their strength and solidarity . . . by attacking. Hitler showed this in his attack on the Jews. You can always bolster your own shaky position by attacking someone more vulnerable than you are. Also a major point is that when a person is in terrible trouble, we have to give him more than tea and sympathy, we have to give them part of ourselves, no matter what the cost."

It was all there in Bob's screenplay, and we proceeded to film. One stumbling block, however, still had to be surmounted. The Breen office insisted a prologue and epilogue be included, for the wife should be punished for her transgression. We gritted our teeth, and decided to handle that problem when we had to.

A lesser hurdle was John Kerr's recalcitrance about a scene suggested in the play, his abortive attempt to prove his manhood with a town whore. Both Bob and I agreed that the scene should be presented in the picture. John felt the boy's impotence was established before he arrived for the meeting, and that he should be established as the aggressor, although he would be unable to perform at the last moment.

Bob thought the boy was licked before he started, and the difference about his failure is his violent reaction to it: attempted suicide. He has been persecuted by his classmates for the last time. (The head bully, by the way, was played by Tom Laughlin, who later directed and starred in *Billy Jack.*)

John finally saw it our way, and after the scene was shot, with Norma Crane performing a brilliant vignette as the town whore, he agreed that Bob's approach was the right one.

All the elements were developed in the screenplay, so that the filming of it seemed like going through those pre-established motions. The players knew the play inside it. They'd confronted many kinds of audiences with it, so that they'd shaded their delineations of their characters over the many times they'd performed it. It was all there, and there was no need to gild it with any ornamentation.

There was, however, no way the picture was going to be released without the Breen office's prologue and epilogue, and the retribution required. The Deborah Kerr character would have to pay with her life.

(After I'd completed the picture, I saw a French production of the play starring Ingrid Bergman. There'd been great difficulty in getting it produced. Everybody said there was no story there, no conflict. "So the boy thinks he's a homosexual," a practical French producer told Bob Anderson, "and the wife of the headmaster gives herself to him to prove that he's not. But what is the problem?")

The picture was released, and with the exception of the hated additional sequences, it received gratifyingly warm notices.

"Surprising as it may seem," Crowther wrote in the *Times*, "in the light of the screen's production code, 'Tea and Sympathy' has been given a strong and sensitive screen rendering by M-G-M . . . it is a drama that teems with nuances . . . and it is a drama that hints not only at some of the nastier types in boys' boarding schools . . . Mr. Kerr's performance is incredibly sure . . . Miss Kerr reveals genuine and tender female character we have not seen on screen in a long, long time . . .

Because the letter at the end, which brings the story into a ten years later reminiscent frame, is so prudish and unnecessary, we strongly suggest that you leave after Miss Kerr has reached her hand gently toward the boy and spoken the unforgettably poignant line, 'Years from now, when you talk about this . . . and you will . . . be kind.' "

And so on to new challenges, to *Designing Woman,* from a resigning one.

What would happen if a fashion designer married a sportswriter? That was the concept Helen Rose presented to the studio, which Dore Schary bought. He would produce the movie himself, and it would turn out to be his swansong at the studio.

I was assigned the project as George Wells started to write the screenplay. The part of the fashion type was originally scheduled for Grace Kelly, but she chose to get married instead. Gregory Peck as the other star had leading lady approval, and he pleased us all when he agreed that Lauren Bacall would be terrific opposite him.

Greg had performed in only one previous light work, *Roman Holiday,* opposite Audrey Hepburn, in 1953. But that was a romantic comedy, and we were stressing the laughs more on this current go-round.

Greg, the king of the underplayers, was raring to go, like a banker at an American Legion convention. Pratfalls, double takes . . . he was ready to do it all. I never thought he would have to be held back.

Betty's part was one she could sail through, which she did, with never a concession to the turmoil her private life was in at the time.

Bogey had been gravely ill, but he had responded to therapy, and Betty was quite sure he was going to be fine. He still wasn't out of danger, and his condition was a constant worry to her. But being the greatest of pros, Betty didn't demand any special consideration during the shooting of the picture.

We were filming at Marineland when Bogey sailed south on his yacht for the day. Betty was ecstatic, for if he was up to sailing down to see us in production, he must be doing even better than she expected. A group of us boarded to have lunch with him.

Bogey took me aside. "How's the girl?" he asked.

"She's marvelous . . . as always."

"Well, you have to watch her," he said, ever so lovingly. "Because—you know—she's full of crap."

We spent a happy couple of hours with Bogey on this, one of his last outings. He would be dead within six months.

The script called for a ballet dancer, and I inveigled Jack Cole, one of the top choreographers in films, to handle the part. His was a pivotal role, in more ways than one, for at the end, his fancy footwork disarms the bad men who've come to raise mischief. Jack didn't want to play the part at first, since he was very shy. He decided to do it on the advice of his psychiatrist.

"He told me this might help bring me out of myself," Jack explained later, adding, "He didn't tell me I'd have to run off to vomit at the end of every scene."

The picture revolved around the worlds of fashion, the theater, and sports in New York. Its approach was sophisticated, and the art direction of Preston Ames and the set decoration of Henry Grace were a marvel . . . slick and colorful.

I thought, to describe Peck's monumental hangover in an early scene, that a device might be used, one not all that far from the truth. Every noise is magnified, down to the pin from his new shirt, being dropped into a wastebasket with an enormous boom.

One of the comic high spots for me was the sequence where Greg has lunch with his former girl friend, Dolores Gray, to inform her he has married another woman.

He tells Dolores. She takes the news very well. Leaning over smiling, she tips a plate of ravioli into Greg's lap. The action is followed by a long wait. Dolores looks around, then says, "Well, I really must be going."

"Of course," Greg answers. "You'll excuse me if I don't rise?"

But the greatest actor of the piece, one of those legendary natural talents, was largely unsung. Dolores is the owner of a standard poodle—a brown one, I specified, since that color would go well with her décor—with the habit of jumping eagerly into strangers' arms.

We'd been testing several dogs, but none of them worked. Finally, the trainer told me that a neighbor of his had a brown poodle, but he was untrained.

"For God's sake," I said, "bring him in. We'll try anything."

The dog came and was interviewed. At first he didn't seem all that eager for the part. It might have been a matter of billing. I forget. Then he capitulated.

When one works with animals, a lot of film has to be shot to get the right reactions. With this dog, however, whole scenes were filmed without interruption. He supplied all the reactions needed, toeing the mark religiously, unlike some actors I could name, jumping in the arms of people at the right second.

In one scene, he was supposed to steal one of Greg's shoes and zigzag through the room. He went around instead. "Stop!" I yelled. "Not that way."

He looked at me in a rather rude way. "What in the hell do you want?" he seemed to ask.

When I explained, he looked at me again. "Why didn't you say so in the first place?"

The scene was done, and the dog jumped into his cage, refusing to have anything to do with us between takes. His aloofness was the match of Garbo's. When his part in the picture was over, he left the set without even saying goodbye.

The picture, after my recent run of dramas, was a happy change of pace. If I'd ever had a comic touch, I was pleased that those who saw the film said I hadn't lost it.

The review in the usually cute and caustic *Time* magazine pleased me no end:

". . . in the last fourteen years, Director Vincente Minnelli has turned out half a dozen of the pleasantest comedies and musical comedies made in Hollywood since the Thirties. And in 'Designing Woman,' restricted still further by a plot that should have gone down the drain with bathtub gin, Director Minnelli has produced an uncommonly slick, prosperity-padded sequel to the emancipated-woman comedies of Depression times.

"Director Minnelli plays his game of pseudo-sociological croquet with the careless good form of a man who does not have to worry about making his satiric points. He plays the box-office score instead, working the six angles and the big names and the 'production values'—yum-yum Metrocolor, flossy furniture, slinky clothes—with the skill of a cold old pro."

Crowther summed up in a different way: "The direction of Vincente Minnelli keeps things moving tolerably until the end, when it bursts in a splurge of ostentation that is silly and in somewhat doubtful taste."

18 | Gigi

Arthur Freed and I, over the fifteen years of our professional association, had discussed hundreds of properties as potential musicals. One of them kept insinuating itself in our conversations.

Colette had tossed off *Gigi* when she was seventy, and though she didn't think the novelette was terribly important, the *fin-de-siècle* story of girlish love brought her a final blaze of fame, as well as her greatest fortune.

I'd found a 1950 French movie version of the story adequate, but the performances didn't seem very striking. It also hadn't captured the marvelous visuals of Paris, as I would have wanted to see them.

A non-musical Broadway production was too farcically played for my taste. It dwelled more on the mother instead of the young girl, who was after all the title role. That version, however, introduced Audrey Hepburn to American audiences and proved her first substantial boost to stardom.

When it became apparent the picture would be made, we consulted with Alan Lerner. He and Frederick Loewe were close to completing their work on *My Fair Lady*. It couldn't have been better timing, for the two agreed to participate in the film.

I've always loved working with Alan. He has a marvelous quality of

305

adapting and synthesizing other people's work to another medium, while maintaining the spirit of the original. He'd become the Gershwins to write the screenplay for *An American in Paris*. His lyrics for *My Fair Lady* could have been written by George Bernard Shaw himself. Now he'd be filling in for Colette by taking on *Gigi*.

I had no doubt he would perfectly capture the bored cynicism of the wealthier Parisian classes, particularly after he'd shown me how he handled a longish sequence in the book. Gossip was revolving around the attempted suicide of Liane, Gaston's courtesan before his involvement with Gigi. Alan had condensed all the talk to one malicious line, one character describing how Liane had tried to end it all: "Oh, the usual way . . . insufficient poison."

We were of the same mind on the script. Wherever there was any doubt, we would revert to the original. The only character not in the book was Honoré Lachaille, the part Maurice Chevalier was to play. Since Colette had introduced him as an actual character in the French picture she worked on, we could say his living embodiment was also based on Colette. Gigi's mother, who seemed so tiresome to me in the Broadway production, would be treated as an off-stage voice. Doors would angrily slam whenever she started practicing her singing. We didn't include her as an actual character for two reasons: Her off-stage presence could be used for comic effect. Since she had forfeited the upbringing of Gigi to Madame Alvarez, her mother, bringing her into the film in any concrete way could detract from the main story line. The loving relationship between the old woman and the young girl could be more clearly developed.

We anticipated problems with the movie code. The story's attitude was French, and of the period. Men of the time were expected to keep mistresses, and to show them off at Maxim's. Courtesans were the movie stars of the day, their every dido elaborately splashed in the pages of mass publications as they might be in fan magazines today. Gigi's grandmother had been a noted courtesan. But her Tante Alicia had been the most famous of them all. She lived in a splendid apartment, never going out, perhaps keeping constant guard on her fabulous jewelry collection. Gigi was sent to her for lessons on how to become a courtesan too. Her unmarried mother, forsaken by Gigi's father, "preferred the sober life of a second-lead singer in a State-controlled theatre to the fitful opulence of a life of gallantry" and "had become prudish too late in life and disgruntled too soon." It's a mistake Madame Alvarez doesn't want her granddaughter to make. She will be trained in *all* the arts of pleasing a man.

Geoffrey Shurlock, the administrator of the industry code, filed his expected objections, primarily that all of the characters were unmarried and opposed marriage as an institution. That the boy had immoral relations with many women and the girl was being trained for a life as a mistress were also cause for objection.

Shurlock ignored an obvious fact, that goodness prevailed in the end and the couple were honorably married. He gradually conceded small points, however, so that there was finally only one major obstacle to overcome when we started filming.

Gaston had first asked Gigi to be nice to him, and he will be nice to her.

"To be nice to you means that I should have to sleep in your bed," Gigi answers. "Then when you get tired of me I would have to go to some other gentleman's bed."

Shurlock wouldn't bend. The line would have to come out. More pleadings, more arguments and another concession. Shurlock would suspend judgment until after the scene was shot. (Leslie Caron spoke the line so innocently that the code administrator's office withdrew its objections.)

The songs gave us no trouble whatever. Arthur and I had no suggestions to offer Alan and Fritz.

We'd agreed with their plan to use the half-spoken singing developed for Rex Harrison in *My Fair Lady,* with the lyrics of songs becoming almost like dialogue, and acting as very important scene-setters.

The device, used as a crutch for Rex's limited vocal range, was more legitimate in *Gigi.* French performers had been reading dramatic songs in character for years. The most famous *diseuse,* Yvette Guilbert, had brought her readings to America with great success.

The first songs written for the film were "Thank Heaven for Little Girls" and "I Remember It Well." Alan and Fritz would call Arthur and me from New York to perform each song as it was completed. We were totally charmed, and eager to start planning the ways in which their songs would be mounted.

But before I could go much further with my plans for *Gigi,* I was sidetracked by another picture.

The Seventh Sin, based on Somerset Maugham's *The Painted Veil,* was a story told once too often . . . an unfaithful wife, a cholera epidemic, the husband's noble death, spiritual regeneration. But all those elements weren't nearly as fraught with conflict as what was happening behind the scenes.

The enterprise was sour from the beginning. The company didn't get along with each other, and the producer and director were having battles royal with the front office. They'd struggled through most of the filming when matters finally became untenable. Producer David Lewis and director Ronald Neame took a walk.

Studio producer Sidney Franklin stepped in to replace Lewis, and I was asked to take up where Neame's direction left off. Before Neame left the city, I called him. "What do you feel is the best approach?" I asked. But Neame was glad to be out of it, and begged off. I would have to fill in the missing parts myself.

Filming hobbled to a conclusion. The only consideration I requested from the studio: I wanted absolutely no credit for my contributions.

Though we'd recently bought a house on Crescent Drive, and Georgette had been decorating it, she was happy to be going back to her homeland for a while. Her parents would also be making the trip with us, delighted to act as baby sitters for Tina. Our two-year-old daughter was the brightest spot in our marriage. Georgette still hadn't overcome her introvert's manner, and I wasn't much help to her, being as shy as she. Working day after day, long into the night, cut drastically into our domestic life. I was no doubt also neglectful.

Alan and Fritz were already in Paris, finishing the score. Once it was completed, Alan would have to expand his rather comprehensive outline into the completed screenplay. Cecil Beaton would be coming over shortly to discuss the costumes and settings.

That summer on the Continent was the hottest in twenty years. The group of us, headquartered at the Georges Cinq, tried to make the best of it.

Fritz and Alan were operating out of a room upstairs from mine. They spent sweltering days at a rented piano, both of them in their underwear, trying to get relief from the heat by taking many cold showers. The songs gradually took shape—and charming ones they were—the last being "Gigi" with all its lovely patter.

When Howard Dietz arrived in Paris for a short visit, Alan and Fritz played the score for him.

"I planned to have this section with a lot of intricate rhymes, and a lot of interior rhymes," Alan explained to him, "but I decided not to . . . to keep it simple."

308

Howard looked slyly at Alan. "Of course," he said, "They would expect that sort of thing from me . . . more than from you."

Alan might have laughed harder at the crack had he not been facing still another dilemma with me.

During the time we were planning the picture in the United States, an amateur theater company in the San Fernando Valley was presenting *Gigi* in a storefront theater. I decided to see it, to give myself an opportunity to listen to the text.

The hard wooden seats were very uncomfortable. The production might have been so absorbing that I was transported to a point that my discomfort was forgotten. It wasn't. I found it totally irritating.

But that irritation turned serendipitous, for suddenly I came up with an approach to the character of Gaston. When a character is bored, he bores the audience. He was the weakness in the play.

The audience had to feel he was an exciting man underneath, a yawning tiger. They would want the boredom to lift to see that their assessment of him was right.

Alan and I tried to work this premise out for a long time. We were in Paris, and we still didn't have any idea who would play Gaston. Perhaps if we knew it would mean the difference in solving the quandary.

Before we knew it, Louis Jourdan was flying in from England to discuss the film. He certainly looked the part. Alan and I thought he could play it quite well. The three of us had lunch.

"You know what I love about this character of Gaston?" Louis piped brightly.

"What?" I asked.

"He's so bored!"

Depression descended on the table. Louis sensed something was amiss, but since we didn't otherwise react he didn't know what to say. We finished lunch and took Louis back to the hotel with us to continue the discussion.

After he left, Alan and I tried to cheer each other up. We were very low. Suddenly Alan had an inspiration.

"You know something?" he asked. "Louis is typically French, and the French can argue the affirmative, the negative, then meet themselves in rebuttal. They can go on and on. And that is the key to the whole thing." That's the way Alan wrote it. Gaston would leave a room in high dudgeon, having made a definite statement, then go all over Paris rationalizing the thing. Then he'd have to come back with his tail between his legs. It was to happen several times in the picture. That vacillation was what made the character, removing the unsympathetic aspect and giving us an attractive protagonist.

There was never any serious doubt that Leslie Caron would be our Gigi. Her gamine quality was still there, but in the few years since *An American in Paris* she had become a beauty. When I'd first met Leslie, she, at seventeen, fit very well Colette's description of the sixteen-year-old Gigi: "As for her features, no one could yet predict their final mould. A large mouth, which showed beautiful strong white teeth when she laughed . . . and, between high cheekbones, a nose—'Heavens, where did she get that button?' whispered her mother under her breath." But now, we would have to dress her down to show her transformation into a beauty at the end. This was not to be the only similarity with *My Fair Lady* to be pointed out by the critics.

But they were completely different stories, as I saw them, the one we were involved in showing the manners and morals of the French aristocracy at the time. Colette wrote about real people. Liane d'Exelmans, the courtesan of our piece, for example, bore considerable resemblance to the famed courtesans Liane de Pougy and La Belle Otero.

Chevalier was an obvious choice for the part of the old roué. He'd been unavailable for *An American in Paris,* but was now between projects, and he gladly took on the assignment.

To cast an actress as hopelessly British as Hermione Gingold for the part of the French grandmother was, I suppose, not to the liking of the purists. But she offered so many other treasures to us—she was warm as well as funny—that we took the liberty. I've never regretted it.

We went through hell finding a romantic creature for the part of Tante Alicia. She'd been the greatest courtesan of them all, and the actress we chose would have to suggest the eminence she'd been through her present mellowing appearance.

I'd worshipped Ina Claire for a long time, but had never worked with her. The part was offered. She was intrigued, but after several days of give-and-take, she decided to stay in retirement.

Cecil Beaton, in effect, did the casting for us. He'd designed settings and costumes for many Oscar Wilde plays, and had himself been hired because we felt no one evoked the Edwardian mood more brilliantly. Cecil recommended Isabel Jeans, who had starred in so many of those productions.

Eva Gabor, like her sisters, was a throwback to the era, with an opulent beauty that made her visually right as the mistress Liane. We'd tested a French boy to play the ice skating instructor she elopes with,

310

but it didn't work out. We quickly contacted Jacques Bergerac. Costumes were fitted on him. It was only after we started filming his scenes that we discovered he couldn't ice skate. We had to fake it.

The rest of the cast was recruited on location. Actors, instead of extras, can be used in France. Since I've always paid a lot of attention to extras, that they should bear relation to the people they surround was especially important to me. The French extras took pride in what they did, and they offered lovely bits which Joe Ruttenberg's camera absorbed like a sponge. Those appearing in the scenes at Maxim's were probably as good at ensemble playing as any group of extras I've ever worked with.

It took great preparation to make sure they looked right. My taste in art has always been catholic. I equally appreciate the talents of Rembrandt and Charles Dana Gibson. Many artists, if not great, reflect their time so accurately that they should be used as basic sources of reference. Such was the case with Sem, the French caricaturist. He'd sketched the actual characters Colette used as her models in the story, in their natural habitats, and he gave us a wealth of material to draw on . . . if only we could locate it.

I'd seen reproductions of Sem's work in the United States. But curiously, the French didn't know much about the early 1900s. They'd turned their back on the period, and Sem had fallen out of favor. Finally, in a little shop on the Left Bank, I found a portfolio of his drawings.

Constantin Guys was to be used as our guide for the opening sequence in the Bois du Boulogne. His work was also of an earlier period, but the look of the Bois in 1900 remained the same . . . the fashionable people in their carriages, bowing to each other on their afternoon rides, passing by equally fashionable pedestrians on their promenades, some of them pausing to sit on benches under the trees. I had a small row of trees transplanted there, because the ones already in the Bois were set too far back from the roadway and didn't resemble Guys' paintings.

When I explained my concept for the Bois sequence, Cecil Beaton looked at me in a rather jaundiced way. "I worked with some British film-makers in the past," he told me. "The picture was in the same period as *Gigi*. There were some scenes in Hyde Park, and they promised me it would look exactly like scenes of the period. But they cut so many corners that it looked awful."

His implication was obvious. "Our scenes will look good," I assured him. "That's part of your responsibility."

I decided to also revert to an earlier period for the beach sequences.

Boudin was our inspiration, as he'd also been to painters of the later period, since so many beach scenes painted around 1900 looked like the ones he'd executed forty years earlier.

Once Cecil was assured we meant to capture the sumptuous look of the period, he became an eager collaborater. Two-thirds of the picture —all except some interiors and the beach scenes—would be shot in France. Cecil and I looked throughout Paris and its environs for the whimsy and style associated with the period.

The revival of Art Nouveau had just started, and I was determined to use the style in the picture. We'd heard that the Louvre was opening a new section of furnishings devoted to Art Nouveau. Cecil and I were given permission to go through it before it opened. We weren't allowed to photograph it, but Cecil's photographic eye caught it all. He then toured the entrances of Métro stations, many of them also executed in Art Nouveau.

Our reason for using the influence in the settings was to show how avant garde Chevalier's character would be, using the brand-new style in his bachelor digs.

For the building housing Madame Alvarez's apartment, we selected a famous building near the Place Furstenberg, an artists' haven known as the Dakota of Paris. The interiors were done in Victorian red.

The interiors of the aunt's apartment were entirely French period in design, the Louis Quinze and Louis Seize furnishings as delicate as she was. The exterior was deliberately Art Nouveau, for I thought it was an amusing contrast to the traditional interiors.

I'd originally wanted to use a house on Place Monceau for Gaston's ancestral home. Bernhardt have lived there in the main building, situated in the middle of a park with lovely Japanese bridges and Italian pavilions. It was unavailable to us. The owners had had a bad experience with a French film company, who'd rented it for their picture and left the place in shambles. We substituted the exterior of a museum, and used the interiors of another mansion instead.

Filming at the Palais de Glace, where the ice skating sequences would be shot, again would borrow from Sem's sketches. We planned to use an actual place on the round point. Since the Palais hadn't been used for years, we faced a big reconstruction job, but we were sure the effort would be worthwhile.

Our days of preparation, of attempting to create the Paris of 1900, were alternated with pleasant evenings at Chevalier's house, of restaurant hopping with Colette's husband and daughter. We'd sought them out, thinking we'd absorb some of Colette's spirit through the people closest to her, and became quite friendly. Yet, they weren't nearly as resourceful as guides to the city as Arthur Freed. He would seek out charming little bistros, and the group of us would descend on them to sample their patés and sauces. Arthur was especially delighted when, one night, we spotted the painter Chagall dining at the next table. Georgette, while enjoying these evenings, maintained her usual reserve.

Filming started at the Bois du Boulogne. I'd instructed the cast to play the story for real. They became completely involved in the period and the situation, and they didn't try to make anything humorous. The players knew there is nothing *less* funny than to wink at the audience, as if to say, "Watch how we do this, it will kill you."

Chevalier's first scene had him talking to the audience and setting up the situation, as well as introducing the first musical number, "Thank Heaven for Little Girls," which he would be performing. It was Gallic lightness and mischief as only Chevalier could perform . . . a perfect way to start the picture.

Chevalier must have thought so too. A note from him awaited me at the hotel after our first day of filming: "If I were a sissy I would be in love with you."

Throughout the filming, he was to maintain a light touch. His performance was a standard by which the whole picture would profit.

The film from the first day's shooting was rushed off to a French laboratory for processing. Metro had at first been loath to trust it to them, studio executives chauvinistically advising us to fly it back instead to the United States. This would delay us too much, and we were reluctantly permitted to have our way.

When the rushes were delivered to us the following day, Arthur and I were thrilled. We'd never seen such beautiful lab work. It was so impressive, in fact, that Metro adapted the French lab's techniques to its facilities in Culver City.

Since *Gigi* was essentially a dramatic story, there was no reason to mount production numbers in the film. Dance sequences, like the songs in the picture, had to look as if they were spontaneous. The buoyancy that dancing often lent a picture would have to be supplied in a different way, and André Previn's orchestrations very effectively supplied this quality.

Thus, Leslie's talent as a dancer wasn't strictly needed. But she was delivering something more valuable, a very pretty French girl giving a charming performance.

Her talents as a singer were minimal, and Leslie's songs would have to be dubbed. The numbers written for Gigi to sing were all soliloquies of sorts, with the exception of "The Night They Invented Champagne," which was played for pure spontaneity. Singing "The Parisians" and "Say a Prayer for Me Tonight" while all alone suggested the character's introspection.

Throughout the script the action kept returning to Maxim's, as a symbol of Paris and the shallow gossip of the time. It became an extension, almost another major character, in the story.

We were given three days—Saturday, Sunday, and Monday—to shoot all of the sequences in Maxim's. These included two musical numbers and several vital scenes. A detailed schedule had to be drawn up and rigorously adhered to.

Joe Ruttenberg and I began plotting a plan of execution. The more we figured, the more we realized it couldn't be done.

"Why don't we have lunch there," Joe offered, "and maybe we can figure out how to do it when we get there."

As we sat in the main dining room, looking at the room, Joe said, "This Tiffany ceiling is so marvelous. We can put black velvet over the mirrors, so that we don't have to worry about the reflection." I let him finish expressing his thoughts.

"Joe," I responded, "I have news for you. The great thing about Maxim's—the signature of Maxim's—are the mirrors and their art nouveau frames. You can see all the sections of the room behind the people. They give the whole room its character. You'll have to shoot into them."

"I was afraid you'd say that," he replied. The problem to him was now even more compounded. I had great faith that Joe could find the solution. He had to find a way to hide the lights so that they wouldn't reflect in the mirrors. Eventually, he put suction cups on photoflood lights and stuck them wherever he wanted. He was later to say that the intimate quality could never have been filmed in Hollywood, because a constructed set would have no ceiling, and the arc lights would tend to wash out the shadings so important to the creation of mood.

Lighting was only one of his problems. We discovered some Sem drawings in the upstairs bar. They showed that the bar had originally been downstairs. To be faithful to the period, it would have to be moved there. This made the set even more confined.

We would be shooting in three rooms of Maxim's: the front room with its relocated bar, with an entrance to the restaurant suggested rather than shown; the narrow passageway with its tables for dining and the big room where the orchestra played.

The solution to filming so many scenes in so short a time, and in such close quarters, was an obvious one. We would just have to go in and do it.

Beaton had designed marvelous clothes for the cocottes to wear, but made do with existing costumes from the wardrobe department for the others in the restaurant scenes.

"The cocottes are beautiful," I told him, "but the other people are disastrous."

"Yes, they are," he agreed, "aren't they?" He called for his three assistants, and the girls brought out cardboard boxes of plumes, flowers, veils, and other decorations.

He took the actors out one by one. By attaching a flower and a veil here and a beard there, he turned the dreary costumes around so that they were marvels to the eye . . . and faithful to Sem's drawings. Different make-up and hair styling completed the transformation.

When you work such long hours, you don't have time to wonder if the picture is going to be a success. (*Gigi,* in fact, so involved me that when it was over I discovered I'd lost thirty-five pounds during the filming.) To be so caught up in a project is actually rather fortunate, for a director can't keep his mind on the job at hand and imagine the sound of cash registers ringing at the same time. The audience is so fickle that what seems like gold today turns to dross tomorrow. We prepared as best we could, according to our own visions. The final result, we knew, would be compared to *My Fair Lady,* since *Gigi* had been written by the same people.

But we were offering a completely different view, especially in one of life's most vital areas. Where the approach to sex in *My Fair Lady* had been virtually non-existent, its rare peeking through showing it to be rather antiseptic, *Gigi* teemed with nuance and possibility, as did all Colette's writing. Though we packaged it discretely, we filmed it more to our taste than that of the censors.

Genet's Letter from Paris column in *The New Yorker* gave us a dispassionate view of how we were doing:

"The film's subsequent hothouse scenes of flirtations, champagne drinking, and waltzes in the summer room (at Maxim's) have been peopled by Vincente Minnelli, the director, with some of the most extraordinary-looking young and old women that Paris has seen in a while. There are dark beauties with white skins and ripe shoulders, such as the

Impressionist artists painted; girls by the dozen with hourglass shapes and hats the size of tea trays, loaded with roses found only in Renoir's gardens, or heavy with black ostrich plumes; and one straw-haired comedienne, dressed in canary yellow, with a face as blank and deadpan as a Puvis de Chavannes fresco. Along with the entrancing period costumes, Cecil Beaton has re-created period faces and heads by discovering elderly actresses who still resemble Sem's famous cartoons of years ago—those eccentric, beak-nosed old grisettes, like macaws with pompadours."

Genêt had visited us during shooting at Palais de Glace on the Champs-Élysées; at the Musée Jacquemart-André, which we were using as Gaston's family mansion; and at an *auberge* at Montfort-L'Amaury.

"To judge by the parts of the picture that have been photographed here and shown to some of Colette's old admirers," the column concluded, "*Gigi* may well be the most authoritative Parisian movie so far filmed, as well as the most sensuous, effective, and respectful one yet made from any of Colette's writings."

Yet, as filming continued, other events were gathering momentum. Past danger signals could no longer be ignored. Marriage to Georgette, as I'd previously known it, abruptly ended. She wouldn't be coming back with me to the United States. She would return only when she decided on her future plans.

I soon returned to the United States with Tina. Mrs. Magnani, Georgette's mother, returned with us to care for her granddaughter.

Once resettled at the house on Crescent, I was given little time for reflection on things past. We were rushing to complete the picture.

The last great challenge was the shooting of the beach scenes. Six of them had to be shot in one day. The first was the one adapted from Boudin. I discovered that Cecil misunderstood what I wanted. He thought I wanted white costumes only, when actually we needed all the color costumes he could find, since this was the look of Boudin.

"Can you wait?" Cecil asked. "I'll send a truck back right away to get the color costumes."

I agreed. But the trip from Trancas to the studio in Culver City would take a while, and this worried the production department, which in turn called and worried Arthur. He came over.

"Vincente," he said, "you know the wonderful thing about Boudin is his use of white costumes."

The observation didn't wash.

"Don't pull that crap on me, Arthur," I answered. "You know Boudin

316

as well as I do, and he's known for his brilliant use of color. But don't worry about a thing, because I have plenty to shoot while we're waiting."

These were scenes between Chevalier and Hermione, the donkey ride with Leslie and Louis and many other setups.

Sure enough, the costumes were ready in plenty of time, and we filmed those establishing scenes as Boudin might have painted them.

The last shot was of the sunset. I was down on the beach and Joe Ruttenberg was on a high platform. "Vincente," he yelled through a horn. "The fog is rolling in."

The donkeys were giving us a bit of trouble, and I thought we were going to lose the shot. But we caught it in time, and used the rolling fog as a transition to the shooting of "I Remember It Well." The song starts at twilight, and during its progress the sun goes down to all the sunset colors. The number itself was pre-lit at the studio. Light was eliminated at the end of sixteen bars, then less light, then even less.

We finished shooting the picture well within our schedule. I could again start to wonder about what was happening in my private life.

Liza and Tina were getting to know each other for the first time. They'd never spent much time together before. I was delighted they got along so well. Liza, ten years older, treated Tina like a fragile doll. She would describe all the costumes Tina would be wearing when she grew a little older, the hand-me-downs by Adrian and Sharaff that Tina could next play in. (And she did, wearing them until they were nothing but rags.)

Every night, Tina and I observed a ritual. I'd go into her room before she fell asleep. "Tell me a story, Daddy," she'd command.

"What kind of story do you want me to tell?"

"The one about the little boy and the electric light and the horse."

Now that she had supplied me with the bare outline of the plot, it was my responsibility to create a story out of it. My imagination was severely taxed.

Tina would listen quietly, raising her voice when I wasn't performing up to her expectations. I'd have to retrace those steps and do a bit better. The story would continue and Tina would slowly fall asleep. I'd leave her in the room, usually passing Mrs. Magnani in the hallway outside Tina's room as she prepared to join her granddaughter in the room they shared.

During the telling of such stories wondrous visions materialized. I fell into a predictable word pattern: "and lo and behold there suddenly appeared . . . and lo and behold the coach turned into . . . and lo and behold the straw turned to . . ."

Tina's eyes went wide with wonder at the telling and retelling of each story. "Now you tell me a story, Tina," I said to her once.

She started jabbering away, combining the elements of almost all of the stories I'd told her. Came the time for the miracle. "And," Tina said, "below and behold . . ."

No miracle, however, could save my marriage to Georgette. She returned to the United States within a few months, to take over the custody of Tina. The divorce was quietly worked out, and Georgette took Tina with her to New York.

Pan Berman had sent me a script to read. It was *The Reluctant Debutante,* an American adaptation of William Douglas Home's successful London play. The American setting of the screenplay struck me as off kilter.

I turned to the original play. It was marvelously British, very uppity, with delicious implications, and very funny. It told of the last group of debutantes to be presented to the Queen, before the practice was abolished and a new era of social democracy was ushered in. There were popular elements to the work, and if these could be developed, I informed Pan I'd gladly direct the picture.

I was editing *Gigi* when Pan called. "How about Rex Harrison and Kay Kendall?"

"Great!"

At our earliest opportunity, we flew to New York to see Rex, who was still appearing in the stage production of *My Fair Lady.*

"We'd love to do it," Rex said, "but the script is no good."

I assured him it was being rewritten, and told him much of the original flavor of the play would be returned to the script.

When we discussed Rex's suggested changes with the scriptwriter, he said, "I'll put all of Harrison's things in, and once he's signed, I can take them out again."

I bristled. *"We* want them too."

The picture would be filmed in Paris, to help the Harrisons' tax situation in both England and the United States. Pan and I flew over to start putting the picture together. By this time, Rex had left *My Fair Lady* and was in Switzerland, where Kay had been hospitalized with an unspecified illness. The rewrites were sent to him there.

Rex called Pan from Switzerland. He was livid. "We wouldn't play one word of that lousy script!"

Pan seethed, but I was exuberant, because I also hated it.

We decided to call Home in England. He gladly accepted our offer to write the screenplay . . . from scratch.

The studios in Paris had been rented, and the sets were being built. There was a danger that all these pre-production expenses would be a total loss.

There was another problem to consider. The delay in filming might mean that Harrison wouldn't be able to do the picture at all, for he had a firm commitment to open in the London production of *My Fair Lady* at the Theatre Royal, Drury Lane, in several weeks.

Angela Lansbury, who would be playing the mother of a rival debutante, had arrived from the United States, ready to start filming the following day.

"Darling," Pan told her, "I think we've gotten you here for nothing."

We explained our dilemma.

Angela was totally cool. She took matters in hand. After soothing our bruised sensitivities, she ordered dinner. Everything would work out.

Home arrived the following day, and proved to be a dynamo. We went into a huddle and were able to devise a whole new concept in three days. That was our deadline, for Rex was expected in Paris by that time.

Rex was enthralled. We could proceed as scheduled.

If his brother, the British Prime Minister, were as proficient at statesmanship as Home was in the writing of screenplays, I'm sure the sun would never have set on the Empire.

Home was to stay with us throughout the shooting, writing one day ahead of us. Sometimes we feared the next day's pages wouldn't be in our boxes at the Georges Cinq, but they flowed uninterrupted from Home's typewriter to the mimeograph department to us.

I'd heard stories from other directors of how adorable Kay was on the set. She would be raucous and vital and lovable, and when the day's work was over, everyone would want to take her home.

Though very thin, Kay looked ravishing in her Balmain costumes. She was wonderfully co-operative, lending all her resources to the enterprise, spelling out only one condition: "Careful how you photograph my Cyrano nose, darling."

I found Rex wonderfully attentive to her, but gave it no special thought. Kay was equally as devoted to him. She was dying of leukemia, though none of us but Rex knew it. But at no time did he ask for special consideration for her . . . as she did for him.

I'd returned to my hotel room late one day, and was having dinner in my pajamas when the two of them arrived. It was apparent that Rex had just let off angry steam and that Kay was all wrought up.

"My husband is the world's greatest actor," she told me. "I have a part that is so good, and he needs more to do. Look at this scene. I have fifty lines of dialogue and he has only three. You've got to rewrite this."

"Kay," I answered. "I bow to no one—not even you—in my admiration for Rex's talent. But you know that part of the wife is a garrulous one. She talks all the time."

The scene in question involved a third actor who also had more lines than Rex. He and Kay would talk on and on about nothing, while Rex stood between them listening. The younger actor would drone on and on about traffic in the city while Rex painfully reacted.

"I assure you," I told Rex and Kay, "that Rex's actions will be so hilarious that it'll be his scene. It all plays off of Rex." And that's exactly what happened.

Filming was proceeding nicely that winter of 1958 when, one day, Georgette's lawyer appeared on the scene. There were papers to be signed before the divorce hearing. He flew back immediately to the United States, once his mission was completed.

Alan Lerner arrived from the United States soon after. He was hosting a party at his hotel, and asked me to drop by after work.

"I'll be all dirty," I protested.

"I don't care how you look," he answered. "I want to see you."

When I arrived, Alan took me into another room. He immediately confirmed some very disturbing reports that had reached me in France.

"You know, the first preview of *Gigi* was all right," he told me. "We went to the studio and told the executives that this was a great picture, but it would be greater still if the 'Gigi' number was reshot. We thought the lyrics were lost by shooting it all over Paris, and recommended that they be reshot in closeup. Fritz and I even volunteered to pay the extra $50,000 it would cost. I don't mind telling you we held our breath, that the studio would take us up on *that* offer.

"They agreed to our suggestion. But they paid for it. The whole number was reshot on the back lot. And you know something? It didn't work. They didn't use one foot of the new sequence. They're releasing it as you shot and edited it. And you'll probably receive an Academy Award for directing it."

I laughed that idea off. When you're in another country and you hear that the picture you made didn't go over well, and that parts of it are being reshot, you tend to believe the picture couldn't have been very good.

I was still in Europe when the picture was released. The studio sent me the notices.

Crowther, among others, predictably smirked at the similarities with *My Fair Lady*. "But don't think this point of resemblance is made in criticism of the book," he wrote, "for 'Gigi' is a charming entertainment that can stand on its own legs. It is not only a charming comprehension of the spicy confection of Colette but it is also a lovely and lyrical enlargement upon that story's flavored mood and atmosphere.

"Mr. Beaton's designs are terrific—a splurge of elegance and whim, offering *fin-de-siècle* Paris in an endless parade of plushy places and costumes. And within this fine frame of swanky settings, Vincente Minnelli has marshaled a cast to give a set of performances that, for quality and harmony, are superb."

I flew back to the United States after finishing my work on *Debutante,* about to be a single man again, but nevertheless content. This new film, I was confident, would be a success. The critics, soon enough, confirmed this hope.

"Transferred to the screen and run through a high-speed Mixmaster of comic invention by Rex Harrison and wife Kay Kendall, this lukewarm cup of tea has been turned into cheery summer punch," *Time*'s review read. "W. D. Home's screenplay, adapted from his own stage version, tinkles with a profusion of grace notes that, in skillful hands, can often substitute for a full score. The pace, thanks to Vincente Minnelli's direction, is Pall Mall."

Newsweek found the picture "lighter than air, entertaining as all get out."

A. H. Weiler, in the New York *Times,* divided the honors: "Equally important are the contributions of director Vincente Minnelli, who handles threadbare romance and situations as he would a priceless tapestry, and the professionally zany performances of Rex Harrison and Kay Kendall, the husband-and-wife team who play the parents of the diffident damsel of the title."

But the reaction to the picture in London, where it opened a few months later, was even more gratifying. I'd shot a film about a society alien to me—and in still another alien land to boot—and those being satirized recognized themselves.

On December 22, the day after the picture opened in London, I received a telegram at the studio:

YOU'RE THE TOAST OF THE TOWN TODAY AND VERY MUCH IN OUR THOUGHTS WE COULDN'T HAVE DONE IT WITHOUT YOU MUCH LOVE AND GRATITUDE FROM REX AND KATE

Metro's London office wired me extracts from local reviews later in the week:

EVENING NEWS: SUMPTUOUS LAUGH-FEAST . . . OUTSTANDING PIECES OF SCREEN ART, AS WELL AS A WITTY SHOW THAT ALL KINDS CAN ENJOY . . . IS KAY KENDALL THE MOST SPLENDID THING IN COMEDIENNES THE SCREEN HAS FOUND SINCE THE WAR? YES! YES! . . . REX HARRISON IS SUPERB.

EVENING STANDARD: A GREAT HIT . . . BRILLIANT ENTERTAINMENT . . . VINCENTE MINNELLI'S DIRECTION GLITTERS LIKE A TIARA . . . A FROTHY DELIGHT.

DAILY HERALD: THE HARRISONS ARE A WOW . . . IT HAS TAKEN 20 YEARS TO DISCOVER A COMEDY PARTNERSHIP TO REPLACE THOSE WONDERFUL TEAMS LIKE MYRNA LOY AND WILLIAM POWELL. M-G-M HAS DONE IT . . . THE MOST JOYFUL THING I'VE SEEN IN A LONG, LONG TIME.

And many more raves.

Now that I had succeeded in capturing the English milieu, perhaps I was now up to doing the same for the United States.

322

19 | The Rat Pack

May of 1958 brought mixed blessings for several members of the *Debutante* company. Rex Harrison opened triumphantly in the London production of *My Fair Lady,* but Kay's health was gradually worsening. Sol Siegel, the new head of Metro, wanted to double as producer on a film project, and asked me to direct *Some Came Running*. It was also the month of my second strikeout. Georgette's divorce was granted.

The readjustment to life alone was surprisingly easy. Friends periodically looked in on me. Others took a much longer look.

I'd returned from work early one evening when I received a call from Oscar Levant.

"I'm leaving the house," he said. "Can I come over?"

"Sure!" I anticipated sharing a quiet drink or two with him. Since he was so busy with his television series I didn't see him as often as I would have liked.

Oscar arrived. He'd said exactly what he meant. He certainly *was* leaving his house, since he arrived with two suitcases.

"I've left June," he said. His tone informed me that the parting was absolutely final . . . as it had been the countless other times Oscar and June had bickered.

Oscar settled in immediately, calling his doctor to come over to give him a sedative. Before he drifted off, he called the housekeeper and informed her when he would want his meals.

Over the next several weeks, he made tentative reunion feelers in June's direction, but she seemed quite resigned to survive without him.

Though he was wonderful company even in his darkest moods, I was beginning to wonder how long I could put up with his smothering presence.

He'd come into my bedroom late at night and wake me up. He had to talk to someone. He'd tell horrendous tales of misadventures and describe the demons who plagued him, who by this time were so familiar that he called them by pet names. Once he'd unburdened himself, he'd take a pill and go off to sleep in his room. I, of course, stayed wide awake.

I don't suppose any advice I could offer would be of any help. Once, my impatience with Oscar got the better of me. I blurted out a not-so-novel observation. "I think it's all in your head."

He looked terrified. "My head? What a terrible place for it to be!"

I'd come home from the studio to find a lot of people in the living room, having drinks and socializing. Oscar would note my arrival and yell out, "Okay, everybody out! He's had a hard day. He wants to be alone." The guests would scatter.

Oscar's making himself at home didn't disturb me at all. What did bother me was that these guests were also my friends and I would have enjoyed having a drink with them. But he didn't think they should take me away from my work.

Finally I rebelled. On one of those evenings when his guests were beating a quick retreat, I called out to Oscar, "Wait just a minute. They're my friends too. And I want them to have a drink with me." I called them back. Oscar resignedly shook his head.

I never knew who June pitied more, Oscar or me, when she decided to give him one last chance. It didn't take him long to clear out. His suitcases had never been fully unpacked.

Neither had mine, since my arrival from France. I was thick in the planning for *Some Came Running*.

The James Jones novel was long and rambling, heavily populated, but I felt the main characters were interesting and well thought out. I never met Jones, nor was he otherwise involved in the production, so our adaptation would be purely our own.

Jones, however, had described the theme of the book as being about "the separation between human beings—the fact that no two people ever

324

totally get together; that everyone wants to be loved *more* than they want to love." Why he should take seven years and 1,266 pages in which to state that premise was a subject of some controversy when the book was published the previous January. Metro had already acquired the motion picture rights.

I suggested that John Patrick and Arthur Sheekman retain this philosophy in their screenplay. I also insisted the motivation that compelled the protagonist to become a writer be clearly spelled out. Dave Hirsh might be drawn to sleazy experiences, perhaps as a symptom of his lack of self worth, but he is a sensitive man. He carries with him the book of his literary idols, but carelessly stuffs his own manuscripts at the bottom of his duffel bag. His standards are high, and since he rarely meets them, he tends to denigrate his quite substantial talent.

Frank Sinatra would be the lead, but there were two flashy roles which we both knew might overshadow his: Ginny, the human and lovable "pig," and Bama, the cynical gambler. We'd been considering several very good character actors for both parts. One evening, I came up with a thought. Why not his buddy, Dean Martin, for the part of Bama? Shirley MacLaine would also be terrific as Ginny. I called Sol Siegel. We had a meeting with Sinatra the following day. He loved the idea.

Dean jumped at the chance. Shirley's part was small, but being a smart actress, she could see that it dominated the picture. She knew she could do it well, and signed on with us.

Martha Hyer as the confused and frigid Gwen rounded out the main characters in the picture.

Madison, Indiana, was selected as our version of Parkman, the city in the novel, and a crew of 130 people went there in early August for three weeks of filming, primarily exteriors. Madison, seventy miles from Cincinnati, had coincidentally been named the typical American small town by the Office of War Information in 1941, which had used its backgrounds for a documentary.

Some Came Running was a story of small town honky-tonks, of cheap low lifes not without charm. The audience had to be knocked out by their vulgarity. I decided to use the inside of a juke box as my inspiration for the settings . . . garishly lit in primary colors.

Even after we'd started filming, I'd roam the streets of Madison. I came across a red brick building with a neon sign, set off the street, and immediately cast it as the house Bama would be living in.

But I had to temper my enthusiasm. Even in such a setting, discretion had to be used. Part of the lore of the theater is to leave the audience wanting more, and this also holds true in films. Though you can do anything in films, you'd better not try. Restraint is always needed.

That was one quality the national press was accusing Frank of lacking after we'd been in Madison only a short time.

Sinatra is as feisty as a rooster, and if you think that doesn't adequately describe the towering rages of which he's capable, have you ever seen a cockfight?

He'd succeeded Humphrey Bogart as head of the Rat Pack. I could claim, I suppose, to be on the fringes of the group while I was married to Judy. There didn't seem to be any conscious effort to make this the most coveted of all social groups in Hollywood, though the charm of its participants certainly made it that. After Bogey's death, its geographical center shifted from Holmby Hills to Las Vegas, and that made a whale of a difference. But it still was the top social group, and Sinatra headed it as a benevolent father figure. Once his friend, you're a friend for life. He's the greatest foul weather friend, and in this up and down business, Frank has meant constancy to so many during the bad times. Of course, he's prone to tell friends how he'll help them rather than ask how he can help. But I suppose that's the prerogative of any leader of the clan.

When he does render assistance he doesn't want to discuss it. A few years later, I wanted to use a song in a picture, but we were having difficulty getting permission. Frank was in the Orient. I called him. "Don't worry," he said, "it's yours." I thanked him, adding, "But how . . ." Frank interrupted. He stressed each of his following words: "It is yours." I wasn't on the phone with him for more than three minutes, but before I'd hung up the cogs had already started moving to get permission to use the song.

The people of Madison, however, weren't aware of what they had in their midst. They thought Frank and his friends were just plain movie stars, to be ogled and fondled. But Frank chooses the subjects of his familiarity . . . they don't choose him. The fireworks were inevitable.

All of us were staying in the same motel. The owner had moved out of his cottage on the grounds, and Frank and Dean took it over. It became the headquarters for the other members of the Pack, and soon friends were flying in from all over. Leo Durocher stayed on for a while, as did a fellow I took to be a small-time Chicago hood. Even if I'd wanted to, I couldn't socialize with Dean and Frank much. Preparations for the following day's filming took many hours of concentration. On one evening, however, I went over to the bungalow for dinner. The friend from

326

Chicago made great pasta, and several of us were invited to sample his cooking.

The "hood" turned out to be one of Illinois' movie censors!

"We cut a lot of scenes and destroy a lot of pictures," he blithely told me. When he noticed my shock, he added, "But none of yours."

As the evening wore on, it became evident the man had taken a liking to me. As I excused myself, to give Dean and Frank a chance to return to their marathon poker game, the censor said, "Glad I met you, Vince. Come visit me in Chicago. We'll stage a raid for you. Maybe we'll break into a couple of whorehouses." I was never able to take him up on the offer.

Frank and Dean were pretty much prisoners during our three weeks in Madison. Every time they ventured out, some incident seemed to occur. The townspeople were offended when Frank was quoted as saying—I don't know how accurately—that Madison was worse than the skid row in Los Angeles. Another time, it was said he'd torn a phone from the wall because an operator was listening in on his conversation. Yet another incident had Sinatra and Dean's manager involved in a shoving match with an elderly hotel clerk, all over an order of hamburgers.

The national press picked up on the incidents. *Time* magazine was particularly critical of Frank's behavior.

I could find no fault in it, not even in his approach to acting, which critics implied showed his basic contempt for the acting craft. Frank hated to rehearse. Prior to shooting each scene, I would work with other members of the cast until the last moment. Frank would then be called in, we'd go over the scene once again, and shoot. He gave me everything I wanted.

When we returned to California to finish the picture, Frank suggested we work from noon to eight instead of from the customary nine to five. "Performers work better in the afternoon," he theorized, "and the girls look better. They don't run out of gas at five like they usually do."

Mayer, had he still been in control, would have strongly objected to such a system, but I didn't, and the hours were instituted for the rest of the film. We would have lunch at four in the afternoon, on a rehearsal stage outfitted as a commissary.

Frank knew what he spoke of, for the performances of all the actors pleased me enormously.

Certainly, the seduction scene with Martha Hyer couldn't have been done better. Her character was frigid, and though she loves the young writer, she can't adjust to his common streak. They are alone in the late afternoon, in her father's house. The room is in shadow. The stages of seduction are like a dance. Frank takes her hair pins out one by one, and her hair gradually comes down. They move toward the darker part of the room, their kissing seen in silhouette before the scene turns almost totally dark. It was, to me, indicative of the Gwen character to have her surrender in this way, instead of in the more direct, less inhibited light of day.

Frank very generously built up Shirley's part by suggesting a change in the original story. Instead of his character being shot in the end, Shirley would be killed trying to protect him. Her impact in the picture was thus considerable. It made her a star.

She'd been trying to get out of her contract with Hal Wallis before she came on to our picture. Consequently she was late in reporting, and I couldn't supervise her make-up test. It was very critical that she be overly made up, that she look vulgar.

On the Saturday before her first week of filming, her make-up test— handled by someone else—arrived from Hollywood. It was dreadful. Her face was a child's made up as a woman. I made her up myself on Sunday. Rouge was put where the shadows would be. I requested a photographer make color shots of her. Shirley stood in the driveway of the motel for the session. The photographer had arranged to get the film quickly developed. It turned out to be a vulgar look, but one that didn't destroy her face. We breathed easier as we resumed filming.

Shirley was now ready to deliver her pathetic performance. Her part represented the failure of sex rather than the triumph that would be implied if a sex bomb had been cast in the role.

"Shirley giggled inanely," Jack Moffitt wrote in *The Hollywood Reporter*, "where other actresses would have gone throaty in big scenes. She ate like a sloven, she sang roisterously and out of tune, she dressed blowsily and she slopped make-up on her face as her beautiful co-star, Martha Hyer, delivered a great speech about the moral latitude that must be allowed men of talent. Shirley never comprehended a word."

The article further described the change in the ending, and the moroseness of the Sinatra character after he marries the "pig" on the rebound. "His looking away when she meltingly turns to kiss him at the ending of the crummy marriage ceremony makes the finale all hers," Moffitt concluded. "So does his gloomy indifference to the wedding certificate she values so highly. 'You don't have to understand,' says Ginny, 'to be able to feel.' That is the most poignant cry from the human heart that the screen has recorded in some time."

328

The culminating action, where a small-time gambler who'd been her previous lover comes gunning for the Sinatra character, used a town carnival as a background. I revived all memories of such midways during my childhood in Delaware.

We couldn't hire an operating carnival, so we put one together, renting its components from several sources. There was progression to its installation. It was just going up when Martin and Sinatra drove into the town; it would be in full swing at the time Ginny is shot.

Folklore suggests that the Ferris wheel had to be moved three inches to satisfy my esoteric tastes. The reason for the move was somewhat more practical. The camera wouldn't pick it up in the long shots unless it was moved six feet. It was important that the Ferris wheel be seen from all angles, since it was the focal point of the scene.

The rest of the filming would be completed, without incident, at the studio.

The picture was released to considerable praise from the national press . . . and more importantly from the paying public.

The mad-on *Time* magazine had with Sinatra, however, seemed to extend to its review of the picture, bemoaning "the spectacle of director Vincente Minnelli's talents dissolving in the general mess of the story, like sunlight in a slag heap." On the other hand, its sister publication, *Life,* called *Some Came Running* "an unforgettable vignette of American life." I didn't know what to make of the contradiction. *Newsweek* said the picture, "despite its lack of thematic purpose (or possibly because of it), shows flashes of brilliance." It summed up: "Prolix prose pretty palatably packaged."

But the greatest praise, one we all agreed with, was a letter from Dwight Taylor, the son of Laurette, raving about Shirley. "I would give anything if my mother could have seen her performance," he wrote me. "Just when one despairs of finding new talent, *real* talent, along comes some one like this girl and the world seems young again. She gets my vote for the Academy."

Since the picture was released at the end of the year, I didn't have too long to wait to determine how *Some Came Running* had been received by other members of the Academy.

Both *Gigi* and *Some Came Running* had been placed on several "Ten Best" lists at year's end. I found myself in the novel position of competing with myself. When the nominations were announced late in January of 1959, *Gigi* was named in nine categories and *Some Came Running* in three. With the exception of Best Costume Design, where

Cecil Beaton was nominated for *Gigi* and Walter Plunkett for *Some Came Running*, there was no overlapping of nominations. *Gigi*, curiously, received no acting nominations. Shirley MacLaine was nominated for Best Actress and Martha Hyer for Best Supporting Actress in *Some Came Running*. The rest of *Gigi*'s nominations were largely in technical categories. But there were two very important ones also: Best Picture and Best Director.

I thought my chances were better this time around. Ginger Rogers was my date for the proceedings on April 6. There were several attractions of human interest during the evening. Ingrid Bergman was making her first visit to Hollywood after ten years of exile, and Elizabeth Taylor and Eddie Fisher—whose notoriety was more current—arrived together. Elizabeth was nominated as Best Actress for *Cat on a Hot Tin Roof*.

But nothing could detract from our total triumph during the evening, not even the fact that the program ran twenty minutes short and we were caught on stage before a national audience, having to improvise an entertainment and failing dismally.

Though none of the nominations for *Some Came Running* won, *Gigi* swept the boards, its nine Oscars setting an all-time Academy record up to that time.

It won as Best Picture. Alan won for Best Screenplay; Joe Ruttenberg for his cinematography; Preston Ames and Keogh Gleason for art direction-set decoration; Alan and Fritz for "Gigi," the best song; and Cecil for costume design. Maurice Chevalier received an honorary award for his fifty years of contributions to the world of entertainment. And I, at last, won for Best Director.

The celebration, my part of it anyway, had to be put off. I wasn't home to accept the messages that arrived the following day. I'd left at five that morning for location on *Home from the Hill*.

I look back at my body of work and notice that critics quite often praised the way I handled a cliché-ridden story, of how I took mundane situations and presented them in new and interesting ways.

Every director worth his salt does the same. For life isn't usually characterized by the piling of one profound experience after the other. When a momentous occasion presents itself, it often comes in the most improbable way, the coincidences implausible and inexplicable. How

330

many times has a friend prefaced his retelling of an experience in this way: "You wouldn't believe what just happened. It's like a B movie."

To take those moments and present them so that they don't look like a B picture—that's the challenge I relish.

William Humphrey's first novel had been published the previous year. The studio's publicity campaign about the film suggested some problems that would have to be overcome, if one only read between the lines: "Its basic theme, revolving around a Texas dynasty, is universal, reflecting the temptations and ambitions, the dreams and disasters of both adult and youthful generations."

Irving Ravetch and Harriet Frank took an arty book and turned out a beautiful screenplay with almost Biblical simplicity. Rafe, the bastard son, was their creation. They had an exact ear for regional dialogue, as they would again prove in a few years with their brilliant script for *Hud*. The script they wrote for me was one of the few film scripts in which I didn't change a word.

We would be using three newcomers to pictures in pivotal parts. George Peppard, cast as the bastard son, had created a reputation in the theater, and he was now making the transition to pictures.

George Hamilton, as the legitimate son, had previously appeared in one picture, *Crime and Punishment, U.S.A.* Sol Siegel, who would again be producing, joined me at Pan Berman's for a screening of the picture.

"That's the boy for your picture," Pan said.

"I don't think so," Sol answered. "He's too sophisticated."

I tended to agree with Pan. "Let me test him," I told Sol. "I'll lighten his hair a little. I like him very much. I think he has something."

After the test was made, Sol agreed.

As the girl the two boys love, Luana Anders—a former child actress—was cast in her first adult role.

Before the production got much farther along, Sol Siegel called to inform me he would have to drop out of the picture. Metro's board of directors felt he should be paying more attention to the greater problems facing the studio. Edmund Grainger stepped in. Since Sol had prepared the picture, it would be released as being "Produced by Edmund Grainger for Sol C. Siegel."

Shooting at our first location in Oxford, Mississippi, went smoothly.

Robert Mitchum, who snipes that the movie should have been called *Minnelli's Texas*, and says the sets got a lot of fan mail, knew the character of the father very well. He'd met many such men in Maryland, where

Bob was a permanent resident. "These kind of men were my acquaintances, and I took my approach from them. I've always felt that whenever possible, if you have anything to bring to a party, you should."

I had sympathy for the man. There were many cruel things happening to him. His outwardly normal world was rattled by the many skeletons in his closet.

Bob, who has an indolent image, could have walked through the part, but he didn't. His scenes with Eleanor Parker, his bitter wife, suggested the frustration of a man who loves a woman, yet she has not let him touch her in nearly twenty years, her revenge for having a bastard son.

George Hamilton delivered the awkward wakening of the timid legitimate son. He was sympathetic and honorable, and true.

George Peppard was from the Actor's Studio. He had to feel! That's fine, except on location. You can't film when the sun goes down.

His first work on location was in the cemetery, the last scene in the picture. Eleanor Parker, playing the wife of the now dead Mitchum, has had the name of the bastard son inscribed on the tombstone, the first time the relationship has been publicly acknowledged.

George went through the scene, trying to show his sensitivity. I didn't think I was getting enough.

"George," I told him, "you might be a seething volcano inside. But I've got news for you. Nothing's happening. You'll have to do it my way."

He bristled. "When we get back to the studio, we can analyze and talk about it as much as you want."

George went grousing to Mitchum, Bob recalls, threatening to walk off the picture. Bob laid the cards on the table. "I assume you want to continue working," he remembers telling George. "You have contracts to follow this. It'll be a very expensive hike. I'm certain it will be your last job. I'm sure the studio can sue you. Even though you think Minnelli is wrong, do it his way."

Throughout the filming, Bob helped the young people enormously . . . and me too. He spoke from the viewpoint of a veteran actor—and star— and the young people were impressed.

"Why shouldn't they be?" Bob cracks today. "They were impressed because I was very impressive. I was like someone an old cameraman used to describe when I was over at RKO. He was an Argentine-Italian, and I think illiterate. He'd probably started out as Bessie Love's gardener of something. To him, a woman artist was anyone who made over $1,000 a week. If she got less, she had to be a whore. Why else would she hang

332

out with foul-mouthed guys and juicers? I was an artist to Peppard and Hamilton in the same way. But I'll tell you something. George Peppard has caught up to me. Next time around he has to play *my* father."

I don't know why Bob puts on his act. Few actors I've worked with bring so much of themselves to a picture, and *none* do it with such total lack of affectation as Mitchum does. He claims that he never sees his own pictures. I personally believe that when the truth comes out after his death, his shameful vice will be revealed. In some dark cellar a celluloid cache will be discovered. It will be revealed as belonging to the late Mitchum and it won't be a year's supply of blue films. They'll be the pictures he made, which he would sneak in to see time and again.

He gives the same uncaring impression to other directors. A few years back, Bob was filming *Ryan's Daughter* with director David Lean. Lean had signed Bob for the picture, "a quiet little love story in Ireland I've always wanted to make," and Bob had found it swelled to elephantine proportions. "It turned out to be $14 million of waiting," he recalls.

Mitchum, perhaps trying to impress on Lean that people were still part of the story, decided to let out all the stops in one scene. Lean, terribly moved, came up to him. "Bob . . . that was extraordinary!"

Mitchum fixed him with a curious stare. "You don't think it was too Jewish?"

To Bob, acting is just a matter of cadence and rhyme. He generously offered the newcomers some of his distinctive poetry.

And I suspect he offered an old-timer assistance on a somewhat lower plane.

I didn't get along with the production manager assigned by the studio. Suddenly I was being told that filming on the Texas location was over, and the rest of the picture would be shot in Culver City. I was so upset by the development that I truly don't recall what happened next. But Mitchum does.

"Minnelli was so totally frustrated that tears of anger came to his eyes," Bob recalls. "He was so angry in fact that he didn't watch where he was going and bumped into a tree. Then to top it all off, he sat down . . . on a copperhead snake. Fortunately, somebody caught him before they made contact. A lot of phoning went back and forth, and we were finally permitted to finish our location work."

When we moved to California, the production manager was replaced. I hadn't complained to anyone, but I'm sure Mitchum told someone I was going nuts with this guy and he should be replaced.

Portions of the wild boar hunt had been filmed at the sulphur flats near Paris, Texas, an area from which clouds of yellow smoke rose, its terrain dotted with quicksand traps.

The fight between the boar and the hunting dogs was to be staged on a back lot at the studio. A boar was flown in from Louisiana, but died on the way. Only then were we told that boars are in fact rather delicate animals. Rather than risk another mishap, we decided to use an enormous pig with false tusks.

The boar was not visible until the end, but as the hunting party comes upon two dead dogs, it's apparent the animal is dangerous and quick.

We composed the shots of the pig with the remaining dog to suggest a fight. The pig was given a sedative in order to make him appear to fall over dead. But he didn't tumble. A representative from the American Society for the Prevention of Cruelty to Animals supervised the administering of the drug. Then I'd call, "Turn them!" But nothing happened.

After this was repeated a few more times, the ASPCA man said, "I'll allow only one more injection." The pig finally fell.

By this time, George Peppard and I had become fast friends. One remaining scene, where he tells how he felt being a bastard son, had to be worked out.

Now that we were back at the studio, we could analyze the scene and talk as much as we wanted. George found the lines full of self-pity.

His legitimate half brother has discovered they share the same father, and comes to him to try to make it up to him in some way.

"Tell it straight, with no emotion," I advised George. "Be totally honest and open."

His reading was perfect: "My mammy would tie me up at the end of a rope to keep me from going over there . . . to his house . . . 'He doesn't want you,' she said. Well, I didn't like it. I howled like a dog at the end of that rope."

By underplaying George created a very unusual scene.

I liked the picture we'd made together.

Reviews of the picture, however, were not favorable. *Time* dismissed it by describing it as having "a certain low Faulknerian likability." Crowther found "the whole thing . . . aimless, tedious and in conspicuously doubtful taste. Under Vincente Minnelli's direction it is garishly overplayed."

If the picture was operatic—tacit narrative periods orchestrated into crescendos—it apparently didn't work for many. And yet, whenever my films are revived, the boar hunt sequence from *Home from the Hill* is

334

run as an example of one of the most operatic scenes in the history of dramatic films.

Bells Are Ringing, my next picture, was a much happier experience. Since the book written by Adolph Green and Betty Comden was near-perfect, their main challenge in adapting the picture to the screen was to rephrase it in cinematic terms.

Adolph feels I kept more things from the show than I might have, but I disagree. Adding fluidity to the essential stage components seemed a logical approach. Adolph underestimates what the two of them accomplished on the stage.

There were some theatrical conventions, however, that didn't translate to film. We had to attack them in a different way to compensate for these great moments.

Judy Holliday was re-creating her stage role as the owner of a telephone answering service who keeps getting involved in the lives of her clients.

She worked out of a basement apartment on the stage and, though we scouted through the bowels of New York buildings to find something suitable, nothing grabbed us.

Then suddenly there it was. *Life* magazine had just published a double-page spread, showing a lone house standing in the middle of a razed block, its owners holding out for more money. I called the location man and a deal was made to use the house as Judy's home base.

"Drop that Name" was set in a house instead of on the street. In looking for locations, we found a beautiful house on Sutton Place, with a private park behind shared with other houses on the block. It belonged to the divorced wife of Aristotle Onassis. Our location man said she'd refused us permission to use it. "Do you mind if I try?" I asked.

I'd never met Tina Onassis, but I sent her a wire, telling her why we wanted to use the house. She wired back immediately. We would, after all, be able to use it.

We used the actual exteriors, and duplicated its interiors at the studio. The production number progressed through all the rooms of the house, flowing up a stairway and back, with the celebrity conscious people dropping all the names and the Judy Holliday character failing to catch any of them.

"Just in Time" was filmed in the park next door.

Another number, originally with a subway setting, was transplanted to a city street, with traffic zooming by. Judy tells Dean Martin that people will be friendly if one extends himself. She proves it by stopping

335

people on the street to say hello. We picked dour-looking types as extras, with their faces lighting up as they were approached.

Judy's performance was an easy transition from her stage role, even though she was like Astaire in thinking she wasn't doing it right. I kept reassuring her, but Judy was a constant worrier and I don't know how effective I was at convincing her how marvelous she was.

Dean Martin, on the other hand, would rather die than have you believe he cared. He wasn't particularly challenged by the part of the writer. But what he did was done amusingly and well.

The picture was Judy's, as the reviews pointed out.

"In this $3,000,000 Metrocolore musical based on her Broadway boff of 1956," the *Time* magazine review started, "Judy Holliday employs her limited vocal resources with showmanly style, supports them with a comic gift that is a major wonder of the entertainment world, and with some skillful assistance from Director Vincente (*Gigi*) Minnelli manages to jog and jazz and jigger a merely middling book and some fairly forgettable tunes into one of the year's liveliest and wittiest cinemusicals."

Crowther was also charmed. The picture, he wrote, "owes more to Miss Holliday than it does to its authors, its director or even to Alexander Graham Bell."

20 | Europe on $25,000 a Day

I was in New York, for a round of press interviews in conjunction with the release of *Home from the Hill,* when the studio informed me it had been selected for showing at the Cannes Film Festival. I was included in the package Metro would be sending.

When I returned to California, a script awaited me. I was asked to direct *The Four Horsemen of the Apocalypse,* a remake of the 1921 silent picture which had made a star of Rudolph Valentino. The story was now set in World War II, yet retained the events of the original story in the years leading up to 1914. If the setting would return to the earlier period, I felt something could be made of the script.

"There's plenty of time to worry about that," Sol Siegel told me. "In the meantime, go to Cannes and enjoy yourself."

The festival wasn't starting for a few weeks, and I dawdled them away very pleasantly with Tina and Liza. In Tina's case, this time was fortunately spent. Georgette would soon be marrying a publisher from Mexico, and Tina would move there with her. From that point on, our visits would be limited to one a year, and her upbringing would become more cosmopolitan. It took me aback to discover that my daughter, with Spanish now as her primary language and speaking French to her

337

mother at home, had gradually slipped into a rather clipped English, which was not the mark of a native American.

Lee Gershwin, at about this time, called to invite me to a dinner party. I asked if I could bring a date.

"Of course," she replied. I took a thirteen-year-old. Liza.

Frank Sinatra and Gene Kelly were among the guests that night. Roger Edens, sitting at the piano, accompanied them as they each sang a couple of numbers.

Then Roger turned to Liza and asked her to sing with him.

"Until that time," Gene recalls, "I thought Liza was a sweet gawky kid with big eyes just like her father's. But she had something."

Gene was preparing a television special. He wanted to put Liza on the show. She thought it would be fun. I didn't take this as any indication of interest in a show business career, for Liza had lots of interests as a child and she hadn't given Judy and me any indication one way or another.

I told Gene we should ask Judy if it was all right. Judy quickly consented.

The two decided to perform "For Me and My Gal" together. It was the same number that had introduced Gene to films in 1942, with Judy as his co-star.

I accompanied Liza to the rehearsal hall. Saul Chaplin was at the piano. Gene blocked out the steps for Liza, then sat on the piano bench with Saul as she went through her paces. She picked up the steps immediately. Saul yelled with delight, falling off the piano bench and pounding the floor.

Came time for the telecast. "We were in front of this big audience," Gene remembers, "and I was very scared for Liza. I kept thinking she was going to blow it. I was so concerned that, in fact, *I* almost blew it. But Liza was cool and calm, as if this was her fifty-fourth show.

"I don't know where it came from. It had only been a couple of years since she'd come and play in our back yard. I'd come out and do a couple of steps with her, but I didn't see that she had any greater flair for it than most kids did."

As I drove Liza home that night, she seemed unaffected by the reaction to her performance. She did allow, however, that it was fun.

This was my first vacation in three-and-a-half years, and I was grateful for the studio's generosity. All I had to do in return was to go through all that crazy hoopla associated with the Cannes Festival. Oh, yes, and another thing. While I was there, would I mind going over to Marseilles, where Horst Buchholz was filming *Fanny,* and talk to him about his possible appearance in *The Four Horsemen?* Gladly.

When the festival ended, I took the trip to see Horst. But the *Fanny* company had changed its shooting schedule, and Horst was out in the bay filming. It proved impossible to get to him. I moved on.

Ben Thau had recommended a spa on the Italian Riviera, Montecatini, and the studio driver took me there. I thought I'd stay there a couple of days to please Ben. But when I arrived, I discovered it to be such a restful old town that I stayed a full two weeks. William Wyler and David Lean were there, as was Sam Spiegel, whose wife Betty was expected momentarily.

No sooner did Betty arrive than she told me, "I want you to meet somebody. I think you'll like her." We arranged to meet up later in Rome.

For the moment, however, I took the mud baths and waters. I never felt better after taking those morning sessions. The driver would take me to Florence to sightsee every afternoon, and the two weeks quickly passed.

André Previn and George Oppenheimer were among several American acquaintances in Rome at the time of my arrival. So was Betty. She arranged a meeting with a young Yugoslavian woman who'd been married to an Italian and stayed on in Rome after their divorce. Her name was Denise Giganti.

We saw each other for the rest of my stay in Rome. I'd expected the holiday was going to be longer, but a message from the studio showed me otherwise. I was instructed to go to London to test Ingrid Thulin as the female lead in *The Four Horsemen.*

It was apparent I was being rushed, and I didn't like it. The studio would be told when I returned to the United States. I never got the opportunity.

I was next instructed to go to Paris to begin preparing the production. With a firm starting date set by the studio, and daily $25,000 costs starting up at that time, I had no choice. I was drafted.

My objections to the World War II setting were again repeated. I didn't see how the Argentine protagonist living in Paris could remain neutral for so long a time. The Germans hadn't occupied Paris during World War I, as they had in the Second World War. If the studio insisted on setting the story in a later period, the script would have to be changed. Studio head Sol Siegel agreed.

Laying the story in the later period made it necessary to create a plot involving the French Resistance. That story had already been told many times before, and I didn't see why we should have to repeat it.

But we did. Robert Ardrey, who'd written the original screenplay was at work on a new project, so John Gay was sent over to work with me. I'd already written an outline, pinpointing the weaknesses as I saw them.

Gay proved to be of enormous help. The script—with the dreaded World War II setting—took shape. But I never justified the updating in my mind.

When it came time to start casting, I learned the studio was already at work. While in Rome, I'd had lunch with a young French actor, and thought his classically handsome looks, showcased in an epic story, could create the same impact as Valentino had forty years previously. But none of the studio executives had heard of him, and Alain Delon would have to wait for another opportunity to be exposed to American audiences. Glenn Ford had recently signed a multiple picture contract with Metro, and his first film under the agreement, as Metro announced it, would be *The Four Horsemen*.

There I was, stuck with a story I didn't want to do, with a leading actor who lacked the brashness and impulsiveness I associated with his part. I'd wanted new challenges, but I didn't think they'd be *that* challenging.

Yet, if the picture was to be made, I decided it should be as stunning visually as I could make it. The flaws in the story might be overlooked. Some of my previous pictures hadn't held much hope in the beginning, but they'd been saved because I'd had some leeway in the writing. But I didn't have this freedom on *Four Horsemen*. It would be interesting to see what could be accomplished.

I made a quick trip back to the United States to discuss the project. I still wanted to know if there was any chance the setting could be changed to the original period. There wasn't. I would have to go through with it. I began to believe I was the victim of a studio setup.

During the time I was in Southern California, I corresponded with Denise in Rome. She arrived in Paris two weeks after I did, taking a room in the same hotel where I was staying. She would visit the set during the day's shooting, and I found Denise's capacity for making friends quickly most attractive, which was such a contrast to my reserved ways. It was very easy for me to begin having serious thoughts about her, and I hoped she felt the same.

The Thirties were the last elegant decade, and I set out to capture the sophisticated milieu in which the wealthy main characters circulated.

In studying the Blasco-Ibáñez novel, I decided the four horsemen— Conquest, War, Pestilence, Death—were not only a necessary symbolic effect, but an integral part of the story.

Tony Duquette designed a set of andirons incorporating the Four Horsemen, which would come to life to ride in the sky, as a parallel to the unfolding action. He also designed the suits of armor the riders would wear. The andirons are seen in the picture's opening, in the fireplace of the patriarch's Argentine manse, where the French and German branches of the family have arrived for a reunion.

I would again use red as a dominating color, culminating in a red gel over the newsreels, which would be shown in a documentary way to point up the devastation of the war and the insensitivity of the principal actors in taking scant notice of it.

The cast we gathered was as brilliant as it was international. Lee J. Cobb would play Madariaga the patriarch. Charles Boyer would be the head of the French branch of the family, and Paul Lukas the German. Karl Boehm was recruited instead of Horst Buchholz to play the young German son, hired without testing. I felt he could deliver a good performance, my judgment based on some film footage I'd seen on him. Ingrid Thulin would play the married woman Ford becomes involved with, and Paul Henreid her husband, who is a leader in the Resistance. The other major female role, the younger sister of Ford who commits herself to the underground movement, was to be handled by Yvette Mimieux.

Throughout the five months of filming in France, there were streams of memorandums flowing between producer Blaustein, Sol Siegel, John Gay, and me. They were supplemented by many phone conversations with Sol. We seemed compelled to exchange words in proportion to the astronomical numbers being bandied about to describe the production: 15,000 extras, ninety interior sets, 250,000 tons of military equipment.

Program notes published with the picture's release by the studio, though with rather high-flown rhetoric, reviewed the filming:

Paris, one of the world's most glamorous and fabulous cities, became a giant motion picture set for *The Four Horsemen of the Apocalypse.*
This was essential to the telling of the story. For here, less than a generation ago, a valiant people heard in stunned and tearful silence the hobnailed tramp of the invader down its historic streets. Yet so bright did the

341

flame of freedom burn in the hearts of the citizens of Paris, it was to remain for five years a city occupied but never truly conquered.

It was to re-create those unforgettable days of human drama and passions, despair and hope, that Metro-Goldwyn-Mayer set out to capture on film the true flavor of Paris as never before. Although the scope and setting of the production encompassed two hemispheres—from the Pampas of the Argentine to the capitals of Europe—Paris was primarily the colorful stage on which the fascinating Ibáñez characters played out their destinies.

After many months of research and selecting locales, finally on a bright Paris Sunday morning, Director Vincente Minnelli with Cinematographer Milton Krasner and efficiently experienced crews set up equipment in the center of the Place de l'Opèra while the majority of Parisians still slept.

In order to turn back the clock to the years of occupation, Sunday, frequently of necessity, was a shooting day when the normally bustling boulevards and streets were practically deserted. For the same reason, to photograph scenes of Nazi troops entering Paris, August was selected. This is the month when Parisians, themselves, evacuate their city almost en masse for long anticipated holidays at the seashore and resorts.

During the next twelve weeks, Minnelli moved the Cinemascope cameras with the precision of a military maneuver. From the student quarters of St. Germain and the famed Sorbonne to the Left Bank and the steps of Sacré Coeur, the cameras roved over Paris, pausing to photograph the Seine by moonlight, and the impassive gargoyles of Notre Dame.

Outside Paris, scenes were played against a background of the beautiful château countryside, green fields with grazing cattle, ancient stone castles and Gothic arched aqueducts, the latter built by the Romans still defying time.

These unsurpassed settings for a motion picture were used by Minnelli as picturesque frames for the dynamic action of *The Four Horsemen of the Apocalypse*.

Through the magnificently ageless arches of the aqueduct, for example, a speeding Rolls-Royce was photographed, transporting Glenn Ford to a French farmhouse more than 600-years-old. As in the case of innumerable settings, it was selected for reasons of authenticity.

The farmhouse was literally reliving a real life role. In World War II it had valiantly served as headquarters for the French Underground, the center of Nazi harassment.

For the tender love scenes of Glenn Ford and lovely Swedish star Ingrid Thulin, Minnelli appropriately selected Versailles, with its magnificent gardens and musical fountains, the Petit Trianon and the Palace.

Paris, not unaccustomed to a picture company on location on its boulevards, displayed no more than normal curiosity until a morning when Ford was scheduled to play a scene at a table of the Café de la Paix in the shadow of the Paris Opèra.

Suddenly, there was tension in the air as impeccably uniformed Nazi officers mingled with pretty girls and snarling, clattering tanks with Swastika insignia rumbled through the streets. To Frenchmen this was not make-believe. It recalled poignant days of the past and caused them to stop sharply in shocked, indignant surprise.

Time had far from erased the emotional impact of the occupation. Long dormant, it had been aroused that day by the official announcement that German troops were to train on French soil for the first time since World War II in the interest of Europe's common defense. While any antagonism has since simmered down, at the moment it was heated in many quarters, and a matter of concern to the filming of *The Four Horsemen of the Apocalypse*.

Permits for further filming of Occupation scenes on the streets of Paris were cancelled. Fortunately, Minnelli had completed all footage of major importance, particularly the shots of Nazi troops marching through the Arc de Triomphe and Place de la Concorde.

There were no problems on the outskirts of Versailles. Here was recorded the relentless march of the enemy toward Paris. Local residents understandingly worked as extras. Minnelli merely had to set the scene for them. Little direction was necessary. Their faces registered according to the individual—defiance, sadness, fright, and resignation.

Not a few had tears in their eyes. For many, they were reliving a moment in their own lives, a moment in history indelibly burned into their hearts and minds.

The pretentiousness of the foregoing description, coupled with its shameless sentimentality, perhaps describes the thrust envisioned by the studio and haplessly supervised by me. The facts are generally accurate, but the way they were overblown bore direct relation to the story I filmed, and not the story I'd envisioned.

The first sequences I supervised were filmed at Versailles, representing the entry of the German soldiers into Paris. It was easier to shoot the scene there, because the crowds could be easier handled. We'd found a wide street that resembled the Champs Élysées, and dressed it over to make it appear the troops were entering through the Arc de Triomphe.

I re-created a heartbreaking photo in *Life* magazine, showing the tearful face of a middle-aged man as France is occupied by the Germans. The camera panned through the crowd, passing by Glenn Ford and Ingrid Thulin, and rested on the man before moving on.

Claude Renoir, Jean's brother, supervised the photography in the evacuation scenes. I was thrilled by his marvelous sense of composition. But then he comes by it naturally.

We'd already shot scenes in the deserted Place de la Concorde. While preparing, I was standing on a traffic island there, looking through my view finder, when a face suddenly appeared there. It was Simone Signoret. She'd been driving by, recognized me and drawn up to say hello. She was a welcome interruption to the problems I was encountering in filming there.

Modern cars hurtling by made it impossible to shoot during the day. A few years previously, Mike Todd, while filming *Around the World in Eighty Days,* had presumed to tow away cars from in front of the Ritz Hotel. A big mixup resulted, with lots of irritated car owners letting off steam to the Paris police. As a result, the police were reluctant to cooperate with any film companies, and many police units were needed to control traffic on the many blocks we would be shooting. Filming at daybreak proved our best solution, and we sneaked in like thieves to get the sequences.

The actors lent themselves admirably to the monumental filming. (At two hours and thirty-three minutes, *Four Horsemen* is my longest film.) Paul Lukas and Karl Boehm were wonderful as the German father and son, and Boyer as the French father gave a very touching performance. I advised Charles to try something in the scene where he hears of his son's death. Instead of using the Frenchman's typical gestures, I suggested, "Let's try something. This is such a shock. Feel as if your hands are made of lead. There's no life in them. Try not using any gestures at all." The device showed how truly stunned Boyer was at the news.

We returned to the United States to shoot a few remaining interiors.

A couple of weeks after my arrival, Denise was also in California. There was no doubt in our minds that we would soon marry.

There was still one major sequence to handle before the end of filming: the four horsemen in armor appearing in the sky midst clouds and mist. Four horses were drilled for sixty-five working days, trained to gallop at speeds from twenty to thirty miles an hour, under multicolored lights through barrages of fire and smoke.

The picture still wasn't finished when Denise and I accepted an invitation to spend the Christmas holidays in Palm Springs as guests of Joan Cohn and Laurence Harvey. They gladly agreed to be our attendants when we decided to get married.

The wedding, on the eve of the new year of 1961, was held at Joan's house. It was casual and baggy pants. The Justice of the Peace, running

344

late, performed the ceremony very quickly. Denise's English still wasn't very good, and she didn't fully understand him. She was married before she knew it.

We returned to Beverly Hills to start life together. I went back to the studio to finish editing *Four Horsemen*.

The release of the picture confirmed that a man may be a prophet everywhere but in his homeland. Jean De Baroncelli, writing in France's *Le Monde*, said: "Minnelli conceived 'The Four Horsemen of the Apocalypse' with extreme refinement which is the stamp of his talent. Minnelli uses color as no other director in the world. He expresses admirably the poetry of things. All of these qualities are too rare on the screen for them not to be singled out for mention."

Gian Luigi Rondi of Rome's *Il Tempo* wrote: "Vincente Minnelli has succeeded in making a picture which has a sure hold on audiences. He is to be commended most of all for the dignity of style and for the scenes of exquisite beauty which adorn the dramatic story. This is not the first time Minnelli recalls Paris and once again his Paris is evoked in a subtle manner with a palette of colors happily borrowed from the latest Impressionists."

George Ramseger of Berlin's *Die Welt* said: "Again one must admire the daring of the Americans in dealing with a problem of our time and in penetrating recent history. No director ever before caught the psychological situation of World War Two so strongly in his grip. This achievement is remarkable and will go to the heart of audiences."

On this side of the Atlantic, however, critics gave the picture shorter shrift. *Time* concluded: "The tale is trite, the script clumsy and the camerawork grossly faked." Crowther said the picture was "staged by Vincente Minnelli in an incredibly fustian 'Hollywood' style."

In later years, according to some students of film, the picture influenced the look of three extraordinary films: Luchino Visconti's *The Damned*, Bernardo Bertolucci's *The Conformist* and Vittorio de Sica's *The Garden of the Finzi-Continis*. Since I was overcome by these staggering accomplishments, I was immensely flattered.

John Houseman had bought Irwin Shaw's *Two Weeks in Another Town* and asked if I'd like to direct. It was not a successful novel, but it had many of the elements of *The Bad and the Beautiful*.

Could we repeat a past success? We thought we'd try.

The story about a washed-up actor who gets one last chance, filling

345

in as director for his old mentor on a picture shooting in Rome, was also slightly derivative of *La Dolce Vita,* which Fellini had directed the previous year.

Kirk Douglas would again be with us. I was quite surprised when Cyd Charisse suggested herself as the amoral ex-wife who continues as the center of the actor's turmoil. We took her up on the offer.

Charles Schnee's script attempted to create some order out of Shaw's novel, and we felt he'd succeeded. The motivations that weren't spelled out would be filled in by innuendo.

Denise and I flew to Rome for the filming. We would be staying in the apartment she'd kept there.

What we filmed was a better picture than what was released, though one writer on film saw wonders in the picture that few others did.

Peter Bogdanovich, writing in the Winter, 1962, of *Film Culture,* offered his own analysis of the picture:

"Based on an undistinguished novel, Minnelli's new film transforms it into a kind of kaleidoscopic tour of an off-beat underworld. Set in Rome's movie world, it is the story of some has-been American film people making one of those silly period spectacles that appear all the time now as the lower half of neighborhood double bills . . .

"This bizarre group gets together in Minnelli's gaudy, flashy, cynical and debauched Roman world—a picture of perversion and glittering decay that in a few precise and strikingly effective strokes makes Fellini's *La Dolce Vita* look pedestrian, arty and hopelessly social conscious. Just compare Fellini's tiresome, vapid orgy sequences with Minnelli's sexy, colorful ones; Fellini's (like all pseudo-moralists) are slanted so as to appear boring, but Minnelli's look like fun. In an hour and a half, Minnelli implies more than Fellini spelled out in three . . .

"Rather like a companion piece to *The Bad and the Beautiful* (which was about movie-making in Hollywood), *Two Weeks in Another Town* is filled with fascinating incident and sharply sophisticated relationships. Minnelli's flair for melodrama and heightened characterization has never been more apparent: Robinson and Trevor squabbling with each other, acidly cutting at every opportunity; and then, in bed at night, he starts to weep self-pityingly and she mothers him like a small child—it is a devastating scene. Charisse, beautiful, sleekly corrupt, has never been more appealingly evil. It could be said that all the characters are too-dimensional, but it is such an obvious remark that only an idiot could imagine Minnelli didn't know exactly what he was doing: a grand melo-

346

drama, filled with passion, lust, hate and venom, surely the ballsiest, most vibrant picture he has signed."

I wonder if young Bogdanovich and I saw the same picture. Imagine what he might have said if he'd seen it before the unfortunate cuts. So much more was suggested. The orgy scene was arranged so that it was obvious the players were watching an erotic show. It bounced from one character to another and suggested they all were under the influence of drugs. As cut by hands that were less than discerning, the characters seemed to be just looking at each other. Bogdanovich might have liked the studio's orgy. I liked mine much better.

The culprit responsible for the hacking of the picture was the head of the studio in New York, who himself would be out of a job in two months. He found the philosophy of the film immoral—this at a time when the studio was also filming *Lolita,* which emerged intact (the picture, not the girl)—and attacked our picture with a meat cleaver. This was the only time in my career that such a catastrophe befell me.

Not only was the orgy sequence cut, a scene in which Cyd Charisse's character gave her distorted view of life was also inexplicably dropped. Without it, one never knew why she tried to maintain her hold on her husband.

"You've never seen the third floor of my house?" Carlotta asks a friendly reporter. "It's one huge closet. Last time I counted, I had over a thousand dresses. More than four hundred suits. Including the first suit I over owned—a houndstooth gabardine I bought in Macy's basement for nineteen ninety-five . . . It's a trait of mine. I can't stand giving up anything I've ever owned."

My European adventures ended with ashes in my mouth. I didn't like the feeling. It was even more compounded when the picture was released.

One scene had the principal characters screening a film they'd made together in the past. It was to be their symbol of former triumph, a milestone in film-making for others to emulate. We'd wanted to use *Champion,* Kirk's first big hit, but United Artists wanted too much money for us to use it. The only other important picture of Kirk's immediately available to us was *The Bad and the Beautiful.* In using it, we were accused, perhaps justly, of being immodest. One thing was sure, however. In *Two Weeks,* we certainly hadn't matched our past standard.

21 Venice Productions

My contract with Metro ended while I was still shooting *Two Weeks in Another Town*. It would have to be renegotiated upon my return to the United States.

The early 1960s had seen an extraordinary development in the film industry. Studios were losing their economic hold. Some super stars were commanding a million dollars a picture, or were getting a straight percentage of the profits. Some of them, in driving a hard bargain, even managed to obtain title to a film after its initial playing dates. The lunatics, as some cynics persisted in pointing out, were running the asylum.

As a director whose pictures were among the most profitable for Metro, my bargaining position was strengthened. I could now make certain demands. Not having a head for business, I let my agent, Abe Lastfogel of the William Morris Office, put the package together. What came out of his negotiations with the studio was a revelation.

Metro, during our twenty-year association, had steadfastly refused to loan me out to other studios. Now, not only would I be allowed to take any offers coming my way, I could initiate projects through an independent production company. The studio would negotiate for my services with the company and I, as sole owner, would share in the profits of each film as well as getting my usual salary.

It all sounded fine to me, and I became further convinced it should be

348

done when Denise urged me to go along with the plan. Her practical European head for business was better able to grasp such matters than mine could.

We came upon the name for the company in a slightly roundabout way. Since Denise would be an officer of the company, I wanted to combine her name with mine in some way. What we came up with was Vinise. That, easily enough, became Venice.

There was so much easy about my life during that time. Denise was proving to be the most devoted of wives.

She'd always led an active social life, and there was no reason why she shouldn't continue. She already had many friends in Hollywood, some of whom she'd met on her previous trips to New York, and Denise began to renew their acquaintance.

I hadn't given much thought to the fact some people make social careers the end-all of their whole lives, but the point wasn't lost on me as our social life accelerated. Often the whole rationale for going out to fashionable restaurants was to be seen, not much different from the Paris of *Gigi*'s time.

Denise found this life amusing, as did I, but I didn't perceive that she was all that obsessed by it. She's a lovely woman with great charm who makes friends easily, and her company is eagerly sought out. Almost effortlessly, she was soon regarded as one of Hollywood's leading hostesses. With the new standing came added responsibilities.

My wife wisely saw that I could enjoy social pastimes, but if it came to a choice of going to a party with her or staying late at the studio to work out a problem, the studio won every time. But if it was a choice of a quiet evening at home or a night out, that was another matter. There were times when I rebelled against going out night after night, but Denise usually charmed me into going.

On one February night, she informed me we were invited to a party at the Beverly Hilton Hotel. The host was a perfect Southern gentleman . . . I found him a bore. He'd entertained us several times, and we'd repaid each social obligation. The invitations kept coming, and we kept accepting, then we'd have to invite him back. I could just see the three of us, being mutually bored into our old age, as we ping-ponged invitations back and forth. I rebelled.

"No more," I told Denise. "It has to end sometime."

"Now don't be silly, Vincente," she answered. "If you do not come I shall be very cross."

Cecil Beaton was in town, and invited to the same party. He was due shortly, for he'd volunteered to drive us over. I knew I would have to go.

Having already put on a disagreeable grimace, I proceeded with the rest of my dressing.

The three of us arrived at the hotel. As we approached the double doors of the room where the party was being held, we could hear the orchestra playing "Gigi."

"They're playing our song, Cecil," I cracked. The doors opened and inside were all my friends. "Surprise!"

I was delighted, but dumfounded. Why the occasion? This was dispelled by some friends adding, "Happy birthday!" I'd forgotten. It was the first time in my life I'd ever had such a party. Mitzi Gaynor gave a speech, imitating Denise's accent. Rosalind Russell recited a poem she'd written, incorporating the titles of all my movies. I was enormously touched. If being "social" involved such evenings with friends one adores, then I was glad to be part of it.

Inside every introvert, I suppose, is an extrovert dying to get out. Denise knew that, and wouldn't permit me to take the easy way. More often than not, once she'd forced me out among friends, I enjoyed myself more than anyone.

On the other hand, Denise agreed I should concentrate my career on totally creative efforts. She gradually took over all the business matters for the Minnellis.

That summer, the two of us flew to New York to mark a milestone in Liza's life. She was working as an apprentice at the Hyannisport Summer Playhouse, and had been given a small acting part in *Take Me Along*.

We had dinner at Judy's. The three of us, with David Begelman from Creative Management Associates, would fly together to Hyannisport the next day.

Judy and I were both very excited about our daughter's appearance. Liza hadn't told us how serious she was about a show business career, but Judy and I agreed it was a good way for her to spend the summer.

We arrived at the theater in the round. It was housed in a tent. As I walked in with Denise and Judy, it was as if my life had come full circle and I was back at the Minnelli Brothers Tent Theatre.

Liza, of course, was marvelous.

Denise and I flew home, and I was delighted Liza had done us so proud.

Joe Pasternak at Metro wanted to produce a film based on Mark Toby's novel, *The Courtship of Eddie's Father*. Abe Lastfogel worked out my first agreement under the new contract with the studio.

I'd found the book about the efforts of a young son to marry off his widowed father warm and winning. It was real, in the same way *Father of the Bride* had been, and I thought I could bring it off.

Glenn Ford's contract was still in effect at the studio, and he was ideal casting as the father. A gifted young boy, Ronny Howard, who was playing the son on the Andy Griffith television series, was cast as the son. (I find it difficult to reconcile his lovable brashness then with the quietly dignified young man he played in a 1973 picture, *American Graffiti*.)

The father becomes involved with three young women. As Sacred Love, we cast Shirley Jones. Stella Stevens was to play Profane Love, of sorts. Falling in neither category was Dina Merrill as a sophisticate who's actually rather nice, but doesn't really cotton to the idea of taking on the raising of the boy.

The picture was set in Manhattan. We showed the skyline at the opening. A radio announcer's voice greets the new morning as the camera pans across the city, settling on the kitchen where Ford is fixing breakfast.

The sympathetic aspect to his character is immediately suggested, for he's getting his son off to school. It's a new responsibility, taken over after the death of his wife.

Glenn was to deliver a true performance, and a touching one. He was on key throughout the filming. It took a lot of work. He's an actor who requires and demands much help, though I don't know why. I've always found him a very complicated man.

Ronny Howard had an extraordinary hysteria scene, triggered by the death of a goldfish, in which he let out all the stops. He knew how important it was. Ford reacted beautifully, with all the conflicting emotions of the character. He's concerned, but irritated, so his impatience shows. Why would the boy react so violently now, when he'd passively accepted the death of his mother?

One scene, at a penny arcade, was the longest take in the picture, lasting over four minutes. The background had to be continuous, as Stella Steven's character was introduced. She's "picked up" by father and son. Hers was a marvelous performance as a shy sex symbol come to New York to acquire poise so that she can go back home to win a beauty contest. It was a wonderful character, a girl with a wide-eyed innocent look and a body that won't quit.

In a later scene, she goes to a cabaret with a lech, played by Jerry Van Dyke, who is prepared to suffer the agonies of her drum solo, yet another effort to overcome her shyness. ·

She starts off awkwardly, but as she gains confidence, finishes her per-

351

formance quite strongly, to everyone's surprise including her own. I particularly liked the scene.

One of Ford's lines showed his gift of prophecy. Having recently met the Dina Merrill character, she gives her opinions on the equality of women. He rather charmingly answers, "I'm afraid that'll never become a national movement."

The film glided effortlessly from one scene to another, I feel. Though it takes a bit of work to get that effect, it was nevertheless an easy film to direct. The story propelled us along, and John Gay's script must be given great credit. The premise was so affecting that the picture later spun off a television series.

When the picture was about to be released, I was sent to New York for a round of interviews.

Liza had been attending Scarsdale High School in New York the previous year, during the time that Judy was living there. (She and Sid Luft were in the process of divorcing at the time.) She belonged to the school drama club, and had been cast in its production of *The Diary of Anne Frank* in the title role. The production so impressed a sponsor that he underwrote a tour by the students with the play to Israel, Greece, and Italy.

The next fall, Liza took some special courses at the Sorbonne. But she'd had enough of schooling. Only sixteen, she knew what she wanted to do. She'd come back to the United States shortly before my arrival in New York.

This daughter of mine, who'd never settled her attention on one exclusive interest, proceeded to inform me that she wanted to quit school and go into show business. Would I help her convince Judy that she should be allowed to stay in New York while her mother went on tour?

I wasn't positive myself that this was advisable. We talked it out, and Liza convinced me of her dedication. She was prepared to start at the bottom and work.

The years with Judy, both at home and on the road, were unstable at best. Only in such circumstances could a career in show business be considered a form of security for her.

I agreed, finally, that Liza should be allowed to try it on her own. Judy's reluctant permission followed.

Judy would come around within a short time. It wasn't long before she was bragging to Lee Gershwin about Liza's career. "The kid knew exactly who to get to help her," Judy said. "I guess she kept her eyes open whenever she was on her old man's sets." Not to mention the many tours

352

Liza took with Judy. Our daughter knew exactly who to turn to for counsel and training, and the people she worked with at the outset of her career are the same people she's working with today.

I returned to California to discover that negotiations only previously hinted at were now out in the open.

Warner Brothers had outbid all other Hollywood studios for the motion picture rights to *My Fair Lady,* and it was planning to mount a movie version so extravagant that the picture would ultimately cost $17,000,000. I was asked to direct.

The stage production had been so much of a piece and so brilliantly handled that I didn't see how any film version could compete with it. I'd always been hesitant about transforming a successful musical to the screen, particularly ones offering such visual delights as *My Fair Lady.* With the audience already preconditioned to the look the picture should have, as influenced by the look of the stage production, I found it difficult to inject my own vision on such a project.

But the picture was a plum, the most expensive musical ever to be made up to that time, and I'd again be working with Alan Lerner, Fritz Loewe, and Cecil Beaton.

Denise and I talked the matter over. We decided that I would do it if I was allowed the same percentage participation I was receiving under my new contract at Metro. Warner insisted on paying me a straight salary. We never came to terms, and the picture was assigned to another director. My heart didn't break.

My next assignment, my first picture made outside of Metro, wasn't nearly as sublime as *My Fair Lady* . . . it was *Goodbye Charlie.*

It would be filmed at Twentieth Century-Fox, and Marilyn Monroe had originally been announced for the part of Charlie, shot by a jealous husband, who returns to earth reincarnated as a beautiful blonde.

I hadn't seen the stage version with Lauren Bacall, but it had been criticized for some of Betty's masculine antics. She smoked cigars and swatted women on the rump, among other things. The approach, as I saw it, should have been more feminine, and Monroe could well project the vulnerability of the reincarnated, the prey of every predatory male. The original Charlie had been the most predatory of all.

Before much preparation had gone into the film, Monroe was dead. Even had she lived, I was led to believe that her film career was ended, and we should try to cast it with a different actress.

Before getting any further into the production, however, I had to make a very important trip to New York. Liza had been studying musical comedy technique at the Herbert Berghof Studio. She tried out for an off-Broadway revival of *Best Foot Forward,* and landed the third lead.

This was it, her first professional appearance without sponsorship of parents or friends. Judy decided to stay away from the opening, since this was Liza's night, and her appearance in the audience would bring out the press photographers looking for a human interest angle. But nothing could have kept me away, and I was delighted with what I saw. The rough-edged talent would have to be honed, but the presence was there. Whatever was needed, Liza had it. I was sure she would have a very respectable career. She went on to win the Daniel Blum Award that year as the theater's most promising actress.

I could now return to California to resume work on *Goodbye Charlie.*

Debbie Reynolds was not Monroe. She was much more suitably cast in *The Unsinkable Molly Brown,* which she'd just completed, for her unflagging determination came through admirably. But when one combines her self-possession with a tendency to cuteness, you don't get the exact quality I was looking for. Debbie, however, was very big box office at the time, and the studio cast her in the part. We decided that she should look as glamorous as possible.

I started to work with her. She would wind up giving a good performance, but we both knew how much honest sweat was involved.

Debbie came to see the day's rushes one night.

"Hi, Debbie," I called out.

"I don't know if I should answer," she said as she came up. "I haven't said one goddam thing right all day long. I came in the first thing this morning and said, 'Good morning, Vincente.' And you answered, 'No, don't say it that way. Sing it . . . good morning-g-g!'" We'd worked so hard that day that Debbie was kidding me . . . on the level.

Tony Curtis was playing the part of Charlie's best friend, who gets very disturbing feelings about his buddy in his new guise. I found Tony to have a marvelous comedic touch, one he's used in several films. I wish he'd make more.

Pat Boone worked well in the role of the rich young man with the mother fixation who courts the female Charlie.

Walter Matthau performed a marvelous comedy vignette as the Hungarian producer who shot Charlie, then courted him as a female. He piled a phony British accent on top of the Hungarian one he assumed for the role, and his impersonation was uncanny. I've known several men like him in my time.

So apparently did Harry Kurnitz, who adapted George Axelrod's play,

354

into a savage treatment of the climbers in Hollywood. The picture, at the time of its release, however, was dismissed by Crowther as "a bleak conglomeration of outrageous whimsies and stupidities."

I don't think he was referring to one sequence, which Kurnitz took from life.

Our mutual friend, Armand Deutsch, was an heir to the Sears Roebuck fortune. He, in fact, was the intended victim of Leopold and Loeb, who substituted ill-fated Bobby Franks in his place.

Artie Deutsch often talked, not of the infamous kidnapping, but of his sheltered upbringing. Like every other kid on his block he wanted to run a lemonade stand. His parents agreed that he could.

Out came a refectory table and a lace tablecloth, the crystal, the damask napkins. They were set up behind the grilled gate of the family mansion. Bodyguards stood on each side of the fence. Artie wasn't allowed to go on the other side of the fence. Customers would stop to buy the lemonade, which Artie would hand them through the gate. At the end of the day he cleared $1.35 It had cost his parents $1,400.

I insisted to Harry that Pat Boone should tell the story in a drunk scene with Debbie, in which he tells without self-pity the plight of the poor little rich boy.

If the picture didn't do as well as expected, a more extensive analysis found it not all that lacking.

Films and Filming, in May 1965, six months after the picture was released, took a second look: "A director's quality can best be gauged when his material is taxing. Therefore in any thoroughgoing assessment of Minnelli from here on it will be impossible to overlook *Goodbye Charlie*, a victory of décor over dialogue, of pace over pawkiness, and of directorial control over a script that is wild as all getout.

"Everything is managed with the deftness that typifies Minnelli's gift. He has an instinct for withholding exclamation points. Dialogue that ranges erratically from the funny to the desperate is well reined-in, and so is the entire cast."

Then, on the other hand, there was *The Sandpiper*.

I was back at Metro headquarters, and looking around for new projects when producer Martin Ransohoff approached me about directing Elizabeth Taylor and Richard Burton in a picture based on Ransohoff's short story. Richard was originally announced to direct, but the deal didn't work out. The Burtons were then submitted the names of three directors for the picture. One of them was William Wyler, who was next announced as director, and another was Minnelli. Wyler dropped out, and then Ransohoff talked to me.

Richard was appearing in New York in his much-acclaimed *Hamlet,* and I flew back to see him and Elizabeth. Though I found the premise of the story ludicrous and dated, it being an updated version of Reverend Davidson and Sadie Thompson, with superficial philosophizing thrown in, I let the Burtons' enthusiasm color my judgment. I wanted the opportunity to work with them, and I accepted the assignment in the name of Venice Productions.

"It must be wonderful to live in such a place forever," Henry Miller wrote about the Big Sur setting of the story. "But think twice before you try it. For it is land not always quiet and serene—but often dramatic, violent, awesome. This is Big Sur, even today."

We were trying to suffuse the picture with these elements, but the more Dalton Trumbo worked on the story, the more we all realized it was too ponderous and pretentious. Michael Wilson's additions to the script didn't solve the difficulty either.

As we prepared to start filming, I was still plotting ways to improve the script. And then a brouhaha sidetracked these plans.

Elizabeth suggested Sammy Davis to play the sculptor in the film. Neither Ransohoff nor Trumbo liked the idea, for this would add the suggestion of an interracial romance to the already overburdened story. I agreed with them. When the dispute was ended, with Charles Bronson cast in the part, it was time to start the picture.

Because of the Burtons' tax situation, they could only work four weeks in the United States and not at all in England. The shooting at Big Sur would take that much time. From there we would go over to the Boulogne-Billancourt studios in Paris. The name of their game, as the press insisted on repeating, was money, and they were getting a lot of it for *The Sandpiper.* The schedule was designed around them.

In my mind's eye, I can think of no other reason for the Burtons to want to film the story . . . she, playing a free spirit who defies convention and he a minister whose inhibitions vanish through his love for her.

"Both of the characters had philosophies that needed explaining," I was quoted in the August 1965 issue of *Cinema.* "Hers was a completely independent sort of philosophy and makes a very big case out of it. And he, of course, makes an equally good case; he is just as eloquent as she is. But they fall in love and they change each other's point of view. By the time the picture is over, a great deal of him has rubbed off on her and vice versa. He has learned a lot from her philosophy and she has learned a lot from him." All of which, of course, is a rather simplistic explanation of a two-hour film. But perhaps the premise was too simple to warrant that much time.

We spent three-and-a-half weeks shooting exteriors in Big Sur before moving on to Paris.

Metro hosted a cocktail party for the company at the Georges Cinq. One hundred photographers, all of them maniacs, descended on Richard and Elizabeth. Denise and I were caught in this torrential movement toward the Burtons. I was afraid we would all be killed.

Richard and Elizabeth, however, took it in their stride. We were pushed with them into a small office near the ballroom where the party was held, and the four of us had drinks with each other before going back out to brave the mob.

It was constant terror during our stay in Paris. Whenever we went out with the Burtons, there was this frenzy of attention that I couldn't cope with. We did take them one night for a quiet dinner at Elie Rothschild's, but everywhere else we went had a built-in cast of thousands.

We invited the Burtons to join us at the opening of the Lido. Had we known this was one of Paris' top social events, we would have thought better of it. Elizabeth and Richard were sitting on opposite sides of the table. The photographers draped themselves all over Richard to get shots of Elizabeth. He understandably became angry over the mauling.

Aristotle Onassis and Maria Callas were sitting on the other side of the table, which was even with the stage, from Denise and me. The show started, and one of the showgirls swept her cloak around and knocked over a bottle of champagne in a bucket. The champagne spilled over onto the stage. As more showgirls pranced by, they started slipping on the champagne. Onassis and I got up with our napkins and mopped the champagne off the stage. It was typical of that topsy-turvy evening which ended in shambles.

The picture, after all these larger-than-life experiences, was almost an anticlimax.

Some of the press tried to create a feud between Richard and me during the filming. The Burtons were spatting with Ransohoff all during the picture, but I refused to get caught in the crossfire. Eleanor Perry, writing in *Life* magazine, magnified an incident in which Richard and I differed on our approach to a scene. Richard reportedly gave in, adding, "For the money we will dance."

The picture, though it made money, added no new laurels to our careers. But it wasn't totally beneath contempt. "Vincente Minnelli as

357

director has captured the style and charm of an artist's beach house and the clatter and splash of an artist's friends," Crowther wrote in the *Times*.

The three pictures under the Venice Productions banner may have been considered moderate to large successes. But according to studio bookkeeping there were no profits to share. I wasn't totally convinced, but there was no way I could dispute their contentions. So much for my career as a movie mogul.

22 | The Lessening Pace

Metro was again being torn apart by all sorts of power plays. This had been going on since Mayer's demise, and will probably continue until the studio makes way for a housing development or something.

But projects were still being developed in 1964, and I was still being approached to work on them.

One of them, a musical version of *Goodbye, Mr. Chips,* was being prepared by producer Arthur Jacobs. André and Dory Previn had already composed the music and Rex Harrison was set for the title role. Terence Rattigan was writing the screenplay.

Jacobs came over to see me in Paris while I was still filming *The Sandpiper*. He played a record of the Previn music for me. I wasn't enthused.

A few weeks later, Rex was out and Richard Burton had replaced him. But Richard dropped out because he didn't like the lyrics.

That, I suppose, led to the dropping of the Previn music. By this time Peter O'Toole was in. But I was voluntarily out.

Arthur Freed had been talking for some time about a concept for a musical, a cavalcade of Irving Berlin's music, starting in 1901 and coming up to the present. It now looked as if we would go ahead with the project. I informed Arthur Jacobs that I preferred to work on *Say It With Music* than to spend more time with *Mr. Chips.*

We set out to put the picture together. The film, starting at present, would regress from his sophisticated songs of the *Music Box Revue* days and end with the ragtime period, when Berlin's career had started. A ragtime ballet would culminate the picture, incorporating the symbols of the period . . . Frankie and Johnny's revolver, player pianos, card playing, derby hats and sleeve garters, soubrettes and honky-tonks.

It would be great getting back to the musical genre after five years away. The species was dying on the vine, not because I hadn't been doing musicals during that period, but because no one else had been doing them either. Only one of them during that time—*West Side Story*—made any great impact. And rightfully so. Jerome Robbins's choreography was brilliant. If we could end our film with dancing as bold, the picture would be a triumph.

Early on in our preparations, Frank Sinatra and Julie Andrews agreed to star. With these two giant talents to inspire us, Arthur and I intensified our efforts. This would be the bang-up musical to end them all.

During the time we were preparing the picture, I received a letter from a major stockholder asking me why the studio wasn't using my services. I wrote him back to assure him they indeed were, that I was working on a monumental project with Arthur Freed.

In fact we worked on it for a year-and-a-half. During that time, the executives at Metro were more interested in a proxy fight for control of the studio than they were in making pictures. Consequently, no executive would push for such an expensive project and make himself a ready target if it should fail.

Months would go by without hearing from New York. Then a wire would come, asking if we could get the project ready by a certain date. Arthur and I would rush to New York to talk to choreographers and costume designers to get the project ready on time. Then more months of waiting, ended by another special call from New York.

Sinatra would occasionally call to inform us that Metro hadn't even approached him to sign a contract for the picture. Arthur and I were having conferences with Julie during this time too. But the whole project fizzled out.

It was a great disappointment to us all. I didn't mind so much for myself, but I felt Arthur Freed had been ignobly treated. He retired from films soon after.

And I retired from Metro. My five-year contract had ended, and from then on I became a free agent. I spent the rest of the year methodically poring over scripts and finding few to my liking.

360

The career of another Minnelli, however, was beginning to flourish in 1966.

Liza, in England, wrote me a serio-comic letter in which she told of her imagined terrors while preparing her first picture, *Charlie Bubbles,* with Albert Finney.

I immediately wrote back: "I suppose by now you will have gotten deeper into the picture and done some scenes. I know your own intuition and good taste will carry you through and the only advice I can think of, and it's a good general one to follow always, is 'Don't press.' Remember that you register so strongly and so easily that you can project any emotion from ecstasy to anger and still be in control. Do you know what I mean?

"I am delighted that you are doing this picture with Finney and I think it's a marvelous break for you because your first picture won't be some stale, pretentious bore but what sounds to me like a modern and imaginative effort, and I feel absolutely sure that you'll be fresh and great and appealing and something completely new."

And she was.

No sooner did Liza return to the United States than she informed me she was planning to marry Peter Allen, a young Australian singer she'd been seeing.

She was just twenty years old, and I thought she should wait.

Peter wrote me a respectful letter, in which he tried to dispel my reservations about his marriage to Liza. I liked the young man, and I was impressed that he was so tradition-bound that he felt he had to ask for her hand.

My letter to him spelled out my misgivings. They were both quite young, on the brink of professional careers, and I knew that the survival rate of such marriages was infinitesimally small. And yet, marriage to Peter was something Liza very much wanted, I knew. My eventual consent—if one can call it that—was one more request of Liza's I couldn't refuse.

I flew back to New York that March of 1967 for the wedding . . . alone. Denise didn't approve, feeling Liza could have made a better marriage. She was totally honest about it, and Liza understood.

Judy called me at my hotel the day before the marriage. One never knew what to expect when she called. She might say, "Darling, how are you?" Or she might go right into her resentment over some imagined slight.

This time, her mood was somewhere in between.

"If you had any class," she told me, "you'd hire a car and pick me up and take me to our daughter's wedding."

I laughed. "Okay, Judy, when shall I pick you up?"

We got together at the appointed hour and drove to the ceremonies together. Judy was pleased about the marriage. She, in fact, had acted as matchmaker. Peter and his brother appeared with her on the same bill in Australia, and Judy had introduced him to Liza.

Once the wedding was over, though, Judy and I went our separate ways, she to go on with some friends to dinner and I to the hotel and back to California. I had to get ready to go to the Cannes Film Festival in a few days where I'd be serving as First Juror.

David Merrick reached me there and invited me to come to London to talk about a stage musical based on the exploits of Mata Hari. He'd come to me with several projects over the years, but we'd never gotten together before.

The second act hadn't been written, but the first was so affecting that I fell for the idea, and agreed to direct my first Broadway production in almost thirty years.

The theater had changed quite a bit since I'd been away. Where preparing a production had been a great joy in the past, *Mata Hari* proved to be drudgery. All the crafts were highly unionized now, and no one could lift a finger in areas not specifically spelled out in union contracts. Rehearsals were scheduled in three or four different places, and we hopped all over New York to get the musical ready. Having grown accustomed to the more leisurely pace of film-making, I'd forgotten the tension involved in getting a production together on time. Our opening night would be a huge charity benefit in Washington, D.C.

David and I worked on the outline of the second act. I kept in mind a basic attitude. Mata Hari had always been portrayed as a slinky spy, when she was actually a question mark. Many historians felt she'd been unjustly accused and executed. I wanted the audience to leave the theater having great doubts about her.

Though it was arduous work, I felt I was making headway. The second act began with Mata Hari having an idyllic interlude with a detective from the National Bureau, who'd been put on the case to catch her and fell in love with her instead.

I worked out a lyrical setting in a Swiss chalet, with birds singing in the background, to represent the impossible dream. The scenery then separated to show the stark reality, a firing squad in the forest where Mata Hari was to be executed.

362

All the time I was rehearsing the cast, Irene Sharaff was executing the costumes. I'd shown her a lot of clippings from the period. We agreed one color should predominate in every scene. It might be pale yellow changing to mother of pearl or earth tones going into burnt oranges and browns. Though I'd worked with Irene in films, this was our first experience together in the theater. But the theater was her true métier, no matter how highly adaptable she'd been in films, and her work, I felt, was as great as the Oriental costumes she'd done for both stage and film versions of *The King and I*.

I was having greater trouble proving the adaptability of the leads, Marissa Mell as Mata Hari and Pernell Roberts as the detective. The fact that choreographer Jack Cole got sick and had to drop out didn't help much. Neither did the problems we were having with the scenery. It just wouldn't hang right.

Marissa Mell was a great beauty and sang quite well. She did some scenes rather charmingly. In others, however, she needed much work. I don't think she was prepared to offer it. She may have loved the theater, but she loved a mere mortal even more. Her attention wasn't there.

Pernell Roberts hadn't shown his good strong baritone to good advantage on the Bonanza television series, which he'd recently left. But he had shown a full head of hair, which he now refused to don in the name of authenticity. He wanted to perform in his naturally balding head instead of in the toupee we thought would make him more romantic, and insisted on growing a beard. Roberts apparently was rebelling against his Bonanza image. I wasn't willing to hold him down prior to each performance to forcibly put a toupee on him. Roberts is bigger than I am.

The rehearsals staggered on prior to the Washington opening, a benefit which was already sold out. It was impossible to set the opening back the few days it would take to put the production in shape.

What was offered the people of Washington was a dress rehearsal, and Merrick spoke to the audience before the show warning them of this. Everything went wrong. Scenery stuck and costume changes were delayed, resulting in many long waits.

I must say that during the two weeks the show played there the problems were ironed out and many people professed to like the show. I don't know why. The second act never materialized, and it proved to be a lot of nonsense. David, being a realist, forfeited his investment of nearly $1,000,000 and the show never reached New York. I completely agreed with the decision to close *Mata Hari* in Washington and David and I remained good friends.

I might have spent more time licking my wounds, but I wasn't allowed to. The debacle hadn't been fully experienced when I was approached to direct a picture.

Paramount, seeing the extraordinary successs of *Sound of Music* at Twentieth Century-Fox, was making its own high budget musicals in the $20,000,000 bracket, *Darling Lili* and *Paint Your Wagon. On a Clear Day You Can See Forever* wasn't nearly as expensive, though it would have the highest budget of any musical I'd directed.

The Alan Lerner-Burton Lane musical hadn't been a huge success on Broadway, but if mounted with great visual touches could be done well as a film.

Alan adapted his own book for the film. Barbra Streisand was starring in the dual roles of Daisy Gamble and her past incarnation as Melinda, and, in a bit of offbeat casting, Yves Montand was assigned to play her analyst.

(Barbra had received some bad press during the filming of *Funny Girl,* in which she was accused of taking over as director from William Wyler. She had an infallible instinct about what was seemly for her, and occasionally it conflicted with what Wyler wanted. Willie is one director actors don't fool around with. He doesn't like to be told what to do.

(I remember discussing another actor with him when we were both in Europe. He was reputed to be difficult. "I got along with him very well," I told Willie.

("The important thing," he answered, "is that they get along with me. For I'm the boss."

(But I have no ego about such things. The important thing is to make the picture. Consequently, I listened to what Barbra suggested, and implemented some of her suggestions. I found her creative and bright, and we got along beautifully. When the picture ended, Barbra, having noticed that I take only cream in my coffee, presented me with an antique silver coffee service, the sugar bowl missing. On the coffee pot was inscribed, "To Vincente, whom I adore . . . Love, Barbra." On the creamer: "You're the cream in my coffee." It remains one of my great treasures.)

Since I felt the regressions were the weakest part of the play, I perhaps felt they should visually overwhelm the audience. Barbra's past incarnation as Melinda actually wasn't much of a story . . . an artist she posed for, a lover's jealousy, and sudden death. We decided to come into it in a backward way. We first showed her trial, which ended in a verdict of

364

death for treason, before explaining what it was all about. I hoped in this way that suspense would be created, so that the audience couldn't wait to get back to the regressions.

The only condition I placed on Alan in his writing the flashbacks was to shift it to the Regency period. One thing the sequence didn't need was actors in white wigs.

Much of the expense of the picture was accounted for with these scenes at the Royal Pavilion at Brighton. But it would have been even more expensive to re-create it at the studio, as art director John de Cuir was quoted as saying in a newspaper interview, for "it wasn't just duplicating the Pavilion, it was all the fixtures and fittings."

"I think this is a kind of a wild place," he added, "when you think what George IV built it for—he called it his bath house."

Barbra was stunning in a white décolleté dress and turban, studded with beads and diamonds, with pearls dripping from her forehead. The rest of the actors, and the setting, were as expensively outfitted. Place settings were rented. Cecil and I designed the bill of fare for the banquet —capons, lobsters, and suckling pig—and it was catered for the actors. Paramount spared no expense in getting an authentic look to the court of the early nineteenth century. The extraordinary costumes designed by Cecil were part of that budget.

While filming in England, disturbing reports were reaching me from California, suggesting my marriage was at an end. I called Denise after reading an item in a gossip column. "Don't worry about it," she scoffed. "It's nothing."

When I returned to California, I learned otherwise. Denise informed me that she didn't know if she wanted to stay married to me. It was a great shock. We'd grown apart, and I wasn't even aware of it. Until that time, she'd been a marvelous wife who'd made a very happy life for me. But if this was what she wanted, I wouldn't stand in her way. It took her some time to make up her mind, but Denise eventually decided that we would divorce, and she would marry another man. (It took more time for the settlement to be worked out, but the divorce was granted in August of 1971. I was now a three-time loser, and not sure I'd ever marry again. It's extremely difficult to maintain a marriage when one of the parties works so hard and is gone too often. I've always cherished the company of a gentle woman, however. For the last two or three years I've been going everywhere with Lee Anderson, and her warmth and companionship have meant a great deal to me.)

All the while the state of my marriage was in question, work had to continue on the picture. Arnold Scaasi was doing Barbra's costumes now, taking up where Cecil left off. He would be dressing her modern-day role of a little Brooklyn girl whose fiancé wanted her to give up smoking. (So she went to a doctor to help her through hypnosis. The doctor agreed, but under hypnosis she started to tell a strange tale of another life and another time, using an English accent and describing events, when checked on, which proved to be true.)

On Sunday, June 22, I was organizing the shooting for the coming week, when the telephone rang. It was Liza from New York.

"Daddy . . ."

"Darling!"

There was a pause on the other end of the line. "Mama died today."

"Oh, darling . . . I'm so sorry."

Liza was in total control, almost philosophical. But she was also concerned about the job that had to be done.

"I have to make sure she didn't kill herself," Liza said. "Mama couldn't have done that. She was in such a great mood during the last few days."

I comforted Liza as best I could. More long silences. "I'd better go, Daddy."

"Keep me informed, darling."

"Okay."

I hung up the phone and sat at my desk thinking. One of my last meetings with Judy had ended with one of her inward-turned jokes. "That Freddie Fields," she told me, "he's all right." (Since Freddie's firm represented Judy for some time, and their relationship was often stormy, it was reassuring news.)

"What's he done now?" I asked.

"Well, I haven't been too happy with the way they've been representing me. And they have this fellow who's working directly with me. I don't think he's taking very good care of me. I called Freddie and complained. I asked him, 'Why have you assigned me this little man?'

"I guess I called him 'a little man' quite a few times. Know what Freddie did? He called and said he was sending over someone new. And you know who showed up? A midget!"

Once the coroner in London assured her Judy hadn't killed herself, Liza's thoughts could turn to arrangements for the funeral.

Over the next day and a half, Liza would periodically call to tell me what she'd arranged, and to ask if I thought it was right.

"Are you coming to the funeral?" she asked.

"Darling . . . I can't."

366

Liza sensed how awkward I would feel with news photographers around, trying to maneuver all of Judy's ex-husbands so that they could be photographed together. She allowed me to grieve in my own way.

A few days later, Liza and Peter flew to California. I picked them up at the plane. Again, our emotions were kept in control. We needed to be together, but we weren't going to wallow in useless tears. Judy would have been so contemptuous of them.

We'd both gone through so much with Judy, but despite all the difficulties, we never found her as tragic as the public made Judy out to be. She didn't carry herself as a tragic person, and we took the cue from her. Whatever the problem, Judy always had a very good reason for her actions.

The picture I was still working on finished shooting on schedule, despite my sad thoughts about Judy. It was not my greatest musical success, but neither was it Paramount's greatest musical failure.

Arthur Knight's assessment in *Saturday Review* was to my liking.

"What Minnelli does so well is to search out the essential qualities of his star performers, to frame them in ways that heighten the intimacy between them and their audiences, and to surround them with an aura of glamour that makes them at once larger than life and very real. Glamour has become all too rare on the screen today, as have musicals cast with people who can sing with the professionalism of Streisand and Montand. Inevitably *On a Clear Day* will be thought of as their show. But Vincente Minnelli, behind the cameras, has his own brand of professionalism and that is what makes their show sparkle so effortlessly."

When I completed *On a Clear Day,* Liza and I began actively negotiating to do something we'd always talked of: a picture together.

In searching around for a property, we zeroed in on the life story of Zelda Fitzgerald. The crazy hedonism of the Twenties had become a stereotype, with the great elegance of the decade forgotten. It wasn't just a period of the Charleston, flappers, and hot-cha-cha. The Twenties were also dominated by the likes of Otto Kahn, the Metropolitan Opera, and the expatriates in France. Liza and I agreed our approach would be one of style and taste.

Paramount was interested in the project, and we discussed it with executives there. Frank Yablans, the president of the studio, agreed with the elegant approach, and he loaned me a script of *The Great Gatsby,* which he was planning to shoot in the same way. *Zelda,* however, didn't get off the ground.

Another project, on the life of Bessie Smith, which Danny Dare would produce, also fell through. We received permission from her husband to do the film, and worked for a long time on an outline before putting the project in abeyance. We were thinking of Tina Turner in the title role.

Timing, apparently, was premature for both, considering the later revival of interest in Fitzgerald and Diana Ross's subsequent triumph in *Lady Sings the Blues*.

But if you think I'm going to brood about my career's lessening pace, think again. Projects these days fall through with great frequency, and you can't let that get you down.

I'm very aware of what I accomplished, and if my career ended tomorrow I'd still find great satisfaction in what I've done. On the other hand, whenever I start congratulating myself on the way I mastered my craft, an anecdote Alfred Lunt once told me at a dinner party brings me up short.

"I've always been objective in my point of view about a character," he told me. "I could never get inside a character, to get up close to it and play it. But one night it happened. I'd found the secret. I sailed through the part. When I went backstage, people asked me if I was feeling all right. I found out then that I'd given a terrible performance, so I gave that up completely."

But, until his retirement, Alfred didn't give up much else. No one should.

I've been disturbed in recent years with the bitterness and self-pity expressed by veteran directors who can't seem to put current film packages together . . . or have become too lazy to adjust to the new ways of film-making and blame everybody but themselves.

It's really such a bore. When so many of them have contributed films that will stand as landmarks, I don't understand the attitude. I find Billy Wilder's irreverence infinitely more attractive. In a national magazine spread, several directors were asked about their unfulfilled ambitions.

"I've always wanted to do the story of The Crusades," he was quoted as saying, "about the knights in their beautiful armor with caparisoned horses, getting ready to go off to war. They say goodbye to their servants, kiss their wives goodbye and lock them into their chastity belts. They ride off into the sunset to the Holy Land. The rest of the film concerns the village locksmith, Cary Grant."

If someone were to ask me of my unfulfilled hopes, I truly don't know what I'd say, though I know my answer wouldn't be as witty as Billy's.

Throughout my career I was trying to establish a way to adapt the "thinking device" in novels to film. The conventions of the time didn't permit that, however, and these private thoughts would have to be done in a pre-established fantasy way. It wasn't until *Divorce Italian Style* in 1962 that I saw the perfect device used. The hero is talking to a quite boring woman. He murders her. The action reverts to the conversation, showing this to be wishful thinking. I was startled, because I had tried to use the same situation on a picture years before, but it never materialized. And so, director Pietro Germi blazed that trail for us all.

In another area, however, we all need work. The technology of our times hasn't allowed us to implement sound as authentically as we do the visual. Perhaps this is the next great frontier for films. I plan to be part of it. And though I look forward with great optimism, I also look sadly back.

There was more order to films when Leo and I were in our prime. We could cast a project with the best people ever to stand before or behind a camera. Little matter that a particular star or technician wasn't available, when there were equally strong talents serving as backstops. We had the facilities of the world's best set decorating and costume design departments. Though I didn't often use the studio's research departments, preferring to refer to my own files, I knew it was there at the ready. Style and substance weren't an accident at Metro.

I concede there was also the studio politic. It's the stuff of which legends and a proliferating number of books are made, but it couldn't have been all that enjoyable at the time. Fortunately, I was a workhorse with blinders, concentrating on the project at hand. I missed much of the infighting and manipulating, and the who's-sleeping-with-who gossip.

If I rarely took interest in who was getting into whose pants, the times have caused a turnabout of sorts. Today I'm stepping into everyone's shoes. The only way to get a project off the ground is to become a hyphenate producer-screen writer-set decorator-costume designer. All the elements that make up a film have to be synchronized to the second. Only then will a studio be enticed into putting up the money.

None of the gods can be slighted at the christening if the miracle of getting the project underway is to be experienced. Their approval must be treated as the benediction which it, in actuality, is. Then, too often, we lose faith and the gods are offended. Their benevolence evaporates into a dark cloud, followed by the incoherent jumbles that characterize the tempo of films—as well as the careers of film-makers themselves—today.

I'm delighted opportunities in the industry are greater for young people than ever before, but disappointed by the lack of preparation many bring to their work. Their apprenticeship is served in a goldfish bowl, and few careers can withstand that magnified gaze. The work may seem catchy for the moment, but if it doesn't stand the test of time, that career won't go anywhere. It will end just as the young person is on the brink of becoming a seasoned professional . . . and just possibly an artist. For art isn't art unless it haunts you a little, and a person can't become an artist without becoming a craftsman first.

We've learned that hot-air puffery can get a person only a small distance up that steep grade, but a more substantial fuel is needed if he's going to get to the top.

But enough of such preachments. The only time I've ever stood on a soap box was to get a better idea of the angle on the camera behind me. And even when I'm high up in the air behind the camera . . . panning left to right, sweeping in and out, gliding up and down . . . I hope my feet are firmly planted on the ground.

That's the best perspective from which to create magic, and where my veteran colleagues stand today. Though we don't get to the starting gate as often as we once did, you'll notice that whenever we do we somehow muddle through.

23 | Liza, Tina, and Other Wonders

Those in the know had already handed Marlon Brando the 1972 Academy Award for Best Actor in *The Godfather,* but the competition for Best Actress was the keenest in several years. There had been so many excellent women's performances during the year that narrowing them down to five nominations was going to be a difficult job.

Liza was facing the same situation for a second time. She'd been nominated as Best Actress for 1969 in her first starring film, *The Sterile Cuckoo,* along with Genevieve Bujold as *Anne of a Thousand Days;* Jane Fonda in *They Shoot Horses, Don't They;* Jean Simmons in *Happy Ending;* and Maggie Smith for *The Prime of Miss Jean Brodie.*

"The first time I was nominated was really funny," Liza recalls, "because I'd fallen off a motorbike the week before. It wasn't even a good accident . . . it was only a motor scooter . . . not even like a big cycle. So when I went, they kind of patched me all up. Part of my front tooth was missing and the doctor gave me a shot because I had a busted shoulder. I had my arm in a sling, and I was kind of hanging on Daddy . . . a hot twosome. And then they said, 'And the winner is Maggie Smith.' And I applauded, and Daddy said that was it. I didn't even know that was the category. I'd been in such pain, and whatever the doctor had given me had made me a little woozy."

All the while Liza was making *Cabaret* under Bob Fosse's direction, I had the feeling something extraordinary was happening. She'd been very excited about getting the part, and immediately immersed herself in study of Sally Bowles' hedonistic character. She was enthused about Bobby's concept for the film. The production would be taking on the coarse and debauched look of a George Grosz caricature, a perfect device to capture the decadent climate of Berlin, the world's most wicked city in the 1930s. Liza described the touches Bobby planned to suggest the imminent rise of Nazism and the complacency of the Berliners who permitted it. One in particular captured just the right foreboding touch. An innocent boy sings an idealistic message song, "Tomorrow Belongs to Me," falsely lulling the audience with his purity. The camera dollies back to reveal the boy in a Hitler Youth Corps uniform, his face evilly transformed as the tenor of his song becomes militant and strident. It was daring and innovative. I knew Bobby, in only his second picture, would be mastering the medium.

I'd get periodic telephone calls from Liza during the filming in Germany.

"I don't know if I'm doing it right," she'd say.

"Listen to the director," I advised. "He knows if it's fine . . . what are you uncomfortable about anyway?"

"Nothing," she answered, "except that it seems terribly hard."

"How does Bob Fosse feel about it?" I asked.

"Well, he's pleased."

"Then I'm sure it's okay. How does your hair look?" She advised me it was cut in a point at the forehead. "In the rushes," I asked, "do you see yourself or do you see somebody else?"

"I think I see somebody else."

"Then you're on the right track," I assured her. I was positive of it when Liza took me to see a rough cut at the studio. Though she knew the movie was good, she was still unsure about her performance. I wasn't. When the lights came up, I turned to her and said, "It's one of a kind. It's *truly* one of a kind . . . and so are you."

"Do you really think so?"

"Absolutely," I said, "just wait and see."

I liked the style of *Cabaret*. The picture was more vivid than the stage play, which had moved away from the Sally Bowles character through the introduction of an extraneous romance. Bobby, with Geoffrey Unsworth's evocative cinematography, captured the hard and cynical mood of the era with an approach that would have been impossible twenty years ago. And he did it so ingeniously that the experience of seeing *Cabaret* was unique. Less talented directors wouldn't presume to imitate it. It's an important picture, certainly in the progression of the film musical, but also as drama. It dazzled, it thrilled, it filled you with despair, it gave pause for sober thought. *Cabaret*'s sophistication was singular. This wasn't the emptyheaded joy which characterizes the musical genre. *Cabaret* was about *something*.

Liza came through brilliantly, as did Joel Grey in his pseudo-Hitler role. Her fantastic vitality was evident in every frame. Her suggestion of Sally Bowles' defiant quality, lurking beneath the surface, was well thought out. Even in moments of repose, she was an animal ready to spring. But then, I've always thought Liza has a great sense of the character and a superb grasp of motivation. While I reacted emotionally to her Sally Bowles—as one does to all great art—I also had an intellectual appreciation of what Liza had achieved under Bobby's direction.

Instant acclaim knocked Liza off her pins. She knew she was good, but nobody had ever told her she was this good. When she appeared on the covers of *Time* and *Newsweek* during the same week, I knew the momentum had started for her Oscar nomination.

When the announcements were made, Liza found herself in the golden circle. The experts immediately established it as a three-way race. Maggie Smith's dotty old lady in *Travels With My Aunt* came too soon after her last Oscar-winning role, and many found her extravagant theatricality a bit much. Liv Ullman, in her portrayal of the suffering wife in *The Emigrants,* was the victim of poor timing. The picture had been held over from the previous year as a Best Foreign Picture nomination; impact had dissipated. The race was thus restricted to Liza, Diana Ross (*Lady Sings the Blues*), and Cicely Tyson (*Sounder*). Any one of them could squeeze through. We in the industry were engulfed with a trade paper campaign whose like hadn't been seen for many years. Liza found the whole proceedings tasteless, but she had no control over the studio's actions. Neither did the Misses Ross and Tyson. The pressures on them were enormous.

Liza met Diana at an industry function shortly before the March 27, 1973, Award night. "Are they doing to you what they're doing to me?" Liza asked. "Am I supposed to be your enemy?"

"Oh, yes," Diana answered. "But I'm just so happy to be in a good picture. I don't understand all the rest of that." Neither did Liza. She was particularly annoyed by those highly inaccurate sob sister stories that she was penniless because she was paying off all of Judy's debts. Annoy-

373

ance changed to anger, then to impatience. Somehow she got through those agonizing weeks.

That Tuesday had been a busy one for me. I was putting the finishing touches on the material I'd be needing for a meeting with the principals of the picture I was preparing with Liza. Had the meeting been scheduled the day after the Academy Awards to distract Liza in case she didn't win? I don't think so; it just worked out that way. I was also preparing to leave three days later for Dallas, where the U. S. Film Festival would be holding a one-week retrospective of my work. There were many distractions, but none held my interest for long. I was more nervous for Liza than I'd ever been during my nominations for Best Director.

Lee Anderson and I were ready at five o'clock when Liza and Desi Arnaz, Jr., picked us up in the studio limousine.

Liza wore yellow, my favorite color, and she looked adorable. Sensing my nervousness she treated the upcoming adventure as if it were just another premiere the four of us would be attending. We talked in the car, none of us making much sense. Lots of jokes, lots of giggles. Laughing the subject away seemed to be the only way we could get through the ordeal.

As we got out of the car at the Music Center, the cheers of the fans outside seemed to propel me toward the entrance. We had almost an hour to wait before the program started, and the still photographers had free run of the building until the seven o'clock start. Liza and Desi patiently posed for them. They even roped in Lee and me. We inched our way toward the seats reserved for us. Still more than half an hour to kill. Time dragged on. Then I started looking around behind me and, before I knew it, the lights went out. And there on stage was Angela Lansbury going through the brilliant number that opened the show.

All during the proceedings, I felt as if I were watching them through seven layers of gauze and listening to them through an echo chamber. My only touch with reality seemed to be those nervous moments when Liza squeezed my hand. Lee, on my other side, and Desi, to the left of Liza, seemed to be enjoying the show immensely, but I'd occasionally catch their sideways glances to see how Liza and I were holding up under the strain. The tableau was being repeated with dozens of other nominees in the auditorium.

Had I been keeping count, I would have noticed that *Cabaret* was winning most of the major awards. Joel Grey won for Best Supporting Actor, as I expected, but a delightful surprise was Bob Fosse's award as Best Director. This was to be his year. He parlayed his genius in all the major media, also winning an Emmy for Liza's television special, and a

374

Tony for Broadway's *Pippin*. The only category where he didn't win was for directing traffic, but he wasn't in the running that year.

This was a good omen for Liza, as many others noticed. But not me. My nerves were shot, I wasn't thinking, and I was dying for a cigarette to boot.

The show had been scheduled for a fast-moving two hours. It went over the allotted time. But the moment was drawing near. Roger Moore and Liv Ullman were now getting ready to present the Best Actor award. Liza's hand squeezed even harder. Then the Brando bombshell struck. The week before there'd been a great mystery. Brando hadn't acknowledged the Academy's invitation. Finally, he'd requested tickets to be sent to his house the day of the awards. They turned out to be for his pretty American Indian representative. She declined the award for Brando with becoming dignity, I thought. But her poise couldn't forestall the ensuing uproar. I feared it might throw Liza off too.

But after that one lurch, the program continued, in all its inexorable slowness. And now the time had come. "I hope the winner doesn't have a cause too," Raquel Welch cracked.

"And the winner is," Gene Hackman started. He had difficulty tearing open the envelope. Finally he had that precious piece of paper.

"I'm holding onto Daddy's hand," Liza recalls, "and at the time I was going with Desi, and I'm holding onto Desi's hand. And Gene Hackman said, 'The winner is Liza Minnelli.' And Daddy . . . I'm not used to this from him . . . he let out this yell in my ear . . . enough to deafen me for life. And I will never have perfect pitch again because of that yell. It was just the *sha-reek* of the century, and so hysterically funny. Desi let out a yell on the other side, but it didn't compare to Daddy's. You march up there and you immediately forget everything you're going to say. You plan something, even though you're not sure you're going to win. I thought they were going to give it to *Cabaret* because it was a fine movie, and give it to Diana Ross because she did a really good job. And when I saw her change her dress in the middle of the program, I felt she knew something I didn't know."

Whatever Liza's acceptance speech, it was charming and to the point. I beamed proudly at this extraordinary girl who in her father's eyes can do no wrong.

But wait . . . even more agony. The failure of *The Godfather* to sweep its nominations made its shoo-in as Best Picture highly debatable. Could *Cabaret*'s momentum continue? Only rarely are the Best Director and Best Picture awards given to two different films. One of these exceptions occurred in 1951 when *An American in Paris* was Best Picture, but George Stevens beat me out as Best Director for *A Place in the Sun*. Could *Cabaret* win that tenth and most important Oscar? It didn't. The favored picture won, and that was that . . . for the program anyway.

The four of us were then ushered backstage. People reached out to touch Liza as we went through room after room. Just as we thought this would be the last one, the doors to another would open. First the room for the television cameras, then another for still photographers, still another for radio people. Microphones were being shoved up our nostrils.

Liza was asked time and again what she thought of Brando's action. "It's too soon to say," she tactfully answered. "I have no idea how I feel. Maybe I'll know in a few days."

I was asked to describe my feelings. How would any father feel? But with Liza, I've always been more a part of the audience than her father, a super fan who happens to love her very much. "I like what she did," I said. "I thought she deserved it. I was pulling for her, you know." On to another room.

"Then you pose by yourself," Liza describes it, "then you pose with Joel Grey, then you pose with your dad, and then you pose with your dad and Joel Grey, and then Desi gets in the picture, and then they want you all together and then they lead you to another room. And the heat is not to be believed. Daddy is in the same state I am. We're quite bumbling, and 'where do we go? . . . lead us . . . And where should I hold the award? . . . and so on.' And finally we're out. The police take you to your car. We get in, and we're going back. I'm stunned, but calm. And I suddenly look at Daddy. He's totally wrung out. He's in the jump seat and he's slumped way down. 'Are you okay?' I ask. And he answers, *'Never* take me to one of those things again. I will never go through that again. I feel like I've been through World War Three.'"

I was dazed, obviously, but I was also submerged in other thoughts. How Judy would have loved to see this moment. As Liza looked over at me, a happy memory came back . . . another time when her penetrating stare caught me unawares. I'd returned from the studio and was lying on the sofa reading. I suddenly noticed these huge eyes staring down at me. I looked back at my three-year-old. My instinct was to speak baby talk, but some caprice told me to speak to her as an adult. "You know, Liza, I don't know if that coalition government will be good for France. The inflation there is getting terrible." Her eyes widened. She yelled to Judy, who was in the kitchen with the cook. "Mama, come quick! Daddy's

376

talking to me!" Liza didn't know what to make of our laughter, mixed with pride and love as it was.

As her mother, Judy would have been proud. But as an actress? Since the Oscar always evaded her, she may have had the typical actress' jealousy toward a younger competitor getting the award, particularly when Judy's great acting gift was so underestimated.

The fascination that was Judy rarely was shown in her pictures, for her dramatic talent was unfortunately dissipated on films unworthy of her. Judy was uniquely equipped to convey a tragic part's many layers . . . the temper, the madness, the fury, the despair. In only two films— *A Star Is Born* and *Judgment at Nuremberg*—was she able to show what she had in her. Significantly, both pictures won her Academy Award nominations. The times simply didn't allow her to show the facets that Liza has been able to show in all her movie roles. But Judy had so many other enormous successes that she would have happily given over the spotlight this one time to her daughter.

And she probably would have made a joke of it, as she did when she was nominated for Best Actress in *A Star Is Born* . . . but lost to Grace Kelly's *The Country Girl*.

Liza describes a parlor stunt of sorts that Judy and Sid Luft would perform at parties, describing that famous night in 1955. Judy was in the hospital, having given birth to little Joey.

She would describe in detail all the preparations made to telecast from the hospital room if she won. A television camera on a crane was to shoot through the hospital window. "Then they took a mike and stuck it down my throat," Judy would say.

Another camera had been set up in the lobby. Sid, pacing the corridor, would be picked up first by the camera, and say some gracious words before the camera upstairs zoomed in on Judy. Before the ceremonies, Sid claimed he kept saying, "If they don't give my baby the award they don't know what the hell they're doing."

Then Judy would pick up the story. "There I was in bed, preparing for the moment. I vaguely remember Grace Kelly's name being vaguely called."

("And I could have hit Grace Kelly on the head," Liza says, adding jokingly, "but she was going to marry a prince, and Mama was married to Sid Luft!")

"So," Judy would continue, "I next heard someone yell, 'It's a wrap!' Then they tore the mike out. The curtains on the window were closed,

377

and everyone walked out." By this time Judy would be laughing uncontrollably. "And no one said a thing!"

We stayed quite a long time at the Academy banquet with Liza and Desi. Then, by three in the morning, we old folks had had it and excused ourselves. The two young ones went on to finish the celebration at the house of Dino Martin and his wife, Olivia Hussey.

Pandemonium woke me the next morning. Phones rang, telegrams and packages were being delivered. One of the earliest calls was among the most heartwarming. It was Gene Kelly, who's been a part of Liza's life for such a long time.

He was recovering from a cataract operation, and he'd had to cancel the trip to Dallas with me for the Minnelli Retrospective, but his cheery voice gave no indication he'd been under the weather. "Wonderful! Judy would have been thrilled!" he said.

"But you're wasting all this on me, Gene," I laughed. "Liza won't be here until later this afternoon." Sure enough, his was one of the many phone calls which interrupted our business conference.

So where does she go from here? Though Liza has accomplished so much, I don't think the surface of her talent has even been scratched. Her potential is limitless and her range increases daily.

Liza has conquered all the problems she's encountered along the way, and Judy's giant shadow was not the smallest of these. Liza has "overcome" Judy in a wonderful way. She's always been vulnerable when asked about her mother, the hurt and pain still very much with her, but Liza has always shown her devotion to Judy's memory by saying just the right thing. She's a marvelous girl.

And very much her own person. I'm continually asked of the similarities between Liza and Judy. I don't see them as much as others do. To me, Liza is the complete individual, and nothing she does or is capable of surprises me. As a singer, she's inevitably compared to Judy, but so is every other singer who's worth anything.

Liza has a very accurate appraisal of it all. "Mama and I actually went after something different," she once told an interviewer. "She had more of a needing quality. With Mama, it was, 'Help me. Give me.' And it was terrific. She'd get out on that stage and open those little arms. And I'd be very much a part of the audience that reacted to her. I'd stand up too and reach out, and cry my brains out. But I have more defiance in me. If I say, 'Please help me,' I'll always add, 'if you've got the time.' I couldn't sing Mama's special songs. I couldn't do them as well. I would rather present a first-rate version of myself than a second-rate version of

Mama. She understood that people need to cry. And she fed that wonderful thing. When I entertain, I love to create the feeling of a party because I feel people need to laugh as well as cry. To me, it's the same kind of cleansing action."

Liza's approach evolved during the ten years of hard work that went into her development as the consummate performer she is today.

And now her half sister, my daughter Tina, stands at the same threshold that Liza did at the same age. Will she go into show business too? Living with her mother in Mexico City, Tina isn't subject to the same pressures that Liza was. Her interests may lie elsewhere.

Whenever she comes to the United States to visit, Tina gets on famously with Liza. The ten years difference in their ages makes Liza an elder sister-mother to Tina, as she is to Lorna and Joey Luft.

Tina, at nineteen, is a completely different character, consumed by many interests. She's involved in the theater, but she's just as absorbed in art and psychology. Tina writes songs in French, English, and Spanish, accompanying herself on the guitar. She's also cut a record with a thirty-piece orchestra in Mexico. Her environment there is different, and her motivating forces are different. I don't think she knows what she wants as yet. But when she does, I know she'll approach it with the same dedication that Liza did. I like to feel it's in the Minnelli blood.

I never had a son to carry on the family name. It's nevertheless being carried on by Liza today and possibly Tina tomorrow. Actually, I never wanted a son. My daughters are a great joy, and should they decide to give it up for marriage, that's fine with me too. For I've never had any thoughts of immortality.

I leave it to people who like my work to say what my contributions to films have been. I'm always so proud and humble when they tell me about them. People may comment on the timeless quality of my films, but I never had such aspirations when I was making them. My work has been done under great pressure. I accepted the quick decisions that had to be made, filtered them through my particular brand of foolishness at the time, and did the best I could, hoping I'd made the right decision.

In this age, when mankind's frailties and foibles give way to the impersonal efficiency of the computer, I cling to the human comedy with all its cockeyed hopes. A man doesn't marry three times if he isn't an incurable romantic. But my romanticism has never precluded me from my work which, in the final analysis, is the story of my life.

I have never catered to the audience. How could I when its assessment of my work is lauded in one breath as mastery in atmosphere and dismissed as mere decoration in another? Basically, I work to please myself. But I'm the hardest person to please that I know. I'm not an artist in the classical sense. I'm still not sure if movies are an art form. And if they're not, then let them inscribe on my tombstone what they could about any craftsman who loves his job: "Here lies Vincente Minnelli. He died of hard work."

But not quite yet. There are too many projects that excite me, too many films left unmade, too many friends whose company fascinates me, too many experiences to crowd into the time allotted me. But *not* too many daughters to comfort their father in his dotage.

Thank heaven for little girls.

Vincente Minnelli Filmography

All films, except where noted, were made during Mr. Minnelli's twenty-six-year tenure at Metro-Goldwyn-Mayer, the longest studio-director association in that company's history.

1. Cabin in the Sky   1942
2. I Dood It   1943
3. Meet Me in St. Louis   1944
4. Ziegfeld Follies   1945
5. The Clock   1945
6. Yolanda and the Thief   1946
7. Till the Clouds Roll By (Judy Garland sequences)   1946
8. Undercurrent   1946
9. The Pirate   1947
10. Madame Bovary   1948
11. Father of the Bride   1950
12. An American in Paris   1951
13. Father's Little Dividend   1951
14. Lovely to Look At (Fashion Show Sequence)   1951
15. The Story of Three Loves ("Mademoiselle" Sequence)   1952
16. The Bad and the Beautiful   1952
17. The Band Wagon   1952

18. THE LONG, LONG TRAILER 1953
19. BRIGADOON 1953
20. THE COBWEB 1954
21. KISMET 1955
22. LUST FOR LIFE 1955
23. TEA AND SYMPATHY 1956
24. DESIGNING WOMAN 1956
25. GIGI 1957
26. THE RELUCTANT DEBUTANTE 1958
27. SOME CAME RUNNING 1958
28. HOME FROM THE HILL 1958
29. BELLS ARE RINGING 1959
30. THE FOUR HORSEMEN OF THE APOCALYPSE 1961
31. TWO WEEKS IN ANOTHER TOWN 1962
32. THE COURTSHIP OF EDDIE'S FATHER 1962
33. GOODBYE CHARLIE (Twentieth Century-Fox) 1964
34. THE SANDPIPER 1964
35. ON A CLEAR DAY YOU CAN SEE FOREVER (Paramount) 1968

Index

386

387

390